"Black Knights of the Hudson"
History of Army-West Point Football

Wild Blue Yonder!
History of Air Force Falcons Football
AIR FORCE
NAVY BLUE AND GOLD
History of Navy Midshipmen Football
By Steve's Football Bible LLC

Introduction

My love of College Football began in 1966. As a 7-year-old kid I remember watching the Notre Dame-Michigan State "Game of the Century". Next, I remember the 1967 USC-UCLA game and O.J. Simpson weaving through the UCLA defense for the winning touchdown with 6 minutes left in the game. I remember the 1968 Rose Bowl, Indiana vs USC. Who was this Indiana team that went to the Rose Bowl over my beloved Minnesota Golden Gopher's?   I attended my first college football game in 1971. Michigan vs Minnesota at Memorial Stadium on the Campus of the University of Minnesota. My Aunt Roberta took me. I was hooked after that. The Golden Gophers were defeated that day 35-7 by the Wolverines. George Honza of the Golden Gophers scored the only touchdown that day on a pass from Craig Curry. Ironically, I met Mr. Honza in January of 2017 while officiating a basketball game. Growing up in a rural farming town (Alden) in southern Minnesota, as a youth I spent a lot of my Saturdays in the fall watching ABC Sports College games of the week.

This book is for all the College Football fans, casual or diehard, historians or those who just plain love the College game. I hope everyone enjoys it.

Steve Fulton

Contents

Introduction iii

Brief History of Army Football 1

Traditions 1

National Championships 2

Lambert Trophy 2

Commander-In-Chief Trophy 2

Heisman Trophy Winners 4

Retired numbers 6

College Football Hall of Fame 6

National Award winners 7

Army Consensus All-Americans 7

Bowl Games {9-3} 8

Stadiums 8

Rivalries 9

Legendary Coaches 13

1890 Army Cadets 15

1891 Army Cadets 16

1892 Army Cadets 17

1893 Army Cadets 18

1894 Army Cadets 19

1895 Army Cadets 19

1896 Army Cadets 20

1897 Army Cadets 21

1898 Army Cadets 22

1899 Army Cadets 23

1900 Army Cadets 24

1901 Army Cadets 25

1902 Army Cadets 26

1903 Army Cadets 27

1904 Army Cadets 28

1905 Army Cadets 29

1906 Army Cadets 30

1907 Army Cadets 31

1908 Army Cadets 32

1909 Army Cadets 33

1910 Army Cadets 34

1911 Army Cadets 35

1912 Army Cadets 36

1913 Army Cadets 38

1914 Army Cadets {National Champions} 40

1915 Army Cadets 41

1916 Army Cadets {National Champions} 42

1917 Army Cadets 43

1918 Army Cadets 44

1919 Army Cadets 45

1920 Army Cadets 46

1921 Army Cadets 47

1922 Army Cadets 48

1923 Army Cadets 49

1924 Army Cadets 50

    NOTRE DAME {Four Horsemen Legend game} 50

1925 Army Cadets 52

1926 Army Cadets 53

1927 Army Cadets 55

1928 Army Cadets 56

    NOTRE DAME {"Win one for the Gipper" game} 56

1929 Army Cadets 57

1930 Army Cadets 58

1931 Army Cadets 59

1932 Army Cadets 60

1933 Army Cadets 61

1934 Army Cadets 62

1935 Army Cadets 63

1936 Army Cadets 64

1937 Army Cadets 65

1938 Army Cadets 66

1939 Army Cadets 67

1940 Army Cadets 68

1941 Army Cadets 69

1942 Army Cadets 71

1943 Army Cadets 72

1944 Army Cadets {National Champions} 73

    NAVY {@ Memorial Stadium, Baltimore, MD} {#1 vs #2} 74

1945 Army Cadets {National Champions} 75

    Notre Dame {@ Yankee Stadium, Bronx, NY} {#1 vs #2} 76

    NAVY {@ Municipal Stadium, Philadelphia, PA} {#1 vs #2} 76

1946 Army Cadets {National Champions} 77

    Notre Dame {@ Yankee Stadium, Bronx, NY} {#1 vs #2} 78

1947 Army Cadets 81

    Columbia {Columbia ends Army 32 game unbeaten streak-Columbia's greatest win} 81

1948 Army Cadets {Lambert Trophy} 83

1949 Army Cadets {Lambert Trophy} 84

1950 Army Cadets 86

1951 Army Cadets 87

1952 Army Cadets 88

1953 Army Cadets {Lambert Trophy} 89

1954 Army Cadets 90

1955 Army Cadets 91
1956 Army Cadets 92
1957 Army Cadets 93
1958 Army Cadets {Lambert Trophy} 95
1959 Army Cadets 96
1960 Army Cadets 97
1961 Army Cadets 98
1962 Army Cadets 99
1963 Army Cadets 100
1964 Army Cadets 101
1965 Army Cadets 102
1966 Army Cadets 103
1967 Army Cadets 105
1968 Army Cadets 106
1969 Army Cadets 107
1970 Army Cadets 108
1971 Army Cadets 110
1972 Army Cadets {Commander-Chief-Trophy} 111
1973 Army Cadets 113
1974 Army Cadets 114
1975 Army Cadets 115
1976 Army Cadets 116
1977 Army Cadets {Commander-Chief-Trophy} 117
1978 Army Cadets 118
1979 Army Cadets 119
1980 Army Cadets 120
1981 Army Cadets 122
1982 Army Cadets 124
1983 Army Cadets 125
1984 Army Cadets {Commander-Chief-Trophy} 126
    1984 CHERRY BOWL 127
1985 Army Cadets 128
    1985 PEACH BOWL 129
1986 Army Cadets {Commander-Chief-Trophy} 130
1987 Army Cadets 131
1988 Army Cadets {Commander-Chief-Trophy} 132
    1988 SUN BOWL 133
1989 Army Cadets 134
1990 Army Cadets 136
1991 Army Cadets 137
1992 Army Cadets 138
1993 Army Cadets 139
1994 Army Cadets 141
1995 Army Cadets 143

1996 Army Cadets {Commander-Chief-Trophy} **144**

   1996 INDEPENDENCE BOWL 145

1997 Army Cadets **146**

1998 Army Cadets **147**

1999 Army Black Knights **149**

2000 Army Black Knights **150**

2001 Army Black Knights **151**

2002 Army Black Knights **152**

2003 Army Black Knights **153**

2004 Army Black Knights **155**

2005 Army Black Knights **158**

2006 Army Black Knights **160**

2007 Army Black Knights **162**

   TULANE {Miracle at Michie} 162

2008 Army Black Knights **164**

2009 Army Black Knights **166**

2010 Army Black Knights **168**

   2010 ARMED FORCES BOWL 169

2011 Army Black Knights **170**

2012 Army Black Knights **172**

2013 Army Black Knights **174**

2014 Army Black Knights **176**

2015 Army Black Knights **178**

2016 Army Black Knights **180**

   2016 HEART OF DALLAS BOWL 181

2017 Army Black Knights {Commander-Chief-Trophy} **182**

   2017 ARMED FORCES BOWL 183

2018 Army Black Knights {Lambert Trophy} + {Commander-Chief-Trophy} **184**

   2018 ARMED FORCES BOWL 185

2019 Army Black Knights **186**

2020 Army Black Knights {Lambert Trophy} + {Commander-Chief-Trophy} **188**

   2020 LIBERTY BOWL 189

2021 Army Black Knights **191**

   2021 ARMED FORCES BOWL 193

2022 Army Black Knights **194**

2023 Army Black Knights {Commander-In-Chief Trophy} **196**

2024 Army Black Knights **198**

   2024 AAC CHAMPIONSHIP 199

   2024 INDEPENDENCE BOWL 200

2025 Army Black Knights **201**

   2025 FENWAY BOWL 203

Brief History of Army Football
Army Black Knights

The Army Black Knights football team, previously known as the Army Cadets, represents the United States Military Academy in college football. Army is a Division I Football Bowl Subdivision (FBS) member of the NCAA. The Black Knights play home games in Michie Stadium with a capacity of 38,000 at West Point, New York. The Black Knights are coached by Jeff Monken who is entering his eighth season as head coach. Army is a five-time national champion, winning the title in 1914, 1916, and from 1944 to 1946.

Except for seven seasons (1998–2004) where the team was a member of Conference USA, Army has competed as an independent, meaning that they have no affiliation with any conference. As of the next college football season in 2021, Army is one of seven FBS schools whose football teams do not belong to any conference, the others being BYU, Liberty, New Mexico State, Notre Dame, UConn, and UMass. However, for all other sports Army is primarily a member of the Patriot League.

Three players from Army have won the Heisman Trophy: Doc Blanchard (1945), Glenn Davis (1946), and Pete Dawkins (1958).

The three major service academies—Air Force, Army, and Navy—compete for the Commander-in-Chief's Trophy, which is awarded to the academy that defeats the others in football that year (or retained by the previous winner in the event of a three-way tie). Army has won nine CIC Trophies, most recently in 2020.

Army's football program began on November 29, 1890, when Navy challenged the cadets to a game of the relatively new sport. Navy defeated Army at West Point that year, but Army avenged the loss in Annapolis the following year. The academies still clash every December in what the last regular-season Division I college-football game is traditionally. The 2016 Army–Navy Game marked Army's first recent win after fourteen consecutive losses to Navy. From 1944 to 1950, the Cadets had 57 wins, 3 losses and 4 ties. During this time span, Army won three national championships.

Army's football team reached its pinnacle of success during the Second World War under Coach Earl Blaik when Army won three consecutive national championships in 1944, 1945 and 1946, and produced three Heisman trophy winners: Doc Blanchard (1945), Glenn Davis (1946) and Pete Dawkins (1958). Past NFL coaches Vince Lombardi and Bill Parcells were Army assistant coaches early in their careers. For many years, Army teams were known as the "Cadets." In the 1940s, several papers called the football team "the Black Knights of the Hudson." From then on, "Cadets" and "Black Knights" were used interchangeably until 1999, when the team was officially nicknamed the Black Knights.

Traditions
The Long Gray Line

The football team plays its home games at Michie Stadium, where the playing field is named after Earl Blaik. The Brigade of Cadets attendance is mandatory at football games and the Corps stands for the duration of the game. At all home games, one of the four regiments marches onto the field in formation before the team takes the field and leads the crowd in traditional Army cheers.

Songs

Alma Mater is the Army's school song. Army's fight song is On, Brave Old Army Team. Army also plays other organized cheers, Army Rocket Yell, Black, Gold, and Gray, and USMA Cheer.

Mascot

Army's mascots are the Army Mules. While dating back to 1899, they were officially adopted as mascots by USMA in 1936.

National Championships

Army has won five national championships from NCAA-designated major selectors. Army claims the 1944, 1945, and 1946 titles.

Year	Coach	Record
1914	Charles Dudley Daly	9–0
1916	Charles Dudley Daly	9–0
1944	Earl Blaik	9–0
1945	Earl Blaik	9–0
1946	Earl Blaik	9–0–1

Lambert Trophy

The Lambert-Meadowlands Trophy (known as the Lambert Trophy), established in 1936, is an annual award given to the best team in the East in Division I FBS (formerly I-A) college football and is presented by the Metropolitan New York Football Writers. Army has won the Lambert Trophy nine times; seven times under legendary head coach Earl "Red" Blaik in the 1940s and 1950s, and twice under head coach Jeff Monken in 2018 and 2020.

Year	Coach	Record	Final AP Rank
1944	Earl Blaik	9–0	#1
1945	Earl Blaik	9–0	#1
1946	Earl Blaik	9–0–1	#2
1948	Earl Blaik	8–0–1	#6
1949	Earl Blaik	9–0	#4
1953	Earl Blaik	7–1–1	#14
1958	Earl Blaik	8–0–1	#3
2018	Jeff Monken	11–2	#19
2020	Jeff Monken	9–3	NR

Commander-In-Chief Trophy

The Commander-in-Chief's Trophy is awarded to each season's winner of the American college football series among the teams of the U.S. Military Academy (Army Black Knights), the U.S. Naval Academy (Navy Midshipmen), and the U.S. Air Force Academy (Air Force Falcons). The Navy–Air Force game is normally played on the first Saturday in October, the Army–Air Force game on the first Saturday in November, and the Army–Navy Game on the second Saturday in December. In the event of a tie, the award is shared, but the previous winner retains physical possession of the trophy. The Commander-in-Chief's Trophy and the Michigan MAC Trophy are the only NCAA Division I FBS triangular rivalry trophies awarded annually. The few others, such as the Florida Cup and the Beehive Boot, are contested sporadically. Through 2022, the Air Force Falcons hold the most trophy victories with 21. The Navy Midshipmen have won 16. The Army Black Knights trail with 9. The trophy has been shared on five occasions, most recently in 2021.

The Commander-in-Chief's trophy was the brainchild of Air Force General George B. Simler, a former Air Force Academy athletic director who envisioned the trophy to create an annual series of football games for the Air Force Academy against the Military Academy and the Naval Academy. First awarded in 1972 by President Richard Nixon, the trophy itself is jointly sponsored by the alumni associations of the three academies. The trophy is named for the U.S. President, who is the Commander-in-Chief of all U.S. military services under the U.S. Constitution. The President has personally awarded the trophy on several occasions. During the 1980s, for instance, President Ronald Reagan presented the award in an annual White House ceremony. In 1996, President Bill Clinton presented the trophy to the Army team at Veterans Stadium after the Army–Navy Game. From 2003 to 2007, President George W. Bush presented the trophy to Navy teams at ceremonies in the White House.

Years ARMY has won the CIC

1972	1977
1984	1986
1988	1996
2017	2018
2020	2023

Heisman Trophy Winners
Felix "Doc" Blanchard

"Doc" Blanchard was best known as the college football player who became the first junior to win the Heisman Trophy, Maxwell Award and was the first football player to win the James E. Sullivan Award, all in 1945. He played football for the United States Military Academy at West Point, where he was known as "Mr. Inside." Because his father was a doctor, Felix Blanchard was nicknamed "Little Doc" as a boy. After football, he served in the United States Air Force from 1947 until 1971 when he retired with the rank of colonel. During his three years of playing football at West Point, his team under Coach Earl "Red" Blaik compiled an undefeated 27–0–1 record – the tie being a famous 0–0 game against Notre Dame. Notre Dame Coach Edward McKeever was amazed by Blanchard. After his 1944 team lost to Army by a score of 59–0, McKeever said, "I've just seen Superman in the flesh. He wears number 35 and goes by the name of Blanchard.

An all-around athlete, Blanchard served as the placekicker and punter in addition to his primary roles as an offensive fullback and a linebacker on defense. He soon teamed with Glenn Davis on the 1944–45–46 teams (Davis won the Heisman in 1946, the year after Blanchard won it). They formed one of the most lethal rushing combinations in football history. In his three seasons at West Point Blanchard scored 38 touchdowns, gained 1,908 yards and earned the nickname "Mr. Inside." Teammate Davis earned the nickname "Mr. Outside" and in November 1945, they both shared the cover of Time magazine.

Blanchard had the opportunity to play professional football after being selected third overall in the 1946 NFL Draft by the Pittsburgh Steelers. After he was turned down in 1947 for a furlough to play with the NFL, Blanchard then chose to embark upon a career in the United States Air Force and became a fighter pilot. In 1959, while with the 77th Tactical Fighter Squadron and flying back to his base at RAF Wethersfield near London, a gas leak in Major Blanchard's F-100 Super Sabre broke and caught his plane on fire. Rather than escaping and parachuting out safely, he decided to stay with the plane and land it safely, because of a village on the ground that would have been damaged. This garnered him an Air Force commendation for bravery. In the Vietnam War, Blanchard flew 113 missions from Thailand, 84 of them over North Vietnam. He piloted a fighter-bomber during a one-year tour of duty that ended in January 1969. He retired from the Air Force in 1971 as a colonel.

Glenn Woodward Davis

Glenn Davis was known as "Mr. Outside." He was named a consensus All-American three times, and in 1946 won the Heisman Trophy and was named Sporting News Player of the Year and Associated Press Athlete of the Year. At West Point, under Coach Earl Blaik, Davis played fullback in his freshman season. Blaik moved him to halfback for his three varsity seasons, while Doc Blanchard took over at fullback. With Davis and Blanchard, Army went 27–0–1 in 1944, 1945, and 1946. Davis was nicknamed "Mr. Outside", while Blanchard was "Mr. Inside".

Davis averaged 8.3 yards per carry over his career and 11.5 yards per carry in 1945; both results are records which still stand today. Davis led the nation in 1944 with 120 points. He scored 59 touchdowns, including eight on his freshman squad, in his career. His single-season mark of 20 touchdowns stood as a record for 10 years. Blanchard and he set a then-record 97 career touchdowns by two teammates. (The record was broken by USC backs Reggie Bush and LenDale White, who had 99 career touchdowns.) In 2007, Davis was ranked #13 on ESPN's list of Top 25 Players in College Football History.

For all three varsity years at West Point, Davis was a "consensus" All-America player (that is, selected by all the different groups picking All-America teams). In 1944, he won the Maxwell Award and the Walter Camp Trophy and was runner-up for the Heisman Trophy. In 1945, he was again runner-up for the Heisman (won by his teammate Blanchard). In 1946, he won the Heisman and was named the Associated Press Male Athlete of the Year. In 1961, Davis was inducted into the College Football Hall of Fame. Davis also starred in baseball, basketball, and track at West Point.

Davis graduated from West Point in June 1947 and entered the U.S. Army as a second lieutenant. He was offered a contract and $75,000 signing bonus by the Brooklyn Dodgers, but declined, as he was required to serve in the Army and would be a relatively old rookie after that. Davis served three years in the Army. While on leave in 1948, he attended the Rams training camp and played in a preseason game. He then reported for duty in Korea (this was before the Korean War, which began after he returned to the U.S.).

Pete Dawkins

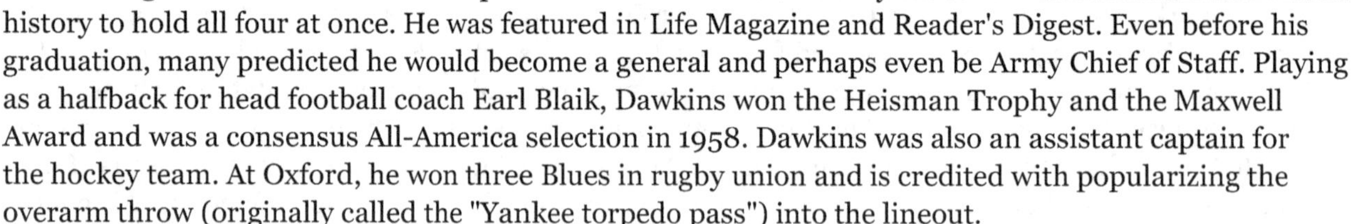

Dawkins attended the United States Military Academy, where he played as halfback on the Army Cadets football team from 1956 to 1958. As a senior in 1958 he won the Heisman Trophy, the Maxwell Award, and was a consensus All-America selection. After graduating from the Military Academy in 1959, he studied at the University of Oxford as a Rhodes Scholar. Dawkins served as an officer in the United States Army until he retired in 1983 with the rank of brigadier general. He earned high honors, serving as First Captain, president of his class, captain of the football team, and a "Star Man" in the top five percent of his class academically. A cadet is considered outstanding if he attains one of these positions. Dawkins was the only cadet in history to hold all four at once. He was featured in Life Magazine and Reader's Digest. Even before his graduation, many predicted he would become a general and perhaps even be Army Chief of Staff. Playing as a halfback for head football coach Earl Blaik, Dawkins won the Heisman Trophy and the Maxwell Award and was a consensus All-America selection in 1958. Dawkins was also an assistant captain for the hockey team. At Oxford, he won three Blues in rugby union and is credited with popularizing the overarm throw (originally called the "Yankee torpedo pass") into the lineout.

After being commissioned from the academy and completing his tenure as a Rhodes Scholar, Dawkins finished Infantry School and Ranger School before being posted for duty in the 82nd Airborne Division. He received two Bronze Stars for Valor for his service in Vietnam and held commands in the 7th Infantry Division and 101st Airborne. From 1971 to 1972, Dawkins, while a lieutenant colonel, was the commander of the 1st Battalion 23rd Infantry, 2nd Infantry Division, Camp Hovey, Korea. In addition to being an instructor at the academy, he was a White House Fellow in the 1973–74 class. During that time, he was chosen to work on a task force, charged with changing the U.S. Army into an all-volunteer force. During the mid-1970's Colonel Dawkins was brigade commander of the 3rd ("Golden Brigade") of the 82nd Airborne Division at Fort Bragg, North Carolina that included the 1st and 2nd 505th and 1/508th battalions. In the late 1970s he was 3rd Brigade Commander (War Eagle Brigade, which included the 1/503, 2/503, and 3/187 Infantry Battalions) of the 101st Airborne Division (Air Assault) at Fort Campbell with the rank of colonel. After serving as the Brigade Commander, he became the Chief of Staff for the 101st Airborne Division and was subsequently promoted to brigadier general. In 1966 Dawkins appeared in uniform on the cover of Life Magazine and participated in a segment of the U.S. Army "Big Picture" film series, "A Nation Builds Under Fire." This was a short documentary reviewing United States progress in South Vietnam, narrated by actor John Wayne.

Retired numbers

No.	Player	Position	Career
24	Pete Dawkins	HB	1956–1958
35	Doc Blanchard	FB	1944–1946
41	Glenn Davis	HB	1943–1946
61	Joe Steffy	G	1945–1947

College Football Hall of Fame

Name	Position	Years at Army	Inducted
Charlie Daly	QB	1901–1902	1951
Chris Cagle	HB	1926–1929	1954
Ed Garbisch	C/OG	1921–1924	1954
Elmer Oliphant	FB	1916–1917	1955
Glenn Davis	HB	1943–1946	1961
John McEwan	C	1913–1916	1962
Doc Blanchard	FB	1944–1946	1964
Paul Bunker	HB/OT	1901–1902	1969
Harry Wilson	HB	1924	1973
Barney Poole	TE/DE		1974
Alex Weyand	OT	1914–1915	1974
Pete Dawkins	HB	1956–1958	1975
Harvey Jablonsky	OG	1931–1933	1978
Bud Sprague	OT	1926–1927	1979
Bill Carpenter	TE	1957–1959	1982
Arnold Galiffa	QB		1983
Doug Kenna	QB	1942–1944	1984
Don Holleder	End/QB		1985
Robin Olds	T		1985
Joe Steffy	OG	1945–1947	1987
John Green	OG	1943–1945	1989
Frank Merritt	OT	1942–1943	1996
Bob Anderson	HB	1957–1959	2004
Arnold Tucker	QB	1945–1946	2008

National Award winners

AFCA Coach of the Year
Earl Blaik – 1946
Tom Cahill – 1966
Eddie Robinson Coach of the Year
Tom Cahill – 1966
Bobby Dodd Coach of the Year
Bob Sutton – 1996
George Munger Collegiate Coach of the Year
Jeff Monken – 2018
Vince Lombardi College Football Coach of the Year
Jeff Monken – 2018
President's Award
Jeff Monken – 2018
Buddy Teevens Award
Jeff Monken – 2024
Heisman Trophy + Maxwell Award
Glenn Davis – 1944
Doc Blanchard – 1945
Pete Dawkins – 1958
Outland Trophy
Joe Steffy – 1947
William V. Campbell Trophy
Andrew Rodriguez – 2011
James E. Sullivan Award
Doc Blanchard 1945
Arnold Tucker 1946
Andrew Rodriguez – 2011
Defender of the Nation Award
Andrew King – 2016
Joe Moore Award {Nation's best Offensive Line}
2024

Army Consensus All-Americans

Player	Pos	Yrs		Player	Pos	Yrs
Charles Romeyn	B	1898		Red Cagle	B	1927, 1928, 1929
William Smith	E	1900		Milt Summerfelt	L	1932
Charles Daly	B	1901		Casimir Myslinski	L	1943
Paul Bunker	L	1901, 1902		Doc Blanchard	B	1944, 1945, 1946
Robert Boyers	L	1902		Glenn Davis	B	1944, 1945, 1946
Arthur Tipton	L	1904		Tex Coulter	L	1945
Henry Torney	B	1904, 1905		John Green	L	1945
William Erwin	L	1907		Hank Foldberg	E	1946
Leland Devore	L	1911		Joe Steffy	L	1947
Louis Merrillat	E	1913		Arnold Galiffa	B	1949
John McEwan	L	1914		Dan Foldberg	E	1950
Elmer Oliphant	B	1916, 1917		Bob Anderson	B	1957
Ed Garbisch	L	1922		Pete Dawkins	B	1958
Bud Sprague	L	1926		Bill Carpenter	E	1959

Bowl Games {9-3}

12/27/2025	ARMY	vs	CONNECTICUT	41	16	W	Fenway Bowl
12/28/2024	#22 ARMY {12-2}	vs	LOUISIANA TECH	27	6	W	Independence Bowl
12/22/2021	ARMY (8-4)	vs	MISSOURI	24	22	W	Armed Forces Bowl
12/31/2020	ARMY (9-2)	vs	WEST VIRGINIA (5-4)	21	24	L	Liberty Bowl
12/22/2018	#22 ARMY (11-2)	vs	HOUSTON (8-5)	70	14	W	Armed Forces Bowl
12/23/2017	ARMY (9-3)	vs	SAN DIEGO STATE (10-2)	42	35	W	Armed Forces Bowl
12/27/2016	ARMY (8-5)	vs	NORTH TEXAS (5-8)	38	31	W	Heart of Dallas Bowl
12/30/2010	ARMY (7-6)	vs	SMU (7-7)	16	14	W	Armed Forces Bowl
12/31/1996	#24 ARMY (10-2)	vs	AUBURN (8-4)	29	32	L	Independence Bowl
12/24/1988	ARMY (9-3)	vs	#20 ALABAMA (9-3)	28	29	L	Sun Bowl
12/31/1985	ARMY (9-3)	vs	ILLINOIS (6-5-1)	31	29	W	Peach Bowl
12/22/1984	ARMY (8-3-1)	vs	MICHIGAN STATE (6-6)	10	6	W	Cherry Bowl

Stadiums

The Plain {1890-1923}

Army played on the field known as the "The Plain" until Michie Stadium was built and opened in 1924. **The Plain** is the parade field at the United States Military Academy at West Point, New York. The flat terrain of the Plain contrasts with the varied and hilly terrain of the remainder of the campus. The Plain rises approximately 150 feet (45 m) above the Hudson River and has been the site of the longest continually occupied U.S. Army garrison in America since 1778. In its early years, the entire academy was located on the Plain and it was used for varying activities ranging from drill and mounted cavalry maneuvers to an encampment site for summer training to a sports venue. Currently, the Plain refers to just the parade field where cadets perform ceremonial parades.

Michie Stadium {1924-present}

The home field for the Army Black Knights, it opened 97 years ago in 1924 and has a current seating capacity of 38,000. The stadium sits at the upper portion of campus, directly west of Lusk Reservoir. The field is at an elevation of 335 feet above sea level and runs in the traditional north–south configuration, with the press box above the west sideline. Due to the view offered by its location overlooking the Hudson River and the Neo-Gothic architecture of the campus below, it was rated as Sports Illustrated's #3 sports venue of the 20th century.

Michie Stadium is dedicated to the memory of Dennis Michie (1870–1898), who was instrumental in starting the football program while a cadet at the Academy. A member of the Class of 1892, Michie organized, managed, and coached the first football team at West Point in 1890. Six years after graduation, he was killed in Cuba during the Spanish American War. There have been several renovations since the stadium's first game in October 1924, when Army defeated Saint Louis, 17–0.

In 1999, the football field at Michie Stadium was named Blaik Field on September 25, in honor of Earl "Red" Blaik, the head coach at West Point from 1941 to 1958. Blaik led Army to three consecutive national titles from 1944 to 1946.

Rivalries
Air Force

Air Force and Army meet annually and vie for the Commander-in-Chief's Trophy. The Commander-in-Chief's Trophy is awarded to each season's winner of the American college football series among the teams of the U.S. Military Academy, the U.S. Naval Academy, and the U.S. Air Force Academy. The Navy–Air Force game is normally played on the first Saturday in October, the Army–Air Force game on the first Saturday in November, and the Army–Navy Game on the second Saturday in December. In the event of a tie, the award is shared, but the previous winner retains physical possession of the trophy. Through 2020, the Air Force Falcons hold the most trophy victories with 20. The Navy Midshipmen have won 16. The current winners, the Army Black Knights, trail with 9. The trophy has been shared on four occasions, most recently in 1993. Air Force first played Army in 1959 and Navy in 1960; prior to 1972, Air Force met Army in odd years and Navy in even years (and neither in 1961, 1962, 1964). The Commander-in-Chief's trophy was the brainchild of Air Force General George B. Simler, a former Air Force Academy athletic director who envisioned the trophy to create an annual series of football games for the Air Force Academy against the Military Academy and the Naval Academy. First awarded in 1972 by President Richard Nixon, the trophy itself is jointly sponsored by the alumni associations of the three academies. The trophy is named for the U.S. President, who is the Commander-in-Chief of all U.S. military services under the U.S. Constitution. The President has personally awarded the trophy on several occasions. During the 1980s, for instance, President Ronald Reagan presented the award in an annual White House ceremony. In 1996, President Bill Clinton presented the trophy to the Army team at Veterans Stadium after the Army–Navy Game. From 2003 to 2007, President George W. Bush presented the trophy to Navy teams at ceremonies in the White House.

Notre Dame

The Army–Notre Dame football rivalry is between the Army Black Knights football team of the United States Military Academy and Notre Dame Fighting Irish. The rivalry dates to 1913, when both teams were among the top college football programs in the United States.

The first Army–Notre Dame game in 1913 is generally regarded as the game that established the national reputation of the Fighting Irish. In that game, Notre Dame revolutionized the forward pass in a stunning 35–13 victory. For years it was "The Game" on Notre Dame's schedule, played at Yankee Stadium in New York. During the 1940s, the rivalry with the Army Black Knights reached its zenith. This was because both teams were extremely successful and met several times in key games (including one of the Games of the Century, a scoreless tie in the 1946 Army vs. Notre Dame Football game). In 1944, the Black Knights administered the worst defeat in Notre Dame Football history, crushing the Fighting Irish, 59–0. The following year, it was more of the same, a 48–0 blitzkrieg. After meeting every year since 1919, the series went on a ten-year hiatus starting in 1947 and lasting until 1957. The game was played in South Bend for the first time and the Fighting Irish won 27–7. Since then, there have been infrequent meetings over the past several decades, with Army's last win coming in 1958. Like Navy, due to the small capacity of Army's Michie Stadium, the Black Knights would play their home games at a neutral site, which for several years was Yankee Stadium and before that, the Polo Grounds. In 1957, the game was played in Philadelphia's Municipal (later John F. Kennedy Memorial) Stadium while in 1965, the teams met at Shea Stadium in New York. They last met at the old Yankee Stadium in 1969. The 1973 contest was played at West Point with the Fighting Irish prevailing, 62–3. In more recent times, games in which Army was the host have been played at Giants Stadium in East Rutherford, New Jersey. **Notre Dame leads the series 40–8–4** through the 2024 season.

Navy

The Army–Navy game is one of the most traditional and enduring rivalries in college football. It has been frequently attended by sitting U.S. presidents. The game has been nationally televised each year since 1945 on either ABC, CBS or NBC. CBS has televised the game since 1996 and has the rights to the broadcast through 2018. Instant replay made its American debut in the 1963 Army–Navy game. Since 2009, the game has been held the Saturday following FBS conference championship weekend. The game has been held in multiple locations, but outside the 1926 game in Chicago and 1983 game in Pasadena, California, it has been along the East Coast, most frequently in Philadelphia, followed by the New York City area and Baltimore. The series has been marked by several periods of domination by one team or the other, with Navy's 14 game winning streak from 2002 through 2015 being the longest for either side. **Through the 2025 meeting, Navy leads the series 64–54–7.**

The **Thompson Cup** is between the Army West Point Black Knights of the United States Military Academy (USMA) at West Point, New York, and the Navy Midshipmen from the United States Naval Academy (USNA) at Annapolis, Maryland. The Black Knights (formerly the "Army Cadets" and "Army Black Knights") and Midshipmen each represent their service's oldest officer commissioning sources. As such, the game has come to embody the spirit of the inter service rivalry of the United States Armed Forces. The game marks the end of the college football regular season and the third and final game of the season's Commander-in-Chief's Trophy series, which also includes the Air Force Falcons of the United States Air Force Academy (USAFA) near Colorado Springs, Colorado.

Series history - Army and Navy first met on the football field on November 29, 1890. The series has been renewed annually since 1899, except for 1909, 1917, 1918 and 1929. It has been held at several locations throughout its history, including Baltimore and New York City, but has most frequently been played in Philadelphia, roughly equidistant from the two academies. Historically played on the Saturday after Thanksgiving (a date on which most other major college football teams end their regular seasons), the game is now played on the second Saturday in December and is traditionally the last game of the season for both teams and the last regular-season game played in College football. With the permanent expansion of the regular season to 12 games starting in 2006, several conference championship games joined the Army–Navy Game on its then-current date of the first weekend of December. In 2009, the game was moved from the first Saturday in December to the second Saturday; this means that it no longer conflicts with conference championship games and once again is the last non-bowl contest in college football. This game has inter-service "bragging rights" at stake. For much of the first half of the 20th century, both Army and Navy were often national powers, and the game occasionally had national championship implications. However, as the level of play in college football improved nationally and became fueled by prospects of playing in the National Football League (NFL), the high academic entrance requirements, height and weight limits, and the five-year military commitment required has reduced the overall competitiveness of both academies. Since 1963, only the 1996, 2010, and 2016 games have seen both teams enter with winning records. Nonetheless, the game is considered a college football institution. It has aired nationally on radio since the late 1920s and has been nationally televised every year since 1945. The tradition associated with the game assures that it remains nationally broadcast to this day. Arguably, one of the reasons this game has maintained its appeal is that the players are playing solely for the love of the game. Most players are required to fulfill a post-graduation active duty military commitment and, by the time this ends, many players are deemed too old to consider playing competitively again. Nevertheless, some participants in the Army–Navy Game have gone on to professional football careers. Quarterback Roger Staubach (Navy, 1965) went on to a Hall of Fame career with the Dallas Cowboys that included starting at quarterback in two Super Bowls including being named the Most Valuable Player of Super Bowl VI. Wide receiver and Return Specialist Phil McConkey (Navy,

1979) was a popular player on the New York Giants squad that won Super Bowl XXI. Running back Napoleon McCallum (Navy, 1985) was able to complete his commitment to the Navy and play for the then-Los Angeles Raiders in 1986. After satisfying his Navy commitment, he joined the Raiders full-time.

The game is especially emotional for the seniors, called "first classmen" by both academies, since it is typically the last competitive regular season football game they will ever play (though they sometimes play in a subsequent bowl game). During wartime the game is even more emotional, as some seniors will make the ultimate sacrifice once they are deployed. Recognition of those who share the uniform and are deployed overseas is an important part of the day. At the end of the game, both teams alma maters are played and sung. The winning team stands alongside the losing team and faces the losing academy's students; then the losing team accompanies the winning team, facing their students. This is done in a show of mutual respect and solidarity. Since the winning team's alma mater is always played last, the phrase "to sing second" has become synonymous with winning the rivalry game. The rivalry between Annapolis and West Point, while friendly, is intense. Even the mascots (the Navy Goat and Army Mule) have been known to play pranks on each other. The cadets live and breathe the phrase "Beat Navy!" while for midshipmen the opposite phrase, "Beat Army!" is ingrained. They have become a symbol of competitiveness, not just in the Army–Navy Game, but in the service of their country, and are often used at the close of (informal) letters by graduates of both academies. A long-standing tradition at the Army-Navy football game is to conduct a formal "prisoner exchange" as part of the pre-game activities. The prisoners are the cadets and midshipmen currently spending the semester studying at the sister academy. After the exchange, students have a brief reprieve to enjoy the game with their comrades.

The game is the last of three contests in the annual Commander-in-Chief's Trophy series, awarded to each season's winner of the triangular series between Army, Navy, and Air Force since 1972. In years when Navy and Army have each beaten Air Force before the Army-Navy Game (1972, 1977, 1978, 1996, 2005 & 2012) the Army-Navy game has also determined whether Army or Navy would win this trophy. In years when Air Force has split its two games, the Army-Navy game determines whether the trophy is shared or won outright by the winner of the game. The rivalries Army and Navy have with Air Force are much less intense than the Army–Navy rivalry, primarily due to the relative youth of the USAFA, established in 1954, and the physical distance between the USAFA and the other two schools. The Army–Air Force and Navy–Air Force games are usually played at the academies' regular home fields, although on occasion they have been held at a neutral field. Navy won 14 Army-Navy games in a row from 2002 to 2015, the longest winning streak in the history of the series. On December 10, 2016, Army snapped its 14 game losing streak against Navy with a 21–17 victory.

Traditionally, the game is played in Philadelphia, due to the historic nature of the city and the fact that it is approximately halfway between West Point and Annapolis. Additionally, Philadelphia has always had a stadium large enough to accommodate the crowds. Philadelphia's John F. Kennedy Stadium (JFK) hosted the game from 1936 to 1979 (except for three years in World War II) – more than any other venue in the history of the series. It even hosted the game for several years after the 1971 construction of nearby Veterans Stadium, which finally became the game's host in 1980. The Pennsylvania Railroad and its successors offered game-day service to all Army–Navy games (except several during WWII) at John F. Kennedy Stadium, using a sprawling temporary station constructed each year on the railroad's nearby Greenwich freight yard. The service, with 40-odd trains serving as many as 30,000 attendees, was the single largest concentrated passenger rail movement in the country. Franklin Field, on the campus of the University of Pennsylvania, hosted the game in the early twentieth century before it was moved to JFK. New York's Polo Grounds holds the record for most games hosted outside of Philadelphia, even though the last time it hosted one was 1925. The city of Baltimore has hosted several games throughout the history of the series as well, even though Baltimore is closer to Annapolis. The Rose Bowl is the only site west of the Mississippi River to host the Army–Navy game; it did so in 1983. The city of Pasadena, California, paid for the travel expenses of all the students and supporters of both academies – 9,437 in all. A substitute, however, for Bill XXII – the Navy mascot – and four rented Army mules were brought in. The attendance was 81,000. The game was held at the Rose Bowl that year because there are many military installations and servicemen and women, along with many retired military personnel, on the West Coast. The game has been held one other time in a non-East Coast venue, at Chicago's Soldier Field, which played host to the 1926 game.

Currently the game is played primarily at Lincoln Financial Field in Philadelphia, the home of the Philadelphia Eagles. Since the 1980s, the game has been held roughly once every three or four years at a site other than Philadelphia. These sites have included Giants Stadium in East Rutherford, New Jersey (replaced in 2010 by MetLife Stadium, which has yet to host the game), M&T Bank Stadium in Baltimore and FedEx Field in Landover, Maryland. These are still considered neutral site games but provide locations that are closer to one academy or the other.

Historical facts of the Army-Navy game

The first Army-Navy game occurred in 1890 when Army Cadet Dennis Mahan Michie agreed to play the Naval Academy after the Midshipmen issued the challenge. The Army team was new, and the game was played at West Point with Navy blanking Army 24-0. Three years later, Navy defeated Army at Annapolis and a post-game argument between a Navy rear admiral and an Army brigadier general almost ended in a duel. President Grover Cleveland called a cabinet meeting that resulted in the Secretary of the Navy and the Secretary of War declaring that each team was restricted from playing one another at home and may not play each other. In fact, a Navy Midshipman wore what is regarded by many as the first ever football helmet the same game that almost resulted in a duel. His name was Joseph Mason Reeves, and he went on to become an admiral and a major lead of the Navy's aircraft carrier fleet. He had been advised by a Navy doctor that any further trauma to his head would result in "instant insanity" or even death. He asked a local shoemaker to make him a helmet out of leather and the football helmet was born.

- The Army and Navy have faced off a total of 116 times. To date, Navy has 60 wins, and the Army has 49. There have been seven ties.
- Cadets and midshipmen played the first Army-Navy football game on Nov. 29, 1890 on "The Plain" at West Point. Navy had been playing organized football since 1879 and defeated the newly established Army team, 24-0.
- The 271 members of the Corps of Cadets each contributed 52 cents to pay half of the Navy's traveling costs for the 1890 game.
- Although today we know the game as an annual tradition (and it has been such since 1930), there have been 10 times when the Army-Navy game was not played. It's said that the longest interruption, which lasted from 1894 to 1898, came about after an argument between an Army general and a Navy admiral almost resulted in a duel following the 1893 game. The game also wasn't played in 1909. That year, Army canceled its remaining games after Cadet Eugene Byrne died from an injury sustained in an October game against Harvard. Twice during World War I, in 1917 and 1918, games were canceled on orders from the War Department. And in 1928 and 1929, the academies could not reconcile player eligibility standards.
- On Nov. 27, 1926, the game was held in Chicago for the formal dedication of Soldier Field in honor of the American servicemen who had fought in World War I.
- Going into both the 1944 and 1945 games, Army and Navy were ranked #1 and #2, respectively. Army won both games.
- The tradition of mules as mascots for Army dates to 1899, when a quartermaster officer decided the team needed a mascot to counter the Navy goat and chose a white mule used to pull an ice wagon. However, the first "official" mule was a former U.S. Army pack mule named "Mr. Jackson" that arrived at West Point in 1936. Since Mr. Jackson, there have been 17 "official" Army mules. "Buckshot," the only female of the bunch, arrived at West Point in 1964, a gift from the Air Force Academy. Today, three mules serve as Army mascots: Raider, Ranger II and General Scott.
- Instant replay made its American debut in the 1963 Army-Navy game.

- A 1973 episode of "M*A*S*H" referenced a fictional Army-Navy game that ended 42-36 Navy. To this day, no Army-Navy game has ended with that score. The radio announcer in the episode says the game is the 53rd Army-Navy game. That game was played in 1952; Navy won, 7-0.
- The Rose Bowl is the only site west of the Mississippi River to host the Army-Navy game -- it did so in 1983. Only six Army-Navy games have been held on the campus of either academy. Two of those games were during World War II, one in 1942 and the other in 1943.
- New York's Polo Grounds holds the record for the most games hosted outside of Philadelphia, although the last game played there was in the 1920s.
- Following each game, players sing both teams' alma maters. The winning team joins the losing team and sings facing the losing team's students. Then the losing team joins the victors on their side of the field and sings the winner's alma mater to its students. This act is a show of mutual respect and solidarity.

Legendary Coaches
Charles Dudley Daly

Daly was the head football coach at West Point from 1913 to 1916 and again from 1919 to 1922. Known as the "Godfather of West Point Football", he was coach to Dwight Eisenhower, Omar Bradley, Joseph Stilwell, Matthew Ridgway, James Van Fleet, George S. Patton and other American military luminaries of the 20th century. In 1921 he founded the American Football Coaches Association. He retired from coaching in 1925 after serving one season as an assistant coach at Harvard while on military assignment there. He played college football as a quarterback at Harvard University and the United States Military Academy and served as the head football coach at the latter from 1913 to 1916 and 1919 to 1922, compiling a career record of  58−13−3. Daly was inducted into the College Football Hall of Fame as a player in 1951. In 1901, he led Army to an 11 to 5 victory over Navy. In that game he had a 95 yard kickoff return and kicked a field goal and converted one extra point. That same season he kicked a 50 yard field goal in a game against Yale. Army's only loss in 1901 came against Daly old team, Harvard, when Daly's successor as team captain, Robert Kernan, stiff-armed him en route to the game-winning touchdown. Daly was once again named to the All-American team in 1901. Daly graduated from West Point in 1905 and received the rank of 2nd Lieutenant.

Head coaching record

Year	Team	Overall
1913	Army	8−1
1914	Army	9−0
1915	Army	5−3−1
1916	Army	9−0
1919	Army	6−3
1920	Army	7−2
1921	Army	6−4
1922	Army	8−0−2
Army:		58−13−3

Earl Henry "Red" Blaik

Earl "Red" Blaik served as the head football coach at Dartmouth College from 1934 to 1940 and at the United States Military Academy from 1941 to 1958, compiling a career college football record of 166–48–14. His Army football teams won three consecutive national championships in 1944, 1945 and 1946. Blaik was inducted into the College Football Hall of Fame as a coach in 1964. In 1941, Blaik was tapped to be head football coach for the United States Military Academy. Army had suffered two consecutive losing seasons in 1939 and 1940, the first since 1906, and dropped its requirements for its coach to be a serving graduate and that all players meet restrictive height-to-weight limitations.

The latter was a condition Blaik made as a requirement for him to accept the position, believing Army to be severely handicapped in the size of its linemen. The United States Naval Academy did not have the same restrictions, and the Army surgeon general was persuaded to drop the requirement for football players.

At West Point, Blaik coached for 18 seasons compiling a 121–32–10 record. Blaik's Army teams had a 32 game unbeaten streak from 1944 to 1947, won consecutive national titles in 1944 and 1945, and finished second in the nation in 1946 with their record blemished only by a scoreless tie with rival Notre Dame at Yankee Stadium. In 1946, Blaik was selected as the AFCA Coach of the Year. In 1948, he became one of the first college coaches to implement a two-platoon system, using players strictly for offense or defense. Blaik was also one of the first

Year	Team	Overall	Coaches Poll	AP Poll
1941	Army	5–3–1		
1942	Army	6–3		
1943	Army	7–2–1		11
1944	Army	9–0		1
1945	Army	9–0		1
1946	Army	9–0–1		2
1947	Army	5–2–2		11
1948	Army	8–0–1		6
1949	Army	9–0		4
1950	Army	8–1	5	2
1951	Army	2–7		
1952	Army	4–4–1		
1953	Army	7–1–1	16	14
1954	Army	7–2	7	7
1955	Army	6–3	15	20
1956	Army	5–3–1		
1957	Army	7–2	13	18
1958	Army	8–0–1	3	3
Army:		121–33–10		

coaches to analyze the game play-by play, charting a team's tendencies on every down with the use of game film. During his tenure at West Point, Blaik coached three Heisman trophy winners, Doc Blanchard in 1945, Glenn Davis in 1946 and Pete Dawkins in 1958, as well as a total of 11 Hall of Fame players. Twenty of his former assistant coaches became head coaches in their own right: Paul Amen, George Blackburn, Chief Boston, Eddie Crowder, Paul Dietzel, Bobby Dobbs, Sid Gillman, Jack Green, Andy Gustafson, Dale Hall, Tom Harp, Herman Hickman, Stu Holcomb, Frank Lauterbur, Vince Lombardi, John Sauer, Richard Voris, Murray Warmath, Bob Woodruff, and Bill Yeoman. Legendary fighter pilot Colonel Robin Olds also served as an assistant coach to Blaik. Dietzel, while at LSU, and Murray Warmath, while at Minnesota, won national championships as head coaches. Gillman, while head coach of the San Diego Chargers won an AFL championship. Lombardi, as head coach of the Green Bay Packers, won five NFL titles and the first two Super Bowls. During Blaik's tenure, the Army team adopted the nicknames "Black Knights" and "Black Knights of the Hudson", which has now come to refer to all intercollegiate athletic teams at West Point. Among his West Point players, Blaik was known for being a stern and disciplined coach. They nicknamed him "The Colonel."

1890 Army Cadets

In the Academy's first season fielding a team in intercollegiate football, the Cadets compiled a 0–1 record. Football began being played at the Academy in 1889, but only one inter-class match game was played that year. During the 1890 season, the Cadets played only one game, on the West Point grounds, losing to the Navy Midshipmen by a 24 to 0 score in the inaugural Army–Navy Game. A week before the game, The New York Times reported that the planned match "is beginning to assume almost national proportions." During the game, Army's quarterback Kirby Walker was knocked out of the game four times, the last time being carried off the field and to the hospital in an unconscious state. After the victory, Navy cadets in Annapolis "fired twenty-four great guns, and then paraded the streets with horns."

Dennis Michie

A 20-year-old Army player, Dennis Michie, was the captain of the 1890 Army football team, though he is sometimes listed as the team's head coach. Michie was the lightest player on the team at 142 pounds. Michie was killed in 1898 during the Spanish American War. Army's home football stadium, Michie Stadium, was dedicated in his honor when it opened in 1924. No Army Cadets were honored on the 1890 College Football All-America Team.

Home games were played at The Plain

11/29/1890	ARMY	vs	NAVY	0	24	L
Coach: Dennis Michie			**Season Record >>**	**0**	**24**	**0-1**

Schedule Source: Steve's Football Bible LLC

Selected game(s) highlights

NAVY

The Midshipmen arrived by special ferry on game day. Looking for a mascot, the Navy players spotted a feisty goat tired up outside an Army NCO's quarters. The invaders "borrowed" the goat, thus acquiring their mascot which lasts to this day. The game was played on a gridiron marked off on the Plain, the main parade ground at West Point and the site of annual summer camp until 1922. A good crowd of 500 spectators was on hand to see the competition. The "competition" quickly turned into a rout.

Use of the flying wedge by Navy was a huge factor in this game as Army's Kirby Walker was knocked out four times. The last time resulted in him being carried off the field to the hospital after not recovering consciousness. Fights did break out in the game, but the result wasn't a surprise to historians that were on hand. In addition, at one point during the game, Navy scored a touchdown on a fake punt for which Army clearly wasn't prepared for. In fact, Army protested the play to the officials not knowing the fake punt was a legal call for a team to make. Navy had come to West Point to beat the debuting Army football team. The game was one-sided, with Navy prevailing 24-0, and Cadet Michie wasn't pleased with it at all.

1891 Army Cadets

In the first full season of Army football (Army had played a single game in 1890), the Cadets compiled a 4–1–1 record and outscored their opponents by a combined total of 80 to 73. The Cadets opened the season with a 10–6 victory over Fordham, the team's first-ever win. In the final game of the season, the Cadets defeated the Midshipmen by 32-16 in the second annual Army–Navy Game.

Army's head coach in 1891 was 22-year-old Henry L. Williams, who had played football at Yale. Williams remained at the Academy only one year. He later served as head coach at Minnesota for 22 years and was inducted into the College Football Hall of Fame. No Army Cadets were honored on the 1891 College Football All-America Team.

Coach Henry Williams

Home games were played at The Plain

10/24/1891	ARMY	vs	FORDHAM	10	6	W
10/31/1891	ARMY	vs	PRINCETON A.C.	12	12	T
11/7/1891	ARMY	vs	STEVENS (4-7)	14	12	W
11/14/1891	ARMY	vs	RUTGERS (8-6)	6	27	L
11/21/1891	ARMY	vs	Schuylkill NAVY	6	0	W
11/28/1891	ARMY	@	NAVY (5-2)	32	16	W
Coach: Henry Williams			**Season Record >>**	80	73	4-1-1

Schedule Source: Steve's Football Bible LLC

Selected game(s) highlights

Navy

Army avenged its series opening loss to Navy by doubling up the Midshipmen, 32-16, in Annapolis. The Cadets overpowered the Midshipmen on the ground, scoring three first half touchdowns to take an 18-6 lead at intermission. Elmer Clark scored on two touchdown runs, while plebe Fine Smith blocked Worth Bagley's punt and returned it for a touchdown. Navy was not to be embarrassed on its home field and answered with touchdowns from C.F. Maclin and Henry Pearson to open the second half. Nonetheless, the Cadets padded their lead with two more touchdowns to provide the 16-point difference.

1892 Army Cadets

In the second full season of Army football, the Cadets compiled a 3–1–1 record, shut out three of their five opponents, and outscored all opponents by a combined total of 90 to 18. In the third annual Army–Navy Game, the Cadets lost to the Midshipmen by a 12 to 4 score.

No Army Cadets were honored on the 1892 College Football All-America Team. Dennis Michie, who was captain of the Army football team in 1890 and 1891, was the coach of the 1892 team. Michie was killed in 1898 during the Spanish American War. Army's home football stadium, Michie Stadium, was dedicated in his honor when it opened in 1924.

Home games were played at The Plain

10/8/1892	ARMY	vs	WESLEYAN (1-8-1)	6	6	T
10/22/1892	ARMY	vs	STEVENS	42	0	W
10/29/1892	ARMY	vs	TRINITY (Connecticut) (2-4-1)	24	0	W
11/19/1892	ARMY	vs	PRINCETON A.C.	14	0	W
11/26/1892	ARMY	vs	NAVY (5-2)	4	12	L
Coach: Dennis Michie			**Season Record >>**	**90**	**18**	**3-1-1**

Schedule Source: Steve's Football Bible LLC

Selected game(s) highlights

NAVY

Worth Bagley proved to be quite valuable to Navy, accounting for eight of the team's 12 points in a 12-4 win over Army. All the scoring came in the second half. Walter Izard had Navy's first touchdown run, and Bagley added the conversion. Army's Thomas Carson answered with a touchdown for the Cadets, but Bagley put the game away with six more points late in the half.

1893 Army Cadets

In their first and only season under head coach Laurie Bliss, the Cadets compiled a 4–5 record and were outscored by their opponents by a combined total of 109 to 84. In the annual Army–Navy Game, the Cadets lost to the Midshipmen by a 6 to 4 score.

Laurie Bliss

Some notable Cadet team members were Brigadier General Dwight Edward Aultman, Major General William D. Connor, who later became Superintendent of the United States Military Academy, Major General Edward Leonard King, who later became the Commandant of the United State Army Command and General Staff College and Major General Dennis Edward Nolan, who organized the Intelligence Section for the American Expeditionary Forces' general headquarters during WWI.

Home games were played at The Plain

9/30/1893	ARMY	vs	VOLUNTEER A.C.	4	6	L
10/7/1893	ARMY	vs	LAFAYETTE (2-6)	36	0	W
10/14/1893	ARMY	vs	LEHIGH (7-3)	0	18	L
10/21/1893	ARMY	vs	AMHERST (7-6-1)	12	4	W
10/28/1893	ARMY	vs	YALE (10-1)	0	28	L
11/4/1893	ARMY	vs	UNION (New York)	6	0	W
11/11/1893	ARMY	vs	TRINITY (Connecticut) (0-9-2)	18	11	W
11/18/1893	ARMY	vs	PRINCETON (11-0)	4	36	L
12/2/1893	ARMY	@	NAVY	4	6	L
Coach: Laurence Bliss			**Season Record >>**	84	109	4-5

Schedule Source: Steve's Football Bible LLC

Selected game(s) highlights

Navy

Henry Kimball's one yard touchdown run, and two-point conversion was all Navy needed in a 6-4 victory over Army. The Cadets' Thomas Carson responded with his second touchdown in as many years against Navy, but the two-point conversion was unsuccessful.

The 1893 game also debuted the first football helmet, according to "Newton's Football: The Science Behind America's Game." The leather helmet was worn by Joseph Mason Reeves after a doctor told him he risked "instant insanity" or death if he was kicked in the head again. Reeves, who reached the rank of admiral, is perhaps better known as the "father of carrier aviation."

The "resulting post-game brawls and possibly the threat of a duel between an admiral and general" caused Cleveland to cancel future Army-Navy games, the museum said. (President William McKinley would step in and reinstitute the game in 1899.)

1894 Army Cadets

In their first season under head coach Harmon S. Graves, the Cadets compiled a 3–2 record and outscored their opponents by a combined total of 95 to 22. The Army–Navy Game was not played in 1894.

Edward Leonard King, Captain

Home games were played at The Plain

10/6/1894	ARMY	vs	AMHERST (7-5-1)	18	0	W
10/13/1894	ARMY	vs	BROWN (10-5)	0	10	L
10/20/1894	ARMY	vs	M.I.T. (2-5)	42	0	W
10/27/1894	ARMY	vs	YALE (16-0)	5	12	L
11/3/1894	ARMY	vs	UNION (New York) (3-4)	30	0	W
Coach: Harmon Graves			**Season Record >>**	**95**	**22**	**3-2**

Schedule Source: Steve's Football Bible LLC

Selected game(s) highlights

YALE

The Cadets hosted a strong Yale team that would go undefeated and be retroactively named National Champions at the Plain. Army gave the Eli's a tough match but fell 12-5, giving Yale its closest game of the season.

1895 Army Cadets

In their second and final season under head coach Harmon S. Graves, the Cadets compiled a 5–2 record, shut out five of their seven opponents, and outscored all opponents by a combined total of 141 to 32. The Army–Navy Game was not played in 1895. On November 2, 1895, Army lost to Yale by a 28 to 8 score in what one press account called the greatest and most exciting game of football ever played on the West Point grounds."

Home games were played at The Plain

10/5/1895	ARMY	vs	TRINITY (Connecticut) (4-4)	50	0	W
10/12/1895	ARMY	vs	HARVARD (8-2-1)	0	4	L
10/19/1895	ARMY	vs	TUFTS (8-5)	35	0	W
10/26/1895	ARMY	vs	DARTMOUTH (7-5-1)	6	0	W
11/2/1895	ARMY	vs	YALE (13-0-2)	8	28	L
11/16/1895	ARMY	vs	UNION (New York) (0-5)	16	0	W
11/23/1895	ARMY	vs	BROWN (7-6-1)	26	0	W
Coach: Harmon Graves			**Season Record >>**	**141**	**32**	**5-2**

Schedule Source: Steve's Football Bible LLC

1896 Army Cadets

In their first and only season under head coach George P. Dyer, the Cadets compiled a 3–2–1 record and outscored their opponents by a combined total of 93 to 45. The Army–Navy Game was not played in 1896.

George P. Dyer

Home games were played at The Plain

10/3/1896	ARMY	vs	TUFTS (2-6-1)	27	0	W
10/17/1896	ARMY	vs	PRINCETON (10-0-1)	0	11	L
10/24/1896	ARMY	vs	UNION (New York)	44	0	W
10/31/1896	ARMY	vs	YALE (13-1)	2	16	L
11/7/1896	ARMY	vs	WESLEYAN (4-5-1)	12	12	T
11/21/1896	ARMY	vs	BROWN (4-5-1)	8	6	W
Coach: George Dyer			**Season Record >>**	**93**	**45**	**3-2-1**

Schedule Source: Steve's Football Bible LLC

Selected game(s) highlights

YALE

Summerlike Weather and the largest crowd of spectators that has ever been seen on the parade grounds of the military academy greeted the Yale and cadet football teams. Foot by foot the Yale men forced their opponents back and after nine minutes' play Van Every was shoved across the line for a touchdown. Romeyn punted to Yale's goal line and Hinkey fumbled the leather. It rolled over the goal line and the cadets fell upon It, scoring a safety for the cadets, making the score, Yale 4, West Point 2. Towards the close of the first half, when the ball had been about West Point's goal line for fully five minutes there was a touchback attempted, but it only resulted in Yale scoring two more for a safety. Time was called a few minutes later and the score for the first half stood, Yale 6, West Point 2. After about ten minutes' play the ball was forced down to West Point's goal line near the sideline. Romeyn tried to punt but his kick was blocked and Chadwlck carried the leather across the line for a touchdown. Yale soon had the ball down near the goal line. Humphrey, West Point's left guard, who Is the biggest man on the team, worked like a Trojan and resisted all Yale's efforts to gain an Inch. He was" injured, however, in a mass play, and it was rumored that his collar bone was broken. He retired from the game and Morgan took his place, but a minute later Rodgers carried the ball across the line for Yale's third touchdown. The ball was kicked out. This time successfully, and Hinkey kicked the goal. Score Yale 16 West Point. 2.

1897 Army Cadets

Coach Herman Koehler

In their first season under head coach Herman Koehler, the Cadets compiled a 6–1–1 record and outscored their opponents by a combined total of 194 to 41. The Cadets suffered their only loss against Harvard by a 10 to 0 score and played Yale to a 6–6 tie. The Army–Navy Game was not played in 1897.

Three Army Cadets were honored on the 1897 College Football All-America Team. Halfback William Nesbitt received second team honors from Walter Camp. Quarterback Leon Kromer received second team honors from the New York Sun. Tackle Wallace Scales received second team honors from Walter Camp and The New York Sun.

Home games were played at The Plain

10/2/1897	ARMY	vs	TRINITY (Connecticut) (4-4-1)	38	6	W
10/9/1897	ARMY	vs	WESLEYAN (6-7)	12	9	W
10/16/1897	ARMY	vs	HARVARD (10-1-1)	0	10	L
10/23/1897	ARMY	vs	TUFTS (6-7)	30	0	W
10/30/1897	ARMY	vs	YALE (9-0-2)	6	6	T
11/6/1897	ARMY	vs	LEHIGH (3-7)	48	6	W
11/13/1897	ARMY	vs	STEVENS	18	4	W
11/20/1897	ARMY	vs	BROWN (7-4)	42	0	W
Coach: Herman Koehler			**Season Record >>**	194	41	6-1-1

Schedule Source: Steve's Football Bible LLC

Selected game(s) highlights

HARVARD

The Cadets hosted the mighty Crimson of Harvard at The Plain in West Point. Harvard's ground game and smothering defense were too much for the Cadets as they lost 10-0 to one of the East Coast's best teams. It was the only shutout Army suffered during the season.

YALE

The Cadets hosted the highly touted Bulldogs at the Plain and were heavy underdogs. Army played one of its best games of the season, tying the Eli's 6-6. Yale would be retroactively voted Co-National Champions for the 1897 season.

1898 Army Cadets

In their second season under head coach Herman Koehler, the Cadets compiled a 3–2–1 record and outscored their opponents by a combined total of 90 to 51. The Cadets' two losses came against undefeated co-national champion Harvard and Yale. The Army–Navy Game was not played in 1898.

Four Army Cadets were honored on the 1898 College Football All-America Team. Fullback Charles Romeyn was a consensus first team All-American, receiving first team honors from Caspar Whitney and the New York Sun. Quarterback Leon Kromer, tackle Robert Foy, and end Walter Smith were recognized as third team All-Americans by Walter Camp.

Team Captain Leon Kromer

Home games were played at The Plain

10/1/1898	ARMY	vs	TUFTS (1-9)	40	0	W
10/8/1898	ARMY	vs	WESLEYAN (7-3)	27	8	W
10/15/1898	ARMY	vs	HARVARD (11-0)	0	28	L
10/22/1898	ARMY	vs	LEHIGH (3-6-1)	18	0	W
10/29/1898	ARMY	vs	YALE (9-2)	0	10	L
11/5/1898	ARMY	vs	PRINCETON (11-0-1)	5	5	T
Coach: Herman Koehler			**Season Record >>**	**90**	**51**	**3-2-1**

Schedule Source: Steve's Football Bible LLC

Selected game(s) highlights

YALE

Despite a gallant effort, the Cadets fell to Yale in a close, defensive game, 10-0. Yale put up two touchdowns while holding Army to none. Yale's size advantage proved to be too much as they wore down the Cadets as the game progressed into the 4th quarter.

1899 Army Cadets

In their third season under head coach Herman Koehler, the Cadets compiled a 4–5 record and were outscored by their opponents by a combined total of 100 to 57. In the annual Army–Navy Game, the Cadets defeated the Navy by a 17 to 5 score.

Walter Smith was the Army team Captain.

Home games were played at The Plain

10/2/1899	ARMY	vs	TUFTS (7-4)	22	0	W
10/7/1899	ARMY	vs	PENN STATE (4-6-1)	0	6	L
10/14/1899	ARMY	vs	HARVARD (10-0-1)	0	18	L
10/21/1899	ARMY	vs	PRINCETON (12-1)	0	23	L
10/28/1899	ARMY	vs	DARTMOUTH (2-7)	6	2	W
11/4/1899	ARMY	vs	YALE (7-2-1)	0	24	L
11/11/1899	ARMY	vs	COLUMBIA (9-3)	0	16	L
11/18/1899	ARMY	vs	SYRACUSE (4-4)	12	6	W
12/2/1899	ARMY	vs	NAVY (5-3)	17	5	W
Coach: Herman Koehler			**Season Record >>**	57	100	**4-5**

Schedule Source: Steve's Football Bible LLC

Selected game(s) highlights

YALE

The Cadets hosted the Bulldogs at The Plain and Yale dominated with a powerful ground game all afternoon on the way to a 24-0 victory. The Eli's smashed across the Army goal line four times in keeping their record clean having never lost to the Cadets.

NAVY {@ Franklin Field, Philadelphia, PA}

In the first Army-Navy game held at Franklin Field, Army's Verne Rockwell and Bob Jackson combined to score three touchdowns in the Cadets' 17-5 victory. Considering Navy had shut out its previous three opponents – North Carolina, Trinity and Lehigh – by a combined 71-0 score, this game was termed an upset of sorts. After Jackson started the scoring in the first half with a short run, Navy drove to the Army nine yard line before time ran out in the half. Rockwell and Jackson tallied second half scores, as the Cadets took a commanding 17-0 lead. The Midshipmen avoided a shutout when Ward Wortman scored with just seconds left in the game.

1900 Army Cadets

In their fourth and final season under head coach Herman Koehler, the Cadets compiled a 7–3–1 record, shut out seven opponents (including a scoreless tie with Penn State), and outscored all opponents by a combined total of 109 to 68. The team's three losses came in games against Harvard (29–0), national champion Yale (18–0), and Navy (11–7).

Army end Walter Smith is recognized by the NCAA as a consensus first team player on the 1900 College Football All-America Team, having received first team honors from Caspar Whitney and third team honors from Walter Camp. Tackle Edward Farnsworth also received third team honors from Camp.

Home games were played at The Plain

9/29/1900	ARMY	vs	TUFTS (3-6-1)	5	0	**W**
10/6/1900	ARMY	vs	PENN STATE (4-6-1)	0	0	**T**
10/13/1900	ARMY	vs	TRINITY (Connecticut) (4-3-1)	28	0	**W**
10/17/1900	ARMY	vs	LASALLE	11	0	**W**
10/20/1900	ARMY	vs	HARVARD (10-1)	0	29	**L**
10/27/1900	ARMY	vs	WILLIAMS (6-4-1)	6	0	**W**
11/3/1900	ARMY	vs	YALE (12-0)	0	18	**L**
11/7/1900	ARMY	vs	RUTGERS	23	0	**W**
11/10/1900	ARMY	vs	HAMILTON	11	0	**W**
11/17/1900	ARMY	vs	BUCKNELL (3-5-1)	18	10	**W**
12/1/1900	ARMY	vs	NAVY (6-3)	7	11	**L**
Coach: Herman Koehler			**Season Record >>**	109	68	**7-3-1**

Schedule Source: Steve's Football Bible LLC

Selected game(s) highlights

HARVARD

The Cadets hosted the Crimson before over 5,000 fans at The Plain. Harvard dominated on both sides of the ball as they crossed the Army goal line four times, while handing Army their 2nd shutout of the season.

NAVY {@ Franklin Field, Philadelphia, PA}

Navy's Bryon Long may have hit the game-tying field goal in the first half, but his recovery of a blocked punt in the end zone proved more valuable in the Midshipmen's 11-7 win over Army. Emory Land's touchdown run early in the second half snapped a 5-5 tie and made the score 11-5 after Orie Fowler's extra point. Then, with 10 seconds left in the game, the Cadets' Quinn Gray blocked Charles Belknap's punt into the Navy end zone. If Gray recovers the punt, it's an Army touchdown. But if Long recovers it, it's a safety. Fortunately for the Midshipmen, Long pounced on the ball in the end zone, and Navy had itself an 11-7 triumph.

1901 Army Cadets

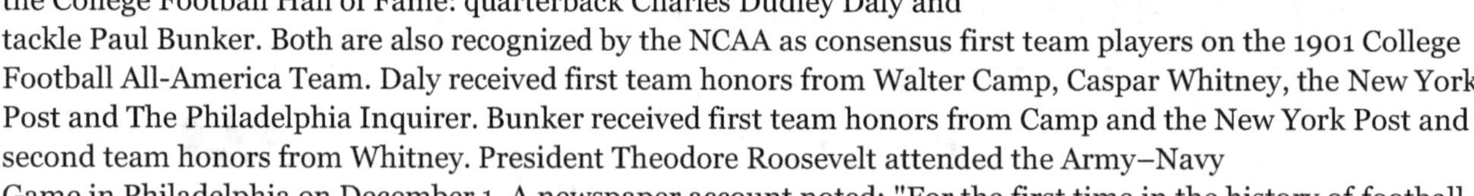

In their first and only season under head coach Leon Kromer, the Cadets compiled a 5–1–2 record, shut out four opponents, and outscored all opponents by a combined total of 98 to 22. The team's only loss was by a 6 to 0 score against an undefeated Harvard team that has been recognized as a co-national champion for the 1901 season.

Two members of the 1901 Army team have been inducted into the College Football Hall of Fame: quarterback Charles Dudley Daly and tackle Paul Bunker. Both are also recognized by the NCAA as consensus first team players on the 1901 College Football All-America Team. Daly received first team honors from Walter Camp, Caspar Whitney, the New York Post and The Philadelphia Inquirer. Bunker received first team honors from Camp and the New York Post and second team honors from Whitney. President Theodore Roosevelt attended the Army–Navy Game in Philadelphia on December 1. A newspaper account noted: "For the first time in the history of football a President of the United States added dignity to a noted contest by his presence."

Home games were played at The Plain

10/5/1901	ARMY	vs	FRANKLIN & MARSHALL	20	0	W
10/12/1901	ARMY	vs	TRINITY (Connecticut) (1-6-1)	17	0	W
10/19/1901	ARMY	vs	HARVARD (12-0)	0	6	L
10/26/1901	ARMY	vs	WILLIAMS (6-4)	15	0	W
11/2/1901	ARMY	vs	YALE (11-1-1)	5	5	T
11/9/1901	ARMY	vs	PRINCETON (9-1-1)	6	6	T
11/23/1901	ARMY	vs	PENNSYLVANIA (10-5)	24	0	W
11/30/1901	ARMY	vs	NAVY (6-4-1)	11	5	W
Coach: Leon Kromer			**Season Record >>**	**98**	**22**	**5-1-2**

Schedule Source: Steve's Football Bible LLC

Selected game(s) highlights

FRANKLIN & MARSHALL

Between two and three thousand football enthusiasts witnessed, the football game here this afternoon between the West Point cadets and the team from Franklin-Marshall College of Lancaster, Penn. It was West Point's first contest for the season and resulted in a score of 20 to 0 in favor of the soldiers. There were three touchdowns, one each by Phipps, Lawson, and Daly, and Daly kicked a goal from the field. West Point scored 10 points in the first half and 10 in the second.

TRINITY

The Military Academy football team shut out Trinity College today by a score of 17 to 0. Daly, West Point's quarterback, not in the game today, he is being in the hospital suffering from an abscess on the hand. Only fifteen minute halves were played. West Point scored 11 in the first half and 6 in the second. Bunker, Graves, and Hackett each made a touchdown, and Bartlett and Farnsworth each kicked a goal.

PENNSYLVANIA

The Quakers made their first visit to The Plain and were sent back to Philadelphia without scoring a point as the Cadets rolled to a 24-0 victory. It was the first meeting between the Eastern Powers.

NAVY {@ Franklin Field, Philadelphia, PA}

Vice President Theodore Roosevelt, who was sworn in as chief executive right after William McKinley was assassinated, became the first president to watch an Army-Navy game. He saw Army quarterback Charles Daly turn in a fine individual performance, leading the Cadets past Navy, 11-5. Daly opened the scoring with a first half field goal, only to have Navy's Newton Nichols tie the score with a touchdown just before intermission. The multi-talented Daly then took the wind out of Navy's sails with a 95 yard kickoff return for a touchdown to open the second half and clinch the 11-5 victory.

1902 Army Cadets

In their only season under head coach Dennis E. Nolan, the Cadets compiled a 6–1–1 record, shut out five of their eight opponents, and outscored all opponents by a combined total of 180 to 28. Army's only loss was 14–6 to Harvard. The Cadets also defeated Syracuse by a 46 to 0 score and tied with an undefeated Yale team that has been recognized as a national co-champion. In the annual Army–Navy Game at Franklin Field in Philadelphia, the Cadets defeated the Midshipmen 22–8.

Two members of this team were inducted into the College Football Hall of Fame: quarterback Charles Dudley Daly and tackle Paul Bunker. In addition, five members of the squad were honored by one or both of Walter Camp (WC) and Caspar Whitney (CW) on the All-America team. They are Bunker (WC-1, CW-1); Daly (WC-3); center Robert Boyers (WC-2, CW-1); tackle Edward Farnsworth (CW-2); and fullback Henry Torney (WC-3).

Home games were played at The Plain

10/4/1902	ARMY	vs	TUFTS (4-6-1)	5	0	**W**
10/11/1902	ARMY	vs	DICKINSON (4-6)	11	0	**W**
10/18/1902	ARMY	vs	HARVARD (11-1)	6	14	**L**
10/25/1902	ARMY	vs	WILLIAMS (3-6-1)	28	0	**W**
11/1/1902	ARMY	vs	YALE (11-0-1)	6	6	**T**
11/8/1902	ARMY	vs	UNION (New York) (0-6)	56	0	**W**
11/15/1902	ARMY	@	Syracuse (6-2-1)	46	0	**W**
11/29/1902	ARMY	vs	NAVY (2-7-1)	22	8	**W**
Coach: Dennis Nolan			**Season Record >>**	**180**	**28**	**6-1-1**

Schedule Source: Steve's Football Bible LLC

Selected game(s) highlights

NAVY {@ Franklin Field, Philadelphia, PA}

Offense, defense and special teams each had a hand in Army's 22-8 victory over Navy. Paul Bunker and quarterback Charles Daly each had rushing touchdowns for the Cadets, while Navy's Ralph Strassburger tackled Daly in the end zone for a safety. Navy cut Army's lead to 10-8 just before halftime when Strassburger returned a punt 55 yards for a touchdown. The Cadets held off the furious Navy comeback with a pair of second half touchdowns. Bunker reached the end zone for the second time that afternoon, while Daly scored a touchdown and added the extra point.

1903 Army Cadets

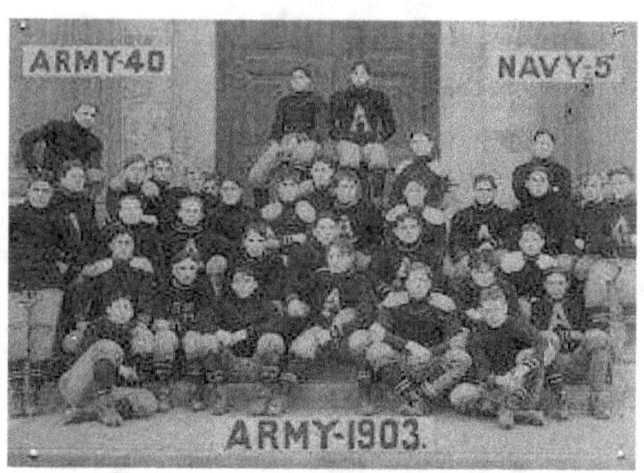

In their first and only season under head coach Edward Leonard King, the Cadets compiled a 6–2–1 record, shut out five of their nine opponents (including a scoreless tie with Colgate), and outscored all opponents by a combined total of 164 to 33. The team's two losses were to Harvard (5–0) and Yale (17–5). In an intersectional game, the Cadets defeated Chicago 10–6. In the annual Army–Navy Game, the Cadets, behind quarterback Horatio B. Hackett, defeated the Midshipmen 40–5.

Three members of the squad were honored by one or both of Walter Camp (WC) and Caspar Whitney (CW) on the All-America team. They are guard Napoleon Riley (WC-2); halfback Edward Farnsworth (CW-2); and fullback Frederick Prince (CW-2).

Home games were played at The Plain

9/26/1903	ARMY	vs	COLGATE	0	0	**T**
10/3/1903	ARMY	vs	TUFTS (5-9)	17	0	W
10/10/1903	ARMY	vs	DICKINSON (7-5)	12	0	W
10/17/1903	ARMY	vs	HARVARD (9-3)	0	5	L
10/24/1903	ARMY	vs	YALE (11-1)	5	17	L
10/31/1903	ARMY	vs	VERMONT (4-5)	32	0	W
11/7/1903	ARMY	vs	MANHATTAN	48	0	W
11/14/1903	ARMY	vs	CHICAGO (12-2-1)	10	6	W
11/28/1903	ARMY	vs	NAVY (4-7-1)	40	5	W
Coach: Edward King			**Season Record >>**	**164**	**33**	**6-2-1**

Schedule Source: Steve's Football Bible LLC

Selected game(s) highlights

VERMONT

The military cadets defeated the University of Vermont here today by a score of 20 to 0. The cadets outclassed the visitors but put up a poor exhibition of football. The Vermont boys played an uphill game, but the soldiers were the stronger, and the Vermont light line gave way before the cadets' attack.

NAVY {@ Franklin Field, Philadelphia, PA}

Army used two Navy fumbles and a blocked field goal attempt to overcome a five-point deficit and overwhelm the Midshipmen, 40-5. Navy took a 5-0 lead on an H.L. Chambers field goal in the first half, but that was the extent of the Midshipmen' offensive output. They mustered just three first downs the rest of the day. Army, on the other hand, boasted a balanced scoring attack. Fred Prince had 15 points, Ray Hill added 10, Tom Doe seven, Russell Davis five, while Ernest Graves, Charles Davis and Horatio Hackett had one point each.

1904 Army Cadets

In their first season under head coach Robert Boyers, the Cadets compiled a 7–2 record, shut out five of their nine opponents, and outscored all opponents by a combined total of 136 to 27. The team's two losses were to Harvard and Princeton. In the annual Army–Navy Game, the Cadets defeated the Midshipmen 11–0.

Five members of the squad were honored by one or both of Walter Camp (WC) and Caspar Whitney (CW) on the All-America team. They are: center Arthur Tipton (WC-1, CW-1); back Henry Torney (CW-1); end Alexander Garfield Gillespie (WC-2); halfback Frederick Prince (CW-2); and tackle Thomas Doe (WC-3).

Coach Robert Boyers

Home games were played at The Plain

10/1/1904	ARMY	vs	TUFTS (2-10-1)	12	0	W
10/8/1904	ARMY	vs	DICKINSON (8-3-1)	18	0	W
10/15/1904	ARMY	vs	HARVARD (7-2-1)	0	4	L
10/22/1904	ARMY	vs	YALE (10-1)	11	6	W
10/29/1904	ARMY	vs	WILLIAMS (3-7-1)	16	0	W
11/5/1904	ARMY	vs	PRINCETON (8-2)	6	12	L
11/12/1904	ARMY	vs	NEW YORK UNIVERSITY	41	0	W
11/19/1904	ARMY	@	Syracuse	21	5	W
11/26/1904	ARMY	vs	NAVY (7-2-1)	11	0	W
Coach: Robert Boyers			**Season Record >>**	136	27	7-2

Schedule Source: Steve's Football Bible LLC

Selected game(s) highlights

NEW YORK UNIVERSITY

In an uninteresting and one sided game the Cadets defeated New York University by a score of 41 to 0. Not once were the collegians dangerous and the Army tore through them for long gains The offensive playing of the New York boys 1 good and several times made a first down, but the beef of the Army was too much and they were unable to gain consistently. Reilly and Reynolds were the mainstays of the New York team and these two heavyweights at the head of tandem formations made all the gains for their team. Early In the first half after the Army had made 12 points, Hill took the ball on a kickoff and went through the entire visiting team for a 110 yard run and a touchdown. The Army gave almost every substitute on the Army squad a trial in the first half made 24 points.

NAVY {@ Franklin Field, Philadelphia, PA}

Midway through the first half, Navy lined up to accept Army's punt at the 50 yard line. The ball apparently touched Navy's Homer Norton, and the Cadets' Art Tipton, racing down the field, kicked the ball ahead of him. The game had suddenly transformed into a modern day soccer match, with Tipton kicking the ball once again toward the Navy goal line. When the ball reached the end zone, Tipton fell on top of it for Army's first touchdown. Despite the controversy surrounding this incident, it was ruled a touchdown and set the tone for Army's 11-0 triumph. This was the Cadets' fourth win in a row over Navy and Army's first shutout in series history.

1905 Army Cadets

In their second and final season under head coach Robert Boyers, the Cadets compiled a 4–4–1 record, shut out three opponents, and outscored all opponents by a combined total of 104 to 60.

Army's losses were to Virginia Tech, Harvard, Yale, and the Carlisle Indians. In the annual Army–Navy Game, the Cadets and Midshipmen tied at six. Halfback Henry Torney was honored as a consensus first team player on the All-America team.

Home games were played at The Plain

9/30/1905	ARMY	vs	TUFTS (5-3)	18	0	**W**
10/7/1905	ARMY	vs	COLGATE (5-4)	18	6	**W**
10/14/1905	ARMY	vs	VIRGINIA TECH (9-1)	6	16	**L**
10/21/1905	ARMY	vs	HARVARD (8-2-1)	0	6	**L**
10/28/1905	ARMY	@	Yale (10-0)	0	20	**L**
11/11/1905	ARMY	vs	CARLISLE (10-4)	5	6	**L**
11/18/1905	ARMY	vs	TRINITY (Connecticut)	34	0	**W**
11/25/1905	ARMY	vs	SYRACUSE (8-3)	17	0	**W**
12/2/1905	ARMY	vs	NAVY (10-1-1)	6	6	**T**
Coach: Robert Boyers			**Season Record >>**	**104**	**60**	**4-4-1**

Schedule Source: Steve's Football Bible LLC

Selected game(s) highlights

VIRGINIA TECH

The upset of the week was VPI's 16–6 win over Army. The army went down today before the Virginia Polytechnic team to the tune of 16 to 6. The visitors outweighed the soldiers and ploughed through their line for steady gains. Carpenter and Tread-well circled the ends repeatedly for long runs. In the first half the army scarcely held the ball at all, and never once threatened the southerner's goal. In justice to the army, it must be said they were weakened by the loss of Erwin, Wilhelm and Beavers. The visitors made their first score on a pretty placement kick from the 25 yard line by Carpenter, who was the star of the game. The army scored in the second half, getting the ball on the fifteen yard line by a fumble. Then, by hard line work, sent Christv over.

NAVY {@ Princeton, NJ}

Princeton President Woodrow Wilson convinced West Point and Annapolis officials to play the 1905 Army-Navy game at Princeton, where the two service academies battled to a 6-6 tie. It was immediately obvious that Princeton was ill-equipped to handle the large crowd in attendance, as a huge traffic jam made both teams late for kickoff. As a result, the game was suspended with four minutes left due to darkness. Henry Torney scored Navy's touchdown early in the first half, while Archibald Douglas tallied Army's touchdown.

1906 Army Cadets

The Cadets compiled a 3–5–1 record, shut out four opponents (including a scoreless tie with Colgate), and outscored all opponents by a combined total of 59 to 37. Henry Smither was the coach in the first game of the season, and Ernest Graves, Sr. was the coach in games two through nine. The team's setbacks included losses to Harvard, Yale, and Princeton. In the annual Army–Navy Game, the Cadets lost to the Midshipmen 10–0.

Two Army players were honored by either Walter Camp (WC) or Caspar Whitney (CW) on the All-America team. They are tackle Henry Weeks (WC-3, CW-2) and guard William Christy (WC-3).

Coach Henry Smither

Home games were played at The Plain

9/29/1906	ARMY	vs	TUFTS	12	0	**W**
10/6/1906	ARMY	vs	TRINITY (Connecticut)	24	0	**W**
10/13/1906	ARMY	vs	COLGATE (4-2-2)	0	0	**T**
10/20/1906	ARMY	vs	WILLIAMS (5-2-2)	17	0	**W**
10/27/1906	ARMY	vs	HARVARD (10-1)	0	5	**L**
11/3/1906	ARMY	vs	YALE (9-0-1)	6	10	**L**
11/10/1906	ARMY	vs	PRINCETON (9-0-1)	0	8	**L**
11/24/1906	ARMY	vs	SYRACUSE (6-3)	0	4	**L**
12/1/1906	ARMY	vs	NAVY (8-2-2)	0	10	**L**
Coach: Henry Smithers			**Season Record >>**	59	37	**3-5-1**

Schedule Source: Steve's Football Bible LLC

Selected game(s) highlights

NAVY {@ Franklin Field, Philadelphia, PA}

"Anchors Aweigh" made its debut at the 1906 Army-Navy game, and the Midshipmen took the song to heart in defeating the Cadets, 10-0. The win over Army was Navy's first since 1900. The 1906 football season was memorable nationwide, as it marked the debut of the forward pass. Navy coach Paul Dashiell added a twist to this new rule to help his team to victory. Thanks to a long field goal by Percy Northcroft, Navy led 4-0 in the second half. On the Midshipmen' next possession, Navy's Homer Norton dropped back in punt formation. Yet, when the ball was snapped, he threw a 25 yard touchdown pass to Jonas Ingram to give Navy the 10-0 victory.

1907 Army Cadets

In their second season (first full season) under head coach Henry Smither, the Cadets compiled a 6–2–1 record, shut out six of their nine opponents, and outscored all opponents by a combined total of 125 to 24. The team's only two losses were to Cornell and to Navy in the annual Army–Navy Game.

Two Army players were honored by either Walter Camp (WC) or Caspar Whitney (CW) on the All-America team. They are guard William Erwin (WC-1, CW-1) and tackle Henry Weeks (WC-3, CW-2).

Home games were played at The Plain

10/5/1907	ARMY	vs	FRANKLIN & MARSHALL	23	0	W
10/12/1907	ARMY	vs	TRINITY (Connecticut)	12	0	W
10/19/1907	ARMY	vs	YALE (9-0-1)	0	0	T
10/26/1907	ARMY	vs	ROCHESTER	30	0	W
11/2/1907	ARMY	vs	COLGATE (4-4-1)	6	0	W
11/9/1907	ARMY	vs	CORNELL (8-2)	10	14	L
11/16/1907	ARMY	vs	TUFTS	21	0	W
11/23/1907	ARMY	@	Syracuse (5-3-1)	23	4	W
11/30/1907	ARMY	vs	NAVY (9-2-1)	0	6	L
Coach: Henry Smithers			**Season Record >>**	125	24	6-2-1

Schedule Source: Steve's Football Bible LLC

Selected game(s) highlights

NAVY {@ Franklin Field, Philadelphia, PA}

Navy combined an early Army turnover with a solid defensive outing to turn back the Cadets, 6-0. The Midshipmen's Percy Wright recovered Frederick Montiford's punt at the Army 25 yard line. It took Navy six plays to score, as Archibald Douglas plowed through from the one yard line to give Navy all the points it would need in its second-straight shutout over Army.

1908 Army Cadets

In their first season under head coach Harry Nelly (at right), the Cadets compiled a 6–1–2 record, shut out five of their nine opponents (including a scoreless tie with Princeton), and outscored all opponents by a combined total of 87 to 21. The team's only loss was to Yale. In the annual Army–Navy Game, the Cadets defeated the Midshipmen 6–4.

Two Army players were honored by Walter Camp (WC) on his All-America team. They are center Wallace Philoon (second team) and end Johnson (third team).[3] Philoon also received first team honors from the Washington Herald, Chicago Inter Ocean, and Fred Crolius. In addition, tackle Daniel Pullen was selected as a first team All-American by the New York World, Fielding H. Yost, T. A. Dwight Jones, and the Kansas City Journal.

Home games were played at The Plain

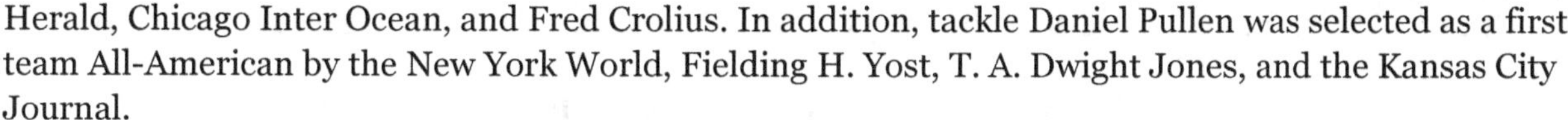

10/3/1908	ARMY	vs	TUFTS	5	0	W
10/10/1908	ARMY	vs	TRINITY (Connecticut)	33	0	W
10/17/1908	ARMY	vs	YALE (7-1-1)	0	6	L
10/24/1908	ARMY	vs	COLGATE (4-3)	6	0	W
10/31/1908	ARMY	vs	PRINCETON (5-2-3)	0	0	T
11/7/1908	ARMY	vs	SPRINGFIELD	6	5	W
11/14/1908	ARMY	vs	WASHINGTON & JEFFERSON (10-2-1)	6	6	T
11/21/1908	ARMY	vs	VILLANOVA (1-6)	25	0	W
11/28/1908	ARMY	vs	NAVY (9-2-1)	6	4	W
Coach: Harry Kelly			**Season Record >>**	**87**	**21**	**6-1-2**

Schedule Source: Steve's Football Bible LLC

Selected game(s) highlights

NAVY {@ Franklin Field, Philadelphia, PA}

Ed Lange's fumble on the opening kickoff proved costly to Navy, as Army's Henry Chamberlain retrieved the loose ball and raced all the way to the Navy one yard line. From there, Bill Dean crossed the goal line for the touchdown (worth five points). He kicked the extra point himself to account for all six points in the 6-4 Army win. Lange somewhat redeemed himself by kicking a second half field goal (worth four points), but it wasn't enough to upend the Cadets.

1909 Army Cadets

In their second season under head coach Harry Nelly, the Cadets compiled a 3–2 record, shut out two of their five opponents, and outscored all opponents by a combined total of 57 to 32. The team's two losses were to Yale and Harvard; the Army–Navy Game was not played in 1909. Army canceled the rest of its season after Cadet Eugene Byrne, a left tackle, died during the game on Oct. 30 against Harvard.

Tackle Daniel Pullen was selected by The New York Times as a second team player on its All-America team.

Home games were played at The Plain

10/2/1909	ARMY	vs	TUFTS	22	0	W
10/9/1909	ARMY	vs	TRINITY (Connecticut)	17	6	W
10/16/1909	ARMY	vs	YALE (10-0)	0	17	L
10/23/1909	ARMY	vs	LEHIGH (4-3-2)	18	0	W
10/30/1909	ARMY	vs	HARVARD (8-1)	0	9	L
Coach: Harry Kelly			**Season Record >>**	57	32	**3-2**

College Football History Books available at www.stevesfootballbible.com

1910 Army Cadets

In their third and final season under head coach Harry Nelly, the Cadets compiled a 6–2 record, shut out five of their eight opponents, and outscored all opponents by a combined total of 96 to 12 – an average of 12.0 points scored and 1.5 points allowed. The Cadets' two losses came against 1910 national champion Harvard by a 6 to 0 score and to the Navy Midshipmen by a 3 to 0 score in the annual Army–Navy Game.

Army's center Archibald Vincent Arnold was selected by sportswriter, Wilton S. Farnsworth, of the New York Evening Journal as a first team player on the All-America team. Arnold was also selected by The New York Times as a second team All-American.

Home games were played at The Plain

10/8/1910	ARMY	vs	TUFTS	24	0	W
10/15/1910	ARMY	vs	YALE (6-2-2)	9	3	W
10/22/1910	ARMY	vs	LEHIGH (2-6-1)	28	0	W
10/29/1910	ARMY	vs	HARVARD (8-0-1)	0	6	L
11/5/1910	ARMY	vs	SPRINGFIELD	5	0	W
11/12/1910	ARMY	vs	VILLANOVA (0-4-2)	13	0	W
11/19/1910	ARMY	vs	TRINITY (Connecticut)	17	0	W
11/26/1910	ARMY	vs	NAVY (8-0-1)	0	3	L
Coach: Harry Kelly			**Season Record >>**	96	12	6-2

Schedule Source: Steve's Football Bible LLC

Selected game(s) highlights

LEHIGH

Despite weather conditions, the football team swept Lehigh before snowed them under bv a score of 28 to 0. The visitors had a chance and never threatened the Army goal. Because of a wet field and a drizzling rain which fell throughout the game, there were many fumbles, the majority of which were recovered by the cadets, who were thus enabled on, several occasions to storm the visitors' goal line for points. Brown was a star for the Army, and both he and Dean thrilled the spectators by spectacular runs, shaking off tacklers and using the straight arm with good effect. Hyatt, the Army quarterback, handled the punts in good shape, but Dean, early in the game fumbled considerably, although the Lehigh ends were to slow to take advantage. Army always recovered the ball. Lehigh tried the forward pass only twice but used (he delayed pass for several good gains until the Army solved It. Louse, the Lehigh tell end. played a star game and did great work for his team on the defensive. The playing was almost entirely in the visitors' territory.

NAVY {@ Franklin Field, Philadelphia, PA}

Seven proved to be a lucky number for both Jack Dalton and his Midshipmen teammates. After missing his first-six field goal attempts in the 1910 Army-Navy game, Dalton connected on his seventh, which was all Navy needed in a 3-0 triumph. This field goal was also valuable in that it capped the Midshipmen' first undefeated season, a year that saw them outscore all nine opponents, 99-0. Dalton's field goal was the lone offensive highlight in a game that saw both clubs combine to punt 40 times.

1911 Army Cadets

In their first and only season under head coach Joseph Beacham (at right), the Cadets compiled a 6–1–1 record, shut out five of their eight opponents (including a scoreless tie with Georgetown), and outscored all opponents by a combined total of 88 to 11 – an average of 11.0 points scored and 1.4 points allowed. The Cadets' only loss came against the Navy Midshipmen by a 3 to 0 score in the annual Army–Navy Game.

Tackle Leland Devore was a consensus first team player on the All-America team. Other notable players on the 1911 Army team include center Franklin C. Sibert, guard Archibald Arnold, and tackle Robert Littlejohn.

Home games were played at The Plain

10/7/1911	ARMY	vs	VERMONT	12	0	W
10/14/1911	ARMY	vs	RUTGERS	18	0	W
10/21/1911	ARMY	vs	YALE (7-2-1)	6	0	W
10/28/1911	ARMY	vs	LEHIGH (5-5-1)	20	0	W
11/4/1911	ARMY	vs	GEORGETOWN (7-1-1)	0	0	T
11/11/1911	ARMY	vs	BUCKNELL (6-3-1)	20	2	W
11/18/1911	ARMY	vs	COLGATE (3-6)	12	6	W
11/24/1911	ARMY	vs	NAVY (6-0-3)	0	3	L
Coach: Joseph Beacham			**Season Record >>**	**88**	**11**	**6-1-1**

Schedule Source: Steve's Football Bible LLC

Selected game(s) highlights

VERMONT

On a wet arid muddy field, making the handling of the ball almost impossible, the Army defeated the University of Vermont here today by a score of 12 to 0. The soldiers played an open game, and the dodging of Milburn and Hobbs through broken fields were features of the game. The Vermont boys once had a chance to score, when Macintosh blocked Salisbury's punt late in the fourth period, but outside of this one instance they never threatened the Army goal.

NAVY {@ Franklin Field, Philadelphia, PA}

On paper, the 1911 Army-Navy game was slated to be an even matchup. Army entered the season finale 6-0-1, while Navy was 5-0-3. Each team had surrendered less than two points per contest, while averaging two touchdowns per outing. The game lived up to its billing, with Jack Dalton's second-quarter field goal proving to be the difference in a 3-0 win. Dalton did much more than kick a field goal, however. He had a pair of 15 yard runs on the Midshipmen' scoring drive and recorded a 72 yard punt.

1912 Army Cadets

Under head coach Ernest Graves Sr., the Cadets compiled a 5–3 record and outscored opponents by a total of 108 to 59. Dwight Eisenhower played at left halfback for the team. Eisenhower's college football career ended on November 16 when he sustained a knee injury against Tufts. On November 9, Army lost by a 27–6 score to a Carlisle team led by Jim Thorpe.

General Eisenhower (3rd from L), General Bradley (far R)

Home games were played at The Plain

10/5/1912	ARMY	vs	STEVENS	27	0	W
10/12/1912	ARMY	vs	RUTGERS	19	0	W
10/19/1912	ARMY	vs	YALE (7-1-1)	0	6	L
10/26/1912	ARMY	vs	COLGATE (5-2)	18	7	W
11/9/1912	ARMY	vs	CARLISLE (12-1-1)	6	27	L
11/16/1912	ARMY	vs	TUFTS	15	6	W
11/23/1912	ARMY	vs	SYRACUSE (4-5)	23	7	W
11/30/1912	ARMY	vs	NAVY (6-3)	0	6	L
Coach: Joseph Beacham			**Season Record >>**	108	59	5-3

Schedule Source: Steve's Football Bible LLC

Selected game(s) highlights

RUTGERS

The Army defeated Rutgers here today in a hard fought game 19 to 0. The Cadets made their first score in the early period, when Rutgers attempt at a forward pass was intercepted by an Army forward and Eisenhower and Hobbs had taken the ball to the visitors' 10 yard line. From this point Hobbs went over, but the trial for goal was missed. In the second period the Army, through steady gains by Hobbs arid Benedict, soon had the ball within striking distance of the Rutgers' goal, and Prichard and Gillespie executed a beautiful forward pass, the latter taking the ball over for the Cadets' second Score. Devore kicked an easy goal. The soldiers then eased up and rushed in substitutes. By hard, straight football the Cadets were again threatening the Rutgers goal, and Prichard and Merrillat essayed another forward pass for thirty yards, Merrillat making the touchdown. Prichard failed to kick goal.

COLGATE

The Army team played Colgate off Its feet hero to-day, winning by a score of 18 to 7. The score was no indication of the relative strength of the teams. The Cadets touchdowns came after the best offensive work seen on the Army gridiron this year, a result of hard straight football Interspersed with several forward passes, with Prlchard and Markoe doing good work in this latter play. Colgate scored the first touchdown in three minutes of play, before the cadets had got their wits together, Riley took Huntington's pass at the extreme left of the field and ran straight down to the Army's 15 yard line before being tackled by Prlchard. The visitors went through the Cadets line for the touchdown in three plays, Swartout carrying the ball. Brooks kicked the goal. Hobbs, Benedict and Keyes, by fine offensive work, put the ball on the Colgate 5 yard line immediately afterward and Hobbs was pushed over for the score. Keyes failed at goal. Keyes scored again in the second period and Prlchard In the last. No Army goals were kicked.

CARLISLE

The fast and tireless Carlisle Indians dropped in here for an afternoon of football and circled and battered the Army eleven for four touchdowns, from which three goals were kicked. The Army made one touchdown and had the honor of scoring first, but that was about all the satisfaction the soldiers derived from the battle. They were beaten by a score of 27 to 6, which decisive drubbing is something they are quite unaccustomed to. There was no help for it, however, for the Redmen were far and away their superiors in the art of rushing the leather over the goal line. It was dark when the game was finished and It was Just about that lime that the whirlwind Thorpe, who had been tearing off great loops mound the ends nil afternoon, tried to kick his fourth goal. That was the only kick of his that went astray, probably on account of the dim light. Whether in the dusk or in the daylight, however, the Indians marched and tore and forward passed their way to the Army goal line, sometimes going us far as seventy yards in one unbroken series of gains.

NAVY {@ Franklin Field, Philadelphia, PA}

At 6-2, 228 pounds, Navy's John "Babe" Brown was not your typical placekicker. In fact, he used his imposing frame to his advantage in the 1912 Army game, and the result benefitted all the Midshipmen. With five minutes left in the game, he lined up to attempt a field goal. But rather than dropkick the ball when it was snapped to him, he took off running before the Cadets tackled him at the five yard line. He booted a 12 yard field goal two plays later and tacked on a 35 yarder with less than a minute left to give Navy a 6-0 victory. The triumph was Navy's sixth in nine decisions and dropped Army's final record to 5-3.

1913 Army Cadets

In their first season under head coach Charles Dudley Daly (at right), the Cadets compiled an 8–1 record, shut out five of their nine opponents, and outscored all opponents by a combined total of 253 to 57 – an average of 28.1 points scored and 6.3 points allowed. The Cadets' only loss was against Notre Dame by a 35 to 13 score. In the annual Army–Navy Game at the Polo Grounds in New York City, the Cadets won 22–9.

End Louis A. Merrilat was a consensus first team player on the All-America team. Tackle Alex Weyand was selected as a second team All-American by Walter Camp and was later inducted into the College Football Hall of Fame. Quarterback Vernon Prichard was selected as a second team All-American by Harper's Weekly.

Home games were played at The Plain

10/4/1913	ARMY	vs	STEVENS	34	0	W
10/11/1913	ARMY	vs	RUTGERS	29	0	W
10/18/1913	ARMY	vs	COLGATE (6-1-1)	7	6	W
10/25/1913	ARMY	vs	TUFTS	2	0	W
11/1/1913	ARMY	vs	NOTRE DAME (7-0)	13	35	L
11/8/1913	ARMY	vs	ALBRIGHT	77	0	W
11/15/1913	ARMY	vs	VILLANOVA	55	0	W
11/22/1913	ARMY	vs	SPRINGFIELD	14	7	W
11/29/1913	ARMY	vs	NAVY (7-1-1)	22	9	W
Coach: Charles Daly			**Season Record >>**	253	57	8-1

Schedule Source: Steve's Football Bible LLC

Selected game(s) highlights

NOTRE DAME

The Notre Dame eleven swept the Army off its feet on the Plains this afternoon and buried the soldiers under a 35-to-13 score. The Westerners flashed the most sensational football that has been seen in the East this year, baffling the Cadets with a style of open play and a perfectly developed forward pass

which carried the victors down the field 30 yards at a clip. Football men marveled at this startling display of open football. Bill Roper, former head coach at Princeton, who was one of the officials of the game, said that he had always believed that such playing was possible under the new rules but that he had never seen the forward pass developed to such a state of perfection. The Eastern gridiron has not seen such a master of the forward pass as Charley Dorais, the Notre Dame quarterback. A frail youth of 145 pounds, as agile as a cat and as restless as a jumping-jack, Dorais shot forward passes with accuracy into the outstretched arms of his ends, Captain Knute Rockne, and Gus Hurst, as they stood poised for the ball, often as far as 35 yards away. The yellow leather egg was in the air half the time, with the Notre Dame team spread out in all directions over the field waiting for it. The Army players were hopelessly confused and chagrined before Notre Dame's great playing, and their style of old-fashioned, close line-smashing play was no match for the spectacular and highly perfected attack of the Indiana collegians. All five of Notre Dame's touchdowns were the result of forward passes. They sprang the play on the Army seventeen times and missed only four. In all they gained 243 yards with the forward pass alone. This was the first time Notre Dame has ever been on the Army schedule, and 5,000 came to the reservation to witness the game. Report had the Indiana team strong, but no one imagined that it knew so much football. Dorais ran the team at top speed all the time. The Westerners were on the jump from the start and handled the ball with few muffs. The little quarterback always displayed great judgment and was never at a loss to take the Cadets by surprise. He got around as if on springs and was as cool as a cucumber on ice when shooting the forward pass. Half a dozen Army tacklers bearing down on him in full charge didn't disconcert the quarterback one bit. He got his passes away accurately, every one before the Cadets could reach him. He tossed the football on a straight line for 30 yards time and again.

NAVY {@ Polo Grounds, New York, NY}

Navy coach Doug Howard could look at the 1913 season from two perspectives. His defense allowed a total of 29 points in nine games, which is quite impressive. But when you consider the Midshipmen allowed 22 in one game, and it was the game against Army, Howard's club did not end the year on a solid note. Indeed, Navy would need more than three Babe Brown field goals to overcome the Cadets. Vernon Prichard and Louis Merrilat caught the Midshipmen defense off-guard with two touchdown passes, and Merrilat's 60 yard run set up West Point's other score in the 13-point victory.

1914 Army Cadets {National Champions}

In their second season under head coach Charles Dudley Daly, the Cadets compiled a 9–0 record, shut out six of their nine opponents, and outscored all opponents by a combined total of 219 to 20 – an average of 24.3 points scored and 2.2 points allowed. In the annual Army–Navy Game, the Cadets defeated the Midshipmen 20 to 0. The Cadets also defeated Notre Dame 20–7.

The team was recognized as the national champion by the Helms Athletic Foundation, the Houlgate System, and the National Championship Foundation, and a co-national champion by Parke H. Davis.

Three Army players were recognized as first team players on the All-America team: end Louis A. Merrilat; center John McEwan; and quarterback Vernon Prichard. Tackle Alex Weyand was selected as a third team All-American by Walter Camp. Four players from the 1914 team were later inducted into the College Football Hall of Fame: McEwan; Weyand; Robert Neyland (later coach at Tennessee); and Elmer Oliphant.

NATIONAL CHAMPIONS						
Home games were played at The Plain						
10/3/1914	ARMY	vs	STEVENS	49	0	W
10/10/1914	ARMY	vs	RUTGERS (5-3-1)	13	0	W
10/17/1914	ARMY	vs	COLGATE (5-2-1)	21	7	W
10/24/1914	ARMY	vs	HOLY CROSS	14	0	W
10/31/1914	ARMY	vs	VILLANOVA	41	0	W
11/7/1914	ARMY	vs	NOTRE DAME (6-2)	20	7	W
11/14/1914	ARMY	vs	MAINE	28	0	W
11/21/1914	ARMY	vs	SPRINGFIELD	13	6	W
11/28/1914	ARMY	vs	NAVY (6-3)	20	0	W
Coach: Charles Daly			Season Record >>	219	20	9-0

Schedule Source: Steve's Football Bible LLC

Selected game(s) highlights

MAINE

The Army defeated Maine 28 to 0. The game was featured by the fine work of Oliphant, the former Purdue star, and McEwan. Oliphant scored three of the Cadets' touchdowns and kicked four goals. He figured largely in the Army's other tally, tossing a long forward pass to Tully who took it across the line for a score.

NAVY {@ Franklin Field, Philadelphia, PA}

Army capped its first undefeated season (9-0) with a "textbook perfect" 20-0 triumph over Navy. The Cadets took advantage of a blocked punt and two Navy fumbles to score their first 14 points. After forcing Navy to punt on its opening possession, Louis Merillat blocked the punt in the end zone for a safety. The Midshipmen' H.C. Blodgett fumbled a second-quarter punt that "Robert Neyland" picked up at the Navy 20 yard line. One play later, Louis Merillat was in the end zone after catching a 20 yard touchdown pass from Vernon Prichard. Finally, Blodgett fumbled a second punt that quarter which resulted in a Paul Hodgson one yard touchdown run.

1915 Army Cadets

In their third season under head coach Charles Dudley Daly, the Cadets compiled a 5–3–1 record, shut out four of their nine opponents, and outscored all opponents by a combined total of 114 to 57. In the annual Army–Navy Game, the Cadets won 14–0.

Three Army players were recognized on the All-America team. Fullback Elmer Oliphant was selected as a first team player by Walter Camp, Monty, and Damon Runyon. Center John McEwan was selected as a first team All-American by Damon Runyon and a second team player by Monty. Tackle Alex Weyand was selected as a second team player by Monty and a third team player by Walter Camp.

Team Captain Alex Weyand

Home games were played at The Plain

10/2/1915	ARMY	vs	HOLY CROSS	14	14	T
10/9/1915	ARMY	vs	GETTYSBURG	22	0	W
10/16/1915	ARMY	vs	COLGATE (5-1)	0	13	L
10/23/1915	ARMY	vs	GEORGETOWN (7-2)	10	0	W
10/30/1915	ARMY	vs	VILLANOVA	13	16	L
11/6/1915	ARMY	vs	NOTRE DAME (7-1)	0	7	L
11/13/1915	ARMY	vs	MAINE	24	0	W
11/20/1915	ARMY	vs	SPRINGFIELD	17	7	W
11/27/1915	ARMY	vs	NAVY (3-5-1)	14	0	W
Coach: Charles Daly			**Season Record >>**	114	57	**5-3-1**

Selected game(s) highlights

HOLY CROSS

In a desperate and hard-fought battle in the Plains today the Army and Holy Cross teams fought to a draw, the score at the finish standing 14 to 14. It was the opening contest of the local football season and for the first time in many years the Cadets were not returned a winner in their initial game. Holy Cross flashed a splendid team, well drilled in forward passing, both in the offense and defense. The visitors threw a scare into the Cadets at the very outset when a long pass of forty yards. "Devlin to McCarthy, netted them their first score. The Army, with its strongest combination in, then ripped up the visitors' defense with line-smashing plays, which finally took the oval to the five yard line, where Ford was shoved over for a touchdown. In the second quarter the Army coaches sent an entire substitute team against the visitors, and within three minutes another long pass Devlin to McCarthy, gave Holy Cross the second touchdown, from which Brawley once more kicked goal. After that the big team went back and managed to stem the tide of defeat by scoring another touchdown in the last quarter. The Army's attempts at forward passing were miserable failures today, not one of the nine trials belng successful.

NAVY {@ Polo Grounds, New York, NY}

The 1915 Army-Navy game marked the first time each team wore numbered jerseys for identification. However, the Navy offense finished with the same number it had a year ago, 0, as Army blanked the Midshipmen, 14-0. Elmer "Ollie" Oliphant certainly left his impression on the Navy defense, accounting for 130 of his team's 196 total offensive yards, along with 11 punt returns for 114 yards. The contest once again fell victim to bad weather, which factored into a combined 30 punts and 10 turnovers between the two teams.

1916 Army Cadets {National Champions}

Team Captain John McEwan

In their fourth season under head coach Charles Dudley Daly, the Cadets compiled a 9–0 record and outscored all opponents by a combined total of 235 to 36. In the annual Army–Navy Game, the Cadets defeated the Midshipmen 15 to 7. The Cadets also defeated Notre Dame by a score of 30 to 10 and Villanova by a 69 to 7 score. The 1916 Army team was selected retroactively as the 1916 national champion by Parke H. Davis.

Fullback Elmer Oliphant from the 1916 Army team was a consensus first team All-American and was later inducted into the College Football Hall of Fame in 1955. Center John McEwan received second team honors from Walter Camp, the United Press, the International News Service, and Walter Eckersall.

NATIONAL CHAMPIONS
Home games were played at The Plain

9/30/1916	ARMY	vs	LEBANON VALLEY	3	0	W
10/7/1916	ARMY	vs	WASHINGTON & LEE (5-2-2)	14	7	W
10/14/1916	ARMY	vs	HOLY CROSS	17	0	W
10/21/1916	ARMY	vs	TRINITY (Connecticut)	53	0	W
10/28/1916	ARMY	vs	VILLANOVA	69	7	W
11/4/1916	ARMY	vs	NOTRE DAME (8-1)	30	10	W
11/11/1916	ARMY	vs	MAINE	17	3	W
11/18/1916	ARMY	vs	SPRINGFIELD	17	2	W
11/25/1916	ARMY	vs	NAVY (6-3-1)	15	7	W
Coach: Charles Daly			**Season Record >>**	235	36	9-0

Schedule Source: Steve's Football Bible LLC

Selected game(s) highlights

NAVY {@ Polo Grounds, New York, NY}

Through 103 Army-Navy games, there has been one constant – neither team can ill-afford to miss an extra point. Of course, there are exceptions to this standard. Take 1916, when "Ollie Oliphant" missed the extra point on Army's first score of the afternoon. Army coach Charles Daly could not have been that upset, considering Oliphant had carried the ball three times for 89 yards during that drive. It was just a sign of things to come for Navy, which suffered a 15-7 defeat at the hands of the Cadets. Oliphant added a field goal late in the first quarter, and the Cadets used a trick play for their final score

of the day. Army was attempting a field goal when holder Charles Gerhardt took the snap and threw to fullback Eugene Vidal for the touchdown. Navy scored its first series touchdown since 1907 when Harry Goodstein blocked a punt and returned it for a touchdown.

1917 Army Cadets

Team Captain Elmer Oliphant

In their first and only season under head coach Geoffrey Keyes, the Cadets compiled a 7–1 record, shut out four of their eight opponents, and outscored all opponents by a combined total of 203 to 24. All eight games were played at home and the Cadets' sole loss came to Notre Dame by a 7–2 score. The Army–Navy Game was not played this season or the next.

Halfback Elmer Oliphant was a consensus first team player on the All-America team and was later inducted into the College Football Hall of Fame.

Home games were played at The Plain

10/6/1917	ARMY	vs	CARNEGIE TECH	28	0	W
10/13/1917	ARMY	vs	VMI (4-4-1)	34	0	W
10/20/1917	ARMY	vs	TUFTS	26	3	W
10/27/1917	ARMY	vs	VILLANOVA	21	7	W
11/3/1917	ARMY	vs	NOTRE DAME (6-1-1)	2	7	L
11/10/1917	ARMY	vs	CARLISLE (3-6)	28	0	W
11/17/1917	ARMY	vs	LEBANON VALLEY	50	0	W
11/24/1917	ARMY	vs	BOSTON COLLEGE	14	7	W
Coach: Geoffrey Keys			**Season Record >>**	**203**	**24**	**7-1**

Schedule Source: Steve's Football Bible LLC

Selected game(s) highlights

NOTRE DAME

Notre Dame won from the Army today in their annual football game. The contest, which was hard but cleanly fought, was interesting throughout. Elmer Oliphant was the whole show for the Cadets, but he could not beat the Fighting Irish alone, as he has done to some other teams heretofore, and the Soldiers had to bite the dust. The final score was 7-2 for Notre Dame.

1918 Army Cadets

In their only season under head coach Hugh Mitchell (at right), the Cadets played just one game, on campus at West Point. They defeated a team from Mitchel Army Air Service on Long Island, New York.

Due to a combination of the end of World War I and the Spanish Flu outbreak, many teams canceled their season.

Home games were played at The Plain

9/28/1918	ARMY	vs	MITCHELL FIELD	20	0	**W**
Coach: Hugh Mitchell			**Season Record >>**	**20**	**0**	**1-0**

Schedule Source: Steve's Football Bible LLC

Selected game(s) highlights

College Football History Books available at www.stevesfootballbible.com

1919 Army Cadets

In their fifth non-consecutive season under head coach Charles Dudley Daly (Daly was Army's coach from 1913 to 1916), the Cadets compiled a 6–3 record, shut out five of their nine opponents, and outscored all opponents 140 to 38. In the annual Army–Navy Game at the Polo Grounds in New York City, the Cadets lost to the Midshipmen 6–0. Army defeated Villanova by a lopsided 62 to 0 score but lost to Notre Dame 12–9.

End Earl Blaik was selected by Walter Camp as a third team player on the All-America Team.

Home games were played at The Plain

9/27/1919	ARMY	vs	MIDDLEBURY	14	0	**W**
10/4/1919	ARMY	vs	HOLY CROSS	9	0	**W**
10/11/1919	ARMY	vs	SYRACUSE (8-3)	3	7	**L**
10/18/1919	ARMY	vs	MAINE	6	0	**W**
10/25/1919	ARMY	vs	BOSTON COLLEGE (5-3)	13	0	**W**
11/1/1919	ARMY	vs	TUFTS	24	13	**W**
11/8/1919	ARMY	vs	NOTRE DAME (9-0)	9	12	**L**
11/15/1919	ARMY	vs	VILLANOVA	62	0	**W**
11/29/1919	ARMY	vs	NAVY (7-1)	0	6	**L**
Coach: Charles Daly			**Season Record >>**	**140**	**38**	**6-3**

Schedule Source: Steve's Football Bible LLC

Selected game(s) highlights

NOTRE DAME

The Cadets hosted the Fighting Irish at West Point in a much anticipated game. George Gipp was the catalyst for the Irish as he ran, passed and played stellar defense to lead Notre Dame to a 12-9 victory. Gipp's first touchdown cut the Army lead to 9-6 just before halftime. Gipp's passing in the 2nd half set up Walter Miller's touchdown run to give the Irish the lead, 12-9.

NAVY {@ Polo Grounds, New York, NY}

After a two-year series hiatus due to World War I, Army and Navy renewed their heated rivalry in 1919. Despite posting seven times as much total offensive yardage as the Cadets, Navy could only manage a pair of Clyde King field goals. Fortunately for Naval Academy fans, that was enough for a 6-0 win. The victory marked the fourth time in 10 years that Navy had beaten Army strictly by kicking field goals. Although the game was played in a steady downpour, neither team lost a fumble nor committed a turnover. The Midshipmen finished the year 6-1, while the Cadets were 6-3.

1920 Army Cadets

In their sixth season under head coach Charles Dudley Daly, the Cadets compiled a 7–2 record, shut out five of their nine opponents, and outscored all opponents by a combined total of 314 to 47. In the annual Army–Navy Game, the Cadets lost to the Midshipmen 7–0. The Cadets also defeated Lebanon Valley College 53–0 and Bowdoin College 90–0.

Two players were recognized on the All-America team. Fullback Walter French was selected as a first team All-American by Football World magazine and as a second team All-American by Walter Camp and the United Press. Guard Fritz Breidster was selected as a second team All-American by Walter Eckersall and a third team player by Walter Camp.

Home games were played at The Plain

10/2/1920	ARMY	vs	UNION	35	0	W
10/2/1920	ARMY	vs	MARSHALL	38	0	W
10/9/1920	ARMY	vs	MIDDLEBURY	29	0	W
10/16/1920	ARMY	vs	SPRINGFIELD	26	7	W
10/23/1920	ARMY	vs	TUFTS	28	6	W
10/30/1920	ARMY	vs	NOTRE DAME	17	27	L
11/6/1920	ARMY	vs	LEBANON VALLEY	53	0	W
11/13/1920	ARMY	vs	BOWDOIN	90	0	W
11/27/1920	ARMY	vs	NAVY	0	7	L
Coach: Charles Daly			**Season Record >>**	316	47	7-2

Schedule Source: Steve's Football Bible LLC

Selected game(s) highlights

NOTRE DAME

For the third consecutive season, the Fighting Irish defeated the Cadets of West Point. "It was the struggle of a good team against a great one," writes a prominent New York critic. "Beaten though the Army, by a score of 27 to 17, the glory of a gallant fight against a too powerful foe remains with West Point. Against a machine capable of pounding its way for successive marches of seventy five and eighty five yards, the Cadets went down as almost any other eleven in the East must have if it had faced the Notre Dame eleven that took the field today.

NAVY {@ Polo Grounds, New York, NY}

Navy's first offensive touchdown in 10 Army-Navy games proved to be a big one, handing the Cadets a 7-0 defeat. This also evened the all-time series mark at 11-11-2. Army was unable to convert on any of its three first half field goal attempts, forcing the teams into halftime deadlocked in a scoreless tie. This remained until Vic Noyes tossed a seven yard touchdown to Ben Koehler for the score. The Midshipmen nullified any hopes of an Army comeback with an interception at midfield to end the game.

1921 Army Cadets

In their seventh season under head coach Charles Dudley Daly, the Cadets compiled a 6–4 record, shut out five of their ten opponents, and outscored all opponents by a combined total of 217 to 65. In the annual Army–Navy Game, the Cadets lost to the Midshipmen 7–0. The Cadets also lost to Yale and Notre Dame.

Three Army players were recognized on the All-America team: halfback Walter French was selected as a third team All-American by Walter Camp, guard Fritz Breidster was selected as a third team All-American by Jack Veiock, sports editor of the International News Service, and a center named Larsen was selected as a second team All-American by Walter Camp and Football World.

Home games were played at The Plain

10/1/1921	ARMY	vs	SPRINGFIELD	28	6	W
10/1/1921	ARMY	vs	NEW HAMPSHIRE	7	10	L
10/8/1921	ARMY	vs	MIDDLEBURY	19	0	W
10/8/1921	ARMY	vs	LEBANON VALLEY	33	0	W
10/15/1921	ARMY	vs	WABASH	21	0	W
10/22/1921	ARMY	vs	YALE	7	14	L
10/29/1921	ARMY	vs	SUSQUEHANNA	53	0	W
11/5/1921	ARMY	vs	NOTRE DAME	0	28	L
11/12/1921	ARMY	vs	VILLANOVA	49	0	W
11/26/1921	ARMY	vs	NAVY	0	7	L
Coach: Charles Daly			**Season Record >>**	**217**	**65**	**6-4**

Schedule Source: Steve's Football Bible LLC

Selected game(s) highlights

NOTRE DAME

In the finest exhibition of football ever shown in the east, Notre Dame met and defeated the Army eleven after the latter was conceded to win by most of the critics. However, it only goes to show that critics are· often wrong and that the eastern brand of football is not superior to the west. The day was ideal for football and as the teams took the field the stands gave vent to a tremendous cheer which threatened the historic walls of Fort Putnam. The first of the game was given to a punting duel and had no material effect as to the score. However, in the second period after a brief exchange of punts, the ball was in the Army's territory and a 35 yard pass to Kiley from Mohardt was good for the initial marker. Injuries were weakening the Army team and after a few minutes, Mohardt passed to Wynne and another touchdown. In the second half, Kiley again came into the spotlight when he again caught a pretty pass and trotted for the third touchdown. Mohardt broke away with his sensational runs for long gains and one of these resulted in the garnering of the remaining tally. Buck Shaw repeated, and his every attempt was perfect.

NAVY {@ Polo Grounds, New York, NY}

Allowing just 124 yards of total offense, Navy posted its sixth shutout in its last-seven wins with a 7-0 victory over Army. Vince Conroy gave Navy all the points it needed with a short touchdown run midway through the first quarter. The Midshipmen defense sealed the deal with a superb effort, halting the Cadets on two key occasions. Army had driven to the Navy 33 yard line in the fourth quarter, as Denis Mulligan's field goal attempt fell short. The Midshipmen's Ira McKee spoiled Army's next hope with an interception at the Navy eight yard line. This win was Navy's third-straight victory over its archrival. In addition to outscoring Army 20-0 in the last three quarters, Navy had a 40-13 advantage in first downs and had outgained the Cadets, 683-230.

1922 Army Cadets

In their eighth season under head coach Charles Dudley Daly, the Cadets compiled a 8–0–2 record, shut out seven of their ten opponents, and outscored all opponents by a combined total of 228 to 27, an average of 22.8 points scored and 2.7 points allowed. In the annual Army–Navy Game, the Cadets defeated the Midshipmen 17–14. Two Army players were recognized as first team players on the All-America team: guard Fritz Breidster and center Edgar Garbisch (pictured at right). Garbisch was later inducted into the College Football Hall of Fame.

Home games were played at The Plain

9/30/1922	ARMY	vs	SPRINGFIELD	35	0	W
9/30/1922	ARMY	vs	LEBANON VALLEY	12	0	W
10/7/1922	ARMY	vs	KANSAS (3-4-1)	13	0	W
10/14/1922	ARMY	vs	AUBURN (8-2)	19	6	W
10/21/1922	ARMY	vs	NEW HAMPSHIRE	33	0	W
10/28/1922	ARMY	@	Yale (6-3-1)	7	7	T
11/4/1922	ARMY	vs	ST. BONAVENTURE	53	0	W
11/11/1922	ARMY	vs	NOTRE DAME (8-1-1)	0	0	T
11/18/1922	ARMY	vs	BATES	39	0	W
11/25/1922	ARMY	vs	NAVY (5-2)	17	14	W

Schedule Source: Steve's Football Bible LLC

Selected game(s) highlights

NEW HAMPSHIRE

West Point vanquished the New Hampshire State eleven here this afternoon by a score of 33 to 0: The collegians were no match for the Army regulars, although they did make it interesting for the soldiers' second eleven, which aggregation essayed to carry the burden of responsibility at the outset of the contest. The cadets today were again without the services of Bill Wood and Garbisch, two of their best men, but Gillmore, a flashy backfield man who can kick and carry the ball, filled Wood's shoes satisfactorily. The speedy Army back was the outstanding star in most of the victor's advances to-day. The result of the game was pleasing to Army's supporters and was sweet revenge for the cadets, who were beaten last season by New Hampshire, 10 to 7. Last season, Conner, a husky back on State's team, kicked a field goal which beat the Army. Today Conner was back, and once more he threatened the cadets' goal posts with his field goal ability, but the oval went low and into the line of scrimmage on Army's 12 yard line. This after Lawrence had fumbled and Christensen, for State, had fallen on the loose ball in the second period. At the beginning of this same period the New Hampshire lads were driving Army's substitute eleven back until they had the ball on the cadets' 10 yard line. Here the big team was jammed into the breach and the visitors were stopped. At this point Lawrence made his costly fumble. The cadets scored in every period and were going strong at the end.

NAVY {@ Franklin Field, Philadelphia, PA}

Army's George Smythe proved to be a thorn in Navy's side, as his 47 yard punt return set up his seven yard touchdown pass to Fran Dodd and gave the Cadets a 17-14 win before 55,000 fans at Philadelphia's Franklin Field. Trailing 10-7, momentum swung to Navy's side as Vince Conroy's one yard touchdown run gave the Midshipmen a 14-10 lead at the start of the fourth quarter. However, the excitement shifted back to the Army sideline, as Smythe's punt return and touchdown pass gave the Cadets a lead they would not relinquish. The Army defense clinched the victory by stopping Navy at the Cadet 22 yard line late in the game. Despite the outcome, the Midshipmen won the statistical battle, outgaining Army, 283-154.

1923 Army Cadets

In their first season under head coach John McEwan {pictured at right}, the Cadets compiled a 6–2–1 record, shut out five of their nine opponents, and outscored all opponents by a combined total of 237 to 56. In the annual Army–Navy Game, the Cadets and Midshipmen played to a scoreless tie at the Polo Grounds in New York City.

Two Army players were recognized on the All-America team. Center Edgar Garbisch was selected as a first team player by Tom Thorp and Percy Haughton and a second team player by Athletic World magazine, Norman E. Brown and Davis Walsh. Garbisch was later inducted into the College Football Hall of Fame. Guard August Farwick received second team honors from Norman E. Brown and Tom Thorp.

Home games were played at The Plain

9/29/1923	ARMY	vs	TENNESSEE (5-4-1)	41	0	W
10/6/1923	ARMY	vs	FLORIDA (6-1-2)	20	0	W
10/13/1923	ARMY	vs	NOTRE DAME (9-1)	0	13	L
10/20/1923	ARMY	vs	AUBURN (3-3-3)	28	6	W
10/27/1923	ARMY	vs	LEBANON VALLEY	74	0	W
11/3/1923	ARMY	@	Yale (8-0)	10	31	L
11/10/1923	ARMY	vs	ARKANSAS TECH	44	0	W
11/17/1923	ARMY	vs	BETHANY (WEST VIRGINIA)	20	6	W
11/24/1923	ARMY	vs	NAVY (5-1-3)	0	0	T
Coach: John McEwan			**Season Record >>**	**237**	**56**	**6-2-1**

Schedule Source: Steve's Football Bible LLC

Selected game(s) highlights

FLORIDA

The Gators to the surprise of many held Coach John McEwan's Army team scoreless in the first half but managed to lose the game 20–0 in the second. Edgar Garbisch missed two first half field goals. In the third quarter Army's passing game began to work, leading to a touchdown by William H. Wood. A blocked punt led to another Wood score. In the fourth quarter, Tiny Hewitt broke through the line for a 35 yard run, leading to the final score by quarterback George Smythe.

NAVY {@ Polo Grounds, New York, NY}

The 1923 Army-Navy game may have resulted in a scoreless tie, but that doesn't mean the afternoon was lacking in excitement. After all, when the two teams combine to punt 26 times, something is bound to happen – maybe even more than once. On the first play of the fourth quarter, Army's Henry Baxter blocked Navy punter Carl Cullen's kick. The alert Cullen scrambled to recover the punt inside his own 10 yard line, which under the rules allowed Navy to retain possession. Although this was long before instant replay existed, the 65,000 fans were treated to the same incident on Navy's next punt. Again, the Midshipmen were inside their own 10 yard line as August Farwick got a hand on Cullen's kick, which the Navy punter also recovered. Navy closed its season with a 14-14 tie against Washington in the Rose Bowl to finish 5-1-3 on the year.

1924 Army Cadets

In their second season under head coach John McEwan, the Cadets compiled a 5–1–2 record, shut out four of their eight opponents, and outscored all opponents by a combined total of 111 to 41. In the annual Army–Navy Game, the Cadets defeated the Midshipmen 12–0; the team's only loss came to undefeated national champion Notre Dame, by a 13 to 7 score.

Five Army players were recognized on the All-America team. Center Edgar Garbisch was selected as a first team player by Walter Camp, Football World magazine, and All-Sports Magazine. Garbisch was later inducted into the College Football Hall of Fame. Guard August Farwick received first team honors from the All-America Board, the Newspaper Enterprise Association, Billy Evans, and Walter Eckersall. End Frank Frazer was selected as a third team player by Walter Camp. Harry Ellinger received third team honors from Davis J. Walsh. Halfback Harry Wilson was selected as a third team player by All-Sports Magazine.

Home games were played at Michie Stadium

10/4/1924	ARMY	vs	ST. LOUIS	17	0	W
10/11/1924	ARMY	vs	DETROIT MERCY	20	0	W
10/18/1924	ARMY	vs	NOTRE DAME (10-0)	7	13	L
10/25/1924	ARMY	vs	BOSTON U (1-5)	20	0	W
11/1/1924	ARMY	@	Yale (6-0-2)	7	7	T
11/8/1924	ARMY	vs	FLORIDA (6-2-2)	14	7	W
11/15/1924	ARMY	vs	COLUMBIA (5-3-1)	14	14	T
11/29/1924	ARMY	vs	NAVY (2-6)	12	0	W
Coach: John McEwan			**Season Record >>**	**111**	**41**	**5-1-2**

Schedule Source: Steve's Football Bible LLC

Selected game(s) highlights

NOTRE DAME {Four Horsemen Legend game}

On Oct. 18, 1924, Knute Rockne's Notre Dame Squad took on Army at the Polo Grounds in New York City. Led by the backfield of Harry Stuhldreher, Don Miller, Jim Crowley, and Elmer Layden, the Irish upset the Black Knights, 13-7. After the game, New York Herald Tribune sportswriter Grantland Rice penned one of the most famous leades in sports history. Rice's iconic memorable headline appeared in the paper's evening edition, as well as the Sunday, Oct. 19 printing. The Four Horsemen helped lead Notre Dame to its first ever national championship, and the quartet of backs became college football icons.

{Excerpted from Loyal Sons by Jim Lefebvre} - Saturday, October 18 dawned sunny and pleasant in New York City. By late morning, the subway lines came alive with the bustling activity of college football fans. The sports event of the year was about to unfold amidst the green grass and grandstands of the Polo Grounds. As many in the huge crowd settled into their seats, the ceremony began. To the roar of the crowd, in marched the West Point Band, playing grand marches as they led column after column of gray-clad cadets into the stadium. Once the game began, many in the huge crowd were mesmerized by the Notre Dame attack that had flummoxed opponents the past three seasons. The shift, and its myriad of fakes and feints, along with cross-blocking in the line, in which Army's linemen were never sure who would be coming at them, was creating confusion through the West Point defense. The Notre Dame rooters were frenzied as their heroes marched downfield and went ahead, 6-0, as Layden scored.

Up in the wooden press box, newspapermen were marveling at the precision and skill shown by Notre Dame. Grantland Rice, considered the dean of newspaper sports writers, was holding court with Damon Runyan and several other notable scribes. Into this conclave strolled young George Strickler, Rockne's publicist and South Bend Tribune correspondent. Part of his assignment from Rockne was to keep an ear open for scuttlebutt and analysis from the "big guys" in the newspaper business. The conversation revolved around the exceptional work of the Notre Dame backfield. "Yeah, just like the Four Horsemen," Strickler piped up, recalling the Rudolph Valentino film much of the team had watched Wednesday night at Washington Hall before leaving on the trip east. No reaction was noted from among the professional writers. The second half started, and Notre Dame continued its charge. Again, the crowd was buzzing at the tremendous coordination and sophistication of the Irish attack. Notre Dame, lining up quickly, going into the shift and snapping off plays in rapid succession, seemed to be catching the Cadets flat on their feet. A dazzling run by Crowley gave ND the final margin in a 13-7 victory.

Grantland Rice, in the evening twilight and gathering chill, sat at his typewriter in the press box and pondered his opening. Something about Strickler's halftime comment and the imagery of horses stuck in Rice's mind when he reflected on the Notre Dame backfield. His fingers hit the typewriter keys:

Outlined against a blue-gray October sky, the Four Horsemen rode again. In dramatic lore they are known as Famine, Pestilence, Destruction and Death. These are only aliases. Their real names are Stuhldreher, Miller, Crowley and Layden. They formed the crest of the South Bend cyclone before which another fighting Army football team was swept over the precipice at the Polo Grounds yesterday afternoon as 55,000 spectators peered down on the bewildering panorama spread on the green plain below."

- Grantland Rice, New York Herald Tribune, October 18, 1924

FLORIDA

The Gators traveled to West Point to play Coach John McEwan's Army Cadets and lost 14 to 7. The close loss was felt bitterly. The Gators were expected to lose 16 to 0. Army's Harry Wilson scored the first touchdown. Ark Newton ran the second half kickoff for a 102 yard touchdown. A second third quarter Gator touchdown was waved off, and Army scored in the final moments to evade the tie.

NAVY {@ Memorial Stadium, Baltimore, MD}

Given the choice of where to play the 1924 Army-Navy game, Annapolis officials chose Baltimore's 80,000-seat stadium. But this supposed home field advantage did not pay the dividends the Midshipmen had hoped, as Edgar Garbisch booted four field goals to give Army a 12-0 win. He may have accounted for all 12 points, but Garbisch had the opportunity to score 21 against the Midshipmen. Army's opening drive ended with Garbisch attempting a 30 yard dropkick field goal, however, it was blocked. Garbisch recovered the block, but his 40 yard attempt four downs later fell short. He also had a 45 yard  attempt midway through the second quarter that sailed wide. Navy may not have reached the end zone, but it wasn't due to a lack of effort. The Midshipmen set a then series record by completing 12-of-22 passes for 50 yards. The Army victory gave the Cadets a 13-12-2 series advantage, a lead it would not relinquish for 56 years.

1925 Army Cadets

In its third season under head coach John McEwan, the team compiled a 7–2 record and outscored opponents by a total of 185 to 71.

When an ill Babe Ruth could not lead the Yankees to the World Series in 1925, college football took center stage at Yankee Stadium that fall. The fiercely competitive Army–Notre Dame rivalry game moved there and remained through 1946. The Army–Navy Game was played on November 28 at the Polo Grounds in New York City, Army won 10–3.

Home games were played at Michie Stadium

10/3/1925	ARMY	vs	DETROIT MERCY	31	6	W
10/10/1925	ARMY	vs	KNOX	26	7	W
10/17/1925	ARMY	vs	NOTRE DAME (7-2-1)	27	0	W
10/24/1925	ARMY	vs	ST. LOUIS	19	0	W
10/31/1925	ARMY	@	Yale (5-2-1)	7	28	L
11/7/1925	ARMY	vs	DAVIS & ELKINS	14	6	W
11/14/1925	ARMY	@	Columbia (6-3-1)	7	21	L
11/21/1925	ARMY	vs	URSINUS	44	0	W
11/28/1925	ARMY	vs	NAVY (5-2-1)	10	3	W
Coach: John McEwan			**Season Record >>**	**185**	**71**	**7-2**

Schedule Source: Steve's Football Bible LLC

Selected game(s) highlights

Notre Dame {@ Yankee Stadium, Bronx, NY}

Not since back in 1916 has an Army football team trampled the Hoosiers under foot. But they did it and there was no doubt about the way they did it. The score was 27 to 0. Before more than 70.000, the largest football crowd in New York's long history, saw Knute Rockne's bewildered cohorts fall beneath the onslaught of the determined, tough, but not particularly brilliant squad from the military academy. Notre Dame tried an aerial game tried it  desperately. But the Army mule knocked those tactics flat. Twenty four forward passes were tried. Only four were successful. Only once did the Hoosiers get past midfield while they were in possession of the ball.

DAVIS & ELKINS

The Army football team defeated Davis and Elkins College, today 14 to 6. The Cadets found the West Virginians strong in every department of the game. Wilson scored for the Army In the second period and Trapnell went over in the final quarter after receiving a pass from Harding. Powell scored the visitors touchdown, running 25 yards after receiving a forward pass. In the final period the Army added another touchdown when Trapnell received a pass from Harding and ran twenty yards to make the score. Harding kicked the goal.

NAVY {@ Polo Grounds, New York, NY}

Six turnovers proved to be Navy's demise, as Army held on for a 10-3 triumph before 60,000 fans at the Polo Grounds. After driving to the Army three yard line early in the second quarter, Navy had to settle for a 12 yard field goal by Tom Hamilton. The Cadets, on the other hand, were able to capitalize upon a fourth down situation just before halftime. On fourth-and-four from the nine, Neil Harding hit Henry Baxter for the touchdown and the 7-3 win. Russell Reeder tacked on a field goal in the fourth quarter for the victory.

1926 Army Cadets

In their first season under head coach Biff Jones (pictured at right), the Cadets compiled a 7–1–1 record, shut out four of their nine opponents, and outscored all opponents by a combined total of 240 to 71. In the annual Army–Navy Game, the Cadets tied the Midshipmen at 21. The team's only loss came to Notre Dame by a 7 to 0 score.

Four Army players were recognized on the All-America team. Tackle Bud Sprague was a consensus first team honoree with first team designations from the Associated Press (AP) and the Central Press Association (CP). Sprague was later inducted into the College Football Hall of Fame. Halfback Harry Wilson was selected as a first team honoree by Walter Camp, the All-America Board, Collier's Weekly, the International News Service, and the Newspaper Enterprise Association. Guard Ernest Schmidt was selected as a first team player by the New York Sun. Center Maurice Daly was selected as a second team honoree by the New York Sun.

Home games were played at Michie Stadium

10/2/1926	ARMY	vs	DETROIT MERCY	21	0	**W**
10/9/1926	ARMY	vs	DAVIS & ELKINS	21	7	**W**
10/16/1926	ARMY	vs	SYRACUSE (7-2-1)	27	21	**W**
10/23/1926	ARMY	vs	BOSTON U	41	0	**W**
10/30/1926	ARMY	@	Yale (4-4)	33	0	**W**
11/6/1926	ARMY	vs	FRANKLIN & MARSHALL	55	0	**W**
11/13/1926	ARMY	vs	NOTRE DAME (9-1)	0	7	**L**
11/20/1926	ARMY	vs	URSINUS	21	15	**W**
11/27/1926	ARMY	vs	NAVY (9-0-1)	21	21	**T**
Coach: Biff Jones			**Season Record >>**	**240**	**71**	**7-1-1**

Schedule Source: Steve's Football Bible LLC

Selected game(s) highlights

NAVY {@ Soldier Field, Chicago, IL}

Army kicked off to open the game, and surprisingly, Coach Jones of the Cadets had a half dozen of his first string players on the sideline. After the teams exchanged punts, the offensive fireworks began. Starting from its 45 yard line, Navy began to mix an array of short passes with its running attack. After several plays moved the ball to Army's 34, Jim Schuber of Navy faked an end sweep but instead rifled a long pass that Hank Hardwick plucked out of the air at the eight yard line before being dragged down at the one. Two plays later Howard Caldwell blasted in for the touchdown, and Tom Hamilton's drop-kick made it 7-0, Navy. Again, the teams returned to an exchange of possessions although Navy clearly held the upper hand, and writer Walter Eckersall later declared that "the Middies appeared unbeatable in the first quarter." Late in the period Navy began a drive from its 43 yard line and, after a penalty set them back to the 32, Hamilton connected on a pass to Schuber that was good for 23 yards. After a couple more plays, Coach Jones rushed the rest of his Army first string into the game just before the quarter ended with the Middies at the Army 22. Several plays later Schuber blasted in from one yard out for the TD, and Hamilton's PAT made it 14-0. Later in the second quarter Army finally got its offense on track behind the hard running of Chris Cagle and Harry Wilson. Starting from their 37 yard line after a punt, the Cadets got rolling as Wilson broke off a dazzling change of pace run of 23 yards to the Navy 40. Two plays later Cagle swept around right end on a 21 yard gallop, and on the next snap Wilson slashed PAGE 11 through the left side of the line and sailed 17 yards to Army's first touchdown. Wilson's placekick made it 14-7. The next time Army had the ball it was unable to move, and so Red Murrell dropped back to his 20, from where he boomed a towering punt that came down to the Middies' Howard Ransford on the Navy 25. Attempting a running catch, Ransford fumbled the ball, and the bouncing pigskin caromed off the foot of Army's Skip Harbold and toward the Navy goal line. Catching up with the ball near the 15, Harbold picked it up and rumbled toward paydirt, and despite falling at the one, the weary cadet managed to squirm into the end zone for the touchdown. Wilson's PAT made it 14-14, and the wild first half soon ended.

1926 game at Soldier's Field

The second half got underway as Army started from its 26 after Cagle's 20 yard run back of the kickoff. Several plays later Wilson swept around left end for a gain of 15 yards to the Navy 44, and on the next snap Cagle broke up the middle and dashed all the way for the touchdown that put Army ahead 21-14 after Wilson's PAT. Despite the stunning comeback by the Cadets, the Middies returned to the attack. Both high-powered offenses fought back and forth until late in the third quarter when Navy started from its 43 yard line after a punt. Slowly the Middies headed up the field as the action moved into the fourth quarter. Hamilton completed two key passes to Alan Shapley on the drive, and Ransford chipped in a critical gain of eight yards for a first down at Army's 15. The 12 play drive was capped off in sensational fashion when Shapley swept around right end on a fourth down and three play for an eight yard touchdown run. With the entire stadium holding its breath, Hamilton calmly drop-kicked the extra point to tie it at 21-21. With just over seven minutes left to play, the surrounding gloom and darkness had gathered to the point where it was increasingly difficult for fans and writers in the press box to distinguish the players on the field. Still, Army mounted one last attempt at the win, starting from its 27 yard line after the following kickoff. On the second play of the series Wilson broke through left tackle for a 28 yard dash into Navy territory, and then he and Murrell alternated in pounding the Middies' line. Finally, checked just inside the 20, Wilson dropped back to attempt a place-kick from the 26. The ball was spotted directly in front of the goal posts, but incredibly Wilson's kick sailed just wide. The final couple minutes were played in "almost total darkness," as the electric lights over the stadium's entrance tunnels and, on the Scoreboard, twinkled in the gloom. On the last play of the game Hamilton attempted a desperate pass for Navy, but the aerial was intercepted by (and here's where the darkness contributed to the confusion) either Wilson, Cagle, or Chuck Harding -- depending on which game account you choose to accept. The runback was finally halted deep in Navy territory, and so the monumental battle ended in a 21-21 tie.

1927 Army Cadets

In their second season under head coach Biff Jones, the Cadets compiled a 9–1 record, shut out six of their ten opponents, and outscored all opponents by a combined total of 197 to 37. In the annual Army–Navy Game, the Cadets defeated the Midshipmen 14–9. The team's only loss came to national champion Yale by a 10 to 6 score. Four Army players were recognized on the All-America team. Halfback Red Cagle was a

consensus first team honoree and was later inducted into the College Football Hall of Fame. Tackle Bud Sprague was selected as a first team honoree by the Associated Press (AP), the International News Service (INS), and the Central Press Association (CP). End Charles Born was selected as a second team honoree by the United Press (UP), Hearst newspapers, New York Sun, and Billy Evans. Tackle George Perry was selected as a first team honoree by the New York Sun.

Home games were played at Michie Stadium

9/24/1927	ARMY	vs	BOSTON U	13	0	W
10/1/1927	ARMY	vs	DETROIT MERCY (7-2)	6	0	W
10/8/1927	ARMY	vs	MARQUETTE (6-3)	21	12	W
10/15/1927	ARMY	vs	DAVIS & ELKINS	27	6	W
10/22/1927	ARMY	@	Yale (7-1)	6	10	L
10/29/1927	ARMY	vs	BUCKNELL	34	0	W
11/5/1927	ARMY	vs	FRANKLIN & MARSHALL	45	0	W
11/12/1927	ARMY	vs	NOTRE DAME (7-1-1)	18	0	W
11/19/1927	ARMY	vs	URSINUS	13	0	W
11/26/1927	ARMY	vs	NAVY (6-3)	14	9	W
Coach: Biff Jones			**Season Record >>**	197	37	9-1

Schedule Source: Steve's Football Bible LLC

Selected game(s) highlights

Notre Dame {@ Yankee Stadium, Bronx, NY}

In what was called the greatest game that Army played in several years, Notre Dame went down to a crushing defeat. Before an immense gathering in Yankee Stadium, the West Point team played an alert, heady game causing the biggest upset of the season. No doubt Red Cagle was the outstanding start, but to forget William Nave would be a crime in fact, not to mention anyone who played on that inspired team would be an injustice. However, Cagle with his runs from pass formation, his beautiful forward passes, his receiving a pass from Richard Hutchinson, and his air-tight defense was the star. Nave distinguished himself as field general. The line was perfect, charging with coordination and precision, and holding down the plucky Notre Dame forwards when it was necessary. To say that Notre Dame was unimpressive is most unworthy. We have never seen a Rockne coached team which did not typify good football. To stop Niemic, Voedish, Smith and Flannigan required almost superhuman endeavor, but that day Army was worthy of the task set before them.

NAVY {@ Polo Grounds, New York, NY}

In the last Army-Navy game played at the Polo Grounds, the Cadets overcame a pesky Midshipmen club to claim a 14-9 victory. Navy held a 2-0 lead at halftime, but it could have just as easily been 16-0. On its first possession, Navy reached the Army eight yard line but came away without a point. Midway through the second quarter, the Midshipmen' Carl Giese blocked a punt out of the end zone to give Navy a 2-0 lead. Navy had another chance to reach the end zone just before halftime, but Army stopped Joe Clifton on a fourth-and-goal from the one yard line. A two yard run by Lighthorse Harry Wilson gave the Cadets a 7-2 advantage early in the third quarter. Army added another touchdown to its lead when Chris Cagle intercepted an Ed Hannegan pass and returned it 41 yards to the Navy four yard line. Wilson scored again, and Army was on its way to the win.

1928 Army Cadets

Led by head coach Biff Jones, the team finished the season with a record of 8–2. The 1928 season was one of the few years in which Army did not play the Navy Midshipmen in the Army–Navy Game. Against Notre Dame at Yankee Stadium, with the game scoreless at halftime, legendary Notre Dame coach Knute Rockne gave his "win one for the Gipper" speech (with reference to All-American halfback George Gipp, who died in 1920); Notre Dame went on to win, 12–6. Army participated in the best-attended college football game at Yankee Stadium on December 1, when Army lost to Stanford 26–0 before 86,000.

Home games were played at Michie Stadium

9/29/1928	ARMY	vs	BOSTON U	35	0	W
10/6/1928	ARMY	vs	SMU (6-3-1)	14	13	W
10/13/1928	ARMY	vs	PROVIDENCE	44	0	W
10/20/1928	ARMY	@	Harvard (5-2-1)	15	0	W
10/27/1928	ARMY	@	Yale (4-4)	18	6	W
11/3/1928	ARMY	vs	DEPAUW	38	12	W
11/10/1928	ARMY	vs	NOTRE DAME (5-4)	6	12	L
11/17/1928	ARMY	vs	CARLETON	32	7	W
11/24/1928	ARMY	vs	NEBRASKA (7-1-1)	13	3	W
12/1/1928	ARMY	vs	STANFORD (8-3-1)	0	26	L
Coach: Biff Jones			**Season Record >>**	215	79	**8-2**

Schedule Source: Steve's Football Bible LLC

Selected game(s) highlights

NOTRE DAME {"Win one for the Gipper" game}

Before 80,000 fans at Yankee Stadium, the Fighting Irish rallied from a 6-0 halftime deficit to beat the Army, 12-6, after Coach Knute Rockne gave his famous "Win one for the Gipper speech". The speech had its intended effect as the Irish held on to beat an undefeated Army squad at Yankee Stadium.

"I've got to go, Rock. It's all right. I'm not afraid. Some time, Rock, when the team is up against it, when things are wrong and the breaks are beating the boys, ask them to go in there with all they've got and win just one for the Gipper. I don't know where I'll be then, Rock. But I'll know about it, and I'll be happy."

NEBRASKA

The Cornhuskers traveled to West Point for the first ever meeting of the Cadets with any Big 6 team. The Army squad was an eastern team to be feared, carrying only one loss on their season to date, and it looked to be a major event as Nebraska itself was rolling along with just the scoreless tie of last week making any blemish on the record. The teams seemed evenly matched to start, and it wasn't until the 2nd quarter than Nebraska put the first points on the board. Settling back to hold the three-point lead, the Cornhuskers went into a strong defensive mode, but the Army squad found the end zone in the third quarter anyway. Night fell, and play was complicated by the darkness on the unlit field, yet Army managed a late touchdown to firmly seal the game and hand the Cornhuskers their first and only loss of 1928.

1929 Army Cadets

Led by head coach Biff Jones, the team finished with a record of two wins and nine losses. The Cadets offense scored 276 points, while the defense allowed 132 points. The club started the season with three wins and one tie but finished with a 6–4–1 record. Christian "Red" Cagle was the team's Captain (pictured at right).

The 1929 game between Army and Notre Dame had the highest attendance in the series at 79,408.

Home games were played at Michie Stadium

9/28/1929	ARMY	vs	BOSTON U	26	0	W
10/5/1929	ARMY	vs	GETTYSBURG	33	7	W
10/12/1929	ARMY	vs	DAVIDSON (5-5)	23	7	W
10/19/1929	ARMY	@	Harvard (5-2-1)	20	20	T
10/26/1929	ARMY	@	Yale (5-2-1)	13	21	L
11/2/1929	ARMY	vs	SOUTH DAKOTA	33	6	W
11/9/1929	ARMY	@	Illinois (6-1-1)	7	17	L
11/16/1929	ARMY	vs	DICKINSON	89	7	W
11/23/1929	ARMY	vs	OHIO Wesleyan	19	6	W
11/30/1929	ARMY	vs	NOTRE DAME (9-0)	0	7	L
12/28/1929	ARMY	@	Stanford (9-2)	13	34	L
Coach: Biff Jones			**Season Record >>**	**276**	**132**	**6-4-1**

Schedule Source: Steve's Football Bible LLC

Selected game(s) highlights

Notre Dame {@ Yankee Stadium, Bronx, NY}

In the last game of the season for Notre Dame, the Fighting Irish came into the game sporting an 8-0 record. Army was looking for revenge from last season's "Gipper Speech" loss to the Irish. During the second quarter of the 1929 showdown that had remained scoreless, an Army rush on an Irish punt set up the Cadets at the Notre Dame 13. On a day where opportunities to score were almost non-existent, the Cadets had the game's first chance. On third-and-8 from the 11, star halfback Chris "Red" Cagle scrambled with the ball to his right before throwing across the field to intended receiver Carl Carlmark for what had the makings of a touchdown — until Jack Elder cut in front of him, grabbed the toss and raced past his pursuers with his Olympic-caliber speed for what still stands as an Irish record 100 yard interception return for a touchdown. The Irish defense made that play stand up as they beat the Cadets, 7-0.

1930 Army Cadets

In their first season under head coach Ralph Sasse (pictured at right), the Cadets compiled a 9–1–1 record, shut out seven of their eleven opponents, and outscored all opponents by a combined total of 268 to 22, an average of 24.4 points scored and 2.0 points allowed per game. In the annual Army–Navy Game, the Cadets defeated the Midshipmen 6–0. The team's only blemish was a 7–6 loss to undefeated national champion Notre Dame team in Knute Rockne's final year as head coach.

Two Army players were recognized on the All-America team. Tackle Jack Price received first team honors from the North American Newspaper Association (NANA) and the Los Angeles Times. Guard Charles Humber received second team honors from the International News Service (INS) and third team honors from the Associated Press (AP).

Home games were played at Michie Stadium

9/27/1930	ARMY	vs	BOSTON U	39	0	W
10/4/1930	ARMY	vs	FURMAN	54	0	W
10/11/1930	ARMY	vs	SWARTHMORE	39	0	W
10/18/1930	ARMY	@	Harvard (4-4-1)	6	0	W
10/25/1930	ARMY	@	Yale (5-2-2)	7	7	T
11/1/1930	ARMY	vs	NORTH DAKOTA	33	6	W
11/8/1930	ARMY	vs	ILLINOIS (3-5)	13	0	W
11/15/1930	ARMY	vs	KENTUCKY WESLEYAN	47	2	W
11/22/1930	ARMY	vs	URSINUS	18	0	W
11/29/1930	ARMY	vs	NOTRE DAME (10-0)	6	7	L
12/13/1930	ARMY	vs	NAVY (6-5)	6	0	W
Coach: Ralph Sasse			**Season Record >>**	**268**	**22**	**9-1-1**

Schedule Source: Steve's Football Bible LLC

Selected game(s) highlights

NAVY {@ Yankee Stadium, Bronx, NY}

A disagreement regarding eligibility policies may have cancelled the 1928 and '29 Army-Navy games, but a capacity crowd at Yankee Stadium welcomed the rivalry's return Dec. 13, 1930. Unfortunately for Navy, Army retained its recent series dominance with a 6-0 victory. The final score certainly doesn't reflect Army's commanding performance, as the Cadets finished the afternoon with 265 yards of total offense, compared to 63 for the Midshipmen. Yet, Navy was able to keep Army off the scoreboard until the fourth quarter, when Ray Stecker ran 56 yards for the game's lone score. Navy had a chance to win the game on its final possession. Army's Wendell Bowman fumbled a punt on his own 37 yard line, and the Midshipmen's John Byng recovered. The Midshipmen drove 12 yards but were stopped on downs. The Cadets took over and advanced to the Navy seven yard line as time ran out.

1931 Army Cadets

In their second season under head coach Ralph Sasse, the Cadets compiled an 8–2–1 record, shut out four of their eleven opponents, and outscored all opponents by a combined total of 296 to 72. In the annual Army–Navy Game, the Cadets defeated the Midshipmen 17–7. The Cadets also defeated Notre Dame, 12 to 0. Army's two losses were to Harvard by a point and a 26–0 shutout at Pittsburgh. Right End Richard Brinsley Sheridan, Jr. (pictured at right) broke his neck making a tackle in the tie with Yale and died two days later of his injuries.

Two Army players were recognized on the All-America team. Tackle Jack Price received first team honors from the International News Service (INS) and Central Press Association (CP), and halfback Ray Stecker received third team honors from the INS.

Home games were played at Michie Stadium

9/26/1931	ARMY	vs	OHIO Northern	60	0	W
10/3/1931	ARMY	vs	KNOX	67	6	W
10/10/1931	ARMY	vs	MICHIGAN STATE (5-3-1)	20	7	W
10/17/1931	ARMY	vs	HARVARD (7-1)	13	14	L
10/24/1931	ARMY	@	Yale (5-1-2)	6	6	T
10/31/1931	ARMY	vs	COLORADO COLLEGE (4-4)	27	0	W
11/7/1931	ARMY	vs	LSU (5-4)	20	0	W
11/14/1931	ARMY	@	Pittsburgh (8-1)	0	26	L
11/21/1931	ARMY	vs	URSINUS	54	6	W
11/28/1931	ARMY	vs	NOTRE DAME (6-2-1)	12	0	W
12/12/1931	ARMY	vs	NAVY (5-5-1)	17	7	W
Coach: Ralph Sasse			**Season Record >>**	**296**	**72**	**8-2-1**

Schedule Source: Steve's Football Bible LLC

Selected game(s) highlights

Notre Dame {@ Yankee Stadium, Bronx, NY}

A ripping, tearing Army team, full of fight and flame, struck Notre Dame today with the sweep of a cyclone. This Army team beat the South Bend invaders, 12-0, as 80,000 sat through a swirling snowstorm during the first half of the bitter battle to get the shock of lives. The Army won the game on two great plays. The first was a long pass from Brown to Stecker in the first quarter that picked up 58 yards and led to the first touchdown. The second deadly thrust that found Notre Dame's heart came in the final quarter With the brilliant Stecker, the big star of afternoon, swept around Notre Dame's for 70 yards and the second touchdown. **Grantland Rice – Baltimore Sun**

NAVY {@ Yankee Stadium, Bronx, NY}

The running of Ed Herb and Ray Stecker paced Army to a 17-7 win over Navy at Yankee Stadium. The first of Herb's touchdown runs and a Travis Brown 25 yard field goal gave the Cadets a 10-0 halftime lead. Navy cut the deficit to 10-7 in the third quarter when Lou Kirn and Harvey Tschirgi connected on a 55 yard scoring strike. Herb then erased any hopes of a Navy triumph when he went up and over from the one yard line late in the final stanza. By reaching the end zone twice, Herb certainly garnered most of the headlines. However, the real hero was Stecker, who turned in a workman-like 141 yards on 29 carries.

1932 Army Cadets

In their third and final season under head coach Ralph Sasse, the Cadets compiled an 8–2 record, shut out eight of their ten opponents, and outscored all opponents by a combined total of 261 to 39. In the annual Army–Navy Game, the Cadets defeated the Midshipmen 20–0. The Cadets also defeated Harvard, 40 to 0. The team's two losses were to Pittsburgh by an 18 to 13 score and a 21–0 shutout by Notre Dame at Yankee Stadium. Three Army players were recognized on the All-America team. Guard Milton Summerfelt was a consensus first team player. End Dick King received first team honors from the New York Sun, and second team honors from the Associated Press (AP), Newspaper Enterprise Association (NEA), and International News Service (INS). Quarterback Felix Vidal received third team honors from the AP.

Home games were played at Michie Stadium

10/1/1932	ARMY	vs	FURMAN	13	0	W
10/8/1932	ARMY	vs	CARLETON	57	0	W
10/15/1932	ARMY	vs	PITTSBURGH (8-1-2)	13	18	L
10/22/1932	ARMY	@	Yale (2-2-3)	20	0	W
10/29/1932	ARMY	vs	WILLIAM & MARY (8-4)	33	0	W
11/5/1932	ARMY	@	Harvard (5-3)	46	0	W
11/12/1932	ARMY	vs	NORTH DAKOTA AGRICULTURE	52	0	W
11/19/1932	ARMY	vs	WEST VIRGINIA Wesleyan	7	0	W
11/26/1932	ARMY	vs	NOTRE DAME (7-2)	0	21	L
12/3/1932	ARMY	vs	NAVY (2-6-1)	20	0	W
Coach: Ralph Sasse			**Season Record >>**	261	39	8-2

Schedule Source: Steve's Football Bible LLC

Selected game(s) highlights

WEST VIRGINIA WESLEYAN

Several near drownings occurred here today as the Army waded to a 7 to 0 victory over a gallant fighting eleven from West Virginia Wesleyan in the lake that was Michie Stadium. Army sent in its second team at the start of the game and Wesleyan held them scoreless in the first half. Early in the third period the entire Army varsity went in, scored a touchdown in three minutes and trotted tf the field. The touchdown was scored by Vidal in a spectacular 70 yard run.

Notre Dame {@ Yankee Stadium, Bronx, NY}

Under perfect weather conditions, before 80,000 people, and in a glorious setting, Notre Dame gave one of its most glamorous performances of all-time at Yankee Stadium, and completely outclassed one of the best Army teams in history by a 21-0 score. Notre Dame took to the air and made a quick touch-down on two flashy pass plays, with Melinkovich scoring. The second score came early in the second half and climaxed a 73 yard advance, with Devore getting the score on a 37 yard pass. The final touchdown came late in the third period, when, after Banas kicked Army into a hole on its 3 yard line. Fields fumbled the ball on an attempted punt, and Jim Harris recovered in the end zone.

NAVY {@ Franklin Field, Philadelphia, PA}

Thanks in large part to a Navy offense that mustered just 15 yards on the ground and turned the ball over seven times, Army rolled to a 20-0 win over the Midshipmen. Rip Miller's club had an early indication this may not be its day when its opening drive was halted by an interception at the Army six yard line. On first down, the Cadets' Kenneth Field "quick-kicked" the ball 85 yards to the Navy 15 yard line. Peck Vidal opened the scoring with a two yard touchdown run in the first quarter, and Army added two more scores in the final half. Jack Buckler scored one on a short run and took a lateral from Tom Kilday and passed 43 yards to Bill Frentzer for the other touchdown.

1933 Army Cadets

In their first year under head coach Garrison H. Davidson (pictured at right), the Cadets compiled a 9–1 record, shut out seven of their ten opponents, and outscored all opponents by a combined total of 227 to 26. In the annual Army–Navy Game, the Cadets defeated the Midshipmen 12–7. In the final game of the season at Yankee Stadium, the undefeated Cadets were upset by struggling Notre Dame, 13–12.

Four Army players were recognized on the All-America team. Halfback Jack Buckler received first team honors from the Associated Press (AP), United Press (UP), Newspaper Enterprise Association (NEA), Central Press Association (CP), and New York Sun. Quarterback Paul Johnson received second team honors from the AP and NEA. Guard Harvey Jablonsky received second team honors from the NEA, CP, and International News Service (INS). End Peter James Kopcsak received third team honors from the CP.

Home games were played at Michie Stadium

9/30/1933	ARMY	vs	MERCER (4-3-2)	19	6	W
10/7/1933	ARMY	vs	VMI (2-7-1)	32	0	W
10/14/1933	ARMY	vs	DELAWARE	52	0	W
10/21/1933	ARMY	vs	Illinois (5-3)	6	0	W
10/28/1933	ARMY	@	Yale (4-4)	21	0	W
11/4/1933	ARMY	vs	COE	34	0	W
11/11/1933	ARMY	@	Harvard (5-2-1)	27	0	W
11/18/1933	ARMY	vs	PENNSYLVANIA Military	12	0	W
11/25/1933	ARMY	vs	NAVY (5-4)	12	7	W
12/2/1933	ARMY	vs	NOTRE DAME (3-5-1)	12	13	L
Coach: Gar Davidson			**Season Record >>**	**227**	**26**	**9-1**

Schedule Source: Steve's Football Bible LLC

Selected game(s) highlights

NAVY {@ Franklin Field, Philadelphia, PA}

Army scored a pair of first half touchdowns and held on for a 12-7 win over a feisty Rip Miller-coached Navy club. The win was Army's ninth in as many games, and a Dec. 2 victory over 2-5-1 Notre Dame would all but guarantee the Cadets the 1933 national title. However, the Fighting Irish spoiled these hopes by handing Army a 13-12 setback. For the first time since 1916, Army scored in the opening quarter against Navy. Paul Johnson took Bill Clark's punt and returned it 81 yards for the touchdown. But the extra point was blocked, which enabled Navy to take a 7-6 lead when Red Baumberger galloped 38 yards to the Cadet end zone. Nonetheless, Army's Jack Buckler, whose extra point was blocked on his team's first score, raced 25 yards for the winning touchdown in the second half.

Notre Dame {@ Yankee Stadium, Bronx, NY}

The Black Knights lost 13-12 to Notre Dame at the old Yankee Stadium. Army held Notre Dame scoreless for three quarters, but then Irish bounced back to score 13 in the final period, winning in front of about 80,000 fans.

1934 Army Cadets

In their second year under head coach Garrison H. Davidson, the Cadets compiled a 7–3 record, shut out five of their ten opponents, and outscored all opponents by a combined total of 215 to 40. In the annual Army–Navy Game, the Midshipmen won 3–0. The Cadets also lost to Notre Dame 12–6 and Illinois by a 7 to 0 score.

Halfback Jack Buckler (pictured at right) was selected by the College Sports Writers as a second team player on the All-America team.

Home games were played at Michie Stadium

9/29/1934	ARMY	vs	WASHBURN	19	0	W
10/6/1934	ARMY	vs	DAVIDSON (4-4-1)	41	0	W
10/13/1934	ARMY	vs	DRAKE (3-6-1)	48	0	W
10/20/1934	ARMY	vs	SEWANEE (2-7)	20	0	W
10/27/1934	ARMY	@	Yale (5-3)	20	12	W
11/3/1934	ARMY	@	Illinois (7-1)	0	7	L
11/10/1934	ARMY	@	Harvard (3-5)	27	6	W
11/17/1934	ARMY	vs	THE CITADEL (3-5-1)	34	0	W
11/24/1934	ARMY	vs	NOTRE DAME (6-3)	6	12	L
12/1/1934	ARMY	vs	NAVY (8-1)	0	3	L
Coach: Gar Davidson			**Season Record >>**	**215**	**40**	**7-3**

Schedule Source: Steve's Football Bible LLC

Selected game(s) highlights

Notre Dame {@ Yankee Stadium, Bronx, NY}

Before over 80,000 spectators, the Army and Notre Dame once again waged an epic battle that wasn't decided until the final minutes. The Fighting Irish struck first on a 52 yard pass from Bill Shakespeare to Dominic Vairo. With the scored tied 6-6, Andy Pilney threw a touchdown pass to Dan Henley for the winning score late in the 4th quarter.

NAVY {@ Franklin Field, Philadelphia, PA}

Despite the driving rainstorm at Franklin Field, Navy kicker Slade Cutter's 28 yard field goal ended an 11 game drought, as the Midshipmen's 3-0 win marked their first triumph over Army since 1921. Nothing indicates the treacherous weather conditions better than the final statistics. Army and Navy combined to record five first downs and 132 yards of total offense between them. Collectively, they also completed three-of-eight passes and punted 25 times.

1935 Army Cadets

In their third year under head coach Garrison H. Davidson,
the Cadets compiled a 6–2–1 record, shut out four of their nine
opponents, and outscored all opponents by a combined total of 176 to
62. In the annual Army–Navy Game, the Cadets defeated
the Midshipmen 28–6. The Cadets' two losses came
against Mississippi State and Pittsburgh, and they played Notre

Dame to a 6–6 tie at Yankee Stadium. Two Army players were recognized on the All-America team. End
William R. Shuler received first team honors from the Associated Press (AP). Halfback Charles R.
Meyer received second team honors from the United Press (UP) and North American Newspaper Alliance.

Home games were played at Michie Stadium

10/5/1935	ARMY	vs	WILLIAM & MARY (3-4-3)	14	0	W
10/12/1935	ARMY	vs	GETTYSBURG	54	0	W
10/19/1935	ARMY	vs	HARVARD (3-5)	13	0	W
10/26/1935	ARMY	@	Yale (6-3)	14	8	W
11/2/1935	ARMY	vs	MISSISSIPPI STATE (8-3)	7	13	L
11/9/1935	ARMY	@	Pittsburgh (7-1-2)	6	29	L
11/16/1935	ARMY	vs	NOTRE DAME (7-1-1)	6	6	T
11/23/1935	ARMY	vs	VERMONT	34	0	W
11/30/1935	ARMY	vs	NAVY (5-4)	28	6	W
Coach: Gar Davidson			**Season Record >>**	176	62	**6-2-1**

Schedule Source: Steve's Football Bible LLC

Selected game(s) highlights

VERMONT

Pointing for Its annual battle with Navy next week, Army gave its reserves a workout today as the
soldiers defeated Vermont, 34-0, before 5,000 shivering fans in Michle Stadium. The Cadets scored two
touchdowns in the opening period and three more in the final. Vermont's attack was woefully weak, giving the
Mountaineers only two first downs through the entire game. Pell and Goldenberg produced the longest runs of
the battle. Pell went 46 yards for a score in the last period, while Goldenberg went 40 in the same session.
Monk Meyer, star back fielder, was the only soldier varsity player to see action.

MISSISSIPPI STATE

The game was arranged by Coach Major Ralph Sasse, a WWI veteran and regarded as an armored
warfare genius by no less of an authority than George Patton. He'd been a good coach at Army too, before a
player's death broke him emotionally. Sasse was lured back into football thanks to a chance meeting with
State's president, and accounts are he inherited a good club recruited by the campus secretary. Army doesn't
seem to have taken their guests, the 'Farm Boys from Mississippi' as media labeled them, lightly either. Bobby
Thames scored the day's first touchdown; Army tied it in the second quarter and were driving in the third
before Ike Pickle picked off a pass at the State ten yard line. Minutes into the final period Pee Wee Armstrong
and Fred Walters hooked up for a 35 yard touchdown pass. That lead held and all 'Farm Boys' fans who'd paid
the $37 round trip fee to watch the game went back to their fields well-rewarded.

NAVY {@ Franklin Field, Philadelphia, PA}

The 1935 matchup was a tale of two halves. In the first two quarters, Army piled up 303 yards of total
offense, holding Navy to just 37. Yet, in the second half, the Midshipmen had more than eight times the total
offense than that of the Cadets – 259 yards to 31 for Army. Despite these similarities, there was also one visible
difference. Army scored four times in its half, while the Midshipmen were unable to reach the end zone. Final
score: Army 28, Navy 6. Quarterback "Monk Meyer" had 35- and 40 yard touchdown passes in the opening half,
while Whitey Grove added an 80 yard touchdown run on a reverse. Sneed Schmidt's four yard touchdown
plunge in the fourth quarter was the only offensive highlight in the Midshipmen's season finale.

1936 Army Cadets

In their fourth year under head coach Garrison H. Davidson, the Cadets compiled a 6–3 record and outscored their opponents by a combined total of 238 to 71. In the annual Army–Navy Game, the Cadets lost to the Midshipmen by a 7 to 0 score. The Cadets' other two losses came against Colgate and Notre Dame.

No Army players were recognized on the 1936 College Football All-America Team.

Home games were played at Michie Stadium

10/3/1936	ARMY	vs	WASHINGTON & LEE (4-5)	28	0	W
10/10/1936	ARMY	vs	COLUMBIA (5-3)	27	16	W
10/17/1936	ARMY	@	Harvard (3-4-1)	32	0	W
10/24/1936	ARMY	vs	SPRINGFIELD	33	0	W
10/31/1936	ARMY	vs	COLGATE (6-3)	7	14	L
11/7/1936	ARMY	vs	MUHLENBERG	54	7	W
11/14/1936	ARMY	vs	NOTRE DAME (6-2-1)	6	20	L
11/21/1936	ARMY	vs	HOBART	51	7	W
11/28/1936	ARMY	vs	NAVY (6-3)	0	7	L
Coach: Gar Davidson			**Season Record >>**	**238**	**71**	**6-3**

Schedule Source: Steve's Football Bible LLC

Selected game(s) highlights

NAVY {@ Municipal Stadium, Philadelphia, PA}

In 1936, Army and Navy faced off in Philadelphia in front of the largest crowd to ever attend a football game up to that time. The result was an officiating controversy that changed the rules on defensive pass interference. The game was scoreless through three-and-a half quarters. Most observers agreed Army had seemed to have the better of the battle, but fumbles had stymied the Cadets' efforts to  mount a scoring drive. In the last five minutes, Navy recovered the fourth Army fumble of the afternoon on their own 27 yard-line. A few plays later Army's Jimmy Schwenck batted down a pass from Navy's quarterback Bill Ingram, but field judge E.E. Miller ruled it was illegal interference. The call gave the Middies the six yards and kept the drive alive. Navy continued down the field and reached the 17 yard-line. From there Ingram threw a pass to receiver Bob Antrim on the goal line. The ball bounced out of his hands and into the arms of an Army player. At first the referee seemed to place the ball as if there was a change of possession, but the field judge overruled him and, once again, declared it to be pass interference by Army's Henry Sullivan. Instead of a turnover, the Midshipmen had the ball on the three yard-line with four downs to try and score. Navy's Sneed Schmidt plunged into the line twice to no avail but on his third attempt he was able to cross the goal line. With a successful point after kick Navy led 7-0 and that would prove the final score.

To meet the supreme ticket demand, the 1936 game was moved from 88,000-seat Franklin Field to 102,000-seat Municipal Stadium. Despite driving deep into Navy territory in the first half, Army was unable to capitalize, as John Schmidt's three yard touchdown run in the fourth quarter was all Navy needed for a 7-0 win over the Cadets. Following the series' first scoreless opening half since 1930, the third quarter was even less exciting. Army fumbled the football away on three of its next-four possessions, while the Midshipmen were unable to reach the Cadet end zone on three possessions. However, Navy was able to take advantage of a "Monk Meyer" fumble in the fourth quarter. Aided by a pass interference call against the Cadets' Jim Craig, Schmidt scored his touchdown with two minutes left.

1937 Army Cadets

In their fifth and final year under head coach Garrison H. Davidson, the Cadets compiled a 7−2 record and outscored their opponents by a combined total of 176 to 72. In the annual Army–Navy Game, the Cadets defeated the Midshipmen by a 6 to 0 score. The Cadets' two losses came against Yale and Notre Dame.

No Army players were recognized on the 1937 College Football All-America Team.

Home games were played at Michie Stadium

10/2/1937	ARMY	vs	CLEMSON (4-4-1)	21	6	W
10/9/1937	ARMY	vs	COLUMBIA (2-5-2)	21	18	W
10/16/1937	ARMY	@	Yale (6-1-1)	7	15	L
10/23/1937	ARMY	vs	WASHINGTON (MISSOURI) (4-6)	47	7	W
10/30/1937	ARMY	vs	VMI (5-5)	20	7	W
11/6/1937	ARMY	@	Harvard (5-2-1)	7	6	W
11/13/1937	ARMY	vs	NOTRE DAME (6-2-1)	0	7	L
11/20/1937	ARMY	vs	ST. JOHN'S (MARYLAND)	47	6	W
11/27/1937	ARMY	vs	NAVY (4-4-1)	6	0	W
Coach: Gar Davidson			**Season Record >>**	176	72	7-2

Schedule Source: Steve's Football Bible LLC

Selected game(s) highlights

Notre Dame {@ Yankee Stadium, Bronx, NY}

In a driving rainstorm, the Army Cadets came up short vs the Fighting Irish, losing 6-0 in front of a capacity crowd at Yankee Stadium. The Irish dominated in time of possession, but the Cadets defense held strong, as Notre Dame was inside the Army five yard line five different times and the Army's defense repelled the Irish each time.

NAVY {@ Municipal Stadium, Philadelphia, PA}

In a game that saw the two teams punt a combined 32 times, Army's Jim Craig managed to score a three yard touchdown run to give his team a 6-0 victory. Craig's run capped off a 44 yard scoring drive highlighted by a 19 yard pass from Woody Wilson to Jim Schwenk. The teams had a combined 255 yards of total offense, as Craig was the game's high rusher with 47 yards on 20 carries.

1938 Army Cadets

In their first year under head coach William H. Wood (pictured at right), the Cadets compiled an 8–2 record and outscored their opponents by a combined total of 243 to 95. In the annual Army–Navy Game, the Cadets defeated the Midshipmen by a 14 to 7 score. The Cadets' two losses came against Columbia and Notre Dame and were unranked in the AP poll.

No Army players were recognized on the All-America team.

Home games were played at Michie Stadium

9/24/1938	ARMY	vs	WICHITA STATE	32	0	**W**
10/1/1938	ARMY	vs	VIRGINIA TECH (3-5-2)	39	0	**W**
10/8/1938	ARMY	vs	COLUMBIA (3-6)	18	20	**L**
10/15/1938	ARMY	@	Harvard (4-4)	20	17	**W**
10/22/1938	ARMY	vs	BOSTON U	40	0	**W**
10/29/1938	ARMY	vs	NOTRE DAME (8-1)	7	19	**L**
11/5/1938	ARMY	vs	FRANKLIN & MARSHALL	20	12	**W**
11/12/1938	ARMY	vs	TENNESSEE-CHATT	34	13	**W**
11/19/1938	ARMY	@	Princeton (3-4-1)	19	7	**W**
11/26/1938	ARMY	vs	NAVY (4-3-2)	14	7	**W**
Coach: William Wood			**Season Record >>**	**243**	**95**	**8-2**

Schedule Source: Steve's Football Bible LLC

Selected game(s) highlights

NAVY {@ Municipal Stadium, Philadelphia, PA}

In front of 102,000 fans, the largest crowd to see a sporting event in 1938, Woody Wilson scored on a one yard touchdown run in the third quarter to help Army to a 14-6 win over Navy. Army's Charley Long brought Cadet faithful to their feet in the first quarter when he returned Lem Cooke's punt 79 yards for a touchdown. Navy drove deep into Army territory on each of its next-two possessions, only to be stopped once on downs and once on a Wilson interception. However, Cooke tied the score with a one yard touchdown run before halftime. Navy opened the third quarter poised to take the lead, but Emmette Wood fumbled on the Cadet 17 yard line. Army more than capitalized on this miscue, driving the length of the field to take the lead, and eventually the win, on Wilson's touchdown.

1939 Army Cadets

In their second year under head coach William H. Wood, the Cadets compiled a 3–4–2 record and outscored their opponents by a combined total of 106 to 105. In the annual Army–Navy Game, the Midshipmen won 10–0. The Cadets' three other losses came against Yale, Notre Dame, and Harvard.

Army tackle Harry Stella was selected by the United Press (UP), International News Service (INS), and Newsweek magazine as a first team player on the All-America team.

Home games were played at Michie Stadium

Date	Team		Opponent			
9/30/1939	ARMY	vs	FURMAN (5-4)	16	7	W
10/7/1939	ARMY	vs	CENTRE	9	6	W
10/14/1939	ARMY	@	Columbia (2-4-2)	6	6	T
10/21/1939	ARMY	@	Yale (3-4-1)	15	20	L
10/28/1939	ARMY	vs	URSINUS	46	13	W
11/4/1939	ARMY	vs	NOTRE DAME (7-2)	0	14	L
11/11/1939	ARMY	@	Harvard (4-4)	0	15	L
11/18/1939	ARMY	vs	PENN STATE (5-1-2)	14	14	T
12/2/1939	ARMY	vs	NAVY (3-5-1)	0	10	L
Coach: William Wood			**Season Record >>**	106	105	3-4-2

Schedule Source: Steve's Football Bible LLC

Selected game(s) highlights

NAVY {@ Municipal Stadium, Philadelphia, PA}

When Emory "Swede" Larson took over the Navy program in 1939, no one had to define the magnitude of the Army-Navy rivalry to him. A three-year letter winner (1919-21), Larson had played on three teams victorious over the Cadets. In fact, Larson arranged to have Billy VIII, Navy's mascot, wear the same blanket that adorned the 1921  goat. This superstition must have paid off, as the Midshipmen shut out Army, 10-0. Navy scored on its opening drive, as Ulmont Whitehead booted a 33 yard field goal between the uprights to give the Midshipmen a 3-0 lead. Halfback Dick Shafer added a 22 yard touchdown run in the last quarter, as Navy utilized six Army turnovers to finish 3-5-1 on the season.

1940 Army Cadets

In their third and final year under head coach William H. Wood, the Cadets compiled a 1–7–1 record and were outscored their opponents by a combined total of 197 to 54. The season was the first since 1899 in which the Army football team was outscored by its opponents. In the annual Army–Navy Game, the Cadets lost to the Midshipmen by a 14 to 0 score. The Cadets also suffered blowout defeats to Cornell (45-0) and Penn (48-0).

No Army players were honored on the All-America team. Three weeks after the end of the 1940 season, the War Department ordered coach Wood back to active troop duty and named Earl Blaik as head coach for the 1941 season.

Home games were played at Michie Stadium

10/5/1940	ARMY	vs	WILLIAMS	20	19	W
10/12/1940	ARMY	vs	CORNELL (6-2)	0	45	L
10/19/1940	ARMY	@	Harvard (3-2-3)	6	6	T
10/26/1940	ARMY	vs	LAFAYETTE	0	19	L
11/2/1940	ARMY	vs	NOTRE DAME (7-2)	0	7	L
11/9/1940	ARMY	vs	BROWN (6-3-1)	9	13	L
11/16/1940	ARMY	@	Pennsylvania (6-1-1)	0	48	L
11/23/1940	ARMY	@	Princeton (5-2-1)	19	26	L
11/30/1940	ARMY	vs	NAVY (6-2-1)	0	14	L
Coach: William Wood			**Season Record >>**	54	197	1-7-1

Schedule Source: Steve's Football Bible LLC

Selected game(s) highlights

Princeton

The Army Cadets traveled to Palmer Stadium to play the Princeton Tigers in front of over 26,000 fans. Army trailed 20-6 at halftime and pulled within a point but couldn't overcome the brilliant play of the Tigers Dave Allerdice, who threw for three touchdown passes leading Princeton to a 26-19 victory over Army.

NAVY {@ Municipal Stadium, Philadelphia, PA}

Navy celebrated the 50th anniversary of the Army-Navy game with a solid, all-around effort, resulting in a 14-0 triumph. Navy scored on its first drive, as Bill Busik went the final-two yards for the touchdown to make it 7-0. The Midshipmen covered 54 yards in 12 plays, with Busik accounting for 50 of those 54 yards. Although the Army offense could muster just 107 yards of total offense on the afternoon, the Cadet defense held Navy without a point on its next-two drives, which were halted deep in Army territory. However, the Midshipmen tallied their final score in the third quarter when Howie Clark tossed a nine yard touchdown pass to Everett Malcolm.

1941 Army Cadets

In their first year under head coach Earl Blaik (pictured at right), the Cadets compiled a 5–3–1 record and outscored their opponents by a combined total of 105 to 87. The season represented a four game improvement on the prior year's record of 1–7–1. Army opened with four wins, then played a scoreless tie with undefeated Notre Dame at Yankee Stadium. The eleventh-ranked Cadets then lost on the road in consecutive weeks to Harvard and Penn. In the annual Army–Navy Game, the Midshipmen won for the third straight year.

Army halfback Hank Mazur was selected by Life magazine as a third team player on the All-America team. Mazur was also selected by the Associated Press as a second team player on the 1941 All-Eastern football team.

Home games were played at Michie Stadium

10/4/1941	ARMY	vs	THE CITADEL (4-3-1)	19	6	W
10/11/1941	ARMY	vs	VMI (4-6)	27	20	W
10/18/1941	ARMY	@	Yale (1-7)	20	7	W
10/25/1941	ARMY	vs	COLUMBIA (3-5)	13	0	W
11/1/1941	ARMY	vs	NOTRE DAME (8-0-1)	0	0	T
11/8/1941	ARMY	@	Harvard (5-2-1)	6	20	L
11/15/1941	ARMY	@	Pennsylvania (7-1)	7	14	L
11/22/1941	ARMY	vs	WEST VIRGINIA (4-6)	7	6	W
11/29/1941	ARMY	vs	NAVY (7-1-1)	6	14	L
Coach: Earl "Red" Blaik			**Season Record >>**	105	87	**5-3-1**

Schedule Source: Steve's Football Bible LLC

Selected game(s) highlights

THE CITADEL

Earl Blaik made his debut as Army's first civilian coach in 30 years here this afternoon as the Cadet footballers opened their season against The Citadel. Over 7,000 witnessed the game. Army won, 19-6. Army scored on the fifth play, Mazur passing 43 yards to Kelleher, who caught it on the 12 and stumbled across. Mazur's placement was wide. Near the end of the quarter, Citadel's Andy Victor passed to Campbell from the Army 45 to the 3, where Campbell was tackled by Mazur. Victor plunged for the score on the second play. Victor's try for the extra point was wide. Midway through the period, Jere Maupin galloped 42 yards through the left side of the Citadel line for Army's second touchdown after the Cadets had driven from their own 25 yard stripe. Johnny Hatch blocked the Citadel safety man to make the touchdown possible. Roberts converted. In the third quarter, Mazur broke loose from the Citadel 21 and zig-zagged his way into the end zone for the Cadets third touchdown. The run climaxed a 66 yard drive from Army's own 34. Roberts placement was wide, and the period ended. Army pushed to the Citadel 5 with a half minute to play but was unable to move. After Stephens and Smith worked the ball to the Citadel 5, Army was penalized 5 yards for offside. Bell intercepted an Army pass on the last play of the game.

Yale

Yale's second half finish failed to materialize today as Army panzered to a 20-7 upset victory before 56,000 fans in misty Yale Bowl. The underdog Cadets thoroughly outclassed the Elis in their 38th meeting. Yale's aerial attack, which had produced five touchdowns in its last two games, was grounded by the ceiling zero alertness of the Soldiers. The Elis' lone scoring thrust came in the first minute and a half when Captain Alan Bartholemy blocked a punt for a touchdown. A 59 yard march, climaxed by ' Hank Mazur s eight yard pass to George Seip, produced Army's first score as the first period ended. Ralph Hill, sub back, sent them ahead in the second period with a 54 yard run from scrimmage, and Fullback Johnny Hatch clinched victory with a 9 yard plunge in the third period.

COLUMBIA

Playing with clocklike precision, Army defeated Columbia, 13-0, before 23,000 fans at Michie Stadium. This victory, following last Saturday's triumph over Yale, assures Army of one of its best seasons in five years. The first touchdown was scored by Ralph Hill, a yearling, on a 16 yard run. The extra point was kicked by Gene Smith making his first appearance in the varsity lineup. The second touchdown was scored by Hank Mazur, who intercepted a Governali pass and ran 25 yards.

Notre Dame {@ Yankee Stadium, Bronx, NY}

A band of soggy, mud-stained Army football players emerged with a moral victory in rain-swept Yankee Stadium yesterday as they outplayed Notre Dame to a 0-0 tie before 76,000 hardy souls who braved some of the worst weather in the 28-year history of the classic. Army didn't hold Notre Dame, Notre Dame held Army! And the closest thing to a touchdown in the bitter fight was the second period drive of the Cadets which knifed the crumbling Irish defenses to the 10 yard stripe before a penalty spiked the assault. All the statistics were in Army's favor and so were most of the cheers. Hank Mazur kept the Army in the game with his clever running, his sure fielding of a sloppy pigskin and his long-range boots upset all calculations of the favored westerners.

WEST VIRGINIA

The Army Mule's kick had a point to it today. And that point provided the Cadets with a squeaky 7-6 victory over West Virginia before 25,000 in Michie Stadium. Ridden ruthlessly by the Mountaineers for three quarters, the Mule struck with sudden savagery in the fourth period to wipe out a 6-0 deficit and salvage its fifth victory of the season. Fading deep, Hank Mazur flung a -13 yard toss to Ralph Hill, who outfought a Mountaineer defender to collect the pay-off pitch smack on the goal-line and step into the end zone for the touchdown. Bill Smith, who had huddled in a blanket on the bench all day awaiting this call to arms, dashed out and booted a placement for the extra and desperately needed point. The hard fighting West Virginia eleven had scored in the second period on a three yard pass from Jake Martin to Dick McElwee, climaxing a 43 yard march.

NAVY {@ Municipal Stadium, Philadelphia, PA}

As a Naval Academy player from 1919-21, Swede Larson never lost to Army. And in his first-two years as head coach, his teams shut out the Cadets by a combined score of 24-0. But prior to the 1941 Army-Navy contest, the Marine major was informed he was being sent to the Naval War College in Newport, R.I., immediately after the football season. As you can imagine, he wanted nothing more than a final victory over Army, which is why he was less than pleased when his club trailed West Point, 6-0, at halftime. Challenging his team to win its last battle on the football field, the Midshipmen answered the call in the second half. Bill Busik's effective running and passing set up touchdowns by Phil Hurt and Howie Clark, which led to a 14-6 Navy win.

1942 Army Cadets

In their second year under head coach Earl Blaik, the Cadets compiled a 6–3 record and outscored their opponents by a combined total of 149 to 74. In the annual Army–Navy Game, the Cadets lost to the Midshipmen by a 14 to 0 score. The Cadets also lost to Penn and Notre Dame. Four Army players were honored on the 1942 College Football All-America Team. Tackle Robin Olds was selected as a first team player by Grantland Rice for Collier's Weekly. Tackle Francis E. Merritt was selected as a second team player by both the Central Press Association (CP) and the Newspaper Enterprise Association (NEA) and was later inducted into the College Football Hall of Fame. Halfback Henry Mazur was selected as a second team player by the International News Service (INS). End James Kelleher was selected as a third team player by the Sporting News and NEA.

Home games were played at Michie Stadium

10/3/1942	ARMY	vs	LAFAYETTE	14	0	W
10/10/1942	ARMY	vs	CORNELL (3-5-1)	28	8	W
10/17/1942	ARMY	@	Columbia (3-6)	34	6	W
10/24/1942	ARMY	@	Harvard (2-6-1)	14	0	W
10/31/1942	ARMY	@	Pennsylvania (5-3-1)	0	19	L
11/7/1942	ARMY	vs	NOTRE DAME (7-2-2)	0	13	L
11/14/1942	ARMY	vs	VIRGINIA TECH (7-2-1)	19	7	W
11/21/1942	ARMY	vs	PRINCETON (3-5-1)	40	7	W
11/28/1942	ARMY	@	Navy (5-4)	0	14	L
Coach: Earl "Red" Blaik			**Season Record >>**	**149**	**74**	**6-3**

Selected game(s) highlights

Princeton {@ Yankee Stadium, Bronx, NY}

The Army Mule was flawless, and the Princeton Tiger was clawless yesterday before 40,000 at Yankee Stadium. So, the mule kicked the tiger up and down the gridiron throughout the first half to roll up a 20-0 score. Trying to keep the score to modest proportions and not wanting to take any chances with the Navy game coming up next Saturday, Army sent in many reserves, but they did more damage on the Tigers than the regulars. Army won 40-7. After the first team scored a touchdown in the first period on an 82 yard march, climaxed by Hank Mazur's five yard touchdown toss to Tom Lombardo who trotted 10 yards, the subs rang up two quick tallies in the second period on Bob Woods' 26 yard dash from scrimmage and his catch of Carl Anderson's nine yard pass in the end zone. Princeton made only one first down in the half, compared to Army's 10.

Navy

To conserve transportation resources due to World War II, the Army-Navy game was moved to Annapolis in 1942 and West Point for 1943. This meant the West Point Corp of Cadets, except for two cheerleaders, would not be permitted to attend the game, nor would anyone else outside a 10-mile radius of the Maryland state capital. Thus, half of the Brigade of Midshipmen would serve as the Army cheering section, while the other half would root for the Midshipmen. As it turns out, the Cadets would need much more help than this, as Navy turned back Army, 14-0. Backup halfback Joe Sullivan opened the scoring with a short touchdown run in the second quarter. Hillis Hume set up the other touchdown with an interception deep in Cadet territory midway through the third stanza. Hal Hamberg proceeded to hit Ben Martin with an 18 yard scoring strike. Hume clinched the win with another interception of Army quarterback Doug Kenna at the Navy seven yard line.

1943 Army Cadets

In their third year under head coach Earl Blaik, the Cadets compiled a 7–2–1 record, shut out five of their ten opponents, and outscored all opponents by a combined total of 299 to 66. In the annual Army–Navy Game, the Cadets lost to the Midshipmen by a 13 to 0 score. The Cadets also lost to Notre Dame by a 26 to 0 score, but won convincing victories over Colgate (42-0), Temple (51-0), Columbia (52-0), and Brown (59-0).

Two Army players were honored on the 1943 College Football All-America Team. Center Cas Myslinski was a consensus first team honoree, and tackle Francis E. Merritt was selected as a first team player by Football News and a second team player by the Associated Press.

FINAL RANK: #11 AP						
Home games were played at Michie Stadium						
9/25/1943	ARMY	vs	VILLANOVA (5-3)	27	0	W
10/2/1943	ARMY	vs	COLGATE (5-3-1)	42	0	W
10/9/1943	ARMY	vs	TEMPLE (2-6)	51	0	W
10/16/1943	ARMY	@	Columbia (0-8)	52	0	W
10/23/1943	ARMY	@	Yale (4-5)	39	7	W
10/30/1943	ARMY	@	Pennsylvania (6-2-1)	13	13	T
11/6/1943	ARMY	vs	NOTRE DAME (9-1)	0	26	L
11/13/1943	ARMY	vs	SAMPSON NTS	16	7	W
11/20/1943	ARMY	vs	BROWN (5-3)	59	0	W
11/27/1943	ARMY	vs	NAVY (8-1)	0	13	L
Coach: Earl "Red" Blaik			Season Record >>	299	66	7-2-1

Selected game(s) highlights

Notre Dame {@ Yankee Stadium, Bronx, NY}

The Yankee Stadium crowd had big expectations as the #1 Irish invaded the Bronx to battle #3 Army. Despite playing without quarterback Angelo Bertelli who would win the Heisman that year, the Irish defense stifled Army's offense.

NAVY

For the first time in 50 years, West Point, N.Y., played host to an Army-Navy game. The Midshipmen were less than gracious guests on the field, however, scoring two touchdowns in the second half of a 13-0 triumph. In the first half, Army got inside the Navy 40 yard line three times but failed to reach the end zone. Navy finally cracked the scoreboard midway through the third quarter when Bob Jenkins capped a 42 yard drive with a one yard touchdown run. Jim Pettit then contributed two of the game's biggest plays, one on each side of the ball. His one yard touchdown run stretched the lead to 13-0, and he halted an Army drive at the Navy 24 when he intercepted Doug Kenna's pass.

1944 Army Cadets {National Champions}

The 1944 Army Cadets football team was led by head coach Earl Blaik, the team finished with a perfect 9–0 season. The Black Knights offense scored 504 points, while the defense allowed 35 points. At the season's end, the team won a national championship. The team captain was Tom Lombardo. In 1950, Lombardo was killed in action during the Korean War.

Tom Lombardo led the team in passing with 444 yards and threw 7 touchdown passes. Glenn Davis led the team in rushing with 667 yards and 14 touchdowns. Davis led the team in receiving with 13 catches for 221 yards and 4 touchdown receptions. Davis led the team in scoring with 108 points. Davis {RB} and Felix "Doc" Blanchard {RB} were selected as consensus first team All-Americans.

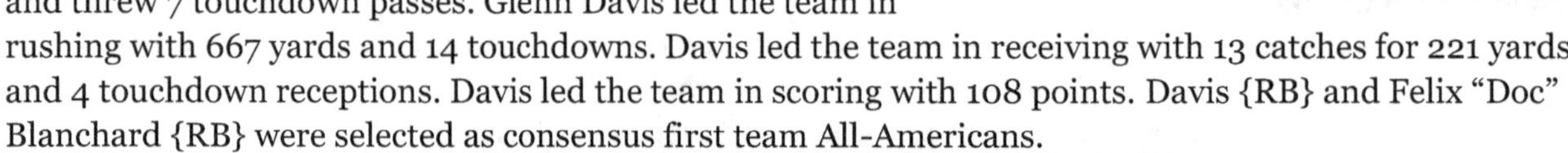

National Champions {AP, Helms}
Home games were played at Michie Stadium

9/30/1944	ARMY		vs		NORTH CAROLINA (1-7-1)	46	0	W
10/7/1944	ARMY		vs		BROWN (3-4-1)	59	7	W
10/14/1944	ARMY	#1	vs		PITTSBURGH (4-5)	69	7	W
10/21/1944	ARMY	#2	vs		COAST GUARD	76	0	W
10/28/1944	ARMY	#2	vs		DUKE (6-4)	27	7	W
11/4/1944	ARMY	#1	vs		VILLANOVA (4-4)	83	0	W
11/11/1944	ARMY	#1	vs	#5	NOTRE DAME (8-2)	59	0	W
11/18/1944	ARMY	#1	@		Pennsylvania (5-3)	62	7	W
12/2/1944	ARMY	#1	vs	#2	NAVY (6-3)	23	7	W
Coach: Earl "Red" Blaik					Season Record >>	504	35	9-0

Schedule Source: Steve's Football Bible LLC

Selected game(s) highlights

Notre Dame {@ Yankee Stadium, Bronx, NY}

This game played at Yankee Stadium remains the worst loss ever suffered by the Irish. The game was a highly anticipated match-up, as Cadets entered the game as the top ranked team and the defending champion Irish ranked #5. Notre Dame simply had no answer for Army, which used the game to propel them to the team to 1944 national championship. It had been thirteen years since Army had beaten Notre Dame. In fact, the last time Army had scored against the Irish was in 1938. The Irish were the defending national champions but lost many key players to graduation and the armed services. The Irish even lost head coach Frank Leahy to military service and were now being led by Ed McKeever. Notre Dame went into the game 5–1 and ranked #5, coming off a 32–13 loss to Navy. The Army squad was being led by Glenn Davis and Doc Blanchard. The Cadets also had a quarterback named Doug Kenna, and a transfer from the University of Texas, sprinter Max Minor.

Army overwhelmed the Irish. Kenna opened the scoring with a run for touchdown. He wasn't done, as he played defense as well, intercepting an Irish pass, which led to a scoring run by Minor. Kenna then pulled a trifecta of sorts, when he passed for a third score. Davis, a late scratch as a starter, also intercepted a pass, and had two offensive runs for scores. By halftime, Army had a commanding 33–0 lead.

Kenna added another scoring pass, and Davis another run for a score. Even Army's back-ups got into the act. Harold Tavzel, a second string tackle, intercepted a poorly thrown pass from the Irish quarterback, and jogged a few yards for a score. When the game was over, Army won 59–0, handing the Irish the worst loss in the program's history. The Irish would recover, winning their last three games to finish 8–2 and ranked #9 in the nation. When asked by a reporter about the score, Army halfback Doc Blanchard said "If there was anyone to blame for the size of the margin, it was Notre Dame, which fired our desire to win with its long humiliation of Army teams."

NAVY {@ Memorial Stadium, Baltimore, MD} {#1 vs #2}

With the country at war and the dominance of the service academies over the rest of college football, the 1944 Army vs. Navy game was one of the most anticipated matchups in the history of the rivalry. The battle on the gridiron that resulted became the stuff of legend. As the days ticked down in 1944 for the 46th edition of the Army vs. Navy annual gridiron engagement, the success of the two squads that season had propelled public interest to a fever pitch unparalleled in the series. Breathless media declared the matchup of the #1 Cadets and the #2 Midshipmen the de facto national championship, and the interest of the public at large seemed to cement that sentiment. As the Dec. 2 Army vs. Navy game approached, the two were the best in the land by a wide margin. For the Cadets, that marked a dramatic change from the recent past.

On Dec. 2, 1944, a sold-out crowd of 66,659 gathered in Municipal Stadium on a frigid but clear Saturday afternoon to see the much-anticipated contest. The cold temperatures were exacerbated by a brisk wind that blew through the stadium the entire game. The Navy contingent arrived on boats sailed across Chesapeake Bay, and the Army party was carried on troopships escorted by Navy destroyers.

Despite a series of turnovers, neither team could capitalize on the opportunities. Navy finally managed a first down in the final minutes of the first quarter but relied on a Statue of Liberty pass to do it. Several plays later, they were forced to punt again. Army began to gain momentum in the second quarter when the Cadets' offensive line began opening holes for the tandem of Blanchard and Davis. Army rolled 66 yards on six plays and scored on a 24 yard touchdown run by Dale Hall. Army led 7-0 – the first time the Cadets had done so in six years – and that was where the score stood at the intermission. The first half proved costly to Navy. The Midshipmen's standout former Crimson Tide players, Whitmire and Jenkins, were forced out of the game due to injuries. The depletion to the defense would prove critical in the final 30 minutes of play.

In the third quarter, Army blocked a Navy punt and scored a safety when kicker Jack Hansen was downed in the end zone after recovering the ball. The Midshipmen defense stiffened after the kickoff, and a string of tackles for loss and penalties quickly had the Cadets facing third and 47. Navy's offense picked up where the defense had left off and went on a 73 yard touchdown drive. Army stopped the Midshipmen once on the goal line but Clyde "Smackover" Scott then smashed it across for the score on the second attempt. As the third period ended it was Army 9, Navy 7, and it remained anybody's ball game.

The Midshipmen started the fourth quarter driving for the score that would give them the lead, but Army's Davis intercepted a pass and took it to midfield. The Cadets turned to Blanchard, giving him the ball eight consecutive times on a scoring drive that covered 52 yards. Army 16, Navy 7. The Midshipmen were forced to punt their next possession, and the Cadets got the ball back on their own 32 yard line. Four plays later, Glen Davis dashed 50 yards for the final touchdown of the game. A few minutes later, the final whistle sounded, and Army had finally beaten its archrival, 23-7. Despite throwing five interceptions and fumbling the ball three times, Army kept control of the contest from start to finish. The Cadets outgained the Midshipmen 181-71 on the ground, and Navy was only able to complete 14 of 24 passes for 98 yards.

1945 Army Cadets {National Champions}

The 1945 Army Cadets football team was coached by Earl Blaik in his fifth year and finished the season undefeated with a record of nine wins and zero losses (9–0). The squad was also recognized as consensus national champions for the 1945 season. For the season, the Cadets' offense scored 412 points, while the defense allowed 46 points.

Arnold Tucker led the team in passing with 320 yards. Glenn Davis led the team in rushing with 930 yards. Doc Blanchard led the team with 16 rushing touchdowns. Hank Foldberg led the team in receptions with 11. Davis led in receiving yards with 213. Blanchard and Davis led the team in scoring with 102 points. Blanchard {RB}, Davis {RB}, Tex Coulter {OL} and John Green {OL} were selected as consensus first team All-Americans.

National Champions {AP, Helms, NCF}
Home games were played at Michie Stadium

9/29/1945	ARMY		vs		LOUISVILLE Field	32	0	W
10/6/1945	ARMY		vs		WAKE FOREST (5-3-1)	54	0	W
10/13/1945	ARMY	#1	vs	#9	MICHIGAN (7-3)	28	7	W
10/20/1945	ARMY	#1	vs		MELVILLE PT BOATS	55	13	W
10/27/1945	ARMY	#1	vs	#19	DUKE (6-2)	48	13	W
11/3/1945	ARMY	#1	vs		VILLANOVA (4-4)	54	0	W
11/10/1945	ARMY	#1	vs	#2	NOTRE DAME (7-2-1)	48	0	W
11/17/1945	ARMY	#1	@	#6	Pennsylvania (6-2)	61	0	W
12/1/1945	ARMY	#1	vs	#2	NAVY (7-1-1)	32	13	W
Coach: Earl "Red" Blaik					Season Record >>	412	46	9-0

Schedule Source: Steve's Football Bible LLC

Selected game(s) highlights

LOUISVILLE

The season began with a challenging tune-up against a team formed at Louisville's Air Force personnel distribution command. Louisville unleashed the most aggressive defense it could manage, and it slowed the Cadets down. Army's depth advantages were obvious from the start, though. Davis opened the scoring with a weaving, brilliant 87 yard run in the first quarter, but with entirely different personnel coming in for the second quarter, Army scored twice. A 25 yard Bob Stuart punt return set up a two yard McWilliams plunge. Davis reentered and caught a 55 yard touchdown pass from Dick Walterhouse. Army led 19-0 at halftime and rolled.

WAKE FOREST

Wake Forest barely fell to Tennessee in the first week and lost by only seven to Duke the week after Army. The Demon Deacons would finish 19th in the AP poll after going 5-0-1 down the stretch. But in rainy West Point (you'll notice Army didn't have to leave New York too much), Wake had no chance. Just two minutes in, Fuson burst around left end for a 51 yard score. Davis one-upped him with a 55 yarder, then McWilliams outdid them both with a 79 yarder. Army rushed for 443 yards to Wake Forest's 78 and scored twice in the first quarter, twice in the second, and three times in the third.

MICHIGAN

A crowd of 70,000 welcomed Army and Fritz Crisler's Wolverines to Yankee Stadium for what was supposed to be Army's first significant test. Michigan's line play frustrated Army, but star power carried the day. McWilliams scored on a seven yard run for Army's first touchdown, and Blanchard rumbled 68 yards just two minutes later. Michigan's misdirection offense caused Army some problems, but a strong defensive day from Blanchard kept the Wolverines at bay. Up 21-7 in the fourth quarter, Army put the game away with a 70 yard sprint by Davis.

DUKE

Duke would go undefeated against teams not named Army or Navy in 1945, but the Blue Devils suffered a program-worst 35-point defeat in front of 42,287 at New York's Polo Grounds. The deficit was only that small because of penalties: Army gained 524 yards and scored seven touchdowns but had a couple more called back. McWilliams opened two minutes in with a 54 yard touchdown run, Bob Stuart and Blanchard scored twice each (once on a pass from Davis), and Davis added a tally. It was obvious to the 42,287 in attendance, almost from the kickoff, how the game was going to end up. It was 28-0 at halftime before Army reserves let Duke find a little bit of an offensive rhythm.

VILLANOVA

Army and Villanova played for six consecutive years between 1943 and 1948. Final score of these six hours: Cadets 240, Wildcats 0. The only encouragement 'Nova could get from playing Army in 1945 was that the final score wasn't as bad as it had been the year before, when the Cadets laid a devastating 83-0 score on the board. The total yardage from this one was almost inhumane: Army 506, VU 25. Blanchard romped to two early scores, then scored two more later. Villanova had one first down, even with the Army backups playing a considerable amount of the game.

Notre Dame {@ Yankee Stadium, Bronx, NY} {#1 vs #2}

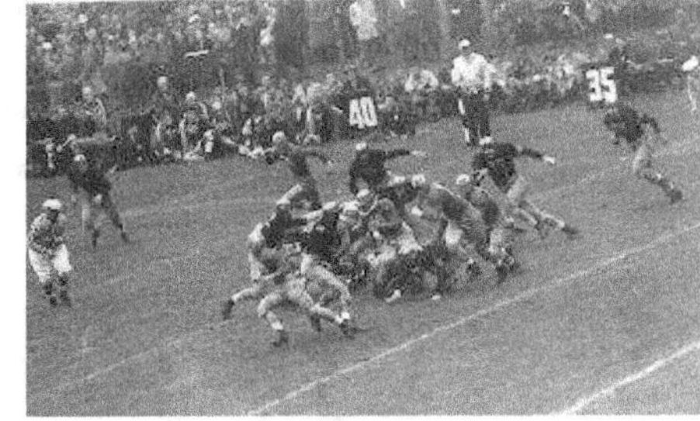

Again, this wasn't as bad as it had been the year before. Reeling from a loss to Navy a year earlier, Notre Dame came to Yankee Stadium and got destroyed, 59-0. In 1945, having held Navy to a scoreless tie, the Fighting Irish came in more confident, and it made a difference ... for a few minutes. It was just 7-0 after one quarter before Army began to pour it on. The Cadets scored twice in the second quarter, then Barney Poole blocked a punt, setting up a 21 yard Davis score. For the day, Davis had three touchdowns, Blanchard two. Notre Dame gained 184 yards and threatened a couple of times. But against the second-best team in the country, Army gained a cool 441 yards and cruised. Again.

NAVY {@ Municipal Stadium, Philadelphia, PA} {#1 vs #2}

Because of the war America had just won, the 1945 Army-Navy game might have been one of the most celebratory sporting events in the country's history. A crowd of 102,000, including President Harry S. Truman packed Municipal Stadium in Philadelphia, which is now the site of a trio of professional ballparks in south Philly: the Wells Fargo Center, Citizens Bank Park, and Lincoln Financial Field, which continues to house Army-Navy games regularly. What might have been the best-ever Navy team battled this incredible Army team to a draw for three quarters. The Midshipmen proved resilient and became the first team all year to score on Army's first team.

The problem: Those three even quarters were the last three. Army had already taken a 20-0 lead in the first 15 minutes. The Cadets took the opening kickoff and took seven plays to set up a Blanchard touchdown. Then Blanchard scored again. Then Davis went 51 yards. From that point forward, Navy outscored the Cadets, 13-12. And that was an achievement. They got to within 20-7 and 26-13, but they couldn't get any closer.

1946 Army Cadets {National Champions}

The 1946 Army Cadets football team was coached by Earl Blaik in his sixth year and finished the season undefeated with a record of nine wins, zero losses and one tie (9–0–1). The squad was also recognized as national champions for the 1946 season by several selectors. The Cadets outscored their opponents, 263 to 80.

This season's Notre Dame game at Yankee Stadium, a matchup of the top two in the rankings, is regarded as one of college football's Games of the Century; it was a scoreless tie. Arnold Tucker led the team in passing with 619 yards. Glenn Davis led the team in rushing with 712 yards. Doc Blanchard led with 9 rushing touchdowns. Davis led the team with 20 receptions for 356 yards and 6 touchdown receptions. Davis led the team in scoring with 78 points. **Arnold Tucker set a team record with 8 interceptions, which was tied by two Army players.** Blanchard {RB}, Davis {RB} and Hank Foldberg {E} were selected as consensus All-Americans.

National Champions {Helms}							
Home games were played at Michie Stadium							
9/21/1946	ARMY		vs		VILLANOVA (6-4)	35	0	W
9/28/1946	ARMY		vs		OKLAHOMA (8-3)	21	7	W
10/5/1946	ARMY		vs		CORNELL (5-3-1)	46	21	W
10/12/1946	ARMY	#2	@	#4	Michigan (6-2-1)	20	13	W
10/19/1946	ARMY	#1	vs	#11	COLUMBIA (6-3)	48	14	W
10/26/1946	ARMY	#1	vs	#13	DUKE (4-5)	19	0	W
11/2/1946	ARMY	#1	vs		WEST VIRGINIA (5-5)	19	0	W
11/9/1946	ARMY	#1	vs	#2	NOTRE DAME (8-0-1)	0	0	T
11/16/1946	ARMY	#1	@	#5	Pennsylvania (6-2)	34	7	W
11/30/1946	ARMY	#1	vs		NAVY (1-8)	21	18	W
Coach: Earl "Red" Blaik				Season Record >>	263	80	9-0-1

Schedule Source: Steve's Football Bible LLC

Selected game(s) highlights

OKLAHOMA

Army hosted Oklahoma, the first meeting of the schools on a football field. President Truman was in the stands, the first time a President attended a game at West Point. It was Oklahoma's season opener, and they were about to unveil the new squad of players they had purchased. It was an ambush in waiting, and Oklahoma almost pulled off a shocker in this one. Their defense put the clamps on Army's offense to a degree not seen since 1943, and though their offense was similarly stymied, early in the 2nd quarter Oklahoma blocked a punt and fell on it in Army's end zone for a surprising 7-0 lead. That lead held up until the final minute of the half.

Oklahoma was using a 7-man line, but the backers were up so close that it was really a 9 man front. With Doc Blanchard out, Army's running game was cut in half already, and Oklahoma's line snuffed it out altogether. Presumably the passing game should have been opened, but Oklahoma's line overwhelmed Army's passers so quickly that they could not get good throws off. But with just over a minute to go in the first half, Army quarterback Arnold Tucker finally connected on a pass to halfback Glenn Davis for 46 yards, setting up a 4 yard touchdown toss to end Hank Foldberg, and the game was knotted up 7-7 at the break. Army end Barney Poole blocked an Oklahoma punt at their 15 in the 3rd quarter, and another Tucker pass to Davis set up a touchdown dive to put Army in front 14-7. But late in the 3rd quarter, Oklahoma's offense came to life. They marched 74 yards, getting a first down at the Army 3, where Arnold Tucker, hero of this game, tackled Darrell Royal (future legendary Longhorn coach) for a

3 yard loss, and on the next play, Tucker intercepted a Royal pass to end the threat. Army promptly fumbled the ball back to Oklahoma at their 18, but on the first play of the 4th quarter, Arnold Tucker struck again, intercepting a pass intended for Royal and returning it 86 yards for a clinching touchdown, making the final score 21-7. Army was held to a paltry 83 yards rushing, an unthinkable number given their previous 2 seasons. Their 82 passing let them edge Oklahoma in total offense 165 yards to 162, but the nation was served notice: Army was beatable.

Michigan

Before 85,000 fans at Michigan, a team they had beaten handily the previous season, more decisively than the 28-7 final score showed. But this win was not nearly so easy. Fullback Doc Blanchard was back for Army, but his knee would be a problem for him the rest of the season, and he often lined up as a flanker in this game. Quarterback Arnold Tucker injured his arm early in the contest and could only throw short passes. But halfback Glenn Davis picked up the passing slack, hitting 7 of 8 for 159 yards. He was the star of the game, running for 2 touchdowns, passing for another in miracle fashion, and grabbing 2 of the 3 interceptions Michigan served up.

Army once again found themselves down 7-0 in this game. A bad punt of just 4 yards gave Michigan the ball at the Army 43, and they drove from there to a 4th down touchdown pass in the opening quarter. Later in the quarter, Glenn Davis erupted for a 57 yard touchdown run, breaking 4 tackles along the way, and the game was even at 7-7. In the 2nd quarter, Davis hit end Barney Poole for a 35 yard pass, but a 10 yard Davis touchdown was negated by a penalty, and the drive was stopped after that. With just under 2 minutes left in the half, Davis hit Doc Blanchard for a 45 yard pass, and Tucker passed to Davis for another 14. The next plays lost yardage, bringing up 4th down and 18 at the Michigan 31 with 29 seconds remaining. Army fumbled a handoff, and Davis scooped the ball up, and, as he was being tackled, threw it to halfback Bob Folsom in the end zone for a 31 yard touchdown, giving Army a miraculous 13-7 halftime lead.

Michigan took the opening kickoff of the 2nd half and marched 83 yards in 13 plays for a touchdown, but Army guard Joe Steffy blocked the extra point try to keep the score 13-13. Early in the final quarter, Army drove 76 yards in 11 plays for a 20-13 lead, Glenn Davis hitting Blanchard for 24 and 8 yard passes, then scoring the touchdown from 7 yards out. Army had another promising drive later in the quarter, but Davis fumbled the ball away. He made up for it by grabbing an interception after Michigan had moved into Army territory. Michigan brought some drama to the game in the final minutes, hitting passes of 15 and 19 yards and driving to the Army 10 with 29 seconds remaining. But they were pushed back by a pair of penalties, and Arnold Tucker intercepted the Hail Mary try on the game's final play, keeping the final score 20-13. Army outgained Michigan 363 yards to 236, that advantage supplied by their 211 yards through the air (on a terrific 12 of 15 passing)

Notre Dame {@ Yankee Stadium, Bronx, NY} {#1 vs #2}

This "Game of the Century" may not have been among the greatest games ever played, but it was arguably the greatest matchup in college football history. Army had scored 0 points in their previous 3 games against a Leahy-coached Notre Dame, 1941-1943, and this game would add to that streak. $5 tickets were going for $250, and Yankee Stadium was filled with 74,000 fans. The game was televised in New York, Philadelphia, and Washington, DC.

In the opening quarter, Army tackle Goble Bryant recovered an Emil Sitko fumble at the Notre Dame 24, but the ensuing drive was halted at the 15. In the

2nd quarter, Army halfback Glenn Davis hit fullback Doc Blanchard (pictured carrying the ball in this game above) for a 23 yard pass to the Notre Dame 23. They lost yardage from there back to the 37, punted, and Notre Dame started their next drive from their own 12. What followed was an 85 yard march, the only sustained drive of this football game, ending in the game's only serious scoring threat. On 4th and 2 at the Army 4, Notre Dame forewent a field goal try, as most teams did in such situations, and tossed a pitch to Bill Gompers around end (as pictured at the top of this article). He looked free and clear for a moment, but he was stopped at the 3, ending the drive a yard short of a first down. Late in the first half, Army recovered a fumble at the Notre Dame 30, but they went no further.

The 3rd quarter was fought out mostly on Notre Dame's side, but Dame guard George Mastrangelo recovered a fumble at Army's 34. That excitement didn't last long, because Army quarterback Arnold Tucker intercepted a pass and returned it 32 yards to his 42. Doc Blanchard got loose for 21 yards on the next play, and Tucker passed to Hank Foldberg to put the ball at the Notre Dame 20. Notre Dame halfback Terry Brennan intercepted a Glenn Davis pass on the next play to stop that drive. In the 4th quarter, Army was stopped inches short of a first down at the Notre Dame 33. Army's next drive was halted when halfback Emil Sitko intercepted a pass at his own 10. He fumbled the ball trying to return it, but Notre Dame quarterback John Lujack fell on the ball at the 5 to avert disaster. Lujack then uncorked a 55 yard punt from his own end zone, which Glenn Davis returned to the Notre Dame 39. That drive ended in another turnover. With 48 seconds left, Doc Blanchard made a spectacular catch of a Glenn Davis bomb at the Notre Dame 20, but he had stepped out of bounds, so the pass was ruled incomplete, and that was the last bit of drama in the game.

The 0-0 stalemate ended Army's 25 game winning streak. Notre Dame outgained Army 225 yards to 190, but they also turned the ball over 7 times to Army's 4. Notre Dame had the one sustained drive and one real scoring threat of the game, but Army had the ball 6 times inside the Notre Dame 33, largely due to turnovers. Notre Dame quarterback Johnny Lujack, who would win the Heisman the next year, threw 4 interceptions, 3 of them grabbed by Army quarterback Arnold Tucker. But Lujack had a great defensive game, including a game saving tackle of Doc Blanchard when he had broken free at one point late in the

game. Glenn Davis carried 17 times for 30 yards, Doc Blanchard 18 for 50, Arnold Tucker 9 for 37, and Notre Dame halfback Terry Brennan was the game's leading rusher with 69 yards on 14 carries. Davis and Blanchard played all 60 minutes for Army, and Lujack was in for all but 2 plays for Notre Dame.

NAVY {@ Municipal Stadium, Philadelphia, PA}

Gen. Dwight D. Eisenhower and Admiral Chester Nimitz were at the game, both giving up their seats for veterans who were wounded in World War II. More than 100,000 fans showed up, and IRS investigators were scattered outside the stadium to tax those who were re-selling the $3 tickets for nearly 20 times face value.

Army was a 28 point favorite, but they were quite fortunate to hold on for a win against a Navy team that was coming in on a 7 game losing streak. The story of this game

was perhaps President Truman's bad juju. He sat on Navy's side for the first half, which was dominated by Army, and he sat on Army's side for the 2nd half, when Navy came back and nearly won. In the opening quarter, Navy advanced a pair of ventures into Army territory, but Army end Barney Poole caused a fumble to end the second advance, tackle Art Gerometta recovering at the Army 37. Army drove to a touchdown from there in 4 plays, quarterback Arnold Tucker hitting halfback Glenn Davis for a 46 yard bomb, and Davis scoring from 13 yards out. Undaunted, Navy responded with an 81 yard drive, including passes of 11 and 32 yards, that ended early in the 2nd quarter with a touchdown. The extra point try was blocked, so Army still led 7-6. Army responded to Navy's response in kind: an 81 yard touchdown drive that featured Glenn Davis bursting up the middle for the last 52 yards on one run. An interception soon gave Army the ball at the Navy 38, and 3 plays later, they scored again, Davis hitting Blanchard for a 26 yard touchdown pass. Army led 21-6 at the half, and at this point, all seemed right with the world. But the 2nd half was a completely different story, not only from the first half, but from every game Army had played for the previous 3 seasons. It seemed completely inexplicable, but Army found themselves with little to no gas left in the tank in this 2nd half, and they barely coasted over the finish line of this season on fumes.

Army opened the 3rd quarter with a drive that was stopped at the Navy 31, where Glenn Davis' punt went awry and only traveled 9 yards. Navy drove 78 yards for a touchdown from there, the drive kept alive by a pass interference penalty. Late in the 3rd quarter, Army went for it on 4th and 1 from their own 35, and Blanchard was stopped short. Navy drove the short field from there, scoring the touchdown early in the 4th quarter on 4th and 3 with a lateral and touchdown pass. Suddenly it was a game, 21-18, the difference being 3 missed extra points by Navy. Army returned the ensuing kickoff to their 32 and moved to the Navy 39 on a 29 yard run by Glenn Davis, but then Davis threw a long pass that was intercepted. Navy launched one last drive deep into Army territory in the game's waning minutes. They picked up 20 yards on a 4th down fullback run that carried to the Army 3 yard line with about 1:30 left. Tackle Goble Bryant and end Hank Foldberg stopped the fullback on the next play, and the other end, Barney Poole, stopped him on the next. A delay of game penalty set the ball back, and Navy's next run was halted at the Army 5. Navy sent in a substitute with 7 seconds left to stop the clock for one more play, but fans were swarming the field at this point (as pictured above: you can see the players still inside the 10 yard line), and the officials never saw the sub, so Navy was unable to get off that last play. Army was off the hook. Except really, they weren't.

A 21-18 win over a 1-8 team, with that team knocking on the goal line at game's end, was just not going to cut it when Notre Dame had been perfect in their games. Navy had a startling 20 first downs to Army's 8, though Navy barely outgained Army 299 yards to 291.

1947 Army Cadets

In its seventh year under head coach Earl Blaik, the team compiled a 5–2–2 record, was ranked #11 in the final AP Poll, and outscored opponents by a total of 220 to 68. The team played its home games at Michie Stadium in West Point, New York. Army's loss to Columbia on October 25, 1947, broke the Cadets' 32 game unbeaten streak dating back to November 1943.

Army guard Joe Steffy was selected by the Football Writers Association of America as the 1947 recipient of the Outland Trophy as the best guard or tackle in the country. Steffy was also a consensus first team pick for the 1947 All-America team, and he was later inducted into the College Football Hall of Fame. Steffy and Army fullback Elwyn "Rip" Rowan received first team honors on the International News Service's 1947 All-East team.

FINAL RANK: #11 AP						
Home games were played at Michie Stadium						
9/27/1947	ARMY	vs	VILLANOVA (6-3-1)	13	0	W
10/4/1947	ARMY	vs	COLORADO (4-5)	47	0	W
10/11/1947	ARMY	vs	ILLINOIS (5-3-1)	0	0	T
10/18/1947	ARMY	vs	VIRGINIA TECH (4-5)	40	0	W
10/25/1947	ARMY	@	Columbia (7-2)	20	21	L
11/1/1947	ARMY	vs	WASHINGTON & LEE (5-5)	65	13	W
11/8/1947	ARMY	@	Notre Dame (9-0)	7	27	L
11/15/1947	ARMY	@	Pennsylvania (7-0-1)	7	7	T
11/29/1947	ARMY	vs	NAVY (1-7-1)	21	0	W
Coach: Earl "Red" Blaik			Season Record >>	220	68	5-2-2

Selected game(s) highlights

VILLANOVA

The remnants of a once great Army football team had to resort to a pair of fumble recoveries yesterday afternoon to gain a 13-0 victory over vengeful Villanova before 28,000 in West Point's Michie Stadium. Bungling backfield assignments, failing to open holes on crucial plays, the Blanchard-less, Davis-less Cadets scored once in the first half and once in the second both tallies were set up by recovered Villanova bobbles, the first 13 yards from the goal line and the second, 23 yards out. Quarterback Bill Gustafson and halfback Winfield Scott Jr. were the scorers.

Columbia {Columbia ends Army 32 game unbeaten streak-Columbia's greatest win}

On October 25, 1947, Columbia halted Army's 32 game unbeaten streak in a dramatic 21-20 upset before a crowd of 35,000 packed into Baker Field's 32,000-seat wooden stadium. The first time Army got the ball it smashed to a touchdown in nine plays from its own 46 with Rip Rowan galloping 24 yards in one piece and Arnold Galiffa, the new T quarterback, firing a rocket pass and ultimately sneaking over. The line power and reckless drive of the Army backs made the game look one-sided at this point. Army barely missed a second TD after intercepting a pass on the Columbia two, but the Cadets scored again early in the second quarter on Bill Gustafson's 25 yard run to the one and Rowan's 1 yard plunge. The first indication that Columbia considered itself anything more than a bystander came after the second touchdown ... the Columbians traveled 69 yards for a touchdown without interruption. In this march was unveiled the passing combination of [Gene] Rossides to [Bill] Swiacki. The former threw three and the latter caught two of them, the second on the 6 yard line with Winfield Scott covering him as with a tarpaulin. Kusserow ran it over and the pattern of the game was revealed ... Army was a running terror capable of 302 yards from scrimmage, which it did, and Columbia was a passing team capable of tapping the air routes for 263 yards, which it did. Furthermore, it gave a vague outline of the clutching ability of the lanky and loose-jointed [Bill] Swiacki. The Cadets scored their third touchdown just six seconds before the end of the half, taking over on their 20 after Columbia missed a field goal. On second down Rip Rowan went through left tackle and broke away. Early in the fourth quarter, Columbia's passing attack began to tell on the Cadets. Early in the game, West Point rushed with a six-man line, hounding and harassing Rossides. West Point ceased rushing, dropping the backers-up [linebackers] and a tackle to help cover the receivers. It didn't help. The Lions always had a halfback open on their right flank. Their short shots to crisscrossing ends were unstoppable.

     Early in the fourth quarter, Rossides started to hit. He fired to Bill Olson for two first downs, moving the Lions to the 28. From the Army 28, he heaved a colossal pass into the end zone. John Shelley apparently had Swiacki covered, but the latter made a headlong dive for the ball as it was about to hit the ground. In some unexplained manner he caught it, virtually off the ground. The Army players argued that he had trapped it, but it was ruled he caught it fairly, and that's the way it looked from the press box. Now up 20-14, the Cadets came back down the field to the Lion 34. They stalled there and were forced to punt. The center snap was high, however, and Rowan just managed to knock it down before he was tackled. Columbia took over on its own 39. Then Rossides fired the crucial pass of the game, almost inexplicably caught by Swiacki. The latter went down, looking over his right shoulder for the ball. At the last minute he took his eye off the ball, turned outward and made a full-length dive, catching the ball as if by magnetism. The ball was on the four. Rossides turned right end for two yards to the two. His next handoff went to Kusserow. The legend of Army's invincibility ... was concluded at 4:16 PM when Kusserow tunneled through left tackle and Ventan Yablonski converted the extra point that won for the Lions, 21 to 20. **{excerpts from New York Herald Tribune}**

Notre Dame

     The Irish welcomed 8th ranked Army to South Bend after having played Army in their back yard in New York for 16 years in a row. The fleet Terry Brennan scored an early 97 yard kickoff return touchdown to put the Irish up. The relentless running attack supplemented Lujack's key passes. Brennan and Sitko would rush for over 400 yards each for the year, but it was the richness of depth that easily carried the Irish to over 2400 rushing yards. Nine backs had over 100 yards rushing. The Irish, for the first time in years, dominated the Cadets and Irish cruised to a 20-0 lead before the Cadets scored. The final score was Notre Dame 27-Army 7.

NAVY {@ Municipal Stadium, Philadelphia, PA}

     In front of 103,000 fans, including President Harry S. Truman, Army scored one touchdown in each of the first-three quarters to cruise to a 21-0 victory over Navy. A Bill Hawkins fumble led to Army's first touchdown, as "Bill Kellum" caught an 18 yard touchdown pass from quarterback Elwyn Rowan. Navy drove right back down the field on the next possession, but turned the ball over on downs inside the Army 10 yard line. On Army's first play from scrimmage, "Rip Rowan" went around the end and down the field 92 yards for the go-ahead score. He finished the afternoon with 148 yards rushing. ("Joe Steffy" once asked Col Blaik what his Greatest Thrill was in Coaching — Rip Rowan's 92 yard run from scrimmage)

1948 Army Cadets {Lambert Trophy}

Led by head coach Earl Blaik, the Cadets offense scored 294 points while the defense allowed 89 points. At season's end, Army was ranked sixth in the nation. Head coach Earl Blaik implemented a two-platoon system, using specialists strictly for offense and defense. Offensive coach Sid Gillman left Army after the season to become the head coach at the University of Cincinnati.

FINAL RANK: #6 AP						
Home games were played at Michie Stadium						
9/25/1948	ARMY	vs	VILLANOVA (8-2-1)	28	0	W
10/2/1948	ARMY	vs	LAFAYETTE	54	7	W
10/9/1948	ARMY	@	Illinois (3-6)	26	21	W
10/16/1948	ARMY	vs	HARVARD (4-4)	20	7	W
10/23/1948	ARMY	@	Cornell (8-1)	27	6	W
10/30/1948	ARMY	vs	VIRGINIA TECH (0-8-1)	49	7	W
11/6/1948	ARMY	vs	STANFORD (4-6)	43	0	W
11/13/1948	ARMY	@	Pennsylvania (5-3)	26	20	W
11/27/1948	ARMY	vs	NAVY (0-8-1)	21	21	T
Coach: Earl "Red" Blaik			Season Record >>	294	89	8-0-1

Schedule Source: Steve's Football Bible LLC

Selected game(s) highlights

HARVARD

Harvard's gridders, with their tricky but erratic single-wing attack, gave unbeaten Army a halftime scare by holding the Cadets to a 7-7 deadlock at intermission yesterday. But the telling cadet power, exploded in the main, by a loose-legged yearling fullback named Gill Stephenson, blasted out two tallies in the third quarter to produce the 20-7 Cadet triumph. Stephenson, the new darling of the 26,921 capacity throng that packed Michie Stadium at West Point, scored all three Soldier touchdowns in this fourth straight Army victory. Chuck Roche's 10- yard flip to quarterback Bill Henry accounted for the lone Harvard score just 42 seconds before the half-time gun.

Cornell

Army's mighty football forces struck into this hilly up-country for the first time in history here today and its grinding ground attack won't be forgotten in a hurry by the 35,000 who packed Schoellkopf Field. For the colossal Cadets smashed Cornell from the ranks of the Unbeaten by a count of 27-6 with a power-parade which featured the line pulverizing play of their, yearling fullback, Gil Stephenson, who racked up two touchdowns as he led his West Point mates to their fifth straight victory. Karl Kuckhahn, sub fullback, and Bobby Jack Stuart were the other touchdown-getters.

NAVY {@ Municipal Stadium, Philadelphia, PA}

Considering Army entered the 1948 season finale with an 8-0 mark, as opposed to Navy's 0-8 record, it should not be a surprise that the Cadets were a 20-point favorite. Yet, the Midshipmen proved the oddsmakers wrong by battling Army to a 21-21 tie. Navy quarterback Reaves Baysinger opened the scoring with a two yard touchdown run midway through the first quarter. However, short touchdown runs by Rudolph Cosentino and Harold Shultz enabled the Cadets to take a 14-7 lead at the half. Navy responded with a one yard Bill Hawkins touchdown run to tie the game at 14 in the third quarter. Army then took its second lead of the game when quarterback Arnold Galiffa scored on a 10 yard bootleg. Finally, Hawkins preserved the tie with clutch plays on both sides of the ball. He followed a one yard touchdown run by knocking away a Galiffa pass on fourth down to end the game.

1949 Army Cadets {Lambert Trophy}

Led by head coach Earl Blaik in his 9th season, The Cadets scored 354 points, while the defense allowed only 68 points. Arnold Galiffa was the starting quarterback, ahead of Earl Blaik's son, Bob. Johnny Trent was the team captain. The Cadets won the Lambert-Meadowlands Trophy as the best college team in the East.

At season's end, Red Blaik confessed that he thoughts of retiring. Sid Gillman left Army to become the head coach for the University of Cincinnati. Head coach Red Blaik interviewed Vince Lombardi, but harbored doubts that Lombardi's background as a high school coach would prepare him for the job. Besides Lombardi, Murray Warmath of Tennessee was the other new face on the coaching staff. Lombardi would focus on offense, while Warmath worked on the defense. They were the only civilian coaches on the staff.

Galiffa {RB} was selected as a consensus first team All-American.

FINAL RANK: #4 AP

Home games were played at Michie Stadium

9/24/1949	ARMY	vs	DAVIDSON (2-8)	47	7	W	
10/1/1949	ARMY	vs	PENN STATE (5-4)	42	7	W	
10/8/1949	ARMY	@	Michigan (6-2-1)	21	7	W	
10/15/1949	ARMY	@	Harvard (1-8)	54	14	W	
10/22/1949	ARMY	vs	COLUMBIA (2-7)	63	6	W	
10/29/1949	ARMY	vs	VMI (3-5-1)	40	14	W	
11/5/1949	ARMY	vs	FORDHAM (5-3)	35	0	W	*-Cain 3 TD catch
11/12/1949	ARMY	@	Pennsylvania (4-4)	14	13	W	
11/26/1949	ARMY	vs	NAVY (3-5-1)	38	0	W	
Coach: Earl "Red" Blaik			Season Record >>	354	68	9-0	

Schedule Source: Steve's Football Bible LLC
***-Single game record**

Selected game(s) highlights

Michigan

Army marched 88 yards for a touchdown in the opening quarter, quarterback Arnold Galiffa hit 3 passes for 52 yards. A Michigan fumble led to a 10 yard drive for another touchdown in the 2nd, giving the cadets a 14-0 halftime lead (Jim Cain is pictured scoring this touchdown above). In the 4th quarter, Army couldn't get off a punt, and Michigan took over and drove a short field to a touchdown to close the gap to 14-7. But Army drove their own short field for a touchdown late in the game to clinch it 21-7. Army outgained Michigan 247 yards to 203, the big difference coming from Michigan's woeful passing game: 3 of 23 for 16 yards and 4 interceptions.

Pennsylvania

Army's football team, which has not lost a game since it tied Penn on this same battleground two years ago, extended its undefeated string to 19 in Franklin Field this afternoon, but suffered extreme travail before escaping with a 14-to-13 decision over an aroused Quaker force which had outplayed the men of West Point. To profit by Penn's failure to convert the point after the first touchdown of this slam-bang engagement, the soldiers had to ground a Quaker pass receiver less than a yard from the goal as time ran out in the first half and to block a field goal attempt from the 20 yard stripe after the Red and Blue had penetrated to the Cadet five in the last quarter. Those were only two of the more breath taking incidents in a gridiron show that blossomed into pure melodrama after an innocuous first period and kept a sellout throng of 78,000 in a dither of excitement Statistics at Philadelphia.

NAVY {@ Municipal Stadium, Philadelphia, PA}

If Navy had any questions about Army's #4 national ranking in 1949, the Cadets erased those doubts with a 38-0 trouncing of the Midshipmen in the 50th meeting between the two academies. The statistics certainly told the story on this afternoon Army had 27 first downs compared to eight for Navy, not to mention a 459-107 advantage in total offensive yardage. The Midshipmen advanced no further than the Army 47 yard line, as Cadet fullback "Gil Stephenson" gained 127 yards on 26 attempts.

1950 Army Cadets

Led by head coach Earl Blaik, the team finished with an 8–1 record. The Cadets offense scored 267 points, while the defense allowed 40 points. Bob Blaik was the starting quarterback.

Tom Lombardo, the captain of the 1944 Army team, was killed in action in Korea. Two weeks before the Army–Navy Game, Johnny Trent, the captain of the 1949 Army team, was killed in action. Trent, and Arnold Galiffa, the starting quarterback of the 1949 Army team, were sent with the Eighth Army to Korea. With President Harry S. Truman in attendance, Navy beat Army by a score of 14–2. It was the first time Navy had beaten Army since 1943. Dan Foldberg {E} was selected as a consensus first team All-American.

FINAL RANK: #2 AP/#5 UPI						
Home games were played at Michie Stadium						
9/30/1950	ARMY	vs	COLGATE (5-3)	28	0	W
10/7/1950	ARMY	vs	PENN STATE (5-3-1)	41	7	W
10/14/1950	ARMY	vs	MICHIGAN (6-3-1)	27	6	W
10/21/1950	ARMY	@	Harvard (1-7)	49	0	W
10/28/1950	ARMY	@	Columbia (4-5)	34	0	W
11/4/1950	ARMY	@	Pennsylvania (6-3)	28	13	W
11/11/1950	ARMY	vs	NEW MEXICO (2-8)	51	0	W
11/18/1950	ARMY	@	Stanford (5-3-2)	7	0	W
12/2/1950	ARMY	vs	NAVY (3-6)	2	14	L
Coach: Earl "Red" Blaik			**Season Record >>**	267	40	8-1

Selected game(s) highlights

MICHIGAN {@ Yankee Stadium, Bronx, NY}

Michigan faced an Army team that was ranked #1 in the AP and Coaches' Polls at Yankee Stadium in New York. The two teams played to a 6-6 tie at halftime, but Army shut out the Wolverines 21-0 in the second half for a final score of 27-6. The game marked the 23rd consecutive victory by Army. Chuck Ortmann threw for 118 yards, and Don Dufek gained 66 yards on the ground and scored Michigan's one touchdown.

NAVY {@ Municipal Stadium, Philadelphia, PA}

The Midshipmen stunned Army, 14-2, earning their first win in in seven matchups. Army entered the game as 21-point favorites, but could not muster any offense, scoring only on a safety. Navy scored both of its touchdowns in the second half. The first came on a seven yard run by quarterback Bob "Zug" Zastrow. Later, Zastrow found end Jim Baldinger in the end zone for a 30 yard score and a 14-0 lead. The high-powered Cadet offense managed just one first down and three paltry yards of offense in the first half, and the second half wasn't much better. Army advanced inside Navy's 20 yard line seven times in the third and fourth quarters but came away with nothing to show for it.

1951 Army Cadets

Led by head coach Earl Blaik, the team finished with a record of 2–7. The Cadets offense scored 116 points, while the defense allowed 183 points. A massive honor code academic violation was revealed in the spring of 1951. There were accusations that football players were distributing unauthorized academic information. This was reported to Colonel Paul Harkins on April 2. It was later revealed that Red Blaik's son, Bob, was part of the honor code violation. On August 3, the violations were announced, and several athletes were implicated in the scandal.

The makeshift team that was assembled were not involved in the honor violation, but they were still a reminder of it. After losing several games to Ivy League schools, Army defeated Columbia for its first win. The team received a congratulatory note from General Douglas MacArthur. In sixth week of the season, the Cadets played Frank Gifford and his USC Trojans squad at Yankee Stadium. Before the Army–Navy Game, the Cadets had a record of 2–6. This was Blaik's only losing season at Army. In the Army–Navy game, Navy scored two touchdowns before Army even ran an offensive series.

Home games were played at Michie Stadium

9/29/1951	ARMY	vs	VILLANOVA (5-3)	7	21	L
10/6/1951	ARMY	@	Northwestern (5-4)	14	20	L
10/13/1951	ARMY	vs	DARTMOUTH (4-5)	14	28	L
10/20/1951	ARMY	@	Harvard (3-5-1)	21	22	L
10/27/1951	ARMY	vs	COLUMBIA (5-3)	14	9	W
11/3/1951	ARMY	vs	USC (7-3)	6	28	L
11/10/1951	ARMY	vs	THE CITADEL (4-6)	27	6	W
11/17/1951	ARMY	@	Pennsylvania (5-4)	6	7	L
12/1/1951	ARMY	vs	NAVY (2-6-1)	7	42	L
Coach: Earl "Red" Blaik			**Season Record >>**	**116**	**183**	**2-7**

Schedule Source: Steve's Football Bible LLC

Selected game(s) highlights

Northwestern

A desperation, 33 yard touchdown pass with a minute and a half left gave Northwestern a 20--14 victory over Army's football team before 40,000 at Dyche Stadium.

NAVY {@ Municipal Stadium, Philadelphia, PA}

For the first time in series history, the Army-Navy game would be shown on live television. However, this was hardly a "made for TV" special, as both the Midshipmen and Cadets entered the annual grudge match with losing records for the first time ever. Nonetheless, Navy ended its season on a much more pleasant note with a 42-7 victory.

Ironically, the game's biggest play was significant in more ways than one. Trailing 14-7, Army was driving to tie the score. On third-and-goal from the Navy six, Freddie Meyers' pass was intercepted by Navy's John Raster who returned it 101 yards for a touchdown. This took what could have been a 14-14 game and made it a 21-7 Navy lead.

1952 Army Cadets

Led by head coach Earl Blaik in his 12th season, the team finished with a record of 4-4-1. The Cadets offense scored 155 points, while the defense allowed 151 points.

Home games were played at Michie Stadium

9/27/1952	ARMY	vs	SOUTH CAROLINA (5-5)	28	7	W
10/4/1952	ARMY	@	Usc (10-1)	0	22	L
10/11/1952	ARMY	vs	DARTMOUTH (2-7)	37	7	W
10/18/1952	ARMY	vs	PITTSBURGH (6-3)	14	22	L
10/25/1952	ARMY	@	Columbia (2-6-1)	14	14	T
11/1/1952	ARMY	vs	VMI (3-6-1)	42	14	W
11/8/1952	ARMY	@	Georgia Tech (12-0)	6	45	L
11/15/1952	ARMY	@	Pennsylvania (4-3-2)	14	13	W
11/29/1952	ARMY	vs	NAVY (6-2-1)	0	7	L
Coach: Earl "Red" Blaik			**Season Record >>**	**155**	**151**	**4-4-1**

Schedule Source: Steve's Football Bible LLC

Selected game(s) highlights

Pennsylvania

It was Army against Penn and the whole world at Franklin Field yesterday, and neither rain nor mud nor fighting Quaker could stay the Cadets in their appointed line of march. The command was forward. They turned impending disaster into glorious victory as they came from behind to erase a 13-point deficit, raced to the tying touchdown and place-kicked the winning point with just 44 seconds to play. They beat Pennsylvania, 14-13. Everything was against them. Penn entered the contest as the favorite, and romped to two first-period touchdowns the first on a three yard dive by Joe Varaitis on the 10th play of a 55 yard march, the second via a 14 yard pass from Glenn (Bones) Adams to Billy Deuber on the 10th maneuver of a 49 yard 'drive.

NAVY {@ Municipal Stadium, Philadelphia, PA}

A first-quarter Navy touchdown would prove to be the difference as the Midshipmen won their third straight over the Black Knights. Phil Monahan scored from two yards out and the two teams combined for 13 turnovers, including six times during a five-minute stretch. Navy advanced inside Army's 35 yard line eight more times but came away with nothing to show for it.

1953 Army Cadets {Lambert Trophy}

Led by head coach Earl Blaik, the team finished with a record of 7–1–1. The Cadets won the Lambert-Meadowlands Trophy, awarded to the top college team in the East.

The Cadets had lost six players, including Freddie Myers, to academic ineligibility. The Cadets defeated Furman, 41–0, the team's first shutout since the 1951 scandal. After a loss to Northwestern, the Cadets were undefeated for the rest of the season. In a scoreless tie against Tulane, future Max McGee starred for the Green Wave. In the Army–Navy Game, Army's 20–7 victory over Navy was its first since 1949. The turning point of the season was an October victory over #7 Duke. The Blue Devils featured stars such as Red Smith and Worth (A Million) Lutz. Tommy Bell ran up the middle. Quarterback Pete Vann switched the ball to his left hand and made a southpaw pass. Red Smith was tackled by Bob Mischak in the final minutes of the game. Mischak ran 73 yards to make the tackle catching up eight yards of separation to save a touchdown. Inspired by Mischak, Army held Duke inside the one yard line, took over on downs, and eventually won the game.

FINAL RANK: #14 AP/#16 UPI						
Home games were played at Michie Stadium						
9/26/1953	ARMY	vs	FURMAN (7-2)	41	0	W
10/3/1953	ARMY	@	Northwestern (3-6)	20	33	L
10/10/1953	ARMY	vs	DARTMOUTH (2-7)	27	0	W
10/17/1953	ARMY	vs	DUKE (7-2-1)	14	13	W
10/24/1953	ARMY	vs	COLUMBIA (4-5)	40	7	W
10/31/1953	ARMY	@	Tulane (1-8-1)	0	0	T
11/7/1953	ARMY	vs	NC STATE (1-9)	27	7	W
11/14/1953	ARMY	@	Pennsylvania (3-5-1)	21	14	W
11/28/1953	ARMY	vs	NAVY (4-3-2)	20	7	W
Coach: Earl "Red" Blaik			Season Record >>	210	81	7-1-1

Schedule Source: Steve's Football Bible LLC

Selected game(s) highlights

Duke {@ Polo Grounds, Manhattan, NY}

In the fourth game of the 1953 season, the unranked cadets, sporting a 2-1 record on the year, upset the number-seven-ranked, 4-0, Duke University Blue Devils, 14-13, in New York City's Polo Grounds. Called by many sports writers "the college game of the year," the victory set Army's team and the Corps of Cadets afire. Tommy Bell ran up the middle. Quarterback Pete Vann switched the ball to his left hand and made a southpaw pass. Red Smith was tackled by Bob Mischak in the final minutes of the game. Mischak ran 73 yards to make the tackle catching up eight yards of separation to save a touchdown. Inspired by Mischak, Army held Duke inside the one yard line, took over on downs, and eventually won the game.

NAVY {@ Municipal Stadium, Philadelphia, PA}

The 1953 Army-Navy game was full of surprises. Navy elected to receive the opening kickoff, but the Cadets recovered their own onsides kick. This set the stage for sophomore fullback Pat Uebel, whose three touchdowns, including a 70 yard punt return, propelled Army past Navy, 20-7. After Uebel's five yard touchdown run made it 7-0, Navy had the chance to tie the score late in the first quarter. The Midshipmen drove to the Army six yard line, but George Welsh's pass was intercepted in the end zone. Navy avoided the shutout when Jack Garrow scored on an eight yard run with 44 seconds left on the clock.

1954 Army Cadets

In their 14th year under head coach Earl Blaik, the Cadets compiled a 7–2 record and outscored all opponents by a combined total of 325 to 127. In the annual Army–Navy Game, the Cadets lost to the Midshipmen by a 27 to 20 score. The Cadets also lost to South Carolina by a 34 to 20 score. Four Army players were honored on the 1954 College Football All-America Team: halfback Tommy Bell (FWAA, INS-1, NEA-2); end Don Holleder (AFCA, INS-2, NEA-1, UP-1, CP-1); guard Ralph Chesnauskas (AP-1, UP-3); and quarterback Pete Vann (INS-2, UP-3, CP-2).

FINAL RANK: #7 AP/#7 UPI

Home games were played at Michie Stadium

9/25/1954	ARMY	vs	SOUTH CAROLINA (6-4)	20	34	L
10/2/1954	ARMY	@	Michigan (6-3)	26	7	W
10/9/1954	ARMY	vs	DARTMOUTH (3-6)	60	6	W
10/16/1954	ARMY	@	Duke (8-2-1)	28	14	W
10/23/1954	ARMY	@	Columbia (1-8)	67	12	W
10/30/1954	ARMY	vs	VIRGINIA (3-6)	21	20	W
11/6/1954	ARMY	@	Yale (5-3-1)	48	7	W
11/13/1954	ARMY	@	Pennsylvania (0-9)	35	0	W
11/27/1954	ARMY	vs	NAVY (8-2)	20	27	L
Coach: Earl "Red" Blaik			Season Record >>	325	127	7-2

Schedule Source: Steve's Football Bible LLC

Selected game(s) highlights

Michigan

Army unleashed a frightening ground game and extended one of college football's most baffling jinxes by beating Michigan, 26-7, before over 69,000 fans at Michigan Stadium. The Cadets scored three times in the first half on end runs by Mike Ziegler, Pat Uebel and Tommy Bell. Bell scored his second touchdown on a 48 yard sprint in the 4th quarter. The Cadets have a perfect 5-0 record against the Wolverines in this intersectional series over the years.

NAVY {@ Municipal Stadium, Philadelphia, PA}

With each team boasting an offense ranked among the top three in the nation, the 1954 Army-Navy game certainly lived up to its billing. The lead was exchanged several times before the #6 Midshipmen, "The Team Named Desire," posted a 27-20 victory over the #5 Cadets. Down 14-6 midway through the first half, Army roared back to take a 20-14 lead. The Cadets' Don Holleder recovered Dick Guest's fumble at the Navy three yard line, and Pat Uebel slammed it home from there to cut the lead to 14-13 after the extra point. A little more than a minute later, quarterback Pete Vann hit Bob Kyarsky with a swing pass, and the swift halfback raced 42 yards for the go-ahead score.

After battling back to take the lead, Army spoiled its fortune by attempting an onsides kick that was unsuccessful. Quarterback George Welsh and his teammates took over at midfield, and six plays later, they led 21-20 after Welsh's five yard run and John Weaver's extra point. Navy opened the second half by driving to Army's nine yard line, only to fumble. Fortunately for Eddie Erdelatz's club, the Cadets were forced to punt on their ensuing possession. Navy made the most of this opportunity, as an Earle Smith five yard touchdown run made it 27-20. The Midshipmen preserved the victory with a dramatic goal-line stand midway through the fourth quarter and held Army at midfield to end the game.

1955 Army Cadets

In their 15th year under head coach Earl Blaik, the Cadets compiled a 6–3 record and outscored all opponents by a combined total of 256 to 72. In the annual Army–Navy Game, the Cadets defeated the Midshipmen by a 14 to 6 score. The Cadets also lost to Michigan, Syracuse, and Yale.

No Army players were honored on the 1955 College Football All-America Team.

FINAL RANK: #20 AP/#15 UPI						
Home games were played at Michie Stadium						
9/24/1955	ARMY	vs	FURMAN (1-9)	81	0	W
10/1/1955	ARMY	vs	PENN STATE (5-4)	35	6	W
10/8/1955	ARMY	@	Michigan (7-2)	2	26	L
10/15/1955	ARMY	vs	SYRACUSE (5-3)	0	13	L
10/22/1955	ARMY	vs	COLUMBIA (1-8)	45	0	W
10/29/1955	ARMY	vs	COLGATE (6-3)	27	7	W
11/5/1955	ARMY	@	Yale (7-2)	12	14	L
11/12/1955	ARMY	@	Pennsylvania (0-9)	40	0	W
11/26/1955	ARMY	vs	NAVY (6-2-1)	14	6	W
Coach: Earl "Red" Blaik			**Season Record >>**	**256**	**72**	**6-3**

Schedule Source: Steve's Football Bible LLC

Selected game(s) highlights

Michigan

After losing the first five games of the series, the Wolverines finally earned a win over Army. The Wolverines, behind Terry Barr and Ed Shannon, throttled the Cadets in a 26-2 victory. At 6 feet tall and 175 pounds, Barr was not the biggest player on the field, but he made some big plays for the Wolverines. He caught a 40 yard pass and scored on the next play to give Michigan an early lead. Fullback Ed Shannon scored on a short run for another Maize and Blue score. However, the biggest play of the day was an 82 yard punt return by the speedy Barr. Michigan's All-American tight end Ron Kramer also contributed with 4 catches for 67 yards.

COLGATE

Don HoIIeder, maturing before "the very eyes of the roaring Cadet Corps and 24,700 amazed civilians, yesterday passed and pranced Army to a 27-7 trouncing of Colgate. He connected for seven of nine passes, most of them long ones and three of them TD's and ripped off 73 yards on carries. His total gain for the day, 254 yards, was far more than he had accounted for in all previous five games combined.

NAVY {@ Municipal Stadium, Philadelphia, PA}

Although he failed to complete either one of his pass attempts, Army quarterback Don Holleder efficiently directed his team past Navy, 14-6. Navy jumped out to a 6-0 lead, thanks to quarterback George Welsh's one yard touchdown run. However, Army's one-two rushing combination of Pat Uebel and Peter Lash wore down the Midshipmen, as both Cadets managed a touchdown in the second half. Thus, despite posting more first downs (19) and more total offensive yards (330) than Army, Navy could not reach the end zone in the second half.

1956 Army Cadets

In their 16th year under head coach Earl Blaik, the Cadets compiled a 5–3–1 record and outscored all opponents by a combined total of 223 to 153. In the annual Army–Navy Game, the Cadets tied the Midshipmen by a 7 to 7 score. The Cadets also lost to Michigan, Syracuse, and Pittsburgh.

Dave Bourland led the team in passing with 394 yards and threw 6 touchdown passes. Bob Kvasky led the team in rushing with 707 yards and rushed for 11 touchdowns. Art Johnson led the team in receptions with 11 for 211 yards. Kvasky led the team in scoring with 66 points. Army guard Stan Slater was honored by the United Press as a third team player on the 1956 College Football All-America Team.

Home games were played at Michie Stadium

9/29/1956	ARMY	vs	VMI (3-6-1)	32	12	**W**	
10/6/1956	ARMY	vs	PENN STATE (6-2-1)	14	7	**W**	
10/13/1956	ARMY	@	Michigan (7-2)	14	48	**L**	
10/20/1956	ARMY	@	Syracuse (7-2)	0	7	**L**	
10/27/1956	ARMY	@	Columbia (3-6)	60	0	**W**	
11/3/1956	ARMY	vs	COLGATE (4-5)	55	46	**W**	*-Stephenson 3 TD catch
11/10/1956	ARMY	vs	WILLIAM & MARY (0-9-1)	34	6	**W**	
11/17/1956	ARMY	@	Pittsburgh (7-3-1)	7	20	**L**	
12/1/1956	ARMY	vs	NAVY (6-1-2)	7	7	**T**	
Coach: Earl "Red" Blaik			**Season Record >>**	**223**	**153**	**5-3-1**	

Schedule Source: Steve's Football Bible LLC
*-Single game record

Selected game(s) highlights

Michigan

Quarterback Jim Van Pelt rushed for a touchdown and caught a 14 yard pass. Sophomore running back Jim Pace ran for 32 yards on 9 carries and scored one of the Wolverine touchdowns. Fullback Ed Shannon scored against Army for the second straight season on a short run. He also completed 2 of 3 passes for twenty-five yards to help the Wolverines to their second straight win over Army – 48 to14.

WILLIAM & MARY

Bob Kyasky scored two touchdowns in Army's 34-6 victory over a stubborn William & Mary team that harried the Cadets with its passing attack. The Army pass defense finally stiffened and ended the day with 5 pass interceptions. Kyasky slashed over twice in 7 yard bursts, going over left guard in the third period and spinning through the middle in the fourth as Army took charge in the second half.

NAVY {@ Municipal Stadium, Philadelphia, PA}

Considering there were nine turnovers between the two teams, it was rather appropriate that the two touchdowns scored in the 1956 game were the result of opponent miscues. In the third quarter, Army's David Bourland intercepted Tom Forrestal's pass and returned it 26 yards to set up Bob Kyasky's four yard touchdown run and a 7-0 lead. In the fourth quarter, one of Army's eight fumbles led to a one yard touchdown run by Rick Dagampat.

1957 Army Cadets

In their 17th year under head coach Earl Blaik, the independent Cadets compiled a 7–2 record and outscored their opponents 251 to 129. In the annual Army–Navy Game at Philadelphia, the Cadets lost 14–0 to the Midshipmen; Army's other loss was in the same stadium, by two points to Notre Dame in mid-October.

Dave Boruland led the team in passing with 513 yards and threw 5 touchdown passes. Bob Anderson led the team in rushing with 983 yards and 13 rushing touchdowns. Bill Graf led the team in receptions with 16. Pete Dawkins led with 225 receiving yards. Anderson led the team in scoring with 84 points. Two Army players were honored on the All-America Team; sophomore back Bob Anderson was a consensus first team selection, and center Jim Kernan was a second team selection of the International News Service (INS).

FINAL RANK: #18 AP/#13 UPI

Home games were played at Michie Stadium

9/28/1957	ARMY	vs	NEBRASKA (1-9)	42	0	W
10/5/1957	ARMY	@	Penn State (6-3)	27	13	W
10/12/1957	ARMY	vs	NOTRE DAME (7-3)	21	23	L
10/19/1957	ARMY	vs	PITTSBURGH (4-6)	29	13	W
10/26/1957	ARMY	@	Virginia (3-6-1)	20	12	W
11/2/1957	ARMY	vs	COLGATE (3-6)	53	7	W
11/9/1957	ARMY	vs	UTAH (6-4)	39	33	W
11/16/1957	ARMY	vs	TULANE (2-8)	20	14	W
11/30/1957	ARMY	vs	NAVY (9-1-1)	0	14	L
Coach: Earl "Red" Blaik			Season Record >>	251	129	7-2

Schedule Source: Steve's Football Bible LLC

Selected game(s) highlights

NEBRASKA

In the first meeting of these teams, the Black Knights of West Point utterly obliterated the Cornhuskers in front of a relatively small Michie Stadium crowd. No matter which way they turned, by air or ground, all of Nebraska's attempts to at least avoid the shutout were thwarted.

NOTRE DAME {@ Municipal Stadium, Philadelphia, PA}

{Notre Dame Football Review} The Notre Dame comeback took a giant stride toward success today as the Fighting Irish came from behind in the last quarter to beat a favored Army team, 23-21. Over 95,000 fans sat in Municipal Stadium and watched Monty Stickles, an unknown sophomore, kick a dramatic 29 yard field goal with only six minutes remaining. The kick took an apparent victory out of the hands of the Cadets and gave Irish coach, Terry Brennan, the greatest victory of his young coaching career. The game was only two and a half minutes old when Bob Anderson, a young sophomore destined for great things, took off on an 81 yard run. Hilliard added the extra point, and Army had a quick 7-0 lead. The Irish took the kickoff and failed to get a first down. A clipping penalty set Army back in a hole and the Cadets decided to quick kick. The ball rolled into the end zone. Notre Dame took over on their 20 and moved 80 yards in 13 plays to tie the score. Quarterback Bob Williams went 14 yards on a keep play. After Frank Reynolds lost two, Williams completed a nine yard screen pass to Reynolds. Williams then hit Dick Prendergast on the Army 49. Fullback Nick Pietrosante netted three, but Williams lost a similar amount trying to pass. Williams was not to be denied though, as he tossed to Bob Wetoska for 16 yards. The lanky quarterback picked up 15 yards after Pietrosante had put the ball on the 24 with the 9 yard gain.

Pietrosante then moved it to the seven. Reynolds banged to the two and just hit inside the one yard line. Pietrosante hit over right side for the score and Don White kicked the extra point. When the first quarter ended. Army was right back down in Irish territory with the ball on the 22. A fourth down Bourland-to-Dawkins pass was good for eight yards but just short of a first down.

Army took the kickoff opening the second half and took just seven plays to score. Highlight of the drive was a 39 yard run by Dawkins that put the ball on the 7. One play later, he went over for the score and Hilliard converted to make it 14-7. It looked like Reynolds might tie the score on the kickoff return but Bourland, the last man between him and the goal, tripped him up on the Army 38, The Irish offense sputtered and then stalled as Army took over on their 26. After an exchange of punts, the Cadets took over on their 19 from where they scored again in 11 plays. Anderson went over from the one after sparking the drive with 31 yards in four attempts. Walters kicked the extra point and with only a minute left in the third quarter, Army led, 21-7. The Irish returned the kickoff to the 35. On the very next play, Pietrosante banged over guard, squirmed out of the arms of two tacklers, broke into the clear, faltered at the 15 but roared into the end zone for the score. Stickles kicked the point, and Notre Dame was back in the ballgame. Army failed to go anywhere and were forced to kick to the Irish 44. Lynch went for 18 and Williams kept for five. Reynolds picked up three and then Pietrosante got a first down on the Army 27. Lynch hit off tackle for seven and, after Pietrosante failed to get the first down, the senior halfback dived to the 15. Lynch then carried four consecutive times. He hit just short of a first down on the five but then picked up four to the one. After being stopped for no gain, he smashed into the end zone for the score. Irish hopes faded as Stickles' placement was too low. In the next series of plays, the Army was guilty of a great tactical error. With second and six, Bourland decided to try a jump pass. Frank Geremia batted the ball into the arms of Pietrosante who was on the ground. The stage was set for Stickles' dramatics. It will long be remembered as one of the highlights of the series which was renewed today after a ten-year lapse. Notre Dame was going for the score but a backfield in motion penalty hurt. With fourth and six on the 22, Brennan sent in Bronko Nagurski with the kicking tee. Williams held as Stickles kicked from the 29. With six and a half minutes to go, Notre Dame had a 23-21 lead. Army picked up one first down before yielding on the 48. The Irish went no place and Pietrosante kicked into the end zone. Bourland failed to find a receiver and ran for two. Three passes fell incomplete and the Irish took over on the 22. Two plays ran out the clock and the most dramatic of Army-Notre Dame games was history.

NAVY {@ Municipal Stadium, Philadelphia, PA}

Just as running back Ned Oldham was a two-time Naval Academy debate champion, the Midshipmen's 14-0 win over Army left little doubt coach Eddie Erdelatz's club was among the top five teams in the nation. While Oldham scampered 44 yards for his second touchdown of the day, the Navy defense slowed Army to just 136 total yards. The Cadets entered the game averaging better than 400 yards per game rushing and passing. Defensive guard Bob Caldwell and defensive back Tom Forrestal preserved the shutout with clutch fourth-quarter plays. Caldwell recovered a fourth-quarter fumble at the Navy nine yard line, and Forrestal picked off a pass in the end zone.

1958 Army Cadets {Lambert Trophy}

Led by head coach Earl Blaik, the team finished with an undefeated 8–0–1 season. The Cadets' offense scored 264 points, while the defense allowed 49 points. At season's end, the team was third in the national rankings. Junior Bill Carpenter was the Cadets' Lonely End. Blaik, in his last season at the helm of Army's squad, took the idea of splitting out an "end" or receiver, 20 or 30 yards wide from the rest of the formation. The "lonely end" as he became known, never entered the huddle, and for Blaik, his presence caused an unbalanced line and generally confused defenses.

Joe Caldwell led the team in passing with 1,097 yards and threw 8 touchdown passes. Bob Anderson led the team in rushing with 564 yards and 5 touchdowns rushing. Bill Carpenter led the ream in receptions with 22. Pete Dawkins led with 494 yards receiving. Dawkins led the team in scoring with 66 points. **Dawkins won Army's third Heisman** while leading the Black Knights to an undefeated season in 1958. Dawkins rushed for 428 yards and five touchdowns, caught another six TDs through the air and totaled another 294 yards on punt and kick returns. He finished with 1,216 all-purpose yards and 12 total TDs as Army finished the season 8-0-1 and ranked third in the country. Dawkins was elected to the National Football Foundation and College Hall of Fame in 1975. Bob Novagratz {Guard} was a 24th round draft pick of the Baltimore Colts in the 1959 NFL draft.

FINAL RANK: #3 AP/#3 UPI						
Home games were played at Michie Stadium						
9/27/1958	ARMY	vs	SOUTH CAROLINA (7-3)	45	8	W
10/4/1958	ARMY	vs	PENN STATE (6-3-1)	26	0	W
10/11/1958	ARMY	@	Notre Dame (6-4)	14	2	W
10/18/1958	ARMY	vs	VIRGINIA (1-9)	35	6	W
10/25/1958	ARMY	@	Pittsburgh (5-4-1)	14	14	T
11/1/1958	ARMY	vs	COLGATE (1-8)	68	6	W
11/8/1958	ARMY	@	Rice (5-5)	14	7	W
11/15/1958	ARMY	vs	VILLANOVA (6-4)	26	0	W
11/29/1958	ARMY	vs	NAVY (6-3)	22	6	W
Coach: Earl "Red" Blaik			**Season Record >>**	264	49	8-0-1

Schedule Source: Steve's Football Bible LLC

Selected game(s) highlights

Notre Dame

The Cadets traveled to South Bend, Indiana, and beat Notre Dame 14-2. Led by senior linebacker Bob Novogratz, who made eighteen tackles and recovered two fumbles against the Fighting Irish, the Army defense, proved it was as devastatingly effective as the offense. It was the only time Army beat Notre Dame as South Bend. It is the last time the Army would beat Notre Dame.

Pittsburgh

Army's only blemish on the season was a 14-14 tie at Pitt Stadium. The Cadets were ranked #1 in the polls going into the game. Trailing 14-6, Pitt took the second half kickoff 58 yards for a touchdown and then made the two-point conversion on a pass from Ivan Toncis to Dick Haley.

NAVY {@ Municipal Stadium, Philadelphia, PA}

All-America running back Pete Dawkins took the opening kickoff and raced down the sideline. But when he cut back, he collided with teammate Bill Rowe, popping the ball loose. Navy recovered on the Army 40 yard line, and Joe Bellino later scored the first touchdown of the game on a three yard run. Nonetheless, the Cadets had the last laugh, capping West Point's undefeated season with a 22-6 victory over Navy. Bob Anderson scored Army's first touchdown just before halftime on a one yard run and added another short score at the start of the final quarter. Trailing 14-6, Navy was driving down the field with two minutes remaining. But Don Usury picked off Joe Tranchini's pass and returned it 38 yards for a touchdown. The Cadets finished the year 8-0-1, as Dawkins captured the Heisman Trophy. Navy closed the year at 6-3.

1959 Army Cadets

In their first year under head coach Dale Hall, the Cadets compiled a 4–4–1 record and outscored all opponents by a combined total of 174 to 141. In the annual Army–Navy Game, the Cadets lost 43–12 to the Midshipmen. The Cadets also lost to Illinois, Penn State, and Oklahoma.

Joe Caldwell led the team in passing with 1.343 yards and threw 9 touchdown passes. Bob Anderson led the team in rushing with 340 yards. Bill Carpenter led the team in receptions with 43 for 591 yards and caught 3 touchdown passes. Carpenter, Anderson and Don Bonko led the team in scoring with 24 points. Army end Bill Carpenter was a consensus first team player on the 1959 College Football All-America Team.

Home games were played at Michie Stadium

9/26/1959	ARMY	vs	BOSTON COLLEGE (5-4)	44	8	W
10/3/1959	ARMY	@	Illinois (5-3-1)	14	20	L
10/10/1959	ARMY	vs	PENN STATE (9-2)	11	17	L
10/17/1959	ARMY	@	Duke (4-6)	21	6	W
10/24/1959	ARMY	vs	COLORADO STATE (6-4)	25	6	W
10/31/1959	ARMY	vs	AIR FORCE (5-4-1)	13	13	T
11/7/1959	ARMY	vs	VILLANOVA (1-9)	14	0	W
11/14/1959	ARMY	@	Oklahoma (7-3)	20	28	L
11/28/1959	ARMY	vs	NAVY (5-4-1)	12	43	L
Coach: Dale Hall			**Season Record >>**	174	141	4-4-1

Selected game(s) highlights

AIR FORCE {Yankee Stadium, Bronx, NY}

In the first ever meeting with the Air Force Academy, the two teams met at Yankee Stadium and played to a 13-13 tie. The Falcons came from behind to tie the game and had a chance to win, but George Pupich missed a 31 yard field goal with 37 seconds left in the game.

Oklahoma

By 1959, the Academy's football dominance had begun to fade. Unfortunately, the same could be said of Bud Wilkinson's program at that point, but the Sooners were able to prevail by a score of 28-20.

NAVY {@ Municipal Stadium, Philadelphia, PA}

Compiling 405 yards of total offense, Navy rolled to a 43-12 victory over Army. Joe Bellino's 113 yards and three touchdowns on 25 carries led a Midshipmen ground game that finished the afternoon with 288 yards. Joe Tranchini added a pair of short rushing scores as the Midshipmen posted 23 first downs compared to 13 for Army.

Despite the statistical difference, Navy held a slim 21-12 lead at the intermission. However, the Midshipmen added three "insurance" touchdowns in the second half. Bellino reached the end zone for the third time in the game, while Tranchini tallied his second touchdown and Roland Brandquist closed the scoring with a one yard run of his own.

1960 Army Cadets

In their second year under head coach Dale Hall (pictured at right), the Cadets compiled a 6–3–1 record and outscored all opponents by a combined total of 222 to 95. In the annual Army–Navy Game, the Cadets lost to the Midshipmen by a 17 to 12 score. The Cadets also lost to Penn State and Nebraska. Tom Blanda led the team in passing with 1,119 yards and threw 8 touchdown passes. Al Rushatz led the team in rushing with 648 yards and rushed for 10 touchdowns. George Kirschenbauer led the team in receptions with 25 for 273 yards. Rushatz led the team in scoring with 60 points. Army guard Al Vanderbush was selected by the Central Press Association as a first team player on the 1960 College Football All-America Team. He was also selected by the UPI as a second team player.

Home games were played at Michie Stadium

9/17/1960	ARMY	vs	BUFFALO	37	0	W
9/24/1960	ARMY	vs	BOSTON COLLEGE (3-6-1)	20	7	W
10/1/1960	ARMY	@	California (2-7-1)	28	10	W
10/8/1960	ARMY	vs	PENN STATE (7-3)	16	27	L
10/15/1960	ARMY	@	Nebraska (4-6)	9	14	L
10/22/1960	ARMY	vs	VILLANOVA (2-8)	54	0	W
10/29/1960	ARMY	vs	MIAMI-OHIO	30	7	W
11/5/1960	ARMY	vs	SYRACUSE (7-2)	9	6	W
11/12/1960	ARMY	@	Pittsburgh (4-3-3)	7	7	T
11/26/1960	ARMY	vs	NAVY (9-2)	12	17	L
Coach: Dale Hall			**Season Record >>**	**222**	**95**	**6-3-1**

Schedule Source: Steve's Football Bible LLC

Selected game(s) highlights

Nebraska

The Cadets struck first with a field goal, and disaster soon followed when Army then recovered a Nebraska fumble on the Cornhusker 5 yard line and promptly converted it into Nebraska's first-ever touchdown against the Cadets. Down 9–0, just two plays later, Nebraska QB Pat Fischer successfully faked a pass before running 64 yards to the Army 14, and soon enough the Cornhuskers were back in it, 9–7. After the halftime break, another bit of trickery by Fischer allowed a 57 yard pass to HB Dillard for another touchdown. The Cadet squad was far more productive than Nebraska on the day, snagging an interception, outgaining them 324–198, and tallying a first down advantage of 18–5. Despite the battle of statistics favoring Army, two outstanding defensive stands by the Cornhuskers on the 5 yard line kept Army scoreless until time expired on a last-ditch Cadet pass play into the end zone that was knocked away and incomplete. The win was Nebraska's first against Army.

NAVY {@ Municipal Stadium, Philadelphia, PA}

Army was not unhappy to see Joe Bellino graduate from the Naval Academy, as the star running back clinched the 1960 Heisman Trophy with an impressive all-around performance against the Cadets in the 1960 regular-season finale. He touched the ball 25 times and accounted for 192 yards. He gained 85 yards on 20 carries, caught two passes for 16 yards, returned two kickoffs for 46 yards and intercepted one pass and returned it 45 yards. All this equaled a 17-12 Midshipmen triumph. Despite Bellino's exploits, Navy nearly squandered a 17-0 halftime advantage. A pair of Al Rushatz touchdown runs made it 17-12, and Army drove down to the Navy 32 yard line with 1:50 remaining. But quarterback Frank Blanda's desperation pass was intercepted, by none other than Bellino.

1961 Army Cadets

In their third year under head coach Dale Hall, the Cadets compiled a 6–4 record and outscored all opponents by a combined total of 224 to 118. In the annual Army–Navy Game, the Cadets lost to the Midshipmen by a 13 to 7 score. The Cadets also lost to Michigan, West Virginia, and Oklahoma.

Dick Eckert led the team in passing with 649 yards and threw 3 touchdown passes. Al Rushatz led the team in rushing with 556 yards and 8 rushing touchdowns. Tom Culver led the team in receptions with 20 for 305 yards. Rushatz led the team in scoring with 48 points. No Army players were selected on the 1961 College Football All-America Team.

Home games were played at Michie Stadium

9/23/1961	ARMY	vs	RICHMOND (5-5)	24	6	W
9/30/1961	ARMY	vs	BOSTON U (4-5)	31	7	W
10/7/1961	ARMY	@	Michigan (6-3)	8	38	L
10/14/1961	ARMY	@	Penn State (8-3)	10	6	W
10/21/1961	ARMY	vs	IDAHO (2-7)	51	7	W
10/28/1961	ARMY	vs	WEST VIRGINIA (4-6)	3	7	L
11/4/1961	ARMY	vs	DETROIT MERCY (5-4)	34	7	W
11/11/1961	ARMY	vs	WILLIAM & MARY (1-9)	48	13	W
11/18/1961	ARMY	vs	OKLAHOMA (5-5)	8	14	L
12/2/1961	ARMY	vs	NAVY (7-3)	7	13	L
Coach: Dale Hall			**Season Record >>**	**224**	**118**	**6-4**

Schedule Source: Steve's Football Bible LLC

Selected game(s) highlights

Michigan

Michigan defeated Army, 38-8, before a crowd of 65,012 at Michigan Stadium. Michigan's point total was its highest in 39 games, dating back to 1956. Michigan touchdowns were scored by Dave Raimey (13 yard run), Bennie McRae (47 yard run), Bill Tunnicliff (three yard run), Bruce McLenna (seven yard run), and Bob Brown (36 yard pass from Bob Chandler). Doug Bickle added a field goal and five extra points.

OKLAHOMA {@ Yankee Stadium, Bronx, NY}

Oklahoma traveled to The Bronx as a heavy underdog for the nationally televised matchup. Oklahoma came out on top, 14-8. Oklahoma scored on a 75 yard lateral pass from Jimmy Carpenter to Mike McClellan and a Bob Page 1 yard run. Oklahoma attempted a total of 6 passes and completed 2. Army attempted 23 passes and completed 9.

NAVY {@ Municipal Stadium, Philadelphia, PA}

Navy may have lost its season opener when it dropped a 20-10 decision to Penn State, but it closed the year in fine fashion with a 13-7 win over Army. Greg Mather, who caught four passes for 36 yards, punted five times for 167 yards and hit 27- and 29 yard field goals, turned in a fine all-around performance. His 27 yarder gave the Midshipmen a 3-0 lead, which they took into the locker room at halftime. Army took the lead early in the third quarter when it went 76 yards in six plays, capped by Al Rushatz's one yard touchdown run. Following an exchange of punts, Navy backup quarterback Bob Hecht took the team 51 yards for the go-ahead score, a 13 yard run by Bill Ulrich. Mather tacked on his second field goal in the fourth quarter to become the first Navy player to score in three series games.

1962 Army Cadets

In their first year under head Coach Paul Dietzel (pictured at right), the Cadets compiled a 6–4 record and outscored all opponents by a combined total of 152 to 104. In the annual Army–Navy Game, the Cadets lost to the Midshipmen by a 34 to 14 score. The Cadets also lost to Michigan, Oklahoma State, and Pittsburgh.

Cammy Lewis led the team in passing with 494 yards and threw 5 touchdown passes. John Seymour led the team in rushing with 539 yards. Seymour led the team in receptions with 7 and Bob Wright led in receiving yards with 92. Seymour and Ray Paske led the team in scoring with 18 points. No Army players were selected on the 1962 College Football All-America Team.

Home games were played at Michie Stadium

9/22/1962	ARMY	vs	WAKE FOREST (0-10)	40	14	W
9/29/1962	ARMY	vs	SYRACUSE (5-5)	9	2	W
10/6/1962	ARMY	@	Michigan (2-7)	7	17	L
10/13/1962	ARMY	vs	PENN STATE (9-2)	9	6	W
10/20/1962	ARMY	vs	VIRGINIA TECH (5-5)	20	12	W
10/27/1962	ARMY	@	George Washington (3-7)	14	0	W
11/3/1962	ARMY	@	Boston U (2-7)	26	0	W
11/10/1962	ARMY	vs	OKLAHOMA STATE (4-6)	7	12	L
11/17/1962	ARMY	vs	PITTSBURGH (5-5)	6	7	L
12/1/1962	ARMY	vs	NAVY (5-5)	14	34	L
Coach: Paul Dietzel			**Season Record >>**	152	104	6-4

Schedule Source: Steve's Football Bible LLC

Selected game(s) highlights

Michigan

Michigan defeated #10 Army by a 17–7 before a crowd of 70,749 at Michigan Stadium. The Wolverines intercepted four Army passes and gave up only four Army completions. Jack Strobel scored Michigan's first touchdown on a one yard run in the first quarter. Dave Raimey scored the Wolverines' second touchdown in the third quarter. Bob Timberlake added a 25 yard field goal and two extra points. Carl Stichweh scored for Army on 73 yard punt return in the fourth quarter. Michigan totaled 276 rushing yards in the game while holding Army to 92 rushing yards.

NAVY {@ Municipal Stadium, Philadelphia, PA}

Enjoying a fine sophomore season, Navy quarterback Roger Staubach stepped into the national spotlight when he completed a series-record 10-of-12 passes in Navy's 34-14 victory over Army. The Midshipmen rode the momentum of an early lead, as Army was held deep in its own territory on the game's opening series and was forced to punt. The snap sailed over Army punter Dick Peterson's head and out of the end zone for a safety, giving Navy a 2-0 lead. This advantage was extended by six points when Staubach hit Neil Henderson for a 12 yard score. Staubach tacked on a 21 yard touchdown run midway through the second quarter for a 15-0 lead.

Although Army scored just before the half to make it 15-6, Navy scored touchdowns on consecutive possessions to take a commanding 28-6 lead. Staubach hooked up with fullback Nick Markoff for a 65 yard touchdown and later added a two yard touchdown himself.

1963 Army Cadets

In their second year under head coach Paul Dietzel, the Cadets compiled a 7–3 record and outscored all opponents by a combined total of 177 to 97. In the annual Army–Navy Game, the Cadets lost to the Midshipmen by a 21 to 15 score. The Cadets also lost to Minnesota and Pittsburgh.

Rollie Stichweh led the team in passing with 454 yards and threw 3 touchdown passes. Ken Waldrop led the team in rushing with 559 yards and 9 rushing touchdowns. Curt Lindler led the team in receptions with 14. Sam Champi led in receiving yards with 146. Waldrop led the team in scoring with 60 points. Army guard Dick Nowak was selected by the UPI and the American Football Coaches Association as a second team player on the 1963 College Football All-America Team.

Home games were played at Michie Stadium

9/21/1963	ARMY	vs	BOSTON U (1-6-1)	30	0	W
9/28/1963	ARMY	vs	CINCINNATI (6-4)	22	0	W
10/5/1963	ARMY	@	Minnesota (3-6)	8	24	L
10/12/1963	ARMY	@	Penn State (7-3)	10	7	W
10/19/1963	ARMY	vs	WAKE FOREST (1-9)	47	0	W
10/26/1963	ARMY	vs	WASHINGTON STATE (3-6-1)	23	0	W
11/2/1963	ARMY	vs	Air Force (7-4)	14	10	W
11/9/1963	ARMY	vs	UTAH (4-6)	8	7	W
11/16/1963	ARMY	@	Pittsburgh (9-1)	0	28	L
12/7/1963	ARMY	vs	NAVY (9-2)	15	21	L
Coach: Paul Dietzel			**Season Record >>**	**177**	**97**	**7-3**

Schedule Source: Steve's Football Bible LLC

Selected game(s) highlights

NAVY {@ Municipal Stadium, Philadelphia, PA}

In a contest that had been postponed one week due to the assassination of President John F. Kennedy, Navy held on for a 21-15 victory over the Cadets. Halfback Pat Donnelly's three touchdowns gave the Midshipmen a commanding 21-7 lead four minutes into the fourth quarter. Yet, as usual, the next 11 minutes would be plenty interesting. Army took the ensuing kickoff and drove 52 yards in nine plays (all running plays), with quarterback Rollie Stichweh taking it in from the one yard line. Stichweh scored the two-point conversion himself, and Navy's lead was cut to 21-15 at the 6:19 mark.

Not only did Stichweh score the touchdown and extra points, but he then recovered the onsides kick at the Navy 49 yard line. The Cadets drove to the Navy four yard line, where on third-and-goal, Stichweh handed off to Ken Waldrop, who was tackled by a horde of Midshipmen defenders in a pile. Stuck at the bottom of the pile, Waldrop was unable to get back to the Army huddle before time ran out.

{From New York Daily New}: President Kennedy's death put into doubt what was already shaping up as the college football game of the year. The Army-Navy game was the Super Bowl of those days, and in 1963, Navy, behind the remarkable Staubach, was the #2 team in the nation. Army, having dropped four straight games in the series, had lost just twice during the season and was primed for the upset. The winner was going to go on to face #1 Texas in the Cotton Bowl. But it was also traditional for the military to observe the 30-day national period of mourning. And so, on Tuesday, Nov. 26, four days after the President's death and the same day the Heisman was awarded to Staubach, it was announced that the game would be moved back one week to Dec. 7 with the approval of the Kennedy family. According to some, it was First Lady Jacqueline Kennedy's ultimate decision that the game be played.

1964 Army Cadets

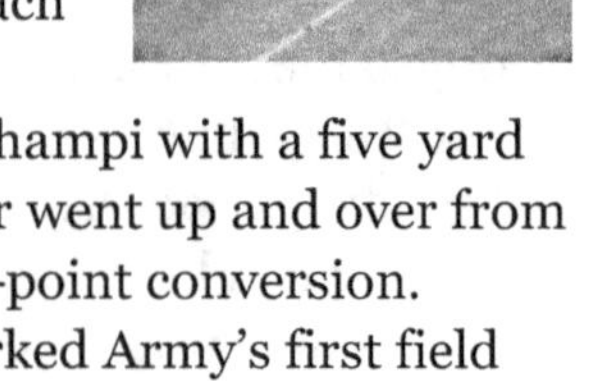

In their third year under head coach Paul Dietzel, the Cadets compiled a 4-6 record and were outscored by opponents, giving up 143 points while scoring 118 points. In the annual Army–Navy Game, the Cadets beat the Midshipmen by an 11 to 8 score. Rollie Stichweh led the team in passing with 816 yards and threw 3 touchdown passes. Stichweh led the team in rushing with 655 yards. Sam Champi led the team in receptions with 25 for 347 yards. Don Parcells, Mark Hamilton and Stichweh led the team in scoring with 18 points. Seven players from this team later fought in the Vietnam War.

Home games were played at Michie Stadium

9/19/1964	ARMY	vs	THE CITADEL (4-6)	34	0	W
9/26/1964	ARMY	vs	BOSTON COLLEGE (6-3)	19	13	W
10/3/1964	ARMY	@	Texas (10-1)	6	17	L
10/10/1964	ARMY	vs	PENN STATE (6-4)	2	6	L
10/17/1964	ARMY	@	Virginia (5-5)	14	35	L
10/24/1964	ARMY	vs	DUKE (4-5-1)	0	6	L
10/31/1964	ARMY	vs	IOWA STATE (1-8-1)	9	7	W
11/7/1964	ARMY	vs	SYRACUSE (7-4)	15	27	L
11/14/1964	ARMY	vs	PITTSBURGH (3-5-2)	8	24	L
11/28/1964	ARMY	vs	NAVY (3-6-1)	11	8	W
Coach: Paul Dietzel			**Season Record >>**	118	143	4-6

Selected game(s) highlights

THE CITADEL

Carl Stichweh covered almost 200 yards on three scoring plays to lead the Army to a 34-0 shutout of The Citadel at Michie Stadium. Stichweh scored on runs of 93 yards and 29 yards and returned a punt 73 yards for a touchdown. Fred Barofsky got the Cadets on the board first with a 72 yard run to give the Cadets a 7-0 lead. Barry Nickerson added three extra points for Army.

BOSTON COLLEGE

Fred Braofsky's 94 yard touchdown on a punt return proved to be the difference in the game as the Cadets had to withstand a furious fourth quarter rally by Boston College. Leading 19-0, the Eagles Ed Foley hit Charlie Smith for a 7 yard TD and Dan Moran scored from 5 yards out to cut the lead to 19-13. BC reached the Army 42 yard line before time ran out.

IOWA STATE

Mark Hamilton scored from 1 yard out in the closing minutes to give Army a 9-7 victory over the Cyclones. A pass interference penalty by Iowa State's Eppie Barney gave the Cadets new life and allowed Hamilton's go ahead touchdown. Iowa State drove to the Army 13 yard line in the last minute and had a chance to win the game, but Ronald Halda missed a 30 yard field goal.

NAVY {@ JFK Stadium, Philadelphia, PA}

Barry Nickerson's 24 yard field goal helped Army snap a five game losing streak to Navy with an 11-8 triumph. The Cadet defense made quite a statement on the opening series, as defensive guard Charlie Stowers sacked Navy's Roger Staubach for a safety less than a minute into the game. Army built upon its lead midway through the second quarter when quarterback Rollie Stichweh hit tight end Sam Champi with a five yard touchdown pass. Navy tied the game just before the half when halfback Tom Leiser went up and over from the Army one yard line. A scrambling Staubach found end Phil Norton for the two-point conversion. When Nickerson hit the game-winning field goal early in the fourth quarter, it marked Army's first field goal against Navy in 33 years. On its final drive, Navy faced a fourth-and-36 from its own 47, and Staubach's pass fell incomplete.

1965 Army Cadets

In their fourth year under head coach Paul Dietzel, the Cadets compiled a 4–5–1 record and were outscored by all opponents by a combined total of 132 to 119. In the annual Army–Navy Game, the Cadets tied the Midshipmen at a 7 to 7 score. The Cadets lost to Tennessee, Notre Dame, Stanford, Colgate, and Air Force.

Curt Cook led the team in passing with 463 yards and threw 4 touchdown passes. Sonny Stowers led the team in rushing with 822 yards and rushed for 4 touchdowns. Terry Young led the team in receptions with 17 for 184 yards. Stowers led the team in scoring with 24 points. No Army players were recognized on the 1965 College Football All-America Team.

Home games were played at Michie Stadium

9/18/1965	ARMY	@	Tennessee (8-1-2)	0	21	**L**
9/25/1965	ARMY	vs	VMI (3-7)	21	7	**W**
10/2/1965	ARMY	vs	BOSTON COLLEGE (6-4)	10	0	**W**
10/9/1965	ARMY	vs	NOTRE DAME (7-2-1)	0	17	**L**
10/16/1965	ARMY	vs	RUTGERS (3-6)	23	6	**W**
10/23/1965	ARMY	@	Stanford (6-3-1)	14	31	**L**
10/30/1965	ARMY	vs	COLGATE (6-3-1)	28	29	**L**
11/6/1965	ARMY	vs	AIR FORCE (3-6-1)	3	14	**L**
11/13/1965	ARMY	vs	WYOMING (6-4)	13	0	**W**
11/27/1965	ARMY	vs	NAVY (4-4-2)	7	7	**T**
Coach: Paul Dietzel			**Season Record >>**	119	132	**4-5-1**

Selected game(s) highlights

RUTGERS

Army's Black Knights got off fast for a 9-6 first half lead at Michie Stadium before a crowd of 31,000. Then stood off the Scarlet Knights of Rutgers to win, 23-6. The Cadets scored three touchdowns and a field goal, halfback Sonny Stowers crossing the goal line twice.

WYOMING

Army struck for two quick second quarter touchdowns and the Cadet defense beat back numerous attempts by the Cowboys to score. Sam Champi scored the first Cadet touchdown when he grabbed a fumble out of mid-air and rambled 42 yards for a touchdown. Tom Schwartz sacked Wyoming quarterback Tom Wilkinson causing the fumble for which Champi scored. Two minutes later, after a Wyoming turnover, Curt Cook fired a 32 yard touchdown strike to Terry Young. The Cadet defense stopped the Cowboys three times at the goal line during the game to gain the shutout.

NAVY {@ JFK Stadium, Philadelphia, PA}

With each team mustering just one first down in the second half, the 1965 Army-Navy tilt struggled to a 7-7 tie. The game jumped out to an exciting start, as Sonny Stowers' 25 yard touchdown run gave Army a 7-0 lead. Quarterback John Cartwright got the Midshipmen on the board with an eight yard touchdown pass to Terry Murray just before intermission. The 353 yards of total offense between the two teams represented the series' lowest total since 1939 (321). This was also the sixth tie in 66 Army-Navy games and the first since 1956 (also by the score of 7-7).

1966 Army Cadets

In their first year under head coach Tom Cahill (pictured at right), the Cadets compiled an 8–2 record and outscored their opponents by a combined total of 141 to 105. In the annual Army–Navy Game, the Cadets defeated the Midshipmen by a 20 to 7 score. The Cadets lost only to Notre Dame by a 35 to 0 score and to Tennessee by a 38 to 7 score.

Steve Lindell led the team in passing with 1,035 yards and threw 7 touchdown passes. Charlie Jarvis led the team in rushing with 450 yards and 3 rushing touchdowns. Terry Young led the team in receptions with 37 for 539 yards and 3 TD receptions. Jarvis led the team in scoring with 30 points. Army linebacker Townsend Clarke was selected by the Central Press Association as a first team player on the 1966 College Football All-America Team.

Home games were played at Michie Stadium

9/17/1966	ARMY	vs	KANSAS STATE (0-9-1)	21	6	**W**
9/24/1966	ARMY	vs	HOLY CROSS (6-3-1)	14	0	**W**
10/1/1966	ARMY	vs	PENN STATE (5-5)	11	0	**W**
10/8/1966	ARMY	@	Notre Dame (9-0-1)	0	35	**L**
10/15/1966	ARMY	@	Rutgers (5-4)	14	9	**W**
10/22/1966	ARMY	vs	PITTSBURGH (1-9)	28	0	**W**
10/29/1966	ARMY	@	Tennessee (8-3)	7	38	**L**
11/5/1966	ARMY	vs	GEORGE WASHINGTON (4-6)	20	7	**W**
11/12/1966	ARMY	@	California (3-7)	6	3	**W**
11/26/1966	ARMY	vs	NAVY (4-6)	20	7	**W**
Coach: Tom Cahill			**Season Record >>**	141	105	**8-2**

Schedule Source: Steve's Football Bible LLC

Selected game(s) highlights

Rutgers

Rutgers made a valiant bid for the brass ring and major upset in college football ranks yesterday but bowed in glory as Army staved off a last period urge to squeeze through with a 14-9 victory. The game, climatic sports event of the Rutgers bicentennial celebration, drew a capacity crowd of 30,000 to the Rutgers Stadium. Included in the throng was the full complement of the U.S. Military Academy cadet corps and more Ail-American football players than one normally sees in a decade. The All-Americans were on hand to join in the ground-breaking ceremonies for the Football Hall of Fame which will be dedicated on the Rutgers com-pus in 1969. The groundbreaking ceremonies served as a morning prelude to the exciting grid battle in the afternoon. Army, a two-touchdown favorite and starting as though it meant to prove its superiority, ate up 30 yards in seven plays for its touchdown and was off to a 7-0 lead before 10 minutes had ticked off the clock. ' That ended the Cadets' domination of the game, for Rutgers fought back to a 7-3 deficit at halftime and almost pulled the decision out of the fire with an offensive display that carried through most of the second half. Fumbles led directly to both Army touchdowns and, ironically, it was the sophomore hero of two previous Rutgers victories who made the bobbles that opened the gates for the Cadets. Bryant Mitchell, unable to break loose for any of the sensational touchdown runs that has marked his play to date, nevertheless wound up as the most productive Scarlet ball carrier with 40 yards in 17 plays. His fumbles came in the first and third period and left Army only 30 yards from the goal line in each instance.

GEORGE WASHINGTON

Army moved within reach of its best record since 1958 by outclassing George Washington, 20-7, today on the running and passing of sophomore quarterback Steve Lindell The victory was Army's sixth in eight games with two remaining. If the Cadets should close by beating California and Navy, they would equal their 1958 victory total. That team, Earl Blaik's last, suffered-only one tie in nine games. The game closed out Army's home schedule and 30,000 were present in the November chill and early twilight at Michie Stadium. They helped the Cadets set a home attendance record of 142,000, topping last year's high of 138,800. Lindell and a defense that held the Southern Conference rivals to only 10 yards rushing, won for the Cadets. George Washington had taken four in a row and boasted a 20-year-old quarterback named after Army's 1946 Heisman Trophy winner, Glenn Davis. But the Colonials had their worst offense day in four years and only punter Bob Schmidt kept the score within bounds. Lindell scrambled for 84 yards on the ground and completed eight of 15 passes for 109 yards and two touchdowns. Chuck Jarvis, a sophomore fullback who has pushed senior Mark Hamilton over to halfback, had his best day. He ran 16 time for 104 yards for 104 yards and caught one of Lindell's TD passes. Army drove 94 yards on only seven plays to lead off the scoring in the first period, and it was almost all Lindell. He sneaked three yards for the initial room to maneuver first down, rolled right end for 52 yards to the Colonial 30 and finally lofted a 28 yard knuckleball to Gary Steele in the end zone. The 6-5 Army end had nine Inches on the GWU defensive back and used the advantage well. Lindell missed this extra point but converted after Army's final two tallies. Army notched its second TD on a 41 yard drive that included Hamilton, back after missing two games with an ankle injury, making his first appearance at halfback.

NAVY {@ JFK Stadium, Philadelphia, PA}

Keyed by a pair of Steve Lindell touchdown passes in the fourth quarter, Army capped off its best season (8-2) since 1958 with a 20-7 win over Navy. Sophomore Charlie Jarvis opened the scoring with a 49 yard touchdown run in the first quarter. Lindell's extra point gave the Cadets a 7-0 lead. Under the efficient direction of quarterback John Cartwright, Navy tied the score at seven when Cartwright and Rob Taylor hooked up on a seven yard touchdown pass. The Midshipmen had three opportunities to take the lead in the third quarter but were unable to convert on any of them. The first drive stalled on the Army 47, Cartwright was intercepted inside the Army 20 yard line and John Church's 42 yard field goal attempt was blocked. Lindell then worked his fourth-quarter magic to ensure Army's victory.

1967 Army Cadets

In their second year under head coach Tom Cahill, the Cadets compiled an 8–2 record and outscored their opponents 183 to 94. In the annual Army–Navy Game in December, the Cadets lost 19–14 to the Midshipmen. Army's other loss was to underdog Duke, by three points in early October; the Blue Devils also defeated Navy, by nineteen in November. After their final home game, a 22–0 shutout of Utah on Veterans Day, the Cadets were 7–1 and prime candidates for the academy's first-ever bowl invitation. During the Vietnam War, Pentagon officials decided against it, citing the "heavy demands on the players' time" as well as an emphasis on football being "not consistent with the academy's basic mission: to produce career Army officers." Steve Lindell led the team in passing with 843 yards and threw 2 touchdown passes. Charlie Jarvis led the team in rushing with 774 yards and 8 rushing touchdowns. Terry Young led the team in receptions with 41 for 516 yards. Jarvis led the team in scoring with 48 points. **Jim Bevans tied the team record for interceptions with 8.**

Home games were played at Michie Stadium

9/23/1967	ARMY	vs	VIRGINIA (5-5)	26	7	W	
9/30/1967	ARMY	@	Boston College (4-6)	21	10	W	
10/7/1967	ARMY	vs	DUKE (4-6)	7	10	L	
10/13/1967	ARMY	@	Smu (3-7)	24	6	W	
10/21/1967	ARMY	vs	RUTGERS (4-5)	14	3	W	
10/28/1967	ARMY	vs	STANFORD (5-5)	24	20	W	
11/4/1967	ARMY	@	Air Force (2-6-2)	10	7	W	
11/11/1967	ARMY	vs	UTAH (4-7)	22	0	W	
11/18/1967	ARMY	@	Pittsburgh (1-9)	21	12	W	
12/2/1967	ARMY	vs	NAVY (5-4-1)	14	19	L	
Coach: Tom Cahill			**Season Record >>**	**183**	**94**	**8-2**	

Schedule Source: Steve's Football Bible LLC
*-Single game record

Selected game(s) highlights

RUTGERS

Rutgers had to play catch-up after Army reeled off a quick touchdown, but the Scarlet Knights never did overtake the Cadets, losing 14-3 before over 31,000 at Michie Stadium. Charley Jarvis scored from 34 yards out and from 7 yards out to give Army a 14-3 lead after 20 minutes of play. The teams battled to a standstill the rest of the game.

UTAH

Quarterback Steve Lindell hit on strikes of 37 and 20 yards for two touchdowns and Charley Jarvis ran for 38 yards to set up another as the Cadets shutout Utah, 22-0 at Michie Stadium. Jarvis then ran 3 yards for a touchdown to finish off the scoring for Army.

NAVY {@ JFK Stadium, Philadelphia, PA}

After operating all season from the T-formation, Navy switched to the I-formation for the annual Army contest. It helped the Midshipmen jump out to a 17-point lead and hold on for a 19-14 victory. The Army defense entered the season finale allowing a mere eight points per game but surrendered twice that many by halftime. Touchdown runs by Dan Pike and Jeri Balsly sandwiched a 29 yard John Church field goal to give the Midshipmen a 17-0 lead. Navy stretched the lead to 19-0 in the third quarter when Bill Dow tackled Army punter Nick Kurilko in the end zone for a safety. To energize his struggling offense, Army Coach Tom Cahill inserted quarterback Jim O'Toole into the game. O'Toole led the Cadets into the end zone on two-straight occasions, including a 52 yard scoring strike to end Gary Steele. Army was driving to take the lead when Charlie Jarvis fumbled on the Navy 23 yard line with four minutes remaining. The Midshipmen then ran out the clock to preserve the five-point triumph.

1968 Army Cadets

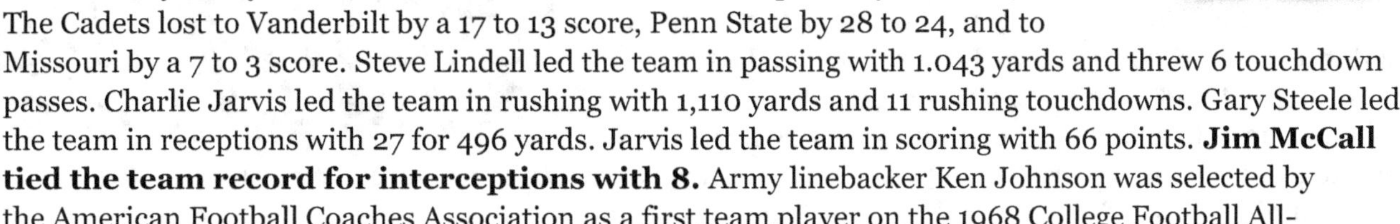

In their third year under head coach Tom Cahill, the Cadets compiled a 7–3 record and outscored their opponents by a combined total of 270 to 137. In the annual Army–Navy Game, the Cadets defeated the Midshipmen by a 21 to 14 score. The Cadets lost to Vanderbilt by a 17 to 13 score, Penn State by 28 to 24, and to Missouri by a 7 to 3 score. Steve Lindell led the team in passing with 1.043 yards and threw 6 touchdown passes. Charlie Jarvis led the team in rushing with 1,110 yards and 11 rushing touchdowns. Gary Steele led the team in receptions with 27 for 496 yards. Jarvis led the team in scoring with 66 points. **Jim McCall tied the team record for interceptions with 8.** Army linebacker Ken Johnson was selected by the American Football Coaches Association as a first team player on the 1968 College Football All-America Team.

Home games were played at Michie Stadium

9/21/1968	ARMY	vs	THE CITADEL (5-5)	34	14	W
9/28/1968	ARMY	vs	VANDERBILT (5-4-1)	13	17	L
10/5/1968	ARMY	@	Missouri (8-3)	3	7	L
10/12/1968	ARMY	vs	CALIFORNIA (7-3-1)	10	7	W
10/19/1968	ARMY	@	Rutgers (8-2)	24	0	W
10/26/1968	ARMY	vs	DUKE (4-6)	57	25	W
11/2/1968	ARMY	@	Penn State (11-0)	24	28	L
11/9/1968	ARMY	vs	BOSTON COLLEGE (6-3)	58	25	W
11/16/1968	ARMY	@	Pittsburgh (1-9)	26	0	W
11/30/1968	ARMY	vs	NAVY (2-8)	21	14	W
Coach: Tom Cahill			**Season Record >>**	**270**	**137**	**7-3**

Schedule Source: Steve's Football Bible LLC

Selected game(s) highlights

Missouri

Mizzou scored early thanks to field position provided by a 53 yard Roger Wehrli punt return. (The future Hall-of-Famer would also pick off a pass and return it for 32 yards later in the game.) Greg Cook plunged in from a yard out, and then the offense set about its self-destruction. The Tigers' defense made a stand when Army recovered a fumble at the Mizzou 26, then stopped most Cadet drives before they started. Army's Arden Jensen hit a 46 yard field goal in the fourth quarter, but the early points were thankfully all Mizzou needed. The Tigers' nine turnovers were offset a bit by Army's six, and Mizzou's run game worked just well enough to control field position.

Penn State

Penn State withstood a fourth quarter Army rally to score a 28-24 victory before over 49,000 fans at University Park. Army outscored Penn State 17-12 in the 4th quarter, but earlier scores by the Nittany Lions and a 53 yard kickoff return for the Lions final score after Army had narrowed the margin to five points clinched it. Bob Campbell scored two touchdowns for the Nittany Lions.

NAVY {@ JFK Stadium, Philadelphia, PA}

Leading by a touchdown midway through the third quarter, Army faced a third-and-eight at its own 35 yard line. Army quarterback Steve Lindell dropped back to pass, only to be hit by defensive end Mike Lettieri. Defensive tackle Tom LaForce caught the fluttering football and raced 36 yards for the tying touchdown. However, backup quarterback Jim O'Toole came on to engineer the game-winning drive late in the third quarter, as running back Charlie Jarvis scored his third touchdown of the day. Early in the fourth quarter, it appeared as if the Midshipmen were poised to take the lead again, driving 63 yards to set up a fourth-and-five at the Cadet 12 yard line. Mike McNallen completed the pass to Mike Clark, but he was stopped two yards short of the first down and Army held on for a 21-14 victory.

1969 Army Cadets

Led by head coach Tom Cahill, the team finished with a record of 4–5–1. The Cadets offense scored 161 points, while the defense allowed 160 points.

Bernie Wall led the team in passing with 814 yards and threw 4 touchdown passes. Lynn Moore led the team in rushing with 983 yards and 9 rushing touchdowns. Joe Albano led the team in receptions with 30 for 394 yards. Moore led the team in scoring with 54 points. No Army players were recognized on the 1969 College Football All-America Team.

Home games were played at Michie Stadium

9/20/1969	ARMY	vs	NEW MEXICO (4-6)	31	14	**W**
9/27/1969	ARMY	@	Vanderbilt (4-6)	16	6	**W**
10/4/1969	ARMY	vs	TEXAS A&M (3-7)	13	20	**L**
10/11/1969	ARMY	vs	NOTRE DAME (8-2-1)	0	45	**L**
10/18/1969	ARMY	vs	UTAH STATE (3-7)	7	23	**L**
10/25/1969	ARMY	vs	BOSTON COLLEGE (5-4)	38	7	**W**
11/1/1969	ARMY	vs	AIR FORCE (6-4)	6	13	**L**
11/8/1969	ARMY	@	Oregon (5-5-1)	17	17	**T**
11/15/1969	ARMY	vs	PITTSBURGH (4-6)	6	15	**L**
11/29/1969	ARMY	vs	NAVY (1-9)	27	0	**W**
Coach: Tom Cahill			**Season Record >>**	161	160	**4-5-1**

Schedule Source: Steve's Football Bible LLC

Selected game(s) highlights

Vanderbilt

Army quarterback Bernie Wall, mixing pinpoint passes with a punishing ground game, led the Cadets to a 16-6 victory over Vanderbilt in Nashville, TN. Wall guided Army on drives of 81 yards and 80 yards and set up a field goal with a 21 yard quarterback sneak up the middle which caught the Commodores defense napping. Wall completed 12 of 18 passes for 114 yards. Lynn Moore rushed for 152 yards on 29 carries and scored two touchdowns.

NAVY {@ JFK Stadium, Philadelphia, PA}

The new power-I offense installed by Army coach Tom Cahill overwhelmed the Navy defense in the 1969 matchup. Tailback Lynn Moore carried the football 40 times for 206 yards as the Cadets rolled over the Midshipmen, 27-0.

While the Army offense was certainly productive, the efforts of the Cadet defense did not go unnoticed. Navy appeared to be on its way to a touchdown just before halftime, but John Bremner picked off quarterback Mike McNallen's pass at the Army 23 yard line. Finally, Navy was inside the Army one yard line late in the fourth quarter, but a dramatic goal-line stand preserved Army's first series shutout in 20 years.

1970 Army Cadets

In their fifth year under head coach Tom Cahill, the Cadets compiled a 1–9–1 record and were outscored by their opponents by a combined total of 281 to 151. In the annual Army–Navy Game, the Cadets were defeated by the Midshipmen by an 11 to 7 score. The Cadets' only victory came in the season opener, a 26 to 0 victory over Holy Cross. Bernie Wall led the team in passing with 970 yards. Dick Atha led with 5 touchdown passes. Ray Rittaco led the team in rushing with 417 yards. Joe Albano led the team in receptions with 54 for 669 yards and 6 TD receptions. Albano led the team in scoring with 36 points. No Army players were selected as first team players on the 1970 College Football All-America Team. **Albano set the single game record for receptions with 13 vs Syracuse.**

Home games were played at Michie Stadium

9/12/1970	ARMY	vs	HOLY CROSS (0-10-1)	26	0	W	
9/19/1970	ARMY	vs	BAYLOR (2-9)	7	10	L	
9/26/1970	ARMY	@	Nebraska (11-0-1)	0	28	L	
10/3/1970	ARMY	@	Tennessee (11-1)	3	48	L	
10/10/1970	ARMY	@	Notre Dame (10-1)	10	51	L	
10/17/1970	ARMY	@	Virginia (5-6)	20	21	L	
10/24/1970	ARMY	vs	PENN STATE (7-3)	14	38	L	
10/31/1970	ARMY	@	Boston College (8-2)	13	21	L	
11/7/1970	ARMY	vs	SYRACUSE (6-4)	29	31	L	*-Albano 13 catch
11/14/1970	ARMY	vs	OREGON (6-4-1)	22	22	T	
11/28/1970	ARMY	vs	NAVY (2-9)	7	11	L	
Coach: Tom Cahill			**Season Record >>**	151	281	1-9-1	

Schedule Source: Steve's Football Bible LLC
***-Single game record**

Selected game(s) highlights

Nebraska

Coach Tom Cahill used three signal-callers today as Army went down to a 28-0 defeat at the hands of nationally ranked Nebraska. The Cornhuskers raked Army's defenses with too many guns while muffling the cadets' attack. Particularly impressive was the Nebraska defense when danger seemed imminent. Army drove inside the Big Red's 25 yard line three times but could not get into the end zone. Early in the fourth quarter, the cadets reached the Nebraska 2 after a 62 yard march sparked by Bernie Wall. But Bruce Simpson was stopped for losses of 1 and 4 yards and two passes fell incomplete as Wall could not find a loose receiver.

OREGON

The Ducks Bobby Moore bolted 59 yards for a touchdown and then caught a two point conversion pass from Dan Fouts to give heavily favored Oregon a 22-22 tie with Army. Dick Atha ran 3 yards for a touchdown and then threw a 19 yard TD pass to Joe Albano to give the Cadets a 22-14 lead. Arden Jensen kicked three field goals for Army.

NAVY {@ JFK Stadium, Philadelphia, PA}

Entering the 1970 season finale, Navy had given up 32 points per game. Yet, it was the Midshipmen defense that came up big in an 11-7 win over Army. Navy defensive back Mark Schickner, who did not even play football the previous fall, intercepted a series-record four passes to preserve the Midshipmen' second win of the year. His last interception was particularly valuable because it came on the Navy 12 yard line with less than a minute to play. The game remained scoreless until the third quarter when Dick Atha and Joe Albano connected on a 42 yard touchdown pass. Navy's Joe Elfein quickly erased that advantage with a 40 yard touchdown run which, combined with a two-point conversion pass from

Mike McNallen to Karl Schwelm, gave Navy an 8-7 lead. Roger Lanning then iced the win with a 33 yard field goal in the fourth quarter.

1971 Army Cadets

In their sixth year under head coach Tom Cahill, the Cadets compiled a 6–4 record but were outscored by their opponents by a combined total of 206 to 146. In the annual Army–Navy Game, the Cadets defeated the Midshipmen by a 24 to 23 score.

Kingsley Fink led the team in passing with 799 yards and threw 8 touchdown passes. Ray Ritacco led the team in rushing with 427 yards. John Simar led the team in receptions with 26. Ed Francis led with 292 receiving yards. Bob Hines led the team in scoring with 24 points. No Army players were selected as first team players on the 1971 College Football All-America Team.

Home games were played at Michie Stadium

9/18/1971	ARMY	vs	STANFORD (9-3)	3	38	L
9/25/1971	ARMY	@	Georgia Tech (6-6)	16	13	W
10/2/1971	ARMY	vs	MISSOURI (1-10)	22	6	W
10/9/1971	ARMY	@	Penn State (11-1)	0	42	L
10/16/1971	ARMY	@	Air Force (6-4)	7	20	L
10/23/1971	ARMY	vs	VIRGINIA (3-8)	14	9	W
10/29/1971	ARMY	@	Miami (4-7)	13	24	L
11/6/1971	ARMY	vs	RUTGERS (4-7)	30	17	W
11/13/1971	ARMY	vs	PITTSBURGH (3-8)	17	14	W
11/27/1971	ARMY	vs	NAVY (3-8)	24	23	W
Coach: Tom Cahill			**Season Record >>**	146	206	6-4

Schedule Source: Steve's Football Bible LLC

Selected game(s) highlights

RUTGERS

Army, tidying up some loose ends before its big date with Navy in three weeks, managed only one sustained touchdown drive today but capitalized on enough opportunities to post an easy 30-17 win over Rutgers in chilly Michie Stadium. Jim Barclay, the Cadets' sophomore place kicker, made good on three of the five field goals he tried, from 2, 28 and 26 yards out, and split end John Simar scored the other West Point TD on a seven yard catch from Kingsley Fink. Rutgers showed a more diversified offense than the Cadets but neither of its quarterbacks, Garry Smolyn or Lon Gasienca, threw with much accuracy. Each was intercepted once. The Cadets amassed a commanding 364-194 offensive yardage advantage, Ray Ritacco rushing for 59 yards and Greg McGuckin for 52 yards, each in 12 carries. Fink completed 11 of 22 passes for 154 yards

NAVY {@ JFK Stadium, Philadelphia, PA}

In typical Army-Navy fashion, the 1971 contest went right down to the wire. This time, however, it was the Cadets who came out on top, 24-23. This marked the first one-point game in series history. Army had jumped out to a 16-0 first-quarter lead, thanks to two Bob Hines touchdowns and a 42 yard field goal by James Barclay (only Army's second series field goal in the last 40 years). By the third quarter, however, the Midshipmen had reached the end zone three times themselves, as a 12 yard Freddie Stuvek-to-Steve Ogden pass gave the Midshipmen a 21-16 lead. Army quarterback Kingsley Fink opened the fourth quarter with a five yard touchdown pass to Ed Francis to help the Cadets regain the lead, 24-21. On the ensuing drive, Navy began a seven-minute drive that was brought to a halt when Stuvek's fourth-down pass was intercepted at the Army four yard line. The Midshipmen regained possession at the Army 39 with less than two minutes to go. Stuvek drove his offense to the seven yard line and appeared to pick up six more yards on an option pitch to George Perry, but officials ruled that Stuvek's knee was down before he gave up the football. Navy turned the ball back over on downs, and Army punter Ron Dahnof ran off the final eight seconds in the end zone, giving Navy a safety, but Army the win.

1972 Army Cadets {Commander-Chief-Trophy}

In their seventh year under head coach Tom Cahill, the Cadets compiled a 6–4 record but were outscored by their opponents by a combined total of 160 to 282. In the annual Army–Navy Game, the Cadets defeated the Midshipmen by a 23 to 153 score.

Kingsley Fink led the team in passing with 1,139 yards and threw 6 touchdown passes. Bob Hines led the team in rushing with 844 yards and 5 rushing touchdowns. Jim Ward led the team in receptions with 32 for 393 yards and 4 TD receptions. Hines led the team in scoring with 30 points. No Army players were selected as first team players on the 1972 College Football All-America Team.

Home games were played at Michie Stadium

9/23/1972	ARMY	vs	NEBRASKA (9-2-1)	7	77	L
9/30/1972	ARMY	@	Texas A&M (3-8)	24	14	W
10/7/1972	ARMY	vs	LEHIGH	26	21	W
10/14/1972	ARMY	vs	PENN STATE (10-2)	0	45	L
10/21/1972	ARMY	@	Rutgers (7-4)	35	28	W
10/28/1972	ARMY	vs	MIAMI (5-6)	7	28	L
11/4/1972	ARMY	vs	AIR FORCE (6-4)	17	14	W
11/11/1972	ARMY	@	Syracuse (5-6)	6	27	L
11/18/1972	ARMY	vs	HOLY CROSS (5-4-1)	15	13	W
12/2/1972	ARMY	vs	NAVY (4-7)	23	15	W
Coach: Tom Cahill			**Season Record >>**	**160**	**282**	**6-4**

Schedule Source: Steve's Football Bible LLC

Selected game(s) highlights

NEBRASKA

Nebraska's Cornhuskers completely overwhelmed Army, 77-7, before a sellout crowd of 42,239 at Michie Stadium and millions watching on ABC-TV's regional telecast. The Cornhuskers scored two TDs in the first quarter, added three in the second, four in the third and two in the fourth before Army finally scored with 35 seconds left in the game. All 49 of Nebraska's players saw action, with the reserves taking over midway in the third quarter. The 77 points were the most scored in the nation in 1972. Johnny Rodgers scored three touchdowns, while Dave Goeller and Steve Runty each scored twice. Dave Humm set a Nebraska and Big 8 percentage record when he hit 14 of 18 passes for 160 yards. As might be expected, Nebraska dominated the total offense statistics, 481 yards to 124. The Husker Black Shirts held Army to minus 12 yards rushing.

Texas A&M

On September 30th, 1972, the Army Black Knights played the Texas A&M Aggies. In one of the biggest upsets to date in College Football, Army defeated Texas A&M, 24-14, despite being a 30-point underdog. Coming off a 77-7 home defeat to Nebraska in its home opener in 1972, Army marched into Texas A&M's Kyle Field. Playing in front of a crowd of 46,680, coach Tom Cahill's Cadets scored 10 points in the second half to break a 14-14 halftime tie. Senior halfbacks Bob Hines and Bruce Simpson led the Army rushing attack. Hines gained 70 yards on 23 carries and scored one touchdown, while Simpson punched in another and ran for 57 yards. Kicker Jim Barclay converted three extra points and booted a career-best 47 yard field goal to put the game out of reach in the fourth quarter. Defensively, Army's entire unit shut down the Aggies' wishbone offense and Matt Wotell intercepted two passes, forced two fumbles and made 14 total tackles. Team captain Steve Bogosian sacked Texas A&M quarterback Lex James three times and finished with 11 stops.

LEHIGH

Army blew a 20 point lead with a rash of 2nd half turnovers, then struck 65 yards in three minutes for a 26-21 victory over Lehigh on Kingsley Fink's 22 yard TD pass to Jim Ward with 3:19 left in the game. Joe Furloni intercepted a pass at the goal line with 17 seconds left to secure the Army victory. Fink ran for a 1 yard touchdown to start the Cadets scoring, followed by Pete Ramsberger scoring from 9 yards out and Jim Ward catching an 11 yard TD pass from Fink. Jim Farrell scored twice on short runs for Lehigh and Bob Stewart caught a 1 yard TD pass from Kim McQuilken to give Lehigh the lead until Fink's pass to Ward for the game winner.

Rutgers

Tom Cahill almost celebrated prematurely. The Army coach put in his second offensive unit with five minutes to go yesterday as his Cadets were enjoying a 15 point lead over Rutgers. Cahill had to sweat out the final minutes of the eventual 35-28 Army triumph. After inserting his second team with the game apparently won, Cahill sat back and watched Rutgers recover an onside kick yards for a touchdown with a Willie Thigpen fumble, the Scarlet Knights convert a pass for two extra points, and Rutgers recovers an onside kick at the Army 42 with three minutes to play. But three running plays and a Leo Gasienica pass attempt on fourth down failed to keep the Scarlet Knights alive, and Cahill put back his first offensive unit to run out the clock before a disappointed homecoming crowd of 20,000.

AIR FORCE

Bob Hines ran 49 yards for a game-breaking touchdown as Army upset heavily favored Air Force, 17-14. Falcons quarterback Rich Haynie was intercepted six times by the Army defense and Hines rushed for 202 yards on 38 carries. Haynie threw for two touchdowns to give the Falcons a 14-10 lead, which set up Hines heroics in the 4th quarter.

HOLY CROSS

Holy Cross, unable to score against an Army team since a 14-14 tie in 1915, did better than that today but Army won, 15-13, before 39,441 Michie Stadium fans in a pre-Navy game tune-up. The Crusaders, who have managed just one tie in the game series, turned Bob Hines fumble into three points early in the second quarter. The Cadets had just recovered a Holy Cross bobble at the Army 15, but four plays later, Lou Kobza lowered the boom on Hines, forcing a turnover, that Tony Konieczny picked up in mid-air. Unable to get closer than the Cadets 21, the Crusaders took a 3-0 lead on a 37 yardr field goal by Jack Kelly. Army overcame a 10-0 deficit behind a Bob Hines 1 yard TD run, a 10 yard TD pass from Kingsley Fink to Jim Ward and a 20 yard field goal by James Barclay.

NAVY {@ JFK Stadium, Philadelphia, PA}

Army and Navy may be well known for their respective efficient, ball-control offenses, but it was a defensive play that keyed Army's 23-15 win in 1972. Army sheared Navy's lead to 12-7 early in the third quarter, thanks to a 43 yard touchdown dash by Bob Hines. Navy drove right back down the field on the ensuing possession, only to stall on the Army 12 yard line. Roger Lanning came on to try a 29 yard field goal, only to have it blocked by the Cadets' Tim Pfister. Scot Beaty retrieved the loose ball and raced 84 yards with the go-ahead touchdown. A Bruce Simpson 21 yard touchdown run extended the lead to 20-12, and Jim Barclay's 23 yard field goal iced the win. Despite the loss, running back Cleveland Cooper etched his name into the Navy record book. His 135 yards on 26 attempts gave him 1,006 yards for the year, the first Midshipmen player to reach this plateau.

1973 Army Cadets

In their eighth and final year under head coach Tom Cahill, the Cadets compiled a 0–10 record and were outscored by their opponents by a combined total of 382 to 67. In the annual Army–Navy Game, the Cadets lost to the Midshipmen by a 51 to 0 score and lost to Notre Dame by a 62 to 3 score. Kingsley Fink led the team in passing with 1,141 yards and threw 4 touchdown passes. Willie Thigpen led the team in rushing with 268 yards. Jim Ward led team in receptions with 35 for 431 yards. Bob Simons and Jim Ward led the team in scoring with 12 points. No Army players were selected as first team players on the 1973 College Football All-America Team.

Home games were played at Michie Stadium

9/22/1973	ARMY	vs	TENNESSEE (8-4)	18	37	L
9/29/1973	ARMY	vs	CALIFORNIA (4-7)	6	51	L
10/6/1973	ARMY	@	Georgia Tech (5-6)	10	14	L
10/13/1973	ARMY	@	Penn State (12-0)	3	54	L
10/20/1973	ARMY	vs	NOTRE DAME (11-0)	3	62	L
10/27/1973	ARMY	vs	HOLY CROSS (5-6)	10	17	L
11/3/1973	ARMY	@	Air Force (6-4)	10	43	L
11/10/1973	ARMY	vs	MIAMI (5-6)	7	19	L
11/17/1973	ARMY	vs	PITTSBURGH (6-5-1)	0	34	L
12/1/1973	ARMY	vs	NAVY (4-7)	0	51	L
Coach: Tom Cahill			**Season Record >>**	67	382	0-10

Schedule Source: Steve's Football Bible LLC

Selected game(s) highlights

TENNESSEE

Condredge Holloway set up Tennessee touchdowns with a 52 yard pass and a 48 yard run as Tennessee won its second straight while Army dropped its third consecutive season opener. Holloway fumbled at his own 12 on the second play of the game, which set up an Army field goal. The slippery QB came back to engineer two first-quarter field goals by Ricky Townsend. Midway through the second period, Holloway evaded the rush and found Emmon Love for a nine yard gain to the 33. On the next play, he found Stanley Morgan deep down the left sideline for a long bomb to the Army 15.

HOLY CROSS

The Army defense kept taking the ball away from Holy Cross, but the Army offense kept giving it back and, in the shadows of a beautiful homecoming day, the failures of the offense finally gave away the game, 17-10. "With 8 minutes 56 seconds left on the Michie Stadium clock, the five times beaten Cadets led the Crusaders, 10-9, and the crowd of 42,267 sensed the first Army triumph of the season. But it was not to be. Army didn't win it; Holy Coss did, for its first victory in the eight game series. It was Army's ball on Its 20 after the defensive platoon 'had stopped the Crusaders for the umpty umph time. Dan Spangler was running at tailback, and, on the second play, he took a pitch-out from quarterback Kingsley Fink, breaking into the clear around the flank for a 14 yard gain. And then he fumbled, and that was the ball game. It was the fifth turnover by the Army offense (three fumbles, two interceptions), and that tore it for Army. When defensive end Chuck Dyer fell on Spangler's bobble at the Army 39 there was 8:56 to go. When quarterback Pete Yass sneaked in from the one (his second TD of the game), there was 4:47 left on the clock

NAVY {@ JFK Stadium, Philadelphia, PA}

A 31-point second quarter fueled the most lopsided victory in series history, as Navy routed Army, 51-0. This bettered the 38-0 win the Cadets posted over the Midshipmen in 1949. In addition, for the first time in series history, a team had two players rush for 100 yards in the same game. Ed Gilmore's 123 yards on 15 carries paced an offense that piled up 460 total yards, while Cleveland Cooper added 102 yards. Of course, it didn't hurt matters that Army turned the ball over five times.

1974 Army Cadets

In their first year under head coach Homer Smith, the Cadets compiled a 3–8 record and were outscored by their opponents by a combined total of 306 to 156. In the annual Army–Navy Game, the Cadets lost to the Midshipmen by a 19 to 0 score. Scott Gillogly led the team in passing with 466 yards. Brad Dodrill led the team in rushing with 558 yards. Gillogly led the team with 9 rushing touchdowns. Jeff Jancek led the team in receptions with 13. Howie Williams led with 207 receiving yards. Gillogly led the team in scoring with 54 points.

Home games were played at Michie Stadium

9/14/1974	ARMY	vs	LAFAYETTE	14	7	W
9/21/1974	ARMY	vs	TULANE (5-6)	14	31	L
9/28/1974	ARMY	@	California (7-3-1)	14	27	L
10/5/1974	ARMY	vs	PENN STATE (10-2)	14	21	L
10/12/1974	ARMY	@	Duke (6-5)	14	33	L
10/19/1974	ARMY	@	Notre Dame (10-2)	0	48	L
10/26/1974	ARMY	vs	HOLY CROSS (5-5-1)	13	10	W
11/2/1974	ARMY	vs	VANDERBILT (7-3-2)	14	38	L
11/9/1974	ARMY	vs	AIR FORCE (2-9)	17	16	W
11/16/1974	ARMY	@	North Carolina (7-5)	42	56	L
11/30/1974	ARMY	vs	NAVY (4-7)	0	19	L
Coach: Homer Smith			**Season Record >>**	156	306	3-8

Schedule Source: Steve's Football Bible LLC

Selected game(s) highlights

Notre Dame

Army was again mismatched, 48-0. The game featured an unexpectedly early fall snowstorm. Bullock scored from the six to lead Fighting Irish backs to 525 yards rushing and 30 first downs, a new record. Bullock scored the second touchdown as well. Clements ran a seven yard keeper before halftime for a touchdown and a 20-0 score. In the third period, Russ Kornman scored twice, from the seven and the four, and Al Samuels went 35 yards on a pitchout to score. Tom Baker scored the same way in the fourth quarter, from the six.

HOLY CROSS

A 24 yard field goal by freshman Mike Castelli with 18 seconds left to play was the winning margin in Army's second win of the season, before a crowd of 39,893. But the key man in the victory was Scott Gillogly, who replaced Greg McGlasker at quarterback with the Cadeis trailing, 7-3, in the closing minutes of the third quarter; and engineered the offense for two scoring drives.

AIR FORCE

Mike Marquez kicked the first field goal of his career, a 33 yarder with 17 seconds left to give the Army a wild 17-16 victory over Air Force. Marquez winning field goal came after Leamon Hall completed three passes for 57 yards before an interference penalty put the ball at the Falcons 16.

NAVY {@ JFK Stadium, Philadelphia, PA}

With President Gerald Ford among the 83,000 fans in attendance, Navy posted its second-straight shutout over Army, 19-0. The Midshipmen once again jumped out to a quick start, as the defense held the Cadets deep in their own territory. Dave Hoopengardner's punt fell at the Army 34 yard line, and Navy quickly went to work. Under the direction of freshman quarterback Mike Roban, the first plebe to start at quarterback for the Midshipmen against Army, Navy managed a 45 yard field goal from Steve Dykes. Bob Jackson added two short touchdown runs, and Navy led 17-0 at halftime. It was time for the Midshipmen' defense to shine in the second half, as it stopped Army on a fourth-and-four from the Navy nine yard line on the first drive of the third quarter. Defensive end Tim Harden recorded a safety midway through the third period when he sacked Army quarterback Scott Gillogly in the end zone. Offensively, Cleveland Cooper became the first player in series history to rush for at least 100 yards in three games. He finished his career with 362 yards on 69 carries versus the Cadets.

1975 Army Cadets

Led by head coach Homer Smith (pictured at right), in his 2nd season. The team finished with a record of 2–9. The Cadets offense scored 165 points, while the defense allowed 337 points. The Cadets won their first two games, then lost 9 straight to close the season.

Leamon Hall led the team in passing with 1,107 yards and threw 7 touchdown passes. Tony Pyne led the team in rushing with 544 yards. Howie Williams led the team in receptions with 37 for 417 yards. Greg King and Pyne led the team in scoring with 24 points.

Home games were played at Michie Stadium

9/13/1975	ARMY	vs	HOLY CROSS (1-10)	44	7	W
9/20/1975	ARMY	vs	LEHIGH	54	32	W
9/27/1975	ARMY	vs	VILLANOVA (4-7)	0	10	L
10/4/1975	ARMY	@	Stanford (6-4-1)	14	67	L
10/11/1975	ARMY	vs	DUKE (4-5-2)	10	21	L
10/18/1975	ARMY	vs	PITTSBURGH (8-4)	20	52	L
10/25/1975	ARMY	@	Penn State (9-3)	0	31	L
11/1/1975	ARMY	@	Air Force (2-8-1)	3	33	L
11/8/1975	ARMY	vs	BOSTON COLLEGE (7-4)	0	31	L
11/15/1975	ARMY	@	Vanderbilt (7-4)	14	23	L
11/29/1975	ARMY	vs	NAVY (7-4)	6	30	L
Coach: Homer Smith			**Season Record >>**	165	337	2-9

Schedule Source: Steve's Football Bible LLC

Selected game(s) highlights

LEHIGH

A lot of people from Bethlehem, Pa., must be wondering if the Lehigh University trip to West Point was necessary, particularly after the 54-32 loss to Army. There were those lapses during the game such as the time center Gene Borgosz made the short snap to quarterback Joe Sterrett, completely missing the waiting hands only to gently lower the ball to the ground for yet another Army recovery and eventual touchdown. Or take the post-game serenade by the Lehigh marching band, which easily won the musical contest because the Army band had walked out of Michie Stadium with most of the 27,872 scoring-sated fans. The Lehigh band skillfully built up to the noisy crescendo that ends Tschaikovsky's 1812 Overture only to see two cadets wheeling the salute gun out of the stadium and there was no cannon roar for the finale. And so, it went for Lehigh. Everything went for the Cadets. It was the first time in 66 games that they had scored more than 50 points. And their total offense, 643 yards, was only four shy of the yardage run up by Glenn Davis, Felix Blanchard and company" against Pitt In 1944. Adding the 44 points scored against Holy Cross last week, Army has 98 points in two games. In eight of the 12 times Army had possession of the ball, the Cadets scored.

NAVY {@ JFK Stadium, Philadelphia, PA}

Navy nearly pitched its third-straight shutout over Army, but Cadet Quarterback Leamon Hall scored a two yard touchdown late in the fourth quarter to make the final score Navy 30, Army 6. Navy kicker Larry Muczynski opened the scoring with a 27 yard field goal in the first quarter. Bob Jackson then scored a two yard touchdown, and Jeff Hoobler blocked an Army punt that Bob DeStafney returned 42 yards for another score. Muczynski not only converted both extra points, but also added a 31 yard field goal just before halftime to give Navy a 20-0 lead heading into the locker room. Jackson (133 yards) and Gerald Goodwin (117 yards) accounted for 250 of Navy's 305 yards on the ground, as the Midshipmen compiled 325 yards of total offense compared to Army's 206.

1976 Army Cadets

Led by head coach Homer Smith, in his 3rd season. The team finished with a record of 5–6. The Cadets offense scored 201 points, while the defense allowed 267 points. Leamon Hall led the team in passing with 2,174 yards **and threw 15 touchdown passes, which was a single season record for Army.** Tony Pyne led the team in rushing with 438 yards. Clennie Brundidge led the team in receptions with 47 for 657 yards and 6 touchdown receptions. Brundidge and Greg King led the team in scoring with 36 points. **Hall established the single game passing yards record with 376 yards vs North Carolina. Hall's 378 total yards is also a record.**

Home games were played at Michie Stadium

9/11/1976	ARMY	vs	LAFAYETTE	16	6	W	
9/18/1976	ARMY	vs	HOLY CROSS (3-8)	26	24	W	
9/25/1976	ARMY	vs	NORTH CAROLINA (9-3)	32	34	L	*-Hall 376 pass yds
10/2/1976	ARMY	vs	STANFORD (6-5)	21	20	W	
10/9/1976	ARMY	@	Penn State (7-5)	16	38	L	
10/16/1976	ARMY	@	Tulane (2-9)	10	23	L	
10/23/1976	ARMY	vs	BOSTON COLLEGE (8-3)	10	27	L	
10/30/1976	ARMY	vs	AIR FORCE (4-7)	24	7	W	
11/6/1976	ARMY	@	Pittsburgh (12-0)	7	37	L	
11/13/1976	ARMY	vs	COLGATE (8-2)	29	13	W	
11/27/1976	ARMY	vs	NAVY (4-7)	10	38	L	
Coach: Homer Smith			**Season Record >>**	**201**	**267**	**5-6**	

Schedule Source: Steve's Football Bible LLC
*-Single game record

Selected game(s) highlights

LAFAYETTE

Army quarterback Leamon Hall teamed up with tight end Clennie Brundidge 10 times for 142 yards and a touchdown Saturday to lead the Cadets to a 16-6 victory over Lafayette in the season opener for both teams. On the final play of the third quarter, with Army holding a tenuous 9-6 advantage, the Cadets were faced with a second and 16 situation at the Lafayette 30 yard line Brundidge ran a turn-in pattern between the Lafayette linebackers, gathered m Hall's pass at the 10 and eluded two would-be tacklers for the touchdown. Hall finished with 16 completions in 27 attempts for 183 yards.

COLGATE

The Colgate Red Raiders, attempting to relive the glories of their famed unbeaten, untied, unscored on and uninvited club of 1932, ran smack into a man of the present, quarterback Leamon Hall, who broke two Army aerial records as the Cadets handed Colgate its first defeat. 29-13, before 29,637 fans in Michie Stadium at West Point. Hall threw three touchdown passes to Don Briggs, Jim Merriken and Clennie Brundidge and completed 14 of 31 tosses for 195 yards. Army built a 16-0 lead in just over a period, but the Red Raiders came back to within three points at 16-13 early in the last quarter. It appeared Colgate, winner of eight straight in its best campaign in 44 years, had the momentum, but Army had other plans. Starting from his own 20 following the kickoff. Hall marched his men 80 yards in 14 plays to go in front. 23-13, with 7:58 remaining in the battle.

NAVY {@ JFK Stadium, Philadelphia, PA}

Quarterback Bob Leszczynski and running backs Joe Gattuso Jr. and Larry Klawinski accounted for 389 of Navy's 428 yards of total offense, which explains the Midshipmen's 38-10 win. Ironically, Navy's punter Art Ohanian played a key role in his team's first two touchdowns. He placed his first kick inside Army's two yard line, which enabled the Midshipmen to get the ball back near midfield after an impressive outing by the Navy defense. Gattuso capped a six play, 50 yard drive with a two yard scoring plunge. Late in the first quarter, Ohanian nailed a 51 yard punt inside the Army seven yard line. Leszczynski and wide receiver Phil McConkey closed out the drive with an 11 yard touchdown to give the Midshipmen an advantage they'd never relinquish.

1977 Army Cadets {Commander-Chief-Trophy}

Led by head coach Homer Smith, in his 4th season. The team finished with a record of 7-4. The Cadets offense scored 287 points, while the defense allowed 245 points. They claimed the Commander-in-Chief's Trophy for the second straight season.

Leamon Hall led the team in passing with 1,944 yards **and threw 15 touchdown passes, tying his team record set in 1976.** Greg King led the team in rushing with 961 yards. Hall led with 8 rushing touchdowns. Clennie Brundidge led the team in receptions with 51 for 84 yards and 4 touchdown receptions. John Hilliard led the team with 5 interceptions. Hall led the team in scoring with 48 points. **Hall threw a single game record 5 touchdown passes vs Massachusetts.**

Home games were played at Michie Stadium

9/10/1977	ARMY	vs	MASSACHUSETTS	34	10	W	*-Hall 5 TD passes
9/17/1977	ARMY	vs	VMI (7-4)	27	14	W	
9/24/1977	ARMY	@	Boston College (6-5)	28	49	L	
10/1/1977	ARMY	vs	COLORADO (7-3-1)	0	31	L	
10/8/1977	ARMY	vs	VILLANOVA (4-7)	34	32	W	
10/15/1977	ARMY	vs	NOTRE DAME (11-1)	0	24	L	
10/22/1977	ARMY	vs	LAFAYETTE	42	6	W	
10/29/1977	ARMY	vs	HOLY CROSS (2-9)	48	7	W	
11/5/1977	ARMY	@	Air Force (2-8-1)	31	6	W	
11/12/1977	ARMY	vs	PITTSBURGH (9-2-1)	26	52	L	
11/26/1977	ARMY	vs	NAVY (5-6)	17	14	W	
Coach: Homer Smith			**Season Record >>**	**287**	**245**	**7-4**	

Schedule Source: Steve's Football Bible LLC
-Single game record {-Fahnestock 3 TD receptions}

Selected game(s) highlights

LAFAYETTE

Army scored early and often with the help of Lafayette miscues and went on to an easy 42-6 college football triumph over the inept Leopards behind Leamon Hall. On the second play from scrimmage. Brian Musician of Lafayette had the ball stripped from his arm by Army's Tiki Traylor. The ball was recovered by Dwain Fuller on the Leopards' 32, from where Hall directed an Army scoring drive capped by Greg King's four yard touchdown dash. Army kicked off, but then Lafayette running back John Orrico coughed up the ball. Army's Mark Berry recovered on the Lafayette 41 and ran the remaining distance for a score. Hall's keeper netted two points, making up for placekicker Mike Castelli's failure after Army's first score. Hall later drove the Cadets 80 yards in 18 plays with King taking a five yard pitch for the TD at the 45-second mark of the second period.

Air Force

Greg King scored on runs of 44 and 15 yards to lead Army to a convincing 31-6 victory over the Falcons in Colorado Springs. King finished with 165 yards on 23 carries. Leading 10-6 at halftime, Army set the tone for the 2nd half on the opening drive by stopping the Air Force cold on three plays and forcing a punt. Leamon Hall led the Cadets on a 14 play, 72 yard drive, culminating with Hall diving over from one yard out for a touchdown. Army never looked back after that.

NAVY {@ JFK Stadium, Philadelphia, PA}

The two service academies added another epic tale to their series when Army knocked off Navy, 17-14. This was the Cadets' first win in the series since 1972. In typical Army fashion, Coach Homer Smith's club used a ball-control offense to roll up a 17-7 lead at halftime. Nonetheless, Navy battled back with some key offensive plays. It was fourth-and-two on the Army 22 yard line with five minutes left in the third quarter, when John Kurowski rumbled down to the four yard line. Joe Gattuso Jr. slammed into the end zone on the next play, and Bob Tata's point after made it 17-14. The two teams exchanged punts for most of the fourth quarter, as Navy drove down to the Army nine yard line with a little over a minute left. It was fourth-and-two as Navy coach George Welsh dug into his bag of tricks, hoping to catch the Cadets off-guard with a halfback pass. However, Gattuso's throw sailed over the head of wide receiver Phil McConkey, sealing the victory for the Cadets.

1978 Army Cadets

In their fifth and final year under head coach Homer Smith, the Cadets compiled a 4–6–1 record and were outscored by their opponents by a combined total of 255 to 188. In the annual Army–Navy Game, the Cadets lost to the Midshipmen by a 28 to 0 score.

Earle Mulrane led the team in passing with 1,419 yards and threw 5 touchdown passes. Jimmy Hill led the team in rushing with 678 yards and 9 rushing touchdowns. Clennie Brundidge led the team in receptions with 44 for 726 yards and 4 TD receptions. Phil Macklin led the team with 4 interceptions. Hill led the team in scoring with 66 points. No Army players were selected as first team players on the 1978 College Football All-America Team.

Home games were played at Michie Stadium

9/16/1978	ARMY	vs	LAFAYETTE	24	14	W
9/23/1978	ARMY	vs	VIRGINIA (2-9)	17	21	L
9/30/1978	ARMY	vs	WASHINGTON STATE (3-7-1)	21	21	T
10/7/1978	ARMY	@	Tennessee (5-5-1)	13	31	L
10/14/1978	ARMY	vs	HOLY CROSS (7-4)	0	31	L
10/21/1978	ARMY	@	Florida (4-7)	7	31	L
10/28/1978	ARMY	vs	COLGATE (3-8)	28	3	W
11/4/1978	ARMY	vs	AIR FORCE (3-8)	28	14	W
11/11/1978	ARMY	vs	BOSTON COLLEGE (0-11)	29	26	W
11/18/1978	ARMY	@	Pittsburgh (8-4)	17	35	L
12/2/1978	ARMY	vs	NAVY (9-3)	0	28	L
Coach: Homer Smith			**Season Record >>**	184	255	**4-6-1**

Schedule Source: Steve's Football Bible LLC

Selected game(s) highlights

COLGATE

Quarterback Jerryl Bennett, making his first start, tossed a pair of touchdown passes and Jim Merriken rambled 49 yards for another score, leading Army to a 28-3 triumph over Colgate yesterday. Playing in place of the injured Earle Mulrane, Bennett hit 19 of 34 passes for 226 yards. He took advantage of a pair of Second period fumbles by Jim Comforti to give the Cadets a 14-3 halftime lead before a Homecoming crowd of 30,673 at Michie Stadium.

BOSTON COLLEGE

Jim Merriken swept left end for three yards and a touchdown on the first play of the fourth quarter, enabling Army to complete a 17 point, second half comeback and defeat Boston College, 29-26. Army scored first on Jimmy Hill's three yard run early in the first period, capping a 12 play, 66 yard drive. Boston College tied the score on a 16 yard sweep around left end by Anthony Brown, who gained 196 yards on 30 carries.

NAVY {@ JFK Stadium, Philadelphia, PA}

Despite a Nov. 18 loss to Florida State, Navy received word that a win over Army would be enough to earn an invitation to the Dec. 22 Holiday Bowl against Brigham Young. The Midshipmen were more than happy to oblige the bowl officials, blanking the Cadets, 28-0.

Quarterback Bob Leszczynski and running backs Mike Sherlock and Steve Callahan proved to be more than the Army defense could handle. Leszczynski and Callahan scored the game's first two touchdowns before the duo collectively put the game out of reach with the Midshipmen's third score of the day. Kicker Bob Tata was set to attempt an 18 yard field goal, only to have the snap sail over holder Leszczynski's head. The Navy quarterback quickly retrieved the ball back at the Cadet 40 yard line, scrambled forward 22 yards and fired to a wide open Callahan in the end zone for six more points.

1979 Army Cadets

Led by Lou Saban (pictured at right) in his first and only season as head coach, Army finished the season with a record of 2–8–1 and were outscored by their opponents by a combined total of 96 to 308. In the annual Army–Navy Game, the Cadets lost to the Midshipmen by a 31 to 7 score.

Earle Mulrane led the team in passing with 656 yards and threw 5 touchdown passes. Jimmy Hill led the team in rushing with 441 yards. Mike Fahnestock led the team in receptions with 19 for 283 yards. Dave Aucoin led the team in scoring with 30 points.

Home games were played at Michie Stadium

9/15/1979	ARMY	vs	CONNECTICUT (3-6-2)	26	10	W
9/22/1979	ARMY	@	Stanford (5-5-1)	17	13	W
9/29/1979	ARMY	vs	NORTH CAROLINA (8-3-1)	3	41	L
10/6/1979	ARMY	vs	DUKE (2-8-1)	17	17	T
10/13/1979	ARMY	@	Penn State (8-4)	3	24	L
10/20/1979	ARMY	vs	BAYLOR (8-4)	0	55	L
10/27/1979	ARMY	vs	BOSTON COLLEGE (5-6)	16	29	L
11/3/1979	ARMY	@	Air Force (2-9)	7	28	L
11/10/1979	ARMY	@	Rutgers (8-3)	0	20	L
11/17/1979	ARMY	vs	PITTSBURGH (11-1)	0	40	L
12/1/1979	ARMY	vs	NAVY (7-4)	7	31	L
Coach: Lou Saban			**Season Record >>**	**96**	**308**	**2-9**

Selected game(s) highlights

BOSTON COLLEGE

Dan Conway ran for two touchdowns, including the clinching score late in the fourth quarter, while totaling 177 yards on 30 carries, as Boston College defeated Army 29-16, ruining a homecoming football celebration for a crowd of 40,162 Saturday. Boston College opened the scoring in the first period when quarterback Jay Palazola hit Bob Rikard with a 50 yard touchdown pass. The Eagles added to their lead early in the second period when Conway plunged over from the one, capping a five play, 55 yard drive. Army scored before the half after recovering a fumble by Palazola on the Cadets' four and marching 96 yards. Quarterback Earle Mulrane hit Kevin Kullander with a six yard toss for the TD. Split end Mike Fahnestock contributed catches of 15 and 40 yards to the drive. Boston College broke open the game in the third period, outscoring Army 10-3. The Cadets' Dave Aucoin reduced the margin to 12-9 at 5:56 of the period with a 25 yard field goal. But the Eagles came right back as Leo Smith burst 64 yards off tackle with a pitchout from reserve quarterback John Loughery, making it 19-9. Smith finished with 12 carries for 114 yards.

NAVY {@ JFK Stadium, Philadelphia, PA}

The Army defense had no answer for Navy's Eddie Meyers, as the Midshipmen running back gained 279 yards and scored three touchdowns in Navy's 31-7 triumph. The performance capped quite an autumn for the 5-9, 205-pound sophomore who started the season fourth on the Navy depth chart at running back.

After starting the season 6-0, the Midshipmen entered the annual battle with the Cadets on a four game losing streak. Coach George Welsh's club was unable to capitalize on its first possession, but kicker Steve Fehr finished the next possession with a 33 yard field goal to give Navy a 3-0 lead. Navy matched an Army touchdown with two of its own to take a 17-7 lead to the locker room at the half. Meyers added his final-two touchdowns midway through the second half to put the contest safely out of reach.

1980 Army Cadets

In their first season under head coach Ed Cavanaugh, the Cadets compiled a 3–7–1 record and were outscored by their opponents 295 to 204. In the annual Army–Navy Game, the Cadets lost to Navy, 33 to 6.

Jerryl Bennett led the team in passing with 1,065 yards and threw 6 touchdown passes. Gerald Walker led the team in rushing with 917 and 6 rushing touchdowns. **Mike Fahnestock led the team in receptions with 47 for 937, which was a single season record for Army** and had 7 TD receptions. Chris Zavie led the team with 5 interceptions. Dave Aucoin led the team in scoring with 48 points.

Home games were played at Michie Stadium

9/13/1980	ARMY	vs	HOLY CROSS (3-8)	28	7	W	
9/20/1980	ARMY	vs	CALIFORNIA (3-8)	26	19	W	
9/27/1980	ARMY	@	Washington State (4-7)	18	31	L	
10/4/1980	ARMY	vs	HARVARD (7-3)	10	15	L	
10/11/1980	ARMY	vs	LEHIGH	24	24	T	*-Fahnestock 186 rec yds
10/18/1980	ARMY	@	Notre Dame (9-2-1)	3	30	L	
10/25/1980	ARMY	@	Boston College (7-4)	14	30	L	
11/1/1980	ARMY	vs	RUTGERS (7-4)	21	37	L	
11/8/1980	ARMY	vs	AIR FORCE (2-9-1)	47	24	W	
11/15/1980	ARMY	vs	PITTSBURGH (11-1)	7	45	L	
11/29/1980	ARMY	vs	NAVY (8-4)	6	33	L	
Coach: Ed Cavanaugh			**Season Record >>**	204	295	3-7-1	

Schedule Source: Steve's Football Bible LLC
*-Single game record

Selected game(s) highlights

HOLY CROSS

Army opened its 1980 season with a rousing 28-7 win over punchless Holy Cross (1-1) before 28,043 in Michie Stadium, who saw quarterback Jerryl Bennett run a marvelously balanced attack. Conversely, the Army defense was muzzling Holy Cross. Of its 218 yards of total offense, 77 came on a late drive that produced its only touchdown. Of its 14 first downs, five came on that drive. Bennett, who completed 14 of 27 passes for 197 yards and two touchdowns and carried 15 times for 72 of the 262 Army yards on the ground, opened right away, isolating wide receiver Mike Fahnestock. He sent Fahnestock deep, brought him across the middle and found him for a 6-0 lead on a 15 yard toss at 13:41 of the opening period. They teamed up again on an 18 yard touchdown play at 9:49 of the second period. Bennett set up the final two touchdowns with pass completions to Dino Harris (17 yards to the one) and Fahnestock (13 to the one). Bennett swept in the first time (7:02, third period) and Harris plunged over (7:34, fourth period) on the second.

LEHIGH

Dave Aucoin set an Army field goal record by kicking a 52 yarder as time ran out, giving the Cadets a 24-24 tie against underdog Lehigh yesterday. Aucoin's kick broke the mark of 50 yards he set last year in a 17-17 deadlock against Duke. Halfback Joe Rabuck had given Lehigh a 24-21 lead on a two yard scoring run with 2:18 remaining. Then Army marched from its 25 to the Lehigh 20, before a penalty set the Cadets back and Aucoin booted his dramatic field goal. **Mike Fahnestock had 186 receiving yards to establish a single game record.**

NAVY {@ Veterans Stadium, Philadelphia, PA}

In rather dominant fashion, Navy regained the series lead for the first time in 58 years, routing Army, 33-6. This was also the first time the Army-Navy game was played at Veterans Stadium. The Midshipmen utilized a balanced attack, as Eddie Meyers' 144 yards on the ground complemented quarterback Fred Reitzel's 138 yards passing. Kicker Steve Fehr was also crucial in Navy's effort, booting four field goals, including a series-record 50 yarder. Once again, turnovers were critical, as the Midshipmen's Travis Wallington recovered Warren Waldorff's fumble at the Navy 15 yard line. Reitzel ran it in from nine yards out, and Fehr's extra point made it 10-0. Navy's defense turned in a stellar effort, limiting Army to 144 yards of total offense. Gerald Walker had one of the Cadets' few offensive highlights with a 26 yard touchdown run.

1981 Army Cadets

In their second season under head coach Ed Cavanaugh, the Cadets compiled a 3–7–1 record and were outscored by their opponents by a combined total of 212 to 126. In the annual Army–Navy Game, the Cadets played the Midshipmen to a 3–3 tie.

Jerryl Bennett led the team in passing with 582 yards and threw 3 touchdown passes. Gerald Walker led the team in rushing with 1,053 yards and 7 rushing touchdowns. Walker led the team with 24 receptions. Al Wynder led with 270 receiving yards. Joe Hampton led the team with 5 interceptions. Walker led the team in scoring with 48 points.

Home games were played at Michie Stadium

9/12/1981	ARMY	@	Missouri (8-4)	10	24	L
9/19/1981	ARMY	vs	VMI (6-3-1)	7	14	L
9/26/1981	ARMY	vs	BROWN (3-7)	23	17	W
10/3/1981	ARMY	@	Harvard (5-4-1)	27	13	W
10/10/1981	ARMY	vs	RUTGERS (5-6)	0	17	L
10/17/1981	ARMY	vs	PRINCETON (5-4-1)	34	0	W
10/24/1981	ARMY	vs	BOSTON COLLEGE (5-6)	6	41	L
10/31/1981	ARMY	@	Air Force (4-7)	3	7	L
11/7/1981	ARMY	vs	HOLY CROSS (6-5)	13	28	L
11/14/1981	ARMY	@	Pittsburgh (11-1)	0	48	L
11/28/1981	ARMY	vs	NAVY (7-4-1)	3	3	T
Coach: Ed Cavanaugh			**Season Record >>**	**126**	**212**	**3-7-1**

Schedule Source: Steve's Football Bible LLC

Selected game(s) highlights

BROWN

Brown staged a second half uprising that had favored Army hanging on in desperation yesterday before the Cadets finally registered their first victory of the season, 23-17. The West Pointers scored two touchdowns and a field goal in the first half, but it took a third touchdown In the final minutes before they finally cemented their sixth triumph in the series with Brown, which dates to 1894. Larry Pruitt, the Army flanker, exploded for a 57 yard punt return for the first score and took a 23- yard toss from sophomore quarterback Bryan Allen for the second. Kicker Dave Aucoln added a 37 yard field goal. It looked like soft pickings for Army as it left the field for the intermission with a 16-3 lead. But it was a delusion as the Bruins dominated third-period action, launching a scoring drive that pulled them within a touchdown with 12:18 left in the game. With quarterback Hank Landers pitching and tailback Vince Stephens ripping apart the Army defense. Brown moved 62 yards in 11 plays, with Landers throwing 16 yards to Steve Gorriaran for the score. The Brown defense halted the next Army thrust on Dave Folsom's pass interception, but Army's Joe Hampton matched the steal, and the Cadets moved out to a 23-1 0 lead with 5:10 to go. The Hampton Interception set the stage for Gerald Walker, Army's stellar runner, who had his greatest career performance with 170 yards on 24 carries. Walker took the ball into the end zone personally in two maneuvers. The second was a 26 yard gallop around his own right end, but the Bruins were far from through. They bounced back behind Landers, who completed 19 of 37 passes for 233 yards on the day - a career high - picking apart the Cadet secondary on an 11 play parade covering 76 yards. The touchdown came on a 14 yard flip by Landers to Stephens, who already had shredded Army for 124 yards on 24 carries, the tailback spearing the ball at the goal line to make it 23-17 with 2:38 remaining on the clock. The Brown defense forced Army to punt, and Landers moved the Bruins to the Army 42 before a Herb Aten interception of a pass intended for Stephens with 27 seconds left sealed the Bruins' fate.

Harvard

Army quarterback Bryan Allem unloaded a long bomb on third-and-14 from his own 21 and wide receiver Al Wynder wrestled the ball away from defender Rocky Delgadillo for a 71 yard gain. Three plays later. Allem bucked the final yard to break a 13-13 tie with 33 seconds left in the third period, and, with durable Gerald Walker controlling the ball in the fourth quarter and going in for the final touchdown. Army frustrated the Crimson. 27-13. before 16,000 at the Stadium. But take away that single play, and the Army quarterback tandem of starter Allem and Jerry Bennett completed just 4 of 20 pass attempts for 29 yards.

BOSTON COLLEGE

Freshman quarterback Doug Flutie riddled Army's pass defense with 15 completions in 21 attempts for 244 yards and three touchdowns, guiding Boston College to a 41-6 triumph over the Cadets. Tight end Scott Nizolek was Flutie's favorite target, catching eight passes for 89 yards and two TDs. He also snared a two-point conversion toss. In five previous games, Nizolek had caught only seven passes. The Eagles, in snapping a four game losing streak, registered all their points before the Cadets scored on a 79 yard pass play from Bryan Allem to Todd Williams late in the fourth period.

NAVY {@ Veterans Stadium, Philadelphia, PA}

If one game ever defined a rivalry, then the 1981 Army-Navy contest speaks volumes about the competition between the Midshipmen and the Cadets. Already bound for a Liberty Bowl appearance against Ohio State, Navy entered the afternoon with a 7-3 record. Army, on the other hand, had struggled to a 3-7 ledger. Despite the fact George Welsh's club entered the game as a 19-point favorite, the Midshipmen escaped Philadelphia with a 3-3 tie against West Point.

The Cadets' offense may have struggled all afternoon, but punter Joe Sartiano was there to kick it out of a hole. He averaged 57.6 yards on his five punts, with a long kick of 79 yards. Veteran kicker Steve Fehr put Navy on the scoreboard first with a 42 yard field goal at the end of the second quarter. Army's Dave Aucoin responded with a field goal in the third quarter, but he missed on a 55 yard attempt as time expired that would have given the Cadets the win.

1982 Army Cadets

In their third season under head coach Ed Cavanaugh, the Cadets compiled a 4–7 record and were outscored by their opponents by a combined total of 271 to 164. Rich Laughlin led the team in passing with 632 yards and threw 2 touchdown passes. Andre Cuerington led the team in rushing with 487 yards. Cuerington and Elton Akins led the team in receptions with 21. Akins led in receiving yards for 391. Mike Williams led the team in interceptions with 4. Craig Stopa led the team in scoring with 52 points.

Home games were played at Michie Stadium

9/11/1982	ARMY	@	Missouri (5-4-2)	10	23	L
9/18/1982	ARMY	vs	LAFAYETTE	26	20	W
9/25/1982	ARMY	@	North Carolina (8-4)	8	62	L
10/2/1982	ARMY	vs	HARVARD	17	13	W
10/9/1982	ARMY	@	Rutgers (5-6)	3	24	L
10/16/1982	ARMY	@	Princeton	20	14	W
10/23/1982	ARMY	vs	BOSTON COLLEGE (8-3-1)	17	32	L
10/30/1982	ARMY	vs	COLUMBIA	41	8	W
11/6/1982	ARMY	vs	AIR FORCE (8-5)	9	27	L
11/13/1982	ARMY	vs	PITTSBURGH (9-3)	6	24	L
12/4/1982	ARMY	vs	NAVY (6-5)	7	24	L
Coach: Ed Cavanaugh			**Season Record >>**	164	271	4-7

Schedule Source: Steve's Football Bible LLC

Selected game(s) highlights

LAFAYETTE

On a day when Army was hurt by penalties at the most inopportune times, when fumbles stymied drives and when Lafayette refused to stay dead, it was the Cadets' "special" special teams which produced a 26-20 win before 31,103 fans at Michie Stadium. Craig Stopa kicked four field goals and Elton Akins returned a kickoff 93 yards for touchdown.

Princeton

Army quarterback Rich Laughlln's 56 yard touchdown run allowed the Cadets to go ahead for the first time in a 20-14 comeback win over Princeton Saturday. But Laughlln had to wait a while before he could fully enjoy the run. The junior had to wait in disbelief as Princeton faked a punt and picked up a first down at the Army 39 with 2:35 remaining. And he had to watch an apparent go-ahead Tiger touchdown pass that was nullified because of an offensive interference call. Finally, with 57 seconds showing on the Palmer Stadium scoreboard and Princeton facing a fourth and 24 situation at the Army 24, defensive back Kevin Murphy broke up a potential touchdown pass in the end zone. Army had its third win in six outings.

NAVY {@ Veterans Stadium, Philadelphia, PA}

Navy turned two first half Army turnovers into 10 points to fuel a 24-7 win. The game was played under the most ideal weather conditions in series history — clear skies and 70 degrees. Despite the sunny skies, Army's afternoon suddenly turned cloudy when the Midshipmen's Rick Pagel recovered Dee Bryant's fumbled punt at the Cadet eight yard line early in the first quarter. Napoleon McCallum punched the ball in from two yards out, and Todd Solomon's conversion gave Navy a quick 7-0 lead. The Midshipmen stretched this advantage to 10-0 when Solomon followed Brian Cianella's interception with a 25 yard field goal shortly thereafter. Army cut the lead to 10-7 in the second quarter when Mike Staver recovered Rich Clouse's fumble at the Navy 15 yard line. Laughlin took it in from three yards out to cut the lead to 10-7. In the third quarter, a pair of McCallum punt returns set up a one yard James Scannell touchdown run, and a 17 yard touchdown pass from Ricky Williamson to split end Bill Cebak.

1983 Army Cadets

In their first season under head coach Jim Young, the Cadets compiled a 2–9 record and were outscored by their opponents by a combined total of 304 to 140. In the annual Army–Navy Game, the Cadets lost to Navy by a 42–13 score. Rob Healy led the team in passing with 913 yards and threw 3 touchdown passes. Elton Akins led the team in rushing with 713 yards. Scott Spellmon led the team in receptions with 34 for 501 yards. Gary Bastin led the team with 4 interceptions. Craig Stopa led the team in scoring with 50 points.

Home games were played at Michie Stadium

9/10/1983	ARMY	vs	COLGATE	13	15	**L**
9/17/1983	ARMY	@	Louisville (3-8)	7	31	**L**
9/24/1983	ARMY	vs	DARTMOUTH	13	12	**W**
10/1/1983	ARMY	@	Harvard	21	24	**L**
10/8/1983	ARMY	vs	RUTGERS (3-8)	20	12	**W**
10/15/1983	ARMY	vs	NOTRE DAME (7-5)	0	42	**L**
10/22/1983	ARMY	vs	LEHIGH	12	13	**L**
10/29/1983	ARMY	@	Air Force (10-2)	20	41	**L**
11/5/1983	ARMY	vs	BOSTON COLLEGE (9-3)	14	34	**L**
11/12/1983	ARMY	@	Pittsburgh (8-3-1)	7	38	**L**
11/25/1983	ARMY	vs	NAVY (3-8)	13	42	**L**
Coach: Jim Young			**Season Record >>**	**140**	**304**	**2-9**

Schedule Source: Steve's Football Bible LLC

Selected game(s) highlights

COLGATE

Mike Powers set a new school record as he kicked five field goals, including the game winner with only 17 seconds to play, as the Red Raiders spoiled the home coaching debut of Army head Coach Jim Young with a 15-13 win in front of a crowd of 22,215 at Michie Stadium.

DARTMOUTH

Army eked out its first win of the season last week at home against Dartmouth. Down 12-3 at the half, the Black Knight defense swarmed over the Big Green in the last 30 minutes, holding Dartmouth to 22 yards offense, if its seven quarterback sacks aren't counted. A touchdown and field goal gave Army the 13-12 decision.

LEHIGH

Lehigh quarterback Marty Horn caught the entire Cadet defense rolling right, while he doubled back left on a busted play that provided the Engineers with a fourth quarter 13-12 win over Army. Horn's winning "bust" climaxed an 11 play, 54 yard drive and set up Horn's unplanned keeper for the winning touchdown with 6:41 remaining.

NAVY {@ The Rose Bowl, Pasadena, CA}

With three touchdowns in the first four minutes of the game, Navy rolled to a 42-13 victory over Army at the Rose Bowl. Other than a trip to Chicago in 1926, the Cadets and Midshipmen had never met farther west than Baltimore. However, Rolfe Arnhym, West Point Class of '53 and then Executive Vice President of the Pasadena Chamber of Commerce, helped arrange for the 1983 contest to be played in California. Navy used a trick play to catch Army off-guard on the opening kickoff, and the Cadets never regained their balance. Craig Stopa's opening kick went to Navy star Napoleon McCallum, who handed it off to return mate Eric Wallace. Wallace then went 95 yards for the game's first touchdown. McCallum added a 14 yard touchdown scamper, and linebacker Steve Brady's 65 yard interception return made it 21-0 just 3:50 into the game. McCallum's 182 yards on 30 carries accounted for a lion's share of the Midshipmen's 296 yards on the ground.

1984 Army Cadets {Commander-Chief-Trophy}

In their second season under head coach Jim Young, the Cadets compiled an 8–3–1 record and outscored their opponents by a combined total of 320 to 218. In the annual Army–Navy Game, the Cadets defeated Navy by a 28–11 score. The Cadets also defeated Michigan State, 10–6, in the 1984 Cherry Bowl.

Nate Sassman led the team in passing with 364 yards. Doug Black led the team in rushing with 1,148 yards and 11 rushing touchdowns. Ben White led the team in receptions with 17 for 241 yards. Doug Pavek led the team with 3 interceptions. Craig Stopa led the team in scoring with 77 points.

Home games were played at Michie Stadium

9/15/1984	ARMY	vs	COLGATE	41	15	W	
9/22/1984	ARMY	@	Tennessee (7-4-1)	24	24	T	
9/29/1984	ARMY	vs	DUKE (2-9)	13	9	W	
10/6/1984	ARMY	vs	HARVARD	33	11	W	
10/13/1984	ARMY	@	Rutgers (7-3)	7	14	L	
10/20/1984	ARMY	vs	PENNSYLVANIA	48	13	W	
10/27/1984	ARMY	@	Syracuse (6-5)	16	27	L	
11/3/1984	ARMY	vs	AIR FORCE (8-4)	24	12	W	*-Stopa 5 FG's
11/10/1984	ARMY	@	Boston College (10-2)	31	45	L	
11/17/1984	ARMY	vs	MONTANA	45	31	W	
12/1/1984	ARMY	vs	NAVY (4-6-1)	28	11	W	
12/22/1984	**ARMY**	**vs**	**Michigan State (6-6)**	**10**	**6**	**W**	**Cherry Bowl**
Coach: Jim Young			**Season Record >>**	**320**	**218**	**8-3-1**	

Schedule Source: Steve's Football Bible LLC
***-Single game record**

Selected game(s) highlights

HARVARD

Army quarterback Nate Sassaman completed just one pass yesterday; but the Cadets ground out 25 first downs and 381 yards on the artificial turf for a 33-11 win over Harvard and a 3-0-1 record. Both teams failed to move the ball in a scoreless first quarter, and it seemed as though the Crimson might spring a surprise before an Army homecoming crowd of 40,504 in Mlchie Stadium. Nine plays later, Sassaman flipped one of his perfectly timed pitches to Dee Bryant, who swept the left side for a 6 yard scoring scamper 12:18 into the quarter. Before the half was over, a feeble Crimson punt gave the Cadets possession at the Harvard 45. Sassaman (15 carries, 127 yards) carried 22 yards, and Craig Stopa kicked a 32 yard field goal with no time left for a 10-0 halftime lead. The Cadets Jumped on a Vignali fumble at the Harvard 43. and turned that into a 17-0 lead when Sassaman completed his only pass of the game, a 20 yard TD toss to tight end Rob Dicker-son 5:12 into the third period.

AIR FORCE

Craig Stopa kicked a team record five field goals for the Cadets as Army rolled to a 24-12 victory over Air Force. Bart Weiss passed for 173 yards but threw two costly interceptions. The Falcons were held to 150 yards rushing and were forced to try and go through the air, which turned out to be unsuccessful. Tom Coleman caught 4 passes for 162 yards and Ken Carpenter caught 6 passes for 102 yards for Air Force.

NAVY {@ Veterans Stadium, Philadelphia, PA}

Dec. 1, 1984, is a day to remember in Army football history. With a 28-11 victory over Navy, the Cadets advanced to their first-ever postseason bowl, the Cherry Bowl. The wishbone offense installed by head coach Jim Young worked to perfection, as fullback Doug Black and quarterback Nate Sassaman rushed for 155 and 154 yards, respectively. Ironically, both players went over the 1,000 yard single season rushing mark during the game.

Although the halftime score was 14-3, it could have just as easily been 14-14. With five minutes left in the first half, Navy had a second-and-six on the Cadet 10 yard line, but quarterback Bob Misch was sacked on successive plays, forcing kicker Todd Solomon to salvage the drive with a 40 yard field goal. On the next possession, tight end Mark Stevens caught a short pass from Misch and appeared headed for the end zone. However, Army's Kermit McKelvy stripped the ball from Stevens at the five, and safety Doug Pavek fell on the ball in the end zone for a touchback.

1984 CHERRY BOWL

Ralf Mojsiejenko's 52 yard field goal attempt went wide left, costing Michigan State three points early. Another chance at the Army 5 for a touchdown led to an interception. A Spartan fumble led to an Army score. Clarence Jones scored the first Army points in a bowl game with a 4 yard touchdown run with 6:31 left in the first half to culminate an 8 play, 46 yard drive. This proved to be the halftime lead for the Cadets. In the fourth quarter, another Spartan fumble led to a score as Craig Stopa  increased the lead to 10 with his 38 yard field goal with 8:40 left in the game. Bob Wasczenski caught a 36 yard touchdown pass to narrow the lead with 4:19 remaining. On their conversion attempt, the pass failed, leaving it at 10-6. From that point, Army and Michigan State played stalemate as Army won their first ever bowl game. The Cadets controlled the clock for 34:05. Nathan Sassaman rushed for 136 yards on 28 carries. Yarema was sacked three times and intercepted three times en route to an 11-of-25 155 yard performance.

1985 Army Cadets

The team was led by head coach Jim Young, in his third year, and played their home games at Michie Stadium in West Point, New York. They finished the season with a record of nine wins and three losses (9–3 overall), and with a victory against Illinois in the Peach Bowl. The Cadets offense scored 396 points, while the defense allowed 232 points.

Rob Healy led the team in passing with 421 yards and threw 4 touchdown passes. Doug Black led the team in rushing with 950 yards. Tory Crawford and Clarence Jones led with 10 rushing touchdowns. Ben White led the team in receptions with 13 for 213 yards. Doug Pavek led the team with 7 interceptions. Craig Stopa led the team in scoring with 71 points.

Home games were played at Michie Stadium

9/14/1985	ARMY	vs	WESTERN MICHIGAN (4-6-1)	48	6	W	
9/21/1985	ARMY	vs	RUTGERS (2-8-1)	20	16	W	
9/28/1985	ARMY	@	Pennsylvania	41	3	W	
10/5/1985	ARMY	vs	YALE	59	16	W	
10/12/1985	ARMY	vs	BOSTON COLLEGE (4-8)	45	14	W	
10/19/1985	ARMY	@	Notre Dame (5-6)	10	24	L	
10/26/1985	ARMY	vs	COLGATE	45	43	W	
11/2/1985	ARMY	vs	HOLY CROSS	34	12	W	
11/9/1985	ARMY	@	Air Force (12-1)	7	45	L	
11/16/1985	ARMY	vs	MEMPHIS (2-7-2)	49	7	W	
12/7/1985	ARMY	vs	NAVY (4-7)	7	17	L	
12/31/1985	**ARMY**	**vs**	**Illinois (6-5-1)**	**31**	**29**	**W**	**Peach Bowl**
Coach: Jim Young			Season Record >>	396	232	9-3	

Schedule Source: Steve's Football Bible LLC

Selected game(s) highlights

Notre Dame

Notre Dame entertained #19 ranked Army in front of over 59,000 fans at Notre Dame Stadium. The Irish jumped out to a 14-0 lead on a Pernell Taylor 1 yard run and a Tim Brown 19 yard TD pass from Steve Buerlein. The Cadets fought back on a Bill Lampley 4 yard TD run and a Craig Stopa 22 yard field goal to cut the lead to 14-10 in the 3rd quarter. Allen Pinkett scored on a 1 yard run and John Carney added a 21 yard field goal to put the game away for the Fighting Irish.

NAVY {@ Veterans Stadium, Philadelphia, PA}

In his final collegiate football game, Napoleon McCallum rushed for 217 yards on 41 carries to lead Navy past Army, 17-7. The Navy senior posted more yards than the entire Army team, who was limited to 192 yards by a stingy Midshipmen defense. Navy took a 7-0 lead when Bob Misch's 13 yard touchdown pass to Troy Saunders finished a 14 play, 73 yard drive. Army's Clarence Jones responded by taking the ensuing kickoff 61 yards to the Navy 36, and then taking the ball into the end zone eight plays later from 10 yards out. Craig Stopa added his 61st consecutive extra point, which made him the first player to score in four Army-Navy games. Navy's Chuck Smith put the Midshipmen ahead to stay with a five yard touchdown run in the fourth quarter, as the Cadets failed to capitalize on two golden offensive opportunities. They were stopped on downs at the Navy two yard line in the second quarter, and Stopa's 37 yard field goal attempt in the third quarter sailed wide right.

1985 PEACH BOWL

On a cold and rainy day in Atlanta, Army scored two touchdowns on halfback option plays and took advantage of four Illini turnovers to carry an eight-point lead into the final five minutes. Trailing 31–23 with less than a minute remaining, Illinois quarterback Jack Trudeau hit All-American receiver David Williams for a 54 yard touchdown to bring the Fighting Illini within two points of a tie. Trudeau's two-point conversion pass attempt was broken up by reserve safety Peel Chronister, and Army handed Illinois its third consecutive Bowl defeat in the 1980s. Trudeau set Peach Bowl records with 38 completions in 55 attempts for 401 yards, and tight end Cap Boso caught a record 9 receptions. The game saw 16 Peach Bowl records broken or tied.

1986 Army Cadets {Commander-Chief-Trophy}

In their fourth season under head coach Jim Young, the Cadets compiled a 6–5 record and were outscored by their opponents by a combined total of 292 to 276. In the annual Army–Navy Game, the Cadets defeated Navy, 27–7. Tory Crawford led the team in passing with 816 yards. Crawford led the team in rushing with 1,078 and 15 rushing touchdowns. Ben White led the team in receptions with 18 for 317 yards. Chance Connor led the team in interceptions with 4. Crawford led the team in scoring with 90 points.

Home games were played at Michie Stadium

9/13/1986	ARMY	vs	SYRACUSE (5-6)	33	28	W
9/20/1986	ARMY	@	Northwestern (4-7)	18	25	L
9/27/1986	ARMY	vs	WAKE FOREST (5-6)	14	49	L
10/4/1986	ARMY	@	Yale	41	24	W
10/11/1986	ARMY	@	Tennessee (7-5)	25	21	W
10/18/1986	ARMY	vs	HOLY CROSS	14	17	L
10/25/1986	ARMY	@	Rutgers (5-5-1)	7	35	L
11/1/1986	ARMY	vs	BOSTON COLLEGE (9-3)	20	27	L
11/8/1986	ARMY	vs	AIR FORCE (6-5)	21	11	W
11/15/1986	ARMY	vs	LAFAYETTE	56	48	W
12/6/1986	ARMY	vs	NAVY (3-8)	27	7	W
Coach: Jim Young			**Season Record >>**	276	292	6-5

Selected game(s) highlights

Yale

The Cadets were leading Yale by only four points, and only because quarterback Tory Crawford had scored his third touchdown with six seconds left by spinning and twisting from 7 yards. And up next was the Yale Precision Marching Band, which had been banned from West Point last year. But when the marching stopped, Crawford scored his fourth touchdown, strong safety Bill Horton intercepted a Kelly Ryan pass in the end zone and Clarence Jones finished an 80 yard trip the other way with a 2 yard run. And a close game was no longer close. Army imposed its wishbone on the Elis and 25,075 more at Yale Bowl, winning, 41-24.

Tennessee

The Army invaded Neyland Stadium and stunned the over 91,000 fans, mostly clad in orange and white. The Vols led 21-7 going into the 4th quarter, but the Cadets rallied with 18 points to leave with a 25-21 victory. Clarence Jones scored on a yard run in the 2nd quarter and a 1 yard run in the 4th quarter to lead the West Point charge. Trailing 21-18 with 35 seconds left, the Vols were forced to punt, and Cadet Chuck Williams blocked the kick, and Reggie Fullwood picked it up at the 2 yard line and fell into the end zone for the winning touchdown.

NAVY {@ Veterans Stadium, Philadelphia, PA}

Army scored on five of its first-eight possessions en route to a 27-7 victory over the Midshipmen. This marked the Cadets' third-most convincing win over Navy, surpassed only by a 38-0 win in 1949 and a 27-0 triumph in 1969. The game certainly lived up to its billing as one of America's purest rivalries, as neither team committed a single penalty. Sophomore Keith Walker put Army on the scoreboard first with a pair of 24 yard field goals. The Cadets gradually cushioned this lead in the second half, thanks in part to a few bounces that went their way. On first-and-10 from the Navy 30, Cadet Quarterback Tory Crawford kept the ball and raced around the end, where he was hit hard at the 20 yard line. The ball popped loose and rolled all the way down to the three yard line, where an alert Benny Wright fell on it. Andy Peterson carried the ball into the end zone two plays later, and Army took a 13-0 lead. Navy took the ensuing kickoff and went 80 yards in 14 plays, with Don Holl plowing through for a three yard touchdown. Ted Fundoukos added the extra point to make it 13-7. Yet, Army tacked on two more scores to provide the final margin.

1987 Army Cadets

In their fifth season under head coach Jim Young, the Cadets compiled a 5–6 record and outscored their opponents by a combined total of 277 to 223. In the annual Army–Navy Game, the Cadets defeated Navy, 17–3. Tory Crawford led the team in passing with 566 yards and threw 5 touchdown passes. Mike Mayweather led the team in rushing with 762 yards. Crawford led with 10 rushing touchdowns. Sean Jordan led the team in receptions with 13 for 292 yards. Dave Berdan led the team with 4 interceptions. Crawford led the team in scoring with 60 points.

Home games were played at Michie Stadium

9/12/1987	ARMY	vs	HOLY CROSS	24	34	L
9/19/1987	ARMY	@	Kansas State (0-10-1)	41	14	W
9/26/1987	ARMY	vs	THE CITADEL	48	6	W
10/3/1987	ARMY	vs	WAKE FOREST (7-4)	13	17	L
10/10/1987	ARMY	@	Boston College (5-6)	24	29	L
10/17/1987	ARMY	vs	COLGATE	20	22	L
10/24/1987	ARMY	vs	RUTGERS (6-5)	14	27	L
10/31/1987	ARMY	vs	TEMPLE (3-8)	17	7	W
11/7/1987	ARMY	@	Air Force (9-4)	10	27	L
11/14/1987	ARMY	vs	LAFAYETTE	49	37	W
12/5/1987	ARMY	vs	NAVY (2-9)	17	3	W
Coach: Jim Young			**Season Record >>**	**277**	**223**	**5-6**

Schedule Source: Steve's Football Bible LLC

Selected game(s) highlights

Kansas State

Tory Crawford ran for three touchdowns and passed for another as the West Pointers left Manhattan with a 41-14 victory over the Wildcats. It was the Cadets first road night game win since 1972. Keith Walker kicked field goals of 25 and 36 yards and was successful on all 5 extra point attempts. Army led 24-0 at halftime. The Cadets had 285 yards rushing to go along with 73 yards passing.

THE CITADEL

The Citadel jumped to an early 6-0 lead, then watched as the Army put up 48 straight points in a blowout 48-6 victory. Andy Peterson scored two touchdowns to lead the Cadets. Sean Jordan caught two TD passes from Tory Crawford. Keith Walker added two field goals. Crawford added a 38 yard touchdown run and Mike Mayweather had a 3 yard touchdown run.

LAFAYETTE

Sean Jordan caught an 89 yard touchdown pass the longest reception in Army history from quarterback Tory Crawford to break a 14-14 second quarter tie and lead the Cadets to a 49-37 victory over Lafayette at Michie Stadium. The game was a repeat of last year's 56-48 shootout with both offenses rolling up big numbers. Army's wishbone gained 323 yards on the ground and six rushing touchdowns, including three by Crawford. Lafayette, 4-6, responded with 400 yards through the air, all by sophomore quarterback Frank Baur, who set a school record for completions, hitting on 32 of 45 passes and two touchdowns.

NAVY {@ Veterans Stadium, Philadelphia, PA}

Mustering just 191 yards of total offense, Navy suffered a 17-3 loss to Army. This marked the first time the Cadets had posted back-to-back victories in the series since 1971-72. Although Army's Mike Mayweather wore down the Midshipmen defense with 119 yards rushing, the only points of the first half came when Cadet kicker Harold "Bit" Rambusch booted a 40 yard field goal in the first quarter. Army stretched its lead to 10-0 with 11:02 left in the game when Andy Peterson scored on a one yard run. Behind the leadership of quarterback Alton Grizzard, Navy battled back. Ted Fundoukos kicked a 30 yard field goal to cut the lead to 10-3, only to have Army clinch the win on a seven yard run by quarterback Tory Crawford.

1988 Army Cadets {Commander-Chief-Trophy}

In their sixth season under head coach Jim Young, the Cadets compiled a 9–3 record and outscored their opponents by a combined total of 336 to 226. In the annual Army–Navy Game, the Cadets defeated Navy, 20–15. They also lost a close game to Alabama, 29–28, in the 1988 Sun Bowl.

Bryan McWilliams led the team in passing with 255 yards. Mike Mayweather led the team in rushing with 1,022 yards and 9 rushing touchdowns. Sean Jordan led the team in receptions with 12 for 289 yards. Earnest Boyd led the team with 5 interceptions. Keith Walker led the team in scoring with 80 points. **Troy Lingley set an Army record for tackles in a season with 161.**

Home games were played at Michie Stadium

9/10/1988	ARMY	vs	HOLY CROSS	23	3	W	
9/17/1988	ARMY	@	Washington (6-5)	17	31	L	
9/24/1988	ARMY	vs	NORTHWESTERN (2-8-1)	23	7	W	
10/1/1988	ARMY	vs	BUCKNELL	58	10	W	
10/8/1988	ARMY	@	Yale	33	18	W	
10/15/1988	ARMY	vs	LAFAYETTE	24	17	W	
10/22/1988	ARMY	@	Rutgers (5-6)	34	24	W	
11/5/1988	ARMY	vs	AIR FORCE (5-7)	28	15	W	
11/12/1988	ARMY	vs	VANDERBILT (3-8)	24	19	W	
11/19/1988	ARMY	vs	Boston College (3-8)	24	38	L	
12/3/1988	ARMY	vs	NAVY (3-8)	20	15	W	
12/24/1988	**ARMY**	**vs**	**Alabama (9-3)**	**28**	**29**	**L**	**Sun Bowl**
Coach: Jim Young			**Season Record >>**	336	226	9-3	

Selected game(s) highlights

HOLY CROSS

Army, using a textbook grind-em-out and wear-em down wishbone offense, put an end to Holy Cross' 12 game winning streak with a 23-3 victory at Michie Stadium yesterday. The loss was the first for Holy Cross since a 56-26 drubbing by Boston College Nov. 11, 1986, and the club's first road defeat since November 1985 at BC. Army pounded out 269 yards on 74 carries and attempted only eight passes. But when sophomore quarterback Otto Leone (who entered the game in the second quarter) did pass, he hit on 4 of 7, including a 68 yard touchdown bomb to Sean Jordan at the end of the third quarter that gave the Cadets their final 20-point lead. Army also scored on a 3 yard run by Mike Mayweather (25 carries, 135 yards), which capped off a 16 play, 86 yard drive on the Cadets' initial second half possession. Army held All-America quarterback Jeff Wiley (13 for 28, 165 yards) without a touchdown pass for the first time in 15 contests.

NORTHWESTERN

Calvin Cass rushed for 142 yards and two touchdowns in leading Army to a 23-7 victory over Northwestern. Army took advantage of two mistakes by the Wildcats early in the 3rd quarter to overcome a 7-3 halftime deficit. Greg Bradshaw's first pass of the second half was intercepted by Army's Mike Thornton at the Northwestern 35. John Barth ran 48 yards up the middle on the next play and Cass scored six plays later.

LAFAYETTE

Benn Barnett ran for 159 yards and two touchdowns and the Army defense intercepted quarterback Frank Baur four times as the Cadets beat Lafayette, 24-17. Barnett scored on runs of 1 and 2 yards as the Cadets rolled up 450 yards on the ground. Mike Mayweather rushed for 156 yards on 20 carries and quarterback Bryan McWilliams ran for 95 yards on 19 carries. Barnett's 1 yard run gave Army a 24-7 lead with 14:15 left in the game.

AIR FORCE

Mike Mayweather rushed for 192 yards and one touchdown and quarterback Bryan McWilliams scored twice, leading Army to a rain soaked 28-15 victory over the Falcons at Michie Stadium.

NAVY {@ Veterans Stadium, Philadelphia, PA}

Army captured the Commander-In-Chief's Trophy with a hard-fought 20-15 victory over Navy. According to Bill Cromartie's "Army-Navy Football: The Greatest Rivalry in Sports, Army coach Jim Young was 25-0 when his team passed the ball no more than three times in a game. This strategy certainly worked against the Midshipmen, as West Point quarterback Bryan McWilliams was the game's top rusher with 100 yards on 21 attempts. When he did drop back to pass, however, McWilliams made the most of the opportunity. With a third-and-six on its own 46 yard line and a 13-9 lead midway through the fourth quarter, McWilliams hit Doug Baker for a 17 yard gain to the Midshipmen 37. He later scored from eight yards out to give his team an 11-point cushion at 20-9.

Alton Grizzard led Navy on the ensuing drive, completing five-of-nine passes to enable James Bradley to reach the end zone from two yards out. The two-point conversion failed, and Army recovered the onsides kick to preserve the win and knot the all-time series record at 41-41-7.

1988 SUN BOWL

The Cadets opened the scoring with a one yard Mike Mayweather touchdown run to take a 7–0 lead. The Crimson Tide responded with a 37 yard Philip Doyle field goal to cut the lead to 7–3 at the end of the first. In the second quarter, Army again scored on the run with Bryan McWilliams reaching the endzone on a 30 yard run. Alabama again responded with a 22 yard Philip Doyle field goal and a 7 yard Marco Battle touchdown reception from David Smith to close the gap to 14–13 at the half. Army went into halftime with a 14–13 lead by putting up 232 yards on the ground.

Alabama put together a 69 yard drive to take its first lead 20–14 in the game halfway through the third quarter on a 23 yard Greg Payne touchdown reception. Army answered with another touchdown on the next drive to take the lead back at 21-20. On Alabama's next drive David Smith was intercepted by Army's O'Neal Miller who returned it 57 yards for a touchdown and a 28-20 lead. In the fourth quarter Alabama put together two scoring drives for a 32 yard Doyle field goal and a 2 yard David Casteal run to regain the lead at 29–28. Army put up 350 yards on the ground against Alabama's 5th-ranked defense that gave up less than 100 yards per game on average during the season. Army Coach Jim Young said about the game "Alabama was one of the better teams in the country. We played them and beat them in everything except the score." The El Paso Times ranks this game 11th among the top Sun Bowl games ever.

1989 Army Cadets

In their seventh season under head coach Jim Young, the Cadets compiled a 6–5 record and outscored their opponents by a combined total of 316 to 212. In the annual Army–Navy Game, the Cadets lost to Navy, 19–17.

Bryan McWilliams led the team in passing with 460 yards and threw 3 touchdown passes. Mike Mayweather led the team in rushing with 1,177 yards and 13 rushing touchdowns. Sean Jordan led the team in receptions with 9 for 220 yards. Ed Givens led the team with 6 interceptions. Mayweather led the team in scoring with 78 yards.

Home games were played at Michie Stadium

9/16/1989	ARMY	@	Syracuse (8-4)	7	10	L
9/23/1989	ARMY	vs	WAKE FOREST (2-8-1)	14	10	W
9/30/1989	ARMY	vs	HARVARD	56	28	W
10/7/1989	ARMY	@	Duke (8-4)	29	35	L
10/14/1989	ARMY	vs	HOLY CROSS	45	9	W
10/21/1989	ARMY	vs	LAFAYETTE	34	20	W
10/28/1989	ARMY	vs	RUTGERS (2-7-2)	35	14	W
11/4/1989	ARMY	@	Air Force (8-4-1)	3	29	L
11/11/1989	ARMY	vs	BOSTON COLLEGE (2-9)	17	24	L
11/18/1989	ARMY	vs	COLGATE	59	14	W
12/9/1989	ARMY	vs	NAVY (3-8)	17	19	L
Coach: Jim Young			**Season Record >>**	**316**	**212**	**6-5**

Schedule Source: Steve's Football Bible LLC

Selected game(s) highlights

HOLY CROSS

Army's wishbone, directed by quarterback Bryan McWilliams and complemented by halfback Mike Mayweather, snapped the Crusaders' 12 game winning streak as the Black Knights grounded Holy Cross, 45-9, before a capacity crowd of 40,869. In the first half alone, the Black Knights gained more yards on the ground (254) than any team has gained against Holy Cross in a game this season. By the end of the third quarter, Army had rolled up 404 yards, nearly as much as the combined total of the Crusaders' five previous opponents. Army put in its second team offense in the fourth quarter and wound up with a whopping 493 rushing yards. Army scored the first five times it touched the football - three TDs and a field goal - while throwing but one pass (on a third-and-1 situation). The pass was incomplete, and it was the only time Army was stopped in the opening half.

NAVY {@ Giants Stadium, East Rutherford, NJ}

In the first Army-Navy game played in East Rutherford, N.J., Frank Schenk hit a 32 yard field goal with 11 seconds left, to give the Midshipmen a come-from-behind 19-17 win over the Cadets. Navy got on the scoreboard first when Alton Grizzard hit B.J. Mason with a 54 yard touchdown pass. However, a bad snap on the extra point left Navy with a 6-0 lead. Schenk added three points to that advantage with a 38 yard field goal midway through the first quarter. Army's efficient wishbone offense consumed most of the second quarter, as Cal Cass notched a pair of one yard touchdown runs to give the Cadets a 14-9 lead at halftime. Rodney Purifoy's three yard touchdown run midway through the third quarter, followed by Schenk's extra point, put Navy back ahead, 16-14. Yet, Army regained the lead with two minutes to go in the third quarter, when Keith Havenstrite nailed a 21 yard field goal. With 5:02 remaining in the game, Navy took over possession on its own 22 yard line. Grizzard and fullback Mike Burns led the Midshipmen down the field, setting the stage for Schenk's game-winning kick. Frank Schenk wasn't exactly given the best name for someone who would become a college football kicker, but he put it in the back of his mind when the Midshipmen called upon him to beat Army. Navy was trailing 17-16 when Alton Grizzard intentionally threw an incomplete pass to Jerry Dawson to stop the clock with 15 seconds remaining. After

Army head coach Jim Young called a timeout with the "ice the kicker" strategy, Schenk stepped up and booted the 32 yard field goal through the uprights. After the kickoff, Army had seven seconds to make magic happen, but Bryan McWilliams' pass to Sean Jordan was incomplete — leaving just one second on the clock. McWilliams pitched to Mike Mayweather for what would have been an option pass, but he was brought down in the backfield, and Schenk was a football hero.

1990 Army Cadets

In their eighth season under head coach Jim Young, the Cadets compiled a 6–5 record and outscored their opponents by a combined total of 295 to 264. In the annual Army–Navy Game, the Cadets defeated Navy, 30–20.

Willie McMillian led the team in passing with 455 yards. Mike Mayweather led the team in rushing with 1,388 yards and 10 rushing touchdowns. Myreon Williams led the team in receptions with 13 for 434 yards and 5 TD receptions. Patman Malcom led the team in scoring with 72 points.

Home games were played at Michie Stadium

9/15/1990	ARMY	vs	HOLY CROSS	24	7	W	
9/22/1990	ARMY	vs	VMI	41	17	W	
9/29/1990	ARMY	@	Wake Forest (3-8)	14	52	L	
10/6/1990	ARMY	vs	DUKE (4-7)	16	17	L	
10/13/1990	ARMY	@	Boston College (4-7)	20	41	L	
10/20/1990	ARMY	vs	LAFAYETTE	56	0	W	*-Williams 3 TD catch
10/27/1990	ARMY	vs	SYRACUSE (7-4-2)	14	26	L	
11/3/1990	ARMY	vs	RUTGERS (3-8)	35	31	W	
11/10/1990	ARMY	vs	AIR FORCE (7-5)	3	15	L	
11/17/1990	ARMY	@	Vanderbilt (1-10)	42	38	W	
12/8/1990	ARMY	vs	NAVY (5-6)	30	20	W	
Coach: Jim Young			**Season Record >>**	295	264	6-5	

Schedule Source: Steve's Football Bible LLC
*-Single game record

Selected game(s) highlights

VIRGINIA MILITARY INSTITUTE

Mike Mayweather rushed for 227 yards and scored three touchdowns leading the Army to a 41-17 rout of the Keydets at Michie Stadium. Myreon Williams caught two passes for 101 yards, including a 69 yard touchdown pass from Willie McMillian. Calvin Cass added a 56 yard touchdown run to give the Cadets a 41-10 lead.

AIR FORCE

Underdog Air Force Academy team spoiled Mike Mayweather's farewell at Michie Stadium when it beat Army, 15-3, in a driving rainstorm. In his final appearance in a football uniform at West Point, Mayweather, Army's career-leading ground gainer, rushed for his season average of 129 yards and became the first Cadet runner to gain more than 4,000 yards. After being blanked, 9-0, in the first half, Army took the kickoff and drove to the Air Force 17 from where Patmon Malcom booted a 34-yard field goal that turned out to be the Cadets' only score.

NAVY {@ Veterans Stadium, Philadelphia, PA}

Navy was unable to stop the vaunted Army rushing attack, as the Cadets used 367 yards on the ground to post a 30-20 win over the Midshipmen. Behind the efficient performances of quarterback Willie MacMillan and tailback Mike Mayweather, Army turned in a 17-0 second-quarter lead. Navy got on the scoreboard before halftime on a six yard touchdown pass from Alton Grizzard to Jerry Dawson, and a Brad Stramanak 45 yard touchdown run in the third quarter made it 17-14. This was as close as the Midshipmen could get, however, as Army kicker Patmon Malcom padded the Cadet advantage with 38- and 25 yard field goals. Army clinched the win by intercepting a Grizzard pass with 6:10 remaining.

1991 Army Cadets

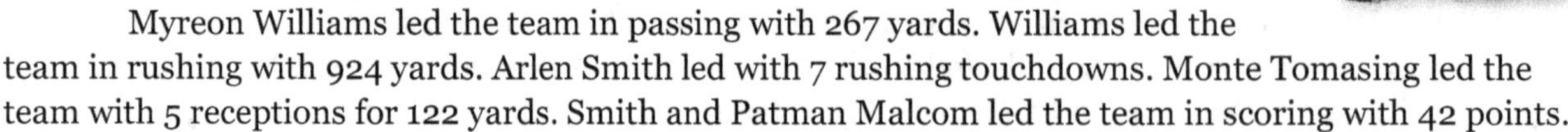

In their first season under head coach Bob Sutton, the Cadets compiled a 4–7 record and were outscored by their opponents by a combined total of 226 to 196. In the annual Army–Navy Game, the Cadets lost to Navy, 24–3.

Myreon Williams led the team in passing with 267 yards. Williams led the team in rushing with 924 yards. Arlen Smith led with 7 rushing touchdowns. Monte Tomasing led the team with 5 receptions for 122 yards. Smith and Patman Malcom led the team in scoring with 42 points.

Home games were played at Michie Stadium

9/14/1991	ARMY	vs	COLGATE	51	22	W
9/21/1991	ARMY	vs	NORTH CAROLINA (7-4)	12	20	L
9/28/1991	ARMY	vs	HARVARD	21	20	W
10/5/1991	ARMY	@	Rutgers (6-5)	12	14	L
10/12/1991	ARMY	vs	THE CITADEL	14	20	L
10/19/1991	ARMY	@	Louisville (2-9)	37	12	W
10/26/1991	ARMY	vs	BOSTON COLLEGE (4-7)	17	28	L
11/2/1991	ARMY	vs	VANDERBILT (5-6)	10	41	L
11/9/1991	ARMY	@	Air Force (10-3)	0	25	L
11/16/1991	ARMY	vs	AKRON (5-6)	19	0	W
12/7/1991	ARMY	vs	NAVY (1-10)	3	24	L
Coach: Bob Sutton			**Season Record >>**	196	226	4-7

Schedule Source: Steve's Football Bible LLC

Selected game(s) highlights

COLGATE

The wishbone spread the defense as it is supposed to do, and the Army backs galloped through the gaps for 500 yards and 26 first downs. The result was a 51-22 victory over Colgate. Willie McMillian, the Black Knights' quarterback scored four touchdowns, all in the first half, and rushed for 170 yards on 16 carries. The score at halftime was 38-8 and the Cadets had outgained the Red Raiders, 376 yards to 106. Army's zeal slackened in the second half and Colgate managed to score two touchdowns after trailing by 44-8. Ahead by 24-8 early in the second period, Army had McMillian throw a pass, the Cadets' only completion of the game, that was good for 30 yards to halfback Edrian Oliver and set up the fourth touchdown. Arlen Smith at left halfback gained 133 yards rushing on 15 attempts.

HARVARD

Harvard, a 30 point underdog, played perhaps its best game of the past decade at Michie Stadium as it bowed to Army, 21-20, when the Cadets put on a tremendous rally by scoring 14 points in the fourth quarter. Even with the clock winding down, Harvard still had a prayer. Sophomore quarterback Mike Giardi threw a Hail Mary pass as time ran out, but it was intercepted by Duncan Johnson. The Cadets, behind backup quarterback Myreon Williams, who replaced starter Willie McMillian, scored after fourth quarter drives of 85 and 69 yards.

NAVY {@ Veterans Stadium, Philadelphia, PA}

On the 50th anniversary of the Japanese attack on Pearl Harbor, Navy posted its only win of the season with a resounding 24-3 triumph over Army. Following Patmon Malcolm's 39 yard field goal, quarterback Jim Kubiak took over, completing 13-of-16 passes for 157 yards. Kubiak and Jason Van Matre were instrumental in Coach George Chaump's offensive scheme. Van Matre would direct the Midshipmen attack up to the opponent's 25 yard line. Van Matre would then shift to tailback to make room for freshman Kubiak as the signal caller. Van Matre and Billy James each added a touchdown on the ground. Defensively, linebacker Byron Ogden led the Midshipmen with 15 tackles.

1992 Army Cadets

In their second season under head coach Bob Sutton, the Cadets compiled a 5–6 record and were outscored by their opponents by a combined total of 251 to 225. In the annual Army–Navy Game, the Cadets defeated Navy, 25–24.

Rick Roper led the team in passing with 708 yards and threw 4 touchdown passes. Steve Weber led the team in rushing with 750 yards. Roper led with 6 rushing touchdowns. Paul Andrzejewski led the team in receptions with 27 for 307 yards. Patman Malcom led the team in scoring with 49 points.

Home games were played at Michie Stadium

9/12/1992	ARMY	vs	HOLY CROSS	17	7	W
9/19/1992	ARMY	@	North Carolina (9-3)	9	22	L
9/26/1992	ARMY	vs	THE CITADEL	14	15	L
10/10/1992	ARMY	vs	LAFAYETTE	38	36	W
10/17/1992	ARMY	@	Rutgers (7-4)	10	45	L
10/24/1992	ARMY	@	Wake Forest (8-4)	7	23	L
10/31/1992	ARMY	vs	EASTERN MICHIGAN (1-10)	57	17	W
11/7/1992	ARMY	vs	AIR FORCE (7-5)	3	7	L
11/14/1992	ARMY	vs	NORTHERN ILLINOIS (5-6)	21	14	W
11/21/1992	ARMY	vs	BOSTON COLLEGE (8-3-1)	24	41	L
12/5/1992	ARMY	vs	NAVY (1-10)	25	24	W
Coach: Bob Sutton			**Season Record >>**	225	251	5-6

Schedule Source: Steve's Football Bible LLC

Selected game(s) highlights

THE CITADEL

Army hosted the Division 1-AA Bulldogs at Michie Stadium. In a back and forth defensive struggle, The Citadel's Jeff Trinh kicked a 37 yard field goal with 2:47 left in the game to give the Bulldogs a 15-14 vicotry over the Cadets. Akili King and Steve Weber scored for Army on short runs. Cedne Sims scored on a 2 yard run in the 3rd quarter to cut the Army lead to 14-12. The subsequent 2 point conversion failed, which set up Trinh's late game heroics.

LAFAYETTE

Patmon Malcom kicked a 43 yard field goal with 19 seconds left in the game to give Army a wild 38-36 victory over Lafayette at Michie Stadium.

NAVY {@ Veterans Stadium, Philadelphia, PA}

Patmon Malcom's career-best 49 yard field goal with 12 seconds remaining won it for Army after the Cadets had fallen behind by 17 points in the third quarter. The Midshipmen, who entered the game at 1-9, raced to a 24-7 advantage only to see the Black Knights come roaring back with three straight scores. A 68 yard touchdown pass from Rick Roper to Gaylord Greene, the longest pass play ever in an Army-Navy contest, and the ensuing two-point conversion (off a fake kick) pulled Army within 24-22 with over seven minutes remaining. Following an exchange of punts, Navy was unable to move the ball and was forced to kick into a stiff wind again. Army took over at the Midshipmen' 33 yard line. On fourth down, Malcom drilled a 44 yard field goal, but the Cadets were flagged for delay of game. His second kick from 49 yards was perfect, capping the greatest comeback in Army-Navy history and a dramatic 25-24 victory for the Cadets.

1993 Army Cadets

In their third season under head coach Bob Sutton, the Cadets compiled a 6–5 record and outscored their opponents by a combined total of 289 to 243. In the annual Army–Navy Game, the Cadets defeated Navy, 16–14.

Rick Roper led the team in passing with 733 yards. Akili King led the team in rushing with 883 yards. Roper led with 9 rushing touchdowns. Leon Gantt led the team in receptions with 21. Paul Andrzejewski led the team with 303 receiving yards. Roper and Rocco Wicks led the team in scoring with 54 points.

Home games were played at Michie Stadium

9/11/1993	ARMY	vs	COLGATE	30	0	W
9/18/1993	ARMY	@	Duke (3-8)	21	42	L
9/25/1993	ARMY	vs	VMI	31	9	W
10/2/1993	ARMY	vs	AKRON (5-6)	35	14	W
10/9/1993	ARMY	@	Temple (1-10)	56	21	W
10/16/1993	ARMY	vs	RUTGERS (4-7)	38	45	L
10/23/1993	ARMY	@	Boston College (9-3)	14	41	L
10/30/1993	ARMY	vs	WESTERN MICHIGAN (7-3-1)	7	20	L
11/6/1993	ARMY	@	Air Force (4-8)	6	25	L
11/13/1993	ARMY	vs	LAFAYETTE	35	12	W
12/4/1993	ARMY	vs	NAVY (4-7)	16	14	W
Coach: Bob Sutton			**Season Record >>**	**289**	**243**	**6-5**

Schedule Source: Steve's Football Bible LLC

Selected game(s) highlights

COLGATE

The Red Raiders fell to the Cadets, 30-0, before a crowd of 26,398 at Michie Stadium. Army threw only one pass while relying on its strong and quick running game in beating Colgate for the third time in a row. Akili King ran for 235 yards in 28 attempts. King's yardage included an 80 yard burst up the middle for Army's first touchdown, in the opening period, and a 1 yard run early in the final quarter for the Cadets' last score. Rick Roper, also was outstanding, scoring touchdowns on runs of 28 and 6 yards, while running 9 times for 72 yards. The Cadets had 496 net yards rushing compared with 84 yards for Colgate.

DUKE

Spence Fischer had his second-straight 300 yard passing performance, and Brad Breedlove added a 44 yard punt return in the fourth quarter yesterday to help Duke break an eight game losing streak with a 42-21 victory over Army in Durham, N.C. Fischer, hit 29 of 36 passes for 357 yards and three touchdowns against the Cadets. The Blue Devils drew to within 14-13 at intermission, then opened the third quarter with a 7 minute 14 second drive ending on Fischer's 9 yard scoring pass to tight end Dan Clark. After a pass interference call on the 2 point conversion try, Fischer used the second chance to hit Breedlove to give Duke a 21-14 lead. Army drove 83 yards and tied the score on Akili King's 22 yard run, on which he broke three tackles, with 3:21 to play. King added 122 yards on 20 carries against the Blue Devils. Duke broke the tie with the help of its third fourth-down gamble against Army's defense. Instead of punting on a fourth-and-6 at the Cadets' 38, punter John Krueger tossed a 13 yard pass to David Lowman to prolong the drive. Five plays later, Tijan Redmon dived in from the 2 with 13:27 left to play. Duke converted its two other fourth-down plays and scored each time.

NAVY {@ Veterans Stadium, Philadelphia, PA}

Navy's furious fourth-quarter rally fell just short, as Army escaped with a 16-14 win. Down 16-0 at the start of the fourth quarter, Navy found the Cadet end zone twice within a two-minute span, as quarterback Jim Kubiak scored on a three yard keeper and found tight end Jim Mill for an eight yard score. The Midshipmen were poised to take the lead with four minutes remaining and the ball on their own 20 yard line. Tailback Billy James gained 60 yards on six carries on the drive, which reached the Army three yard line. Fullback Brad Stramanak picked up a yard on first down, and Kubiak spiked the ball on second down. Stramanak struggled to pick up a yard on third down, and freshman kicker Ryan Bucchianeri's 18 yard field goal attempt sailed wide right.

1994 Army Cadets

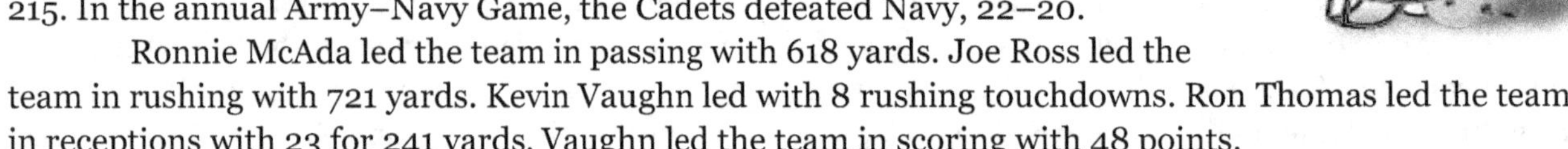

In their fourth season under head coach Bob Sutton, the Cadets compiled a 4–7 record and were outscored by their opponents by a combined total of 252 to 215. In the annual Army–Navy Game, the Cadets defeated Navy, 22–20.

Ronnie McAda led the team in passing with 618 yards. Joe Ross led the team in rushing with 721 yards. Kevin Vaughn led with 8 rushing touchdowns. Ron Thomas led the team in receptions with 23 for 241 yards. Vaughn led the team in scoring with 48 points.

Home games were played at Michie Stadium

9/10/1994	ARMY	vs	HOLY CROSS	49	3	W
9/15/1994	ARMY	@	Duke (8-4)	7	43	L
9/24/1994	ARMY	vs	TEMPLE (2-9)	20	23	L
10/1/1994	ARMY	@	Wake Forest (3-8)	27	33	L
10/8/1994	ARMY	@	Rutgers (5-5-1)	14	16	L
10/15/1994	ARMY	vs	LOUISVILLE (6-5)	30	29	W
10/22/1994	ARMY	vs	THE CITADEL	25	24	W
10/29/1994	ARMY	vs	BOSTON COLLEGE (7-4-1)	3	30	L
11/5/1994	ARMY	vs	AIR FORCE (8-4)	6	10	L
11/12/1994	ARMY	vs	BOSTON U	12	21	L
12/3/1994	ARMY	vs	NAVY (3-8)	22	20	W
Coach: Bob Sutton			**Season Record >>**	**215**	**252**	**4-7**

Schedule Source: Steve's Football Bible LLC

Selected game(s) highlights

LOUISVILLE

Army staged one of its most dramatic victories in recent years, rallying to a 30-29 victory over heavily favored Louisville. The Cadets tied the score at 29-29 on a 10 yard scoring pass from quarterback Ronnie McAda to fullback Joe Ross, capping a 14 play, 77 yard drive with 3 minutes 17 seconds left to play in front of a crowd of 32,125 at Michie Stadium. After place kicker Kurt Heiss put Army ahead with his third conversion -- he also kicked three field goals -- Louisville drove into Army territory, but then David Akers was wide right on a 46 yard field goal attempt with 1:35 left in the game. McAda hit on 7 of 8 passes for 101 yards and gained 93 yards on 14 carries. Army, which trailed by 7-6, at the half, scored on five of its six possessions, including all four in the second half, in a game in which the lead changed hands six times. Two of the last three scoring drives covered 80 yards and the third 77 as Army amassed 317 yards rushing against 199 by Louisville.

NAVY {@ Veterans Stadium, Philadelphia, PA}

For the third straight year, the outcome of the Army-Navy game hinged on the swing of a leg. And for the third consecutive season, the Cadets came out on top, registering another dramatic win over their archrivals after senior Kurt Heiss nailed a career-best 52 yard field goal with 6:19 to play. A crowd of 65,308 witnessed Army's wishbone offense, which amassed 373 rushing yards on the day, wage war against Navy's air attack, which riddled the Cadets for 361 yards passing. All three Navy touchdowns came on plays of 27 yards or longer. Heiss' game-winner, the longest field goal in Army-Navy history, was his third three-pointer of the day. Following the kick, Navy took possession at its own 24 but fell in a big hole when Al Roberts sacked quarterback Jim Kubiak for an eight yard loss. Faced with a fourth down deep in their own territory two plays later, the Midshipmen elected to punt. They would never regain possession as Army's relentless ground attack methodically killed off the clock. Kubiak passed for an Army-Navy record 361 yards, completing 24 of 34 passes with two touchdowns. However, he was intercepted three times, including a critical pickoff by free safety Derek Klein at the Army 2 yard line early in the fourth quarter. The teams exploded for 24 first-quarter points, with Navy leading 14-10 at the break. Heiss' second field goal, from 35 yards out, preceded a 3 yard run by Kevin Vaughn that gave the Cadets a 19-14 lead in the third. But Kubiak hit tight end Kevin Hickman along the left sideline and Hickman rumbled 56 yards to paydirt, shedding several tacklers along the way. Navy's two-point conversion attempt was stuffed by linebacker Ben Kotwica. Quarterback Ronnie McAda rushed for 127 yards and fullback Joe Ross added 120. Vaughn finished with 92 yards rushing.

1995 Army Cadets

In their fifth season under head coach Bob Sutton, the Cadets compiled a 5–5–1 record and outscored their opponents by a combined total of 325 to 211. In the annual Army–Navy Game, the Cadets defeated Navy, 14–13. Ronnie McAda led the team in passing with 761 yards and threw 5 touchdown passes. John Conroy led the team in rushing with 809 yards. McAda led with 10 rushing touchdowns. Ron Leshinski led the team in receptions with 15. John Graves led with 249 yards receiving. Joseph Parker led the team in scoring with 63 points. **Parker set a single season record for field goals with 18.**

Home games were played at Michie Stadium

9/9/1995	ARMY	vs	LEHIGH	42	9	W
9/16/1995	ARMY	vs	DUKE (3-8)	21	23	L
9/23/1995	ARMY	@	Washington (7-4-1)	13	21	L
9/30/1995	ARMY	vs	RICE (2-8-1)	21	21	T
10/14/1995	ARMY	vs	NOTRE DAME (9-3)	27	28	L
10/21/1995	ARMY	@	Boston College (4-8)	49	7	W
10/28/1995	ARMY	vs	COLGATE	56	14	W
11/4/1995	ARMY	vs	EAST CAROLINA (9-3)	25	31	L
11/11/1995	ARMY	@	Air Force (8-5)	20	38	L
11/18/1995	ARMY	vs	BUCKNELL	37	6	W
12/2/1995	ARMY	vs	NAVY (5-6)	14	13	W
Coach: Bob Sutton			**Season Record >>**	**325**	**211**	**5-5-1**

Selected game(s) highlights

NOTRE DAME {@ Giants Stadium, East Rutherford, NJ}

Army came within 2 feet of establishing an unlikely legend of its own, only to see the third-smallest player on the Irish roster make the afternoons biggest play in rescuing a 28-27 victory over the unyielding Cadets. With 39 seconds remaining, Army's clever wishbone offense had threatened a magnificent upset as quarterback Ronnie McAda tossed a 7 yard touchdown pass to split end Leon Gantt. Notre Dame, a three-touchdown favorite, had seen its 28-7 lead crumble to a slim point; its last three possessions had ended with two fumbles and an interception. Coach Bob Sutton unhesitatingly called for Army to attempt a two-point conversion. The ball was placed on the 2 yard line, as a nervous crowd of 74,218 watched at Giants Stadium. Army decided on a "slam-release" pass, in which tight end Ron Leshinski makes a block at the line of scrimmage then slides into the right flat along the goal line. But Leshinski was jostled at the line of scrimmage, and he caught the pass at the 1 yard line. Ivory Covington rushed up from Notre Dame's zone coverage and slammed into the 6-3, 240-pound Leshinski, using the tight end's momentum against him. Covington was moving forward, while Leshinski was running sideways. Despite giving up 77 pounds to the tight end, Covington expertly shoved Leshinski out of bounds 2 feet short of the goal line.

NAVY {@ Veterans Stadium, Philadelphia, PA}

John Conroy's one yard touchdown run with 1:03 left capped a 99 yard drive and gave Army an exciting 14-13 win over Navy. The victory was the Cadets' fourth straight in the series, as those four games were decided by a total of six points. Navy capitalized on an Army turnover on the third play of the game, as Ben Fay found LeBron Butts for a 22 yard touchdown to give the Midshipmen a 7-0 lead. Conroy then tied the game at seven when he scored the first of his two one yard touchdown runs. With the score still tied at halftime, Navy took the second half kickoff and promptly marched 52 yards in 16 plays. Freshman kicker Tom Vanderhorst, playing in his first collegiate football game, connected on a 39 yard field goal to give Navy a 10-7 lead. The Newnan, Ga., native helped extend that advantage to 13-7 with a 22 yard field goal at the start of the fourth quarter. With a fourth-and-goal at the Army one yard line with 8:26 left, the Midshipmen were poised to score again. However, the pass attempt by Chris McCoy fell incomplete in the end zone, and Army took over on downs en route to the game-winning drive.

1996 Army Cadets {Commander-Chief-Trophy}

In their sixth season under head coach Bob Sutton, the Cadets compiled a 10–2 record and outscored their opponents by a combined total of 379 to 224. In the annual Army–Navy Game, the Cadets defeated Navy, 28–24. They also lost to Auburn, 32–29, in the 1996 Independence Bowl.

Ronnie McAda led the team in passing with 954 yards and threw 5 touchdown passes. Joe Hewitt led the team in rushing with 843 yards. Bobby Williams led with 8 rushing touchdowns. Ron Leshinski led the team in receptions with 17 for 259 yards. Joseph Parker led the team in scoring with 94 points.

FINAL RANK: #25 AP/#24 UPI							
Home games were played at Michie Stadium							
9/14/1996	ARMY	vs	OHIO (6-6)	37	20	W	
9/21/1996	ARMY	vs	DUKE (0-11)	35	17	W	
9/28/1996	ARMY	@	North Texas (5-6)	27	10	W	
10/5/1996	ARMY	vs	YALE	39	13	W	
10/12/1996	ARMY	@	Rutgers (2-9)	42	21	W	
10/19/1996	ARMY	vs	TULANE (2-9)	34	10	W	
10/26/1996	ARMY	@	Miami-Ohio (6-5)	27	7	W	
11/2/1996	ARMY	vs	LAFAYETTE	41	21	W	
11/9/1996	ARMY	vs	AIR FORCE (6-5)	23	7	W	
11/16/1996	ARMY	@	Syracuse (9-3)	17	42	L	
12/7/1996	ARMY	vs	NAVY (9-3)	28	24	W	
12/31/1996	ARMY	vs	Auburn (8-4)	29	32	L	Independence Bowl
Coach: Bob Sutton			Season Record >>	379	224	10-2	

Schedule Source: Steve's Football Bible LLC

Selected game(s) highlights

YALE

Yale faced the ultimate of challenges on a pristine Saturday afternoon against Army on the banks of the Hudson River. After trailing 9-7 at halftime, Yale allowed the Cadets to score on three of four possessions to start the second half. But Army still needed two fourth-down conversions against a tiring defense and a deflected pass interception at the Yale 6 before pulling away for a 39-13 victory.

RUTGERS

Army ran the ball 78 times at the wilting Scarlet Knights' defense and amassed 546 yards, the third-highest rushing total in 108 seasons of Cadet football. The result was a 42-21 victory, one that was even more decisive than that final score. Army scored five straight times to take a 35-7 lead midway through the third quarter. The five touchdowns came at the end of drives that covered anywhere from 65 to 81 yards. Quarterback Adam Thompson was the leading rusher with 132 yards. Two fullbacks also each had over 100 yards, Demetrius Perry with 127 and Joe Hewitt with 117. Perry had a straight-ahead touchdown run of 61 yards and Hewitt a similar one of 59 in which he broke three tackles.

NAVY {@ Veterans Stadium, Philadelphia, PA}

Army stopped Navy eight times inside the 10 yard line during the final four minutes of the game to preserve a 28-24 win over the Midshipmen. With the victory, the Cadets clinched their first Commander-In-Chief's Trophy since 1988 and accepted a bid to the Poulan Weedeater Independence Bowl. Despite the loss, Navy accepted a bid to the Jeep Eagle Aloha Bowl, where it defeated California, 42-38. Thanks to touchdown runs from quarterback Chris McCoy and fullback Patrick McGrew and a 15 yard McCoy-to-LeBron Butts touchdown pass, the Midshipmen jumped out to a 21-3 second-quarter lead. The Cadets then used a 44 yard touchdown run from Ronnie McAda and a 22 yard J. Parker field goal to head into the locker room down 21-13 at the half. On the second play of the third quarter, Bobby Williams took the pitch from McAda and went 81 yards for a touchdown. However, the two-point conversion failed, and Navy maintained a 21-19 lead. After the Midshipmen missed a 42 yard field goal, Army drove right back down the field and took a 25-21 lead when Demetrius Perry scored from three yards out. Navy's Tom Vanderhorst brought his team within one, 25-24, when he hit a 31 yard field goal to close the third quarter. Although Parker's 20 yard field goal with 6:35 left in the game provided the game's final margin, Navy drove down inside the Cadet 10 yard line on each of its last two possessions but was unable to score.

1996 INDEPENDENCE BOWL

Auburn quarterback Dameyune Craig was shocked, yet not surprised by what he saw in the fourth quarter of the Independence Bowl. Craig had 440 of his school-record 447 yards by the end of the third quarter, when the Tigers (8-4) led #24 Army by 25 points and had scored on six of nine possessions. But the Cadets then scored 22 fourth-quarter points, and missed a chance to send the game into overtime only after J. Parker missed a 27 yard field goal with 29 seconds left. Craig threw for two touchdowns and ran for one as Auburn avoided its first three game losing streak since 1981. He was 24-of-40 for an Independence Bowl-record 372 yards and ran for 75 yards.

1997 Army Cadets

In their seventh season under head coach Bob Sutton, the Cadets compiled a 4–7 record and were outscored by their opponents by a combined total of 311 to 221. In the annual Army–Navy Game, the Cadets lost to Navy, 39–7.

Johnny Goff led the team in passing with 384 yards. Goff led the team in rushing with 698 yards. Ty Amey led with 6 rushing touchdowns. Brad Miller led the team in receptions with 8. Rod Richards led with 129 receiving yards. Eric Olsen led the team in scoring with 55 points.

Home games were played at Michie Stadium

9/6/1997	ARMY	vs	MARSHALL (10-3)	25	35	L
9/13/1997	ARMY	vs	LAFAYETTE	41	14	W
9/20/1997	ARMY	@	Duke (2-9)	17	20	L
9/27/1997	ARMY	vs	MIAMI-OHIO (8-3)	14	38	L
10/4/1997	ARMY	@	Tulane (7-4)	0	41	L
10/18/1997	ARMY	vs	RUTGERS (0-11)	37	35	W
10/25/1997	ARMY	vs	COLGATE	35	27	W
11/8/1997	ARMY	@	Air Force (10-3)	0	24	L
11/15/1997	ARMY	vs	NORTH TEXAS (4-7)	25	14	W
11/22/1997	ARMY	@	Boston College (4-7)	20	24	L
12/6/1997	ARMY	vs	NAVY (7-4)	7	39	L
Coach: Bob Sutton			**Season Record >>**	221	311	4-7

Schedule Source: Steve's Football Bible LLC

Selected game(s) highlights

LAFAYETTE

Johnny Goff rushed for a career-high 129 yards, including a 30 yard touchdown, as Army easily defeated Division I-AA Lafayette 41-14 at Michie Stadium. Goff completed 1 of 4 passes for 15 yards and watched as Lafayette sophomore Brian Tuma returned an interception 32 yards to tie the game at 7-7 with 1:23 left in the first quarter. The Cadets wishbone attack was as methodically efficient as ever. Army outgained Lafayette 560-176 and had 30 first downs to Lafayette's 12. Junior fullback Ty Amey rushed for a career-high 129 yards. Amey helped Army to a 21-7 halftime lead as he had touchdown runs of 2 and 3 yards in the second quarter.

COLGATE

Brendan Rooney, who gained 33 yards on 9 carries, was one of the eight Army running backs who went to the right places today, totaling 372 yards rushing in a 35-27 victory over Colgate. Joe Hewitt, the Army fullback, fumbled a handoff, and the ball bounced into the hands of Colgate safety Jamal Patterson, who ran 37 yards for a touchdown that tied the score at 14-14 before halftime. Colgate went ahead, 21-14, early in the second half on quarterback Ryan Vena's 40 yard scoring run. But a roughing penalty on a punt sustained an Army drive that ended when Hewitt scored on a 20 yard run. Army (3-4) rolled on for two more touchdowns before Colgate scored again with a minute and a half to play.

NAVY {@ Giants Stadium, East Rutherford, NJ}

With the Navy defense holding Army to just 84 yards of total offense, the Midshipmen rolled to a 39-7 victory over the Cadets in East Rutherford, N.J. The 32-point win was not only Navy's largest margin of triumph over Army since 1973, but it was also the fifth largest for either team in series history. Although Army drove 74 yards in two plays for a game opening touchdown, quarterback Johnny Goff and Co. managed to gain just 13 yards the rest of the afternoon. Meanwhile, Navy quarterback Chris McCoy directed the Mids to a record-setting day on the ground, gaining 205 yards on 31 carries. Fullback Tim Cannada added a career-high 133 yards on 30 carries, as Navy rolled up 383 yards rushing overall. Midshipmen wide receiver LeBron Butts also set a new series standard with his third career touchdown. Defensively, linebacker Travis Cooley had seven tackles, while defensive tackle David Viger and linebacker Jason Coffey added five stops apiece.

1998 Army Cadets

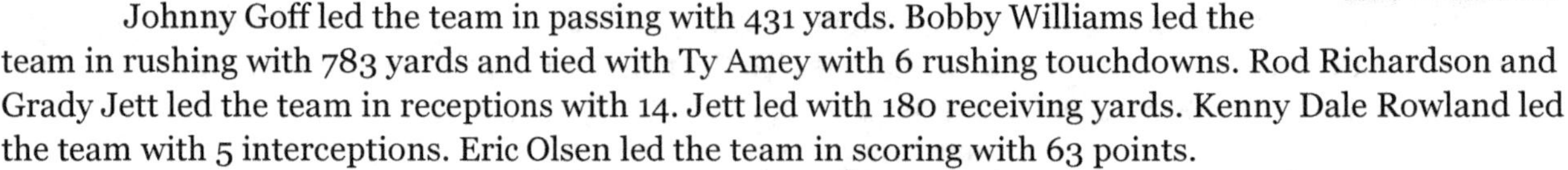

In their eighth season under head coach Bob Sutton, the Cadets compiled a 3–8 record and were outscored by their opponents by a combined total of 325 to 257. In the annual Army–Navy Game, the Cadets defeated Navy, 34–30.

Johnny Goff led the team in passing with 431 yards. Bobby Williams led the team in rushing with 783 yards and tied with Ty Amey with 6 rushing touchdowns. Rod Richardson and Grady Jett led the team in receptions with 14. Jett led with 180 receiving yards. Kenny Dale Rowland led the team with 5 interceptions. Eric Olsen led the team in scoring with 63 points.

Home games were played at Michie Stadium

9/12/1998	ARMY	vs	MIAMI-OHIO (10-1)	13	14	L
9/19/1998	ARMY	vs	CINCINNATI (2-9)	37	20	W
9/26/1998	ARMY	@	Rutgers (5-6)	15	27	L
10/3/1998	ARMY	@	East Carolina (6-5)	25	30	L
10/10/1998	ARMY	@	Houston (3-8)	38	28	W
10/17/1998	ARMY	vs	SOUTHERN MISS (7-5)	13	37	L
10/24/1998	ARMY	@	Notre Dame (9-3)	17	20	L
11/7/1998	ARMY	vs	AIR FORCE (12-1)	7	35	L
11/14/1998	ARMY	vs	TULANE (12-0)	35	49	L
11/21/1998	ARMY	@	Louisville (7-5)	23	35	L
12/5/1998	ARMY	vs	NAVY (3-8)	34	30	W
Coach: Bob Sutton			**Season Record >>**	**257**	**325**	**3-8**

Schedule Source: Steve's Football Bible LLC

Selected game(s) highlights

Rutgers

The Scarlet Knights defeated Army, 27-15, before a Homecoming crowd of 31,879. Army QB Johnny Goff sprained his left ankle early in the second quarter with Rutgers ahead, 14-0, and left the field, never returning. In came Joe Gerena, a sophomore. Gerena performed well enough, except for two intercepted passes, the first giving Rutgers a touchdown and the second ending an Army scoring threat. Gerena wound up attempting 22 passes and completed 12. Once again, Army had the problem of coming from behind without much of a passing attack. Nine backs, Gerena included, rushed for 298 yards. Army scored twice in the second period on dive plays by a backup fullback, Michael Wallace, but missed both conversions and trailed, 14-12. Then came the key play. Gerena, attempting his second pass but under a big rush, was intercepted by cornerback Reggie Stephens, who returned it 50 yards for a touchdown and a 21-12 Rutgers lead.

East Carolina

Bobby Weaver threw two touchdown passes and ran for a third score as East Carolina had to fend off visiting Army in the second half for a 30-25 victory. Weaver burned the Cadets with a 13-for-16, 225 yard effort in the first half. He hit Marcellus Harris on a 9 yard score and ran for a 22 yard touchdown in the first quarter. He found Troy Smith on a 38 yard scoring play just before halftime for the Pirates. Weaver's game came apart in the third quarter, when he was intercepted twice, sacked for a safety and benched in favor of reserve David Garrard. The Cadets spotted the Pirates a 21-0 lead in the first quarter before mounting its comeback. Trailing 27-17, Army sealed Weaver's demise when defensive end David Hageman tackled him by the ankles in the end zone with 5:52 left in the third quarter. The Cadets took the subsequent punt and marched 60 yards to draw to 27-25 on Bobby Williams' 18 yard scoring run with 3:23 left in the period. Army missed the two-point conversion try.

Notre Dame

Notre Dame Kicker Jim Sanson atoned for two missed opportunities with a career-best 48 yard field goal in the final two minutes as the Irish beat Army, 20-17. Sanson, who earlier missed a 48 yard attempt into the wind, had just enough leg to get the low, wobbly kick through the uprights with 1 minute 6 seconds left. Army, which had tried just one pass, then had to abandon its running game, and Johnny Sanders intercepted a pass by Johnny Goff at the Irish 37 with eight seconds left. Notre Dame needed Sanson's heroics after Army tied the game, 17-17, with 10 minutes left, as Craig Stucker scored from 19 yards out for his first career rushing touchdown.

AIR FORCE

When Army crept to within 7 points today, Air Force's Dylan Newman sprinted by the Cadets' confused defensive backs and cradled in a 74 yard touchdown pass. The Falcons defeated the Cadets, 35-7, at Michie Stadium. The Falcons stung Army with three long touchdowns, and their pursuit on defense held the Cadets' rushing attack to 192 yards. Quarterback Johnny Goff completed 4 of 10 passes for 59 yards and an interception. On Air Force's first possession, Matt Farmer sprinted 45 yards on a reverse for a touchdown. On the Falcons' next series, Blane Morgan faked a run, duping cornerback Tony Coaxum and leaving Newman alone for a 54 yard touchdown reception to increase the lead to 14-0. Guiding a triple-option offense like Army's, Morgan completed 7 of 9 passes for 167 yards and two touchdowns and rushed for 51 yards and a touchdown. The Cadets drew to within 14-7 midway in the second quarter when Goff sneaked into the end zone from 1 yard out.

NAVY {@ Veterans Stadium, Philadelphia, PA}

Trailing entering the fourth quarter, Army combined trickery and an old-fashioned wishbone attack to rally for a 34-30 victory over Navy as the teams combined for the most points ever in 99 meetings of this fabled service-academy rivalry. Bobby Williams' 36 yard halfback option pass to backfield mate John Johnson preceded a 70 yard scoring burst by fullback Ty Amey as the Cadets put 15 points on the board in the final stanza. Eric Olsen's 26 yard insurance field goal with 47 seconds left provided the contest's final points. The win was Army's sixth against Navy in a seven game span. Amey's decisive touchdown run capped a day of big plays for the Cadets, who enjoyed five scoring plays of 25 yards or longer, including touchdown runs of 69 yards by quarterback Joe Gerena and 71 yards by fullback Craig Stucker. Army rolled up a season-high 401 yards rushing to seal its third national rushing title in six years. Amey (134) and Stucker (106) each rushed for more than 100 yards from Army's fullback position. Despite the impressive offensive performances by both teams, the game was marred by what took place after Amey's score. A railing collapsed in the Army student section, sending nine Cadets (four West Point students and five military academy prep school students) tumbling 12 feet to the ground.

1999 Army Black Knights

In their ninth season under head coach Bob Sutton, the Black Knights compiled a 3–8 record and were outscored by their opponents by a combined total of 317 to 225. In the annual Army–Navy Game, the Black Knights lost to Navy, 19–9. Joe Gerena led the team in passing with 661 yards. Michael Wallace led the team in rushing with 894 yards and 10 rushing touchdowns. Grady Jett led the team in receptions with 21 for 357 yards. Wallace led the team in scoring with 60 points.

Home games were played at Michie Stadium

9/11/1999	ARMY	vs	WAKE FOREST (7-5)	15	34	L
9/18/1999	ARMY	@	Tulane (3-8)	28	48	L
9/25/1999	ARMY	vs	BALL STATE (0-11)	41	21	W
10/2/1999	ARMY	vs	EAST CAROLINA (9-3)	14	33	L
10/7/1999	ARMY	vs	LOUISVILLE (7-5)	59	52	W
10/16/1999	ARMY	@	Southern Mississippi (9-3)	0	24	L
10/23/1999	ARMY	vs	NEW MEXICO STATE (6-5)	35	18	W
11/6/1999	ARMY	@	Air Force (6-5)	0	28	L
11/13/1999	ARMY	@	Memphis (5-6)	10	14	L
11/20/1999	ARMY	vs	HOUSTON (7-4)	14	26	L
12/4/1999	ARMY	vs	NAVY (5-7)	9	19	L
Coach: Bob Sutton			**Season Record >>**	**225**	**317**	**3-8**

Schedule Source: Steve's Football Bible LLC

Selected game(s) highlights

LOUISVILLE

Quarterback Joe Gerena scored on a 7 yard run in the second overtime, and Michael Wallace rushed for a school-record 269 yards and four touchdowns as Army beat Louisville 59-52. It was the first overtime game for either school. Louisville overcame a 45-17 halftime deficit to force overtime but came up just short in the second extra period. After Gerena scored in the second OT, Louisville started from the Army 25 and gained a first down at the 12. But the drive stalled and, on a fourth-and-7 from the 8, Louisville quarterback Chris Redman threw a pass to Lavell Boyd near the back of the end zone. Boyd jumped and seemed to have the ball in his hands but dropped it under pressure from several Army defenders. Wallace, a junior fullback, rushed for four TDs in the first half as Army built a 45-17 lead. The scoring runs covered 32, 1, 78 and 67 yards. But Louisville rallied to tie it with four touchdowns in the second half -- two 1 yard scoring runs by Moreau and two TD passes by Redman, an 18 yarder to Ibn Green and a 5 yarder to Boyd. Army gained 564 yards, while Louisville had 489. Gerena completed 5 of 10 passes for 84 yards and one touchdown. He also ran 25 times for 98 yards and three touchdowns.

NAVY {@ Veterans Stadium, Philadelphia, PA}

Sophomore quarterback Brian Madden rushed for a career-high 177 yards and one touchdown, while senior kicker Tim Shubzda tied an Army-Navy game record with four field goals to lead Navy over Army, 19-9, in front of a Veterans Stadium record crowd of 70,049. The game was the 100th in the storied rivalry. Madden, who was named the Most Valuable Player of the game by the Philadelphia Sportswriters Association, put Navy on the board first with his two yard touchdown run. It was Navy's only touchdown of the day. Shubzda drilled field goals of 35, 34, 37 and 38 yards, in helping put the Cadets away as the Midshipmen built a 19-3 lead. The Navy defense was sensational all day, holding West Point to just 210 yards of total offense. Gino Marchetti led the way with two fumble recoveries and a forced fumble. John Chavous recorded a team-high tying 10 tackles and intercepted his first career pass, while Daryl Hill also recorded 10 tackles, including two tackles for a loss and a sack. David Ryno, Brad Wimsatt and Chris Lepore had seven tackles apiece. The Midshipmen also got a huge lift from senior punter Tray Calisch, who averaged 50.3 yards per punt over six punts, a Navy record for the Army-Navy game.

2000 Army Black Knights

In their first season under head coach Todd Berry (pictured at right), the Black Knights compiled a 1–10 record and were outscored by their opponents by a combined total of 372 to 224. In the annual Army–Navy Game, the Black Knights lost to Navy, 30–28. Joe Gerena led the team in passing with 779 yards. Michael Wallace led the team in rushing with 1,157 yards and 11 rushing touchdowns. Omari Thompson led the team in receptions with 40 for 451 yards. Wallace led the team in scoring with 72 points.

Home games were played at Michie Stadium

9/4/2000	ARMY	@	Cincinnati (7-5)	17	23	L
9/9/2000	ARMY	vs	BOSTON COLLEGE (7-5)	17	55	L
9/16/2000	ARMY	@	Houston (3-8)	30	31	L
9/23/2000	ARMY	vs	MEMPHIS (4-7)	16	26	L
10/7/2000	ARMY	@	New Mexico State (3-8)	23	42	L
10/14/2000	ARMY	@	East Carolina (8-4)	21	42	L
10/21/2000	ARMY	vs	TULANE (6-5)	21	17	W
11/4/2000	ARMY	vs	AIR FORCE (9-3)	27	41	L
11/11/2000	ARMY	@	Louisville (9-3)	17	38	L
11/18/2000	ARMY	vs	ALABAMA-BIRMINGHAM (7-4)	7	27	L
12/2/2000	ARMY	vs	NAVY (1-10)	28	30	L
Coach: Todd Berry			**Season Record >>**	**224**	**372**	**1-10**

Schedule Source: Steve's Football Bible LLC

Selected game(s) highlights

Houston

Houston's 31-30 win night over Army, was due in large part to the outstanding performance of running back Joffrey Reynolds, who rushed for 201 yards and 3 touchdowns on 34 carries. Army's Brendan Mullen missed a 32 yard field goal with six seconds to play and Houston held on for the victory. Army led 30-25 before Houston drove for the go-ahead touchdown with 1:17 remaining on Jason McKinley's 9 yard pass to Brian Robinson on fourth-and-goal. But Army snuffed the 2-point conversion attempt, and the Cadets drove to the Houston 15 before Mullen missed the field goal. It was his second miss of the night. He couldn't convert on a 31 yard try after Army drove to the Houston 14 in the second quarter.

TULANE

Army avoided a record 11th straight defeat today when quarterback Joe Gerena fired an 18 yard touchdown pass to tight end Clint Dodson with 40 seconds left to lift the Black Knights to a 21-17 victory over Tulane. That touchdown pass capped an 80 yard drive during which Gerena twice completed fourth-down passes. The second fourth-down completion was for 24 yards to tailback Michael Wallace on fourth-and-11 at the Tulane 42 yard line with less than a minute to play. Gerena eluded the grasp of two Tulane defenders before throwing the ball as he ran to his left. On the next play, he found Dodson open in the left corner of the end zone for the final touchdown. With time running out, Tulane reached Army's 45 yard line. But two long passes by quarterback Patrick Ramsey were broken up by Army defenders just short of the Black Knights' end zone as the clock ran out. Gerena finished with 21 completions in 34 attempts for 171 yards.

NAVY {@ PSINet Stadium, Baltimore, MD}

Fifty-six years after they met here for the national championship, Army and Navy staggered in with a combined record of 1-19. In an exciting if error-filled contest, the Midshipmen — aided by two questionable calls by officials — withstood a furious rally by Army to win their first game of the season. Navy's Brian Broadwater passed for one touchdown and ran for another before a then-record crowd of 70,685 at PSINet Stadium.

2001 Army Black Knights

In their second season under head coach Todd Berry, the Black Knights compiled a 3–8 record and were outscored by their opponents by a combined total of 365 to 229. In the annual Army–Navy Game, the Black Knights defeated Navy, 26–17. Chad Jenkins led the team in passing with 1,773 yards and threw 8 touchdown passes. C.J. Young led the team in rushing with 556 yards and 9 rushing touchdowns. Clint Dodson led the team in receptions with 42. Aris Comeaux led with 505 receiving yards. Young led the team in scoring with 54 points.

Home games were played at Michie Stadium

9/8/2001	ARMY	vs	CINCINNATI (7-5)	21	24	L
9/22/2001	ARMY	@	Alabama-Birmingham (6-5)	3	55	L
9/29/2001	ARMY	@	Boston College (8-4)	10	31	L
10/6/2001	ARMY	vs	HOUSTON (0-11)	28	14	W
10/13/2001	ARMY	vs	EAST CAROLINA (6-6)	26	49	L
10/20/2001	ARMY	@	Tcu (6-6)	20	38	L
10/27/2001	ARMY	vs	TULANE (3-9)	42	35	W
11/3/2001	ARMY	@	Air Force (6-6)	24	34	L
11/10/2001	ARMY	vs	BUFFALO (3-8)	19	26	L
11/17/2001	ARMY	@	Memphis (5-6)	10	42	L
12/1/2001	ARMY	vs	NAVY (0-10)	26	17	W
Coach: Todd Berry			**Season Record >>**	**229**	**365**	**3-8**

Schedule Source: Steve's Football Bible LLC

Selected game(s) highlights

Air Force

Larry Duncan returned an interception 95 yards for a touchdown to help Air Force prevent Army from winning consecutive games for the first time in four years. Duncan's interception was one of four turnovers for Army, which finished with 154 more total yards than Air Force and had a 10-minute advantage in time of possession. The Black Knights were rolling offensively until Duncan stepped in front of a pass by Jenkins and sprinted down the left sideline for the longest interception return in school history. The play was a huge momentum swing, giving Air Force a 31-17 lead with 1:33 left in the third quarter. Jenkins rebounded quickly, driving Army 80 yards on the ensuing drive, and C.J. Young scored from 2 yards out with 10 minutes remaining. Army got the ball back less than four minutes later but was forced to punt, and Air Force put the game out of reach when Brooks Walters kicked a 46 yard field goal with 2:36 left.

NAVY {@ Veterans Stadium, Philadelphia, PA}

Army jumped out to a 13-0 lead on its first-two possessions and never looked back, defeating Navy, 26-17-in front of a Veterans Stadium crowd of 69,708. With the loss, Navy finished 0-10, its worst record in school history. The only other Navy teams to go winless were the 1948 squad (0-8-1), the 1883 team (0-1) and the 1879 team (0-0-1). Army set the tone early, stuffing Navy on its first possession and then scoring five plays later on Ardell Daniels' 60 yard touchdown run. Army made it 13-0 on its next possession as Clyde Clark let a sure interception, and possible touchdown, go right through his hands into the arms of Army tight end Brian Bruenton who turned and rumbled 42 yards for a touchdown. The Navy defense settled down after Army's second touchdown, allowing just 197 yards in Army's final 15 possessions after allowing 138 yards on its first-two possessions. Navy, though, was unable to get back into the game as the offense could never get untracked and the special teams made two critical errors that ended any hope of a comeback.

2002 Army Black Knights

In their third season under head coach Todd Berry, the Black Knights compiled a 1–11 record and were outscored by their opponents by a combined total of 491 to 226.[1] In the annual Army–Navy Game, the Black Knights lost to Navy, 58–12. This loss began a 14-game losing streak by Army against Navy.

Zac Dahman led the team in passing with 1,039 yards and threw 5 touchdown passes. Carlton Jones led the team in rushing with 611 yards. Josh Holden led with 8 rushing touchdowns. Aaron Alexander led the team in receptions with 26 for 454 yards. Holden led the team in scoring with 48 points.

Home games were played at Michie Stadium

9/7/2002	ARMY	vs	HOLY CROSS	21	30	L
9/14/2002	ARMY	@	Rutgers (1-11)	0	44	L
9/21/2002	ARMY	vs	LOUISVILLE (7-6)	14	45	L
9/28/2002	ARMY	vs	SOUTHERN MISS (7-6)	6	27	L
10/5/2002	ARMY	@	East Carolina (4-8)	24	59	L
10/12/2002	ARMY	vs	TCU (10-2)	27	46	L
10/19/2002	ARMY	@	Houston (5-7)	42	56	L
10/26/2002	ARMY	vs	ALABAMA-BIRMINGHAM (5-7)	26	29	L
11/9/2002	ARMY	vs	AIR FORCE (8-5)	30	49	L
11/16/2002	ARMY	@	Tulane (8-5)	14	10	W
11/23/2002	ARMY	@	Memphis (3-9)	10	38	L
12/7/2002	ARMY	vs	NAVY (2-10)	12	58	L
Coach: Todd Berry			**Season Record >>**	**226**	**491**	**1-11**

Schedule Source: Steve's Football Bible LLC

Selected game(s) highlights

AIR FORCE

The Falcons rushed for 380 yards, scored on nine of their 10 possessions and snapped a three game losing streak by defeating Army 49-30. Leotis Palmer ran for a touchdown and threw for another on a halfback option pass as the Falcons earned their sixth straight Commander-in-Chief's Trophy. Joey Ashcroft added field goals of 38, 38, 41 and 30 yards, setting a career high and tying a school record for most field goals in a game. Carlton Jones had touchdown runs of 4 and 2 yards for Army. Despite the Falcons' dominating performance on the ground, Army stayed in the game late into the third quarter. Josh Holden, who rushed for two touchdowns, scored from 22 yards out to cut Air Force's lead to 32-24 with 7:18 left in the quarter. The Falcons came right back as Harridge threw a 49 yard touchdown pass to a wide open Adam Strecker 1:17 later to make it 39-24.

NAVY {@ Giants Stadium, East Rutherford, NJ}

Quarterback Craig Candeto rushed for 103 yards and a school-record six touchdowns to lead Navy to a 58-12 rout over Army in the 103rd playing of the Army-Navy game. Candeto also threw a 23 yard touchdown pass to Tony Lane, accounting for seven of Navy's eight touchdowns. The 58 points scored by Navy are the most in series history and the 46-point margin of victory is the second largest in series history (Navy won 51-0 in 1973). Navy played a near perfect game, scoring on its first-eight possessions. The Midshipmen did not have a turnover or a penalty and didn't punt until nine minutes left in the game. The Midshipmen rushed for 421 yards and piled up an Army-Navy game record 508 yards of total offense. The defense played equally well, allowing a season-low 241 yards of total offense, including just 56 yards on the ground. Fourteen different Navy players carried the ball. In addition to Candeto, the Midshipmen got big performances from sophomore fullback Michael Brimage, who had 10 carries for 84 yards; Lane, who carried the ball five times for 65 yards and senior fullback Bryce McDonald, who rushed for 63 yards and a touchdown on 10 carries. Candeto completed four of his five pass attempts for 87 yards and one touchdown as four different receivers caught passes.

2003 Army Black Knights

The Black Knights compiled a 0–13 record and were outscored by their opponents by a combined total of 476 to 206. In the annual Army–Navy Game, the Black Knights lost to Navy, 34–6. Todd Berry began the year in his fourth season as the team's head coach. Berry coached the first six games but was replaced by John Mumford who served as interim head coach for the final seven games.

Zac Dahman led the team in passing with 2,234 yards, which was a single season record and threw 11 touchdown passes. Carlton Jones led the team in rushing with 632 yards and 6 rushing touchdowns. **Aaron Alexander led the team in receptions with 64, which set the single season record for Army**, and had 861 yards and 6 TD receptions. Jones led the team in scoring with 48 points.

Home games were played at Michie Stadium

9/6/2003	ARMY	vs	CONNECTICUT (9-3)	21	48	L
9/13/2003	ARMY	vs	RUTGERS (5-7)	21	36	L
9/20/2003	ARMY	vs	TULANE (5-7)	33	50	L
9/27/2003	ARMY	vs	SOUTH FLORIDA (7-4)	0	28	L
10/4/2003	ARMY	@	Tcu (11-2)	0	27	L
10/11/2003	ARMY	@	Louisville (9-4)	10	34	L
10/18/2003	ARMY	vs	EAST CAROLINA (1-11)	32	38	L
10/25/2003	ARMY	@	Cincinnati (5-7)	29	33	L
11/1/2003	ARMY	@	Alabama-Birmingham (5-7)	9	24	L
11/8/2003	ARMY	@	Air Force (7-5)	3	31	L
11/15/2003	ARMY	vs	HOUSTON (7-6)	14	34	L
11/22/2003	ARMY	@	Hawaii (9-5)	28	59	L
12/6/2003	ARMY	vs	NAVY (8-5)	6	34	L
Coach: John Mumford			**Season Record >>**	**206**	**476**	**0-13**

Selected game(s) highlights

EAST CAROLINA

Army scored first on an Aaron Alexander 28 yard TD reception from Zac Dahman for a 7-0 lead. The Pirates reeled of 21 straight points for a 21-7 lead. Carlton Jones ran 1 yard for a touchdown to cut the lead to 21-14 at halftime. East Carolina then scored 17 straight points for a 38-14 lead early in the 4th quarter. Army tried to rally, scoring on a Jones 20 yard touchdown run, Anthony Zurisko 33 yard field goal and a Lamar Mason 9 yard touchdown to cut the lead to 38-32, which ended up as the final score. Jones rushed for 100 yards and Dahman passed for 235 yards to lead the Black Knights offense.

Air Force

Joey Ashcroft hit three field goals and Marchello Graddy recovered three fumbles, leading Air Force to a 31-3 win over Army. Army had six turnovers and just 199 total yards to match the worst start in school history (1973). The Black Knights have won once in 22 games and haven't beaten Air Force on the road since 1977, a span of 13 games. Graddy gave Air Force plenty of chances with fumble recoveries on three straight possessions in the second quarter - a team record - but the Falcons had trouble capitalizing. Graddy fell on a fumbled snap early in the second quarter at Air Force's 26 yard line, but Air Force settled for Ashcroft's 24 yard field goal after reaching Army's 7. Graddy next recovered a fumble by Recardo Evans at the Falcons' 49 yard line, but that drive ended with Ashcroft pulling a 40 yard field goal to the right. Reggie Nevels fumbled three plays later, and Graddy recovered it at Army's 23. This time, the Falcons gave the ball to Steve Massie five straight times, and he bulled in from one yard out to put Air Force up 13-0. Army had four turnovers and just 94 yards in the first half.

NAVY {@ Lincoln Financial Field, Philadelphia, PA}

Kyle Eckel rushed for 152 yards and two touchdowns as Navy rolled to an easy 34-6 victory over Army in front of a Lincoln Financial Field record crowd of 70,844. The victory was the fourth for Navy over Army in the last five meetings and gave the Midshipmen the Commander-In-Chief's Trophy, which is presented annually to the winner of the football competition among the three major service academies — Army, Navy and Air Force—and is named in honor of the President of the United States. Eric Roberts added two touchdowns rushing, while quarterback Craig Candeto rushed for 58 yards and threw for 55. The 58 yards rushing put Candeto over 1,000 yards making him just the 23rd quarterback in NCAA history and second in Navy history to rush for 1,000 yards and throw for 1,000 yards in a single season. The Navy offense punished the Black Knights for 359 of their 414 yards of total offense on the ground. The Navy defense was just as good, if not better, than the offense as the Midshipmen held the Black Knights to 198 yards of total offense. Bobby McClarin led the way with eight tackles, a pass breakup and the first interception of his career. McClarin's interception came in the third quarter on the Navy six yard line with the Midshipmen nursing a 20-6 lead. Eddie Carthan added eight tackles, including a tackle for a loss, while Eli Sanders chipped in with seven tackles and an interception. Sanders interception also came in the third quarter deep in Navy territory, two plays after a Candeto interception.

2004 Army Black Knights

In their first season under head coach Bobby Ross (pictured at right), the Black Knights compiled a 2-9 record and were outscored by their opponents by a combined total of 388 to 260. In the annual Army–Navy Game, the Black Knights lost to Navy, 42-13.

Zac Dahman led the team in passing with 1,767 yards and threw 9 touchdown passes. Carlton Jones led the team in rushing with 1,269 yards **and 17 rushing touchdowns, which is a single season record for Army.** Aaron Alexander led the team in receptions with 37 for 505 yards. Jones led the team in scoring with 104 points. **Jones set the single game touchdown record with 5 vs South Florida.**

Home games were played at Michie Stadium

9/11/2004	ARMY	vs	LOUISVILLE (11-1)	21	52	L	
9/18/2004	ARMY	@	Houston (3-8)	21	35	L	
9/25/2004	ARMY	@	Connecticut (8-4)	3	40	L	
10/2/2004	ARMY	vs	TCU (5-6)	17	21	L	
10/9/2004	ARMY	vs	CINCINNATI (7-5)	48	29	W	
10/16/2004	ARMY	@	South Florida (4-7)	42	35	W	Jones 5 rush TD's
10/30/2004	ARMY	@	East Carolina (2-9)	28	38	L	
11/6/2004	ARMY	vs	AIR FORCE (5-6)	22	31	L	
11/13/2004	ARMY	@	Tulane (5-6)	31	45	L	
11/20/2004	ARMY	vs	ALABAMA-BIRMINGHAM (7-5)	14	20	L	
12/4/2004	ARMY	vs	NAVY (10-2)	13	42	L	
Coach: Bobby Ross			**Season Record >>**	260	388	2-9	

Schedule Source: Steve's Football Bible LLC
***-Single game record**

Selected game(s) highlights

TCU

Facing a 17-point deficit and mired in a two-game losing streak, TCU turned to banged up quarterback Brandon Hassell. Hassell responded by leading the Horned Frogs to a last minute score for a 21-17 victory over Army on Saturday. Lonta Hobbs scored on a 2 yard run, his second touchdown, with 41 seconds left to seal the victory. Hassell, who replaced an ineffective Kyle Kummer, completed 14 of 23 passes for 158 yards and one touchdown for the Horned Frogs. TCU scored 21 straight points to beat an Army team that has not won at home since beating Tulane 42-37 on Oct. 27, 2001. Carlton Jones ran for 108 yards and a touchdown for Army. Zac Dahman, starting his first game for the Black Knights this season, was 12 of 26 for 214 yards. Dahman threw a 54 yard pass to Jacob Murphy on the second play of Army's first possession, and Tielor Robinson scored on a 3 yard run three plays later, giving the Black Knights their first lead of the season at 7-0. On Army's next possession, Dahman hit Walter Hill with a 35 yard pass to move to the TCU 10. That set up Carlton Jones' 10 yard TD run, extending the Black Knights' lead to 14 points. Austin Miller later capped a 13-play drive with a 25 yard field goal, pushing Army's lead to 17-0 with 2:28 left in the first quarter. An 11 yard touchdown run by Hobbs capped a 75 yard drive and gave TCU its first score with 5:58 left in the third quarter. On its next possession, TCU mounted an 89 yard drive capped by Hassell's 29 yard TD pass to Cody McCarty.

CINCINNATI

The Black Knights snapped the nation's longest losing streak at 19 games Saturday, with Tielor Robinson scoring five touchdowns and Carlton Jones running for 180 yards in a 48-29 victory over Cincinnati. Robinson scored his fifth touchdown on a 93 yard pass from Zac Dahman with 11:32 left to secure the win for Army. Robinson ran for 82 yards as Army amassed 284 yards on the ground and had

111 yards receiving. Thousands of West Point cadets swarmed the field and tore down the goal posts in celebration.

AIR FORCE

Adam Fitch for 115 yards and a touchdown to lead Air Force to a 31-22 win over Army on Saturday. Darnell Stephens added two TDs for the Falcons who amassed 345 yards rushing. Carlton Jones ran for 213 yards and 2 touchdowns to lead Army. Army took a 6-0 lead when Jones broke a 69 yard TD run on the third play of the game. Austin Miller's 47-year field goal on the next possession gave Army a nine-point lead. Air Force, held to just 50 total yards in the first quarter, got the board in the second when Fitch capped a seven-play drive with a 16 yard touchdown. Chris Sutton's interception of Zac Dahman set up the Falcons' next score. Stephens scored from 5 yards out to put Air Force up 14-9 with 8:23 left in the half. After exchanging touchdowns, Army took a 22 21 lead with 17 seconds left in the half on Dahman's 16 yard TD pass to Jacob Murphy. Stephens scored his second TD on a 5 yard run to cap an 11 play drive in the third, giving Air Force a six-point lead with 5:03 remaining in the quarter. Michael Greenaway added a 25 yard field goal with 5:48 remaining to seal the victory for the Falcons.

NAVY {@ Lincoln Financial Field, Philadelphia, PA}

Senior fullback Kyle Eckel rushed for a career-high 179 yards and one touchdown, senior quarterback Aaron Polanco threw for two touchdowns and rushed for another and senior safety Josh Smith came up with a team-high 12 tackles and intercepted a pass returning it 67 yards for a touchdown as Navy dominated Army for the third-consecutive year, 42-13, in front of a sellout crowd of 67,882 that included President George W. Bush at Lincoln Financial Field in Philadelphia. The victory gave Navy the Commander-In-Chief's Trophy, which is presented annually to the winner of the football competition among the three major service academies and is named in honor of the President of the United States, for the second-consecutive year. It is just the second time in school history that Navy has won the trophy two-straight years (1978-79). After a scoreless first quarter, Navy exploded for 28-consecutive points. Polanco got things going with a 10 yard touchdown run with 14:23 remaining in the second quarter and then Eckel, who was named the Philadelphia Sportswriters Most Valuable Player for the second-consecutive year, followed with a 23 yard romp on Navy's next possession. Smith would put the game away on Army's next possession when he intercepted a Zac Dahman pass and returned it 67 yards for a touchdown. Mick Yokitis caught a 12 yard touchdown toss from Polanco with 1:15 left in the half to make it 28-0.

2005 Army Black Knights

In their second season under head coach Bobby Ross, the Black Knights compiled a 4-7 record and were outscored by their opponents by a combined total of 294 to 220. In the annual Army–Navy Game, the Black Knights lost to Navy, 42-23.

Zac Dahman led the team in passing with 1,864 yards and threw 11 touchdown passes. Carlton Jones led the team in rushing with 1,024 yards. Scott Wesley led with 10 rushing touchdowns. Jeremy Trimble led the team in receptions with 42 for 535 yards. Caleb Campbell led the team with 5 interceptions. Wesley led the team in scoring with 66 points.

Home games were played at Michie Stadium

9/10/2005	ARMY	@	Boston College (9-3)	7	44	L
9/17/2005	ARMY	vs	BAYLOR (5-6)	10	20	L
9/23/2005	ARMY	vs	IOWA STATE (7-5)	21	28	L
10/1/2005	ARMY	vs	CONNECTICUT (5-6)	13	47	L
10/8/2005	ARMY	vs	CENTRAL MICHIGAN (6-5)	10	14	L
10/15/2005	ARMY	@	Tcu (11-1)	17	38	L
10/22/2005	ARMY	@	Akron (7-6)	20	0	W
11/5/2005	ARMY	@	Air Force (4-7)	27	24	W
11/12/2005	ARMY	vs	MASSACHUSETTS	34	27	W
11/19/2005	ARMY	vs	ARKANSAS STATE (6-6)	38	10	W
12/3/2005	ARMY	vs	NAVY (8-4)	23	42	L
Coach: Bobby Ross			**Season Record >>**	220	294	4-7

Schedule Source: Steve's Football Bible LLC

Selected game(s) highlights

Air Force

Carlton Jones ran for 146 yards and a touchdown, and Army forced a late fumble to preserve a 27-24 victory over Air Force. Army, which ended an eight-game losing streak against the Falcons and beat Air Force at the academy for the first time in 28 years. Scott Wesley ran for two second half touchdowns for Army. Army took a 3-0 lead on Justin Koenig's 39 yard field goal after Michael Herndon blocked a punt by Chris Carp on Air Force's first possession. The lead changed twice in the second quarter, with Jones running for a 22 yard touchdown for Army. Shaun Carney came right back with a 34 yard touchdown pass to Jason Brown, putting the Falcons ahead 14-10. Army pulled within one point on Koenig's 22 yard field goal, but he missed a 28 yard attempt that would have given it the lead. Army took a 20-14 lead in the third quarter when Wesley broke a tackle at the 5 and ran into the end zone on fourth down. Wesley's 1 yard TD run capped an 11-play, 75 yard drive to put Army ahead 27-17.

MASSACHUSETTS

Zac Dahman completed five passes in the game-winning 61 yard drive that was capped by a 10 yard touchdown strike to Walter Hill with 3:02 to play. Dahman finished 22-of-27 for 224 yards and two TDs. Jeremy Trimble caught seven passes for 86 yards and one TD and Scott Wesley had seven carries for 72 yards and one TD. Army's defense held UMass to just 11 first downs and 275 total yards. The Black Knights also held the ball for 34:58, almost 10 minutes more than the Minutemen. Liam Coen's interception at the beginning of the fourth quarter led to an 11 yard TD run by Carlton Jones. Dahman's pass to Hill on the 2-point conversion gave the Black Knights a 27-20 lead. The Minutemen came back to tie the game when they forced a fumble on fourth-and-1 at the Army 37 with just over 10 minutes remaining. Shannon James picked up the fumble, which slipped through the hands of Dahman and Wesley, and ran it in for the TD.

ARKANSAS STATE

Carlton Jones ran for a season-high 187 yards and two touchdowns Saturday, and the resurgent Black Knights beat Arkansas States 38-10 for their fourth straight victory. Arkansas State fell behind 28-3 at halftime as Army repeatedly pinned the Indians deep in their own territory. Jones scored on runs of 24 and 4 yards in the first quarter and had 131 yards by halftime. Army gained a season-high 300 yards rushing while holding Arkansas State to 165. The Black Knights struck in the 2nd quarter when Army's Kenny Rackers hit punt return man James Johnson and forced a fumble that was recovered by Army's Nicholas Lopez at the Arkansas State 37. Four plays later, Zac Dahman hit Corey Anderson with a 15 yard touchdown pass in the right corner of the end zone with 6:09 left in the half for a 21-3 lead. Scott Wesley scored on a 21 yard run 2:11 before the break.

NAVY {@ Lincoln Financial Field, Philadelphia, PA}

Senior quarterback Lamar Owens rushed for 99 yards and three touchdowns, while sophomore fullback Adam Ballard rumbled for 192 yards and two touchdowns as Navy trounced Army for the fourth-consecutive year, 42-23, in front of a sold out crowd at Lincoln Financial Field (69,322). The win gives Navy the series lead, 50-49-7, for the first time since 1991. The Navy offense, which scored on six-straight possessions, set two Army-Navy game records as the Midshipmen rushed for 490 yards and ran up 531 yards of total offense on a defense that came in ranked 23rd in the nation.

The game turned late in the second quarter with Navy leading 14-10. Rob Caldwell and Keenan Little dropped Army running back Carlton Jones for no gain on a third-and-one play from the Army 40 and forced a West Point punt. The Midshipmen took the ball over at their own 34 yard line with 1:15 left and promptly moved down the field in eight plays with Owens capping the drive off with a one yard dive to make the score 21-10. Army got the ball to start the second half and Caldwell once again stopped Jones for no gain on third and one and forced an Army punt. The Midshipmen moved right down the field, marching 75 yards on seven plays with Ballard putting the nail in Army's coffin with a 28 yard touchdown run. Ballard would later answer an Army touchdown with a 67 yard touchdown run on the first play from scrimmage to make the score 42-17. Reggie Campbell and Marco Nelson didn't let Owens and Ballard have all the fun, as Campbell rushed for 60 yards and a touchdown on three carries, while Nelson rushed for 77 yards on seven carries. Jake Biles led the Navy defense with 13 tackles, while Little and Caldwell recorded 10 tackles each. David Mahoney had three tackles for a loss. Owens was named the Philadelphia Sports Writers Association Most Valuable Player for his efforts, marking the fourth-consecutive year that a Navy player has taken home the honor.

2006 Army Black Knights

In their third season under head coach Bobby Ross, the Black Knights compiled a 3-9 record and were outscored by their opponents by a combined total of 335 to 232. In the annual Army–Navy Game, the Black Knights lost to Navy, 26-14.

David Pevoto led the team in passing with 1,012 yards and threw 6 touchdown passes. Wesley McMahand led the team in rushing with 654 yards. Tony Moore led with 5 rushing touchdowns. Jeremy Trimble led the team in receptions with 52 for 534 yards. Austin Miller led the team in scoring with 52 points.

Home games were played at Michie Stadium

9/2/2006	ARMY	@	Arkansas State (6-6)	6	14	L
9/9/2006	ARMY	vs	KENT (6-6)	17	14	W
9/16/2006	ARMY	@	Texas A&M (9-4)	24	28	L
9/23/2006	ARMY	@	Baylor (4-8)	27	20	W
9/30/2006	ARMY	vs	RICE (7-6)	14	48	L
10/7/2006	ARMY	vs	VMI	62	7	W
10/14/2006	ARMY	@	Connecticut (4-8)	7	21	L
10/21/2006	ARMY	vs	TCU (11-2)	17	31	L
10/28/2006	ARMY	@	Tulane (4-8)	28	42	L
11/3/2006	ARMY	vs	AIR FORCE (4-8)	7	43	L
11/18/2006	ARMY	@	Notre Dame (10-3)	9	41	L
12/2/2006	ARMY	vs	NAVY (9-4)	14	26	L
Coach: Bobby Ross			**Season Record >>**	232	335	3-9

Schedule Source: Steve's Football Bible LLC

Selected game(s) highlights

KENT STATE

Miller made a 36 yard field goal in overtime to give Army a 17-14 victory over Kent State on Saturday. Trailing 14-7, the Golden Flashes tied it with 3:55 remaining in regulation when Edelman lofted a 15 yard pass into the left corner of the end zone to Najah Pruden. Army erased a 7-0 deficit in the first half on two touchdown runs by Tony Moore. Moore's second TD was a 6 yard run on fourth-and-2 that went off left tackle with seven minutes remaining in the second quarter. Wesley McMahand rushed 19 times for 90 yards to lead Army. Kent State scored on a trick play on its first possession. The Golden Flashes lined up for a 34 yard field goal attempt 8:17 into the game, but holder Darren Rogers grabbed the long snap and ran left, untouched into the end zone for a 17 yard score. The Golden Flashes twice threatened inside the Army 20 in the second half but could not score.

VIRGINIA MILITARY INSTITUTE

The Black Knights scored on five of their first six possessions and beat VMI, 62-7. Jeremy Trimble returned a punt 76 yards for a touchdown and caught a TD pass. The Black Knights totaled 426 yards of offense, while holding the Keydets to 191 yards. Five players scored rushing TDs for Army. Army's David Pevoto was 9-for-13 passing for 114 yards.

AIR FORCE

Adam Zanotti returned a fumble 98 yards and Air Force took advantage of an amazing array of mistakes by Army, scoring a school-record 36 points in the second quarter and embarrassing the Black Knights 43-7 at Michie Stadium. This one proved no contest when Army committed turnovers on four consecutive plays from scrimmage in the first half, giving the game away and any chance at the Commander-in-Chief's Trophy.

NAVY {@ Lincoln Financial Field, Philadelphia, PA}

The Navy defense scored nine fourth-quarter points on an interception and safety and set up three more points with a second interception, as Navy blew open a tight game and went on to defeat Army for the fifth-consecutive year, 26-14, in front of a sold-out crowd of 69,943 at Philadelphia's Lincoln Financial Field.

The score was tied at seven at the half, but the Midshipmen scored on their first possession of the second half to take the lead for good when senior Jason Tomlinson scored on a 33 yard reverse. The Navy defense took over from there, holding Army to just 59 yards on its first five possessions. Junior nickel back Jeff Deliz picked off his first-career pass on Army's first drive of the fourth quarter, setting up a 35 yard field goal by sophomore Matt Harmon that gave Navy a 17-7 lead. Three plays later, senior Keenan Little picked off a Carson Williams pass and rumbled 40 yards for a touchdown to give the Midshipmen an insurmountable 24-7 lead with 5:22 remaining. The Navy defense, however, was not finished scoring as senior outside linebacker Tyler Tidwell recorded sacks on consecutive plays, the second one in the end zone for a safety.

Army scored a meaningless touchdown with two seconds left to cut the final margin to 12. Sophomore fullback Eric Kettani, who entered the game on Navy's first series after junior starter Adam Ballard went out with a broken right leg, led the Midshipmen with 67 yards rushing on 15 carries. Sophomore quarterback Kaipo-Noa Kaheaku-Enhada added 64 yards on 15 carries. Junior slot back Reggie Campbell, who scored Navy's first touchdown of the day on a nine yard touchdown run, carried the ball six times for 26 yards. The Navy defense was led by senior Rob Caldwell, who recorded 11 tackles. Little had seven tackles to go along with his interception, while Tidwell and sophomore Clint Sovie were also in on seven tackles. Tomlinson was named the Philadelphia Sportswriters Association Most Valuable Player.

2007 Army Black Knights

The Black Knights, led by first-year head coach Stan Brock, compiled a 3-9 record and were outscored by their opponents by a combined total of 364 to 203. In the annual Army–Navy Game, the Black Knights lost to Navy, 38-3.

Carson Williams led the team in passing with 1,779 yards and threw 11 touchdown passes. Tony Dace led the team in rushing with 330 yards. Jeremy Trimble led the team in receptions with 62 for 912 yards and 7 TD receptions. Trimble led the team in scoring with 48 points.

Home games were played at Michie Stadium

9/1/2007	ARMY	@	Akron (4-8)	14	22	L
9/8/2007	ARMY	vs	RHODE ISLAND	14	7	W
9/15/2007	ARMY	@	Wake Forest (9-4)	10	21	L
9/22/2007	ARMY	@	Boston College (11-3)	17	37	L
9/29/2007	ARMY	vs	TEMPLE (4-8)	37	21	W
10/6/2007	ARMY	vs	TULANE (4-8)	20	17	W
10/13/2007	ARMY	@	Central Michigan (8-6)	23	47	L
10/20/2007	ARMY	@	Georgia Tech (7-6)	10	34	L
11/3/2007	ARMY	@	Air Force (9-4)	10	30	L
11/9/2007	ARMY	vs	RUTGERS (8-5)	6	41	L
11/17/2007	ARMY	vs	TULSA (10-4)	39	49	L
12/1/2007	ARMY	vs	NAVY (8-5)	3	38	L
Coach: Stan Brock			**Season Record >>**	203	364	3-9

Schedule Source: Steve's Football Bible LLC

Selected game(s) highlights

TULANE {Miracle at Michie}

Army trailed Tulane 17-7 with less than 2 minutes to play and was down to third string walk-on senior QB Kevin Dunn, who had thrown one pass in his whole career... He connected on a Hail Mary with no time left to tie the game and Army won in OT. Dunn, a senior, is Army's second-string quarterback. He had thrown one pass in his career before playing Tulane. It was Kevin Dunn's first 2-minute drill at Army. It was also his first touchdown pass. Dunn completed a deflected 36 yard pass to Mike Wright as time expired to send the game into overtime, and Owen Tolson kicked a 25 yard field goal from the left hash to complete a 20-17 comeback over Tulane on Saturday night.

Trailing 17-10 and starting from the Army 20 yard line with 29 seconds remaining, Dunn completed passes of 27 and 17 yards to get to the Tulane 36 before spiking the ball with 4 seconds remaining. On the next snap, Dunn lofted a high pass to the back of the end zone. As the West Point cannon sounded signifying the clock reaching 0:00, the ball was deflected by two defenders and Wright came racing in to make a diving catch, dragging his feet just inside the end line. It was Wright's first career TD reception and only his second catch of the game. The Corps of Cadets rushed the field to join the celebration of Army's second overtime win this season.

Air Force

Chad Hall ran for a school-record 275 yards and a touchdown, leading Air Force over Army 30-10. The Falcons scored the game's first touchdown when Shaun Carney connected with wide receiver Spencer

Armstrong on a 48 yard pass at the beginning of the second quarter. Despite the yards, Hall didn't score until his 58 yard run in the third quarter set up a 1 yard touchdown run that gave the Falcons a two-possession lead. Army only managed 181 yards of total offense, including just 17 yards rushing. The Black Knights' touchdown came after linebacker Frank Scappaticci intercepted Carney at the Air Force 24 and returned it to the 3. Carson Williams found tight end Ernie Bernal in the end zone for a 2 yard touchdown pass three plays later to tie it.

NAVY {@ M&T Bank Stadium, Baltimore, MD}

Senior slot back Reggie Campbell piled up 227 all-purpose yards and two touchdowns to lead Navy to a 38-3 victory over Army in front of 71,610 fans at M&T Bank Stadium in Baltimore. The victory was the Midshipmen' sixth-straight over Army. Navy broke the game open over the final 7:31 of the second half. Army cut Navy's lead to 7-3 on a 28 yard field goal by Owen Tolson, but Campbell returned the ensuing kickoff 98 yards for a touchdown. The return was the second longest in school history and tied an Army-Navy game record.

On Army's first play after the Campbell return, junior defensive end Michael Walsh drilled Army's Wesley McMahand in the backfield, separating the ball from McMahand in the process. Senior linebacker Irv Spencer recovered the fumble at the Army six yard line. Three plays later, Shun White scored from one yard out to make the score 21-3 with 5:49 left. After the two teams traded punts, the Midshipmen were able to get the ball back one more time after Army threw the ball on third-and-one from its own 36. When the pass sailed out of bounds with 11 seconds to go, it forced the Black Knights to punt to Campbell. Campbell returned the punt 46 yards before being tackled at the Army 34 yard line. With one second left, senior Joey Bullen came on and nailed a 51 yard field goal into a tough wind to give Navy an insurmountable 24-3 lead at the half. The field goal by Bullen was the second longest in school history.

The Navy defense pitched a shutout in the second half and the offense picked up 14 more points as Campbell scored on a 12 yard touchdown run and Jarod Bryant scored on a one yard run. Bryant's touchdown was set up by a blocked punt by Bobby Doyle. Navy's defense played its best contest of the year, holding Army to just 217 yards of total offense, including just 100 yards on the ground on 40 carries. Walsh led the way for the Midshipmen with eight tackles, two tackles for a loss and a forced fumble. Ross Pospisil recorded seven stops and a fumble recovery, while Spencer had five tackles, a tackle for a loss, a fumble recovery and two pass break-ups. The Navy rushing attack, which came in averaging a nation's best 357.4 yards per game, was held to just 287 yards on 61 attempts. Senior fullback Adam Ballard rushed for 56 yards on 13 carries, while Zerbin Singleton rushed for 55 yards and a touchdown on five carries. Singleton's touchdown was a 38 yard dash down the right sideline that put Navy up 7-0 in the first quarter. Campbell added 47 yards on five carries. The Midshipmen attempted just five passes, completing two for seven yards.

2008 Army Black Knights

The team was led by second-year head coach Stan Brock (pictured at right), who, amidst pressure from critics, had changed from a pro-style offense to a triple option-like offensive scheme after the previous season. Some pundits dubbed it the "Brock Bone" or "quadruple" option, due to an added passing element. The team finished the season with a disappointing 3–9 record, which culminated in a 34–0 rout by archrival Navy. Brock was subsequently fired and replaced by former Cal Poly head coach, Rich Ellerson. The 2008 Army–Navy Game was the first shut-out of Army by Navy since 1978. One consolation was that in the game's final play, Army fullback Collin Mooney, in the last play of his college football career, broke the school record for single season rushing by a single yard.

Chip Bowden led the team in passing with 282 yards. Collin Mooney led the team in rushing with 1,339 yards and 8 rushing touchdowns. Jameson Carter and Damion Hunter led the team in receptions with 11. Carter led with 157 receiving yards. Mooney led the team in scoring with 48 points.

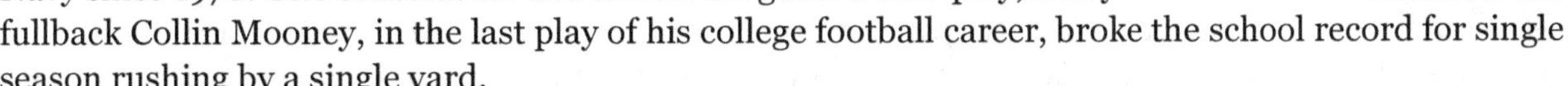

Home games were played at Michie Stadium

8/29/2008	ARMY	vs	TEMPLE (5-7)	7	35	L
9/6/2008	ARMY	vs	NEW HAMPSHIRE	10	28	L
9/20/2008	ARMY	vs	AKRON (5-7)	3	22	L
9/27/2008	ARMY	@	Texas A&M (4-8)	17	21	L
10/4/2008	ARMY	@	Tulane (2-10)	44	13	W
10/11/2008	ARMY	vs	EASTERN MICHIGAN (3-9)	17	13	W
10/18/2008	ARMY	@	Buffalo (8-6)	24	27	L
10/25/2008	ARMY	vs	LOUISIANA TECH (8-5)	14	7	W
11/1/2008	ARMY	vs	AIR FORCE (8-5)	7	16	L
11/8/2008	ARMY	@	Rice (10-3)	31	38	L
11/22/2008	ARMY	@	Rutgers (8-5)	3	30	L
12/6/2008	ARMY	vs	NAVY (8-5)	0	34	L
Coach: Stan Brock			**Season Record >>**	177	284	3-9

Schedule Source: Steve's Football Bible LLC

Selected game(s) highlights

EASTERN MICHIGAN

Collin Mooney had his second straight career high on Saturday with 229 yards rushing. He helped set up Chip Bowden's decisive 9 yard scoring run early in the fourth quarter as Army rallied past Eastern Michigan 17-13 for its second straight victory. Mooney's 54 yard run off right tackle early in the third quarter set up Matthew Campbell's 18 yard field goal that moved Army within 13-10. Army drove 80 yards for the winning score. Mooney gained 48 yards on eight carries to set up Bowden's keeper around the right side after Eastern Michigan's defenders keyed on Mooney's fake up the middle.

LOUISIANA TECH

Ian Smith scored two touchdowns and Army had five sacks for the second consecutive week as the Black Knights earned a 14-7 victory over Louisiana Tech. The Black Knights stopped six other rushes for losses. Army limited Louisiana Tech to 68 yards rushing. Smith, a junior who totaled 17 yards on four carries in six games this season, ran four times for 41 yards and caught a touchdown pass. Collin Mooney led the Black Knights with 57 yards rushing on 17 carries. Army finished with 203 yards rushing. The Black Knights limited the Bulldogs to 18 yards on 19 rushes in the first half. Josh McNary had two sacks. Frank Scappaticci's sack forced a fumble that Fritz Bentler recovered at Louisiana Tech's 18 yard line, setting up Smith's 1 yard TD run with 3:20 to go in the first quarter. Army went up for good when Smith caught a 2 yard pass from quarterback Chip Bowden with 10 minutes remaining.

AIR FORCE

Ryan Harrison kicked three field goals, Tim Jefferson scored on a 1 yard run, and Air Force held off Army 16-7. It was the sixth straight win at Michie Stadium for the Falcons. Harrison kicked field goals of 21, 29 and 48 yards, and averaged 41 yards on eight punts as Army threw for a 47 yard touchdown on the third play of the game. The Falcons led 10-7 halftime lead despite being outgained 148-104 and netting just 72 yards rushing.

NAVY {@ Lincoln Financial Field, Philadelphia, PA}

Senior slot back Shun White and senior fullback Eric Kettani combined for 273 yards rushing and three touchdowns, while the Navy defense held the Army offense to 154 yards of total offense as Navy blasted Army for the seventh-straight year, 34-0, in front of a sold-out crowd of 69,144 at Lincoln Financial Field in Philadelphia. It was Navy's first shutout against Army since 1978. Navy jumped out to a 7-0 lead on the third play of the game when White ran 65 yards off an option pitch from quarterback Kaipo-Noa Kaheaku-Enhada. The Midshipmen made it 10-0 on their third drive of the game when Matt Harmon drilled a 23 yard field goal and went up 17-0 right before the half when Kaheaku-Enhada hit White with an 18 yard touchdown pass.

Navy put the game away with a methodical drive to open the third quarter, marching 72 yards on 14 plays and taking 7:52 off the clock. Kettani ended the drive with a five yard touchdown run and the rout was on. White was the recipient of the 2008 Philadelphia Sports Congress MVP Award for his efforts. The Navy defense was superb all day, holding the Black Knights to just seven first downs. Fifty of Army's 154 yards of total offense came during mop up time in the fourth quarter. Navy's front three of Nate Frazier, Matt Nechak and Jabaree Tuani dominated the Army offensive line and created havoc all day for the Army offense. Frazier was second on the team in tackles with seven, while recording1.5 tackles for a loss and deflecting a pass.

Junior linebacker Ross Pospisil led the Midshipmen with 12 tackles and a forced fumble, while junior outside linebacker Ram Vela had six tackles, a sack and intercepted Army quarterback Chip Bowden's pass and returned it 68 yards for a touchdown. Navy played the game with a heavy heart as it was without the services of senior cornerback Rashawn King who returned home to Raleigh, N.C. on Friday morning to be with his family after the sudden death of his father, Drexel, who suffered a heart attack Thursday night. In memory of Mr. King, the Navy football team wore a sticker on the back of its helmets with the initials DK inside of a black crown.

2009 Army Black Knights

Led by first-year head coach Rich Ellerson (pictured at right), the Black Knights finished the season with a record of 5–7 and were outscored by their opponents by a combined total of 263 to 184. In the annual Army–Navy Game, the Black Knights lost to Navy, 17-3.

Trent Steelman led the team in passing with 637 yards. Steelman led the team in rushing with 706 yards and 5 rushing touchdowns. Alejandro Villanueva led the team in receptions with 34 for 522 yards and 5 TD receptions. Alex Carlton led the team in scoring with 67 points. **Josh McNary set a new team record for sacks with 12.5. McNary set the single game record with 4 sacks vs Temple. Carlton tied the single season record for field goals with 18.**

Home games were played at Michie Stadium

9/5/2009	ARMY	@	Eastern Michigan (0-12)	27	14	W	
9/12/2009	ARMY	vs	DUKE (5-7)	19	35	L	
9/19/2009	ARMY	vs	BALL STATE (2-10)	24	17	W	
9/26/2009	ARMY	@	Iowa State (7-6)	10	31	L	
10/3/2009	ARMY	vs	TULANE (3-9)	16	17	L	
10/10/2009	ARMY	vs	VANDERBILT (2-10)	16	13	W	
10/17/2009	ARMY	@	Temple (9-4)	13	27	L	*McNary 4 sacks
10/23/2009	ARMY	vs	RUTGERS (9-4)	10	27	L	
11/7/2009	ARMY	@	Air Force (8-5)	7	35	L	
11/14/2009	ARMY	vs	VMI	22	17	W	
11/21/2009	ARMY	@	North Texas (2-10)	17	13	W	
12/12/2009	ARMY	vs	NAVY (10-4)	3	17	L	
Coach: Rich Ellerson			**Season Record >>**	**184**	**263**	**5-7**	

Schedule Source: Steve's Football Bible LLC
***-Single game record**

Selected game(s) highlights

VANDERBILT

Alex Carlton kicked a 42 yard field goal in overtime, giving Army a 16-13 victory over Vanderbilt. The field goal, which hit the left upright, was Carlton's third of the game. He also kicked a 51 yarder in the second quarter, Army's longest field goal since 1994. Vanderbilt forced the game into overtime when Ryan Fowler hit a 41 yard field goal with less than 52 seconds remaining for a 13-13 tie. The Commodores' opening possession of overtime fell short when Andrew Rodriguez forced Warren Norman to fumble at the 1 yard line, with the ball falling into the end zone for a touchback. Quarterback Trent Steelman led Army with 97 yards rushing on 25 carries. Army opened the scoring with that 51 yard field goal with 6:22 remaining in the first half. Steelman surged into the end zone for a 2 yard touchdown just 46 seconds into the final quarter for a 10-3 Army lead. Donovan Travis' fourth interception of the season set up Carlton's 23 yard field goal midway through the fourth quarter to give Army a 13-10 advantage.

North Texas

Quarterback Trent Steelman rushed for 132 yards and the winning touchdown with 1:43 left. The Black Knights forced five turnovers and Marcus Hilton blocked a field goal attempt to set up Steelman's 2 yard run. Army was down 13-10 when it turned the ball over on downs at its 36 with 5:29 left. North Texas could have gone ahead by two scores with a touchdown but had to settle for Jeremy Knott's 33 yard try. After the block, Steelman broke down the left sideline for a 55 yard run, then scored the winning TD two plays later. Ty Shrader intercepted Riley Dodge with 1:31 remaining to clinch things.

Air Force

Kevin Fogler caught a 73 yard TD pass and Anthony Wright returned a punt 88 yards for a score, helping Air Force beat Army for a fourth straight time with a 35-7 victory. Asher Clark rushed for two second half scores as the Falcons broke open a tight game to become bowl eligible. Trent Steelman rushed for 102 yards and a touchdown for the Black Knights. Air Force pulled away in the second half, scoring on four of their five drives. Clark got the offense rolling right after halftime, finding a hole in Army's defense and racing 36 yards for his first touchdown of the season. He later added another on an 8 yard burst. Fogler got behind the Black Knights' secondary late in the third quarter and Tim Jefferson hit him in stride. Fogler zigzagged his way into the end zone.

NAVY {@ Lincoln Financial Field, Philadelphia, PA}

The Navy defense kept Army out of the end zone for the third-consecutive year, while junior quarterback Ricky Dobbs ran for a touchdown and threw for another as the Midshipmen beat the Black Knights for the eighth-consecutive time, 17-3, in front of 69,541 at Lincoln Financial Field in Philadelphia. The win gave Navy the Commander-In-Chief's Trophy for the seventh-straight year. The Navy defense was dominant all day, allowing Army just 187 yards of total offense. Army's only score came in the first quarter when Dobbs was intercepted by Army's Steve Erzinger at the Navy 28, and he returned it 16 yards to the Navy 12.

Army could manage just six yards on three plays and had to settle for an Alex Carlton field goal. Navy hurt itself in the first half with missed assignments and penalties, but finally settled down in the third quarter. Dobbs led Navy on an 11 play, 68 yard drive to start the third quarter and capped the drive by hitting a wide open Marcus Curry with a 25 yard touchdown pass to give Navy a 7-3 lead. The Midshipmen made it 10-3 on their next possession, marching 55 yards on 12 plays with Joe Buckley nailing a 36 yard field goal. The Navy defense set up the final score with linebacker Ross Pospisil knocking the ball out of the hands of Army fullback Kingsley Ehie at the Army 32 yard line and outside linebacker Craig Schaefer picking the ball up and running it down to the Army 12 yard line. Four plays later Dobbs scored from the one, giving him his 24th rushing touchdown of the season, an NCAA record for a quarterback.

Dobbs, who was named the Philadelphia Sportswriter's Most Valuable Player, rushed for 113 yards and a touchdown on 33 carries and completed three of his seven pass attempts for 61 yards and a touchdown. Pospisil and Jabaree Tuani led the Navy defense with seven tackles and a tackle for a loss each. Tony Haberer recorded six tackles and a tackle for a loss, while Emmett Merchant (forced fumble, pass broken up), Chase Burge and Schaefer (fumble recovery, pass broken up) had five stops each. Ram Vela had another big day with four tackles, two tackles for a loss, a sack and an interception.

2010 Army Black Knights

The Black Knights, led by second-year head coach Rich Ellerson. By winning six regular season games, Army became bowl-eligible for the first time since the 1996 season. They were invited to the Armed Forces Bowl in University Park, Texas, replacing a team from the Mountain West Conference. They defeated SMU, 16–14, in the bowl game to finish the season 7–6, their first winning season since 1996.

Trent Steelman led the team in passing with 995 yards and threw 7 touchdown passes. Jared Hassin led the team in rushing with 1,013 yards. Steelman led with 11 rushing touchdowns. David Brooks and George Jordan led the team in receptions with 15. Brooks led with 238 receiving yards. Donovan Travis led the team with 5 interceptions. Alex Carlton led the team in scoring with 86 points.

Home games were played at Michie Stadium

9/4/2010	ARMY	@	Eastern Michigan (2-10)	31	27	W	
9/11/2010	ARMY	vs	HAWAII (10-4)	28	31	L	
9/18/2010	ARMY	vs	NORTH TEXAS (3-9)	24	0	W	
9/25/2010	ARMY	@	Duke (3-9)	35	21	W	
10/2/2010	ARMY	vs	TEMPLE (8-4)	35	42	L	
10/9/2010	ARMY	@	Tulane (4-8)	41	23	W	
10/16/2010	ARMY	@	Rutgers (4-8)	20	23	L	
10/30/2010	ARMY	vs	VMI	29	7	W	
11/6/2010	ARMY	vs	AIR FORCE (9-4)	22	42	L	
11/13/2010	ARMY	@	Kent (5-7)	45	28	W	
11/20/2010	ARMY	vs	NOTRE DAME (8-5)	3	27	L	
12/11/2010	ARMY	vs	NAVY (9-4)	17	31	L	
12/30/2010	**ARMY**	**vs**	**SMU (7-7)**	**16**	**14**	**W**	**Armed Forces Bowl**
Coach: Rich Ellerson			**Season Record >>**	346	316	7-6	

Selected game(s) highlights

HAWAII

Scott Enos kicked a 31 yard field goal with 7 seconds remaining in the game to propel Hawai'i to a 31–28 come-from-behind victory over Army. Hawai'i jumped out to a 21–0 lead on quarterback Bryant Moniz's three touchdown passes. But Army rallied with four straight touchdowns of its own, including two by Malcom Brown. The Rainbow Warriors had the final say as they scored late in the third quarter to tie the game. Army was positioning itself for a game-winning field goal when backup quarterback Max Jenkins fumbled the ball while trying to run to the middle of the field to gain position for a field goal attempt. The ball was recovered by the Hawai'i defense. The offense then drove down the field and set up the winning kick.

Duke

The Black Knights got off to a 14–0 start after short TD runs by Brian Cobbs and quarterback Trent Steelman and never looked back. Cobbs finished the game with 2 touchdown runs and Army 248 yards rushing while the Black Knights took advantage of 5 Duke turnovers. Steelman accounted for 62 of Army's rushing yards as well as threw for 85 including his first 2 TD passes of the season to go along with his rushing score. Army nearly doubled up Duke in time-of-possession with the Black Knights holding a 39.57–20.03 advantage for the contest. The win for the Black Knights ended a seven-game losing streak against ACC opponents.

Tulane

Army won its third road game of the season in a 41–23 victory at the Louisiana Superdome against Tulane. Jared Hassin paced Army with 144 yards rushing and 2 TD runs. Quarterback

Trent Steelman also rushed for 85 yards and a score while also throwing a touchdown pass to Davyd Brooks. Steelman only needed to attempt 5 passes all game as the Black Knights torched the Green Wave for 312 yards rushing.

AIR FORCE

Tim Jefferson hit Jonathan Warzeka on touchdown passes of 53 and 63 yards, and Jordan Waiwaiole returned a fumble 63 yards for another score as Air Force beat Army 42-22 to win the Commander-in-Chief's Trophy for the 17th time. Army (5-4) gained a 6-0 lead on field goals of 30 and 41 yards by Alex Carlton before Jefferson got the Falcons going. He scored on a 3 yard run on the first play of the second quarter and hit Warzeka for a 53 yard score to give the Falcons a lead they never relinquished. The Black Knights lost any chance at a comeback when Waiwaiole scooped up a fumble near midfield by Jared Hassin and ran it back 52 yards for a score and a commanding 35-16 lead with 12:39 left. Air Force finished with 277 yards rushing to Army's 244.

NAVY {@ Lincoln Financial Field, Philadelphia, PA}

Senior safety Wyatt Middleton's 98 yard fumble return for a touchdown with 1:03 remaining in the second quarter turned what was shaping up to be a close game into a rout as Navy rolled to its ninth win of the year and ninth-straight win over Army, 31-17, at a sold out (69,223) Lincoln Financial Field in Philadelphia. The 98 yard fumble return was the longest in school history and longest in an Army-Navy game. For his heroics, Middleton was named the Philadelphia Sportswriters Most Valuable Player.

Navy had jumped out to a 17-0 lead as Joe Bukley nailed a 36 yard field goal and quarterback Ricky Dobbs threw touchdown passes of 77 yards to John Howell and 32 yards to Brandon Turner. The touchdown pass to Howell was the longest pass play in series history. The Midshipmen were in total control of the game midway through the second quarter until a pair of Dobbs turnovers gave Army life. Dobbs fumbled the ball on first down from his own 23 and it was recovered by Army's Josh McNary. Six plays later, Army quarterback Trent Steelman hit Malcolm Brown with a five yard touchdown pass to cut the Navy lead to 17-7. It was Army's first touchdown against the Midshipmen since the fourth quarter of the 2006 game. Three plays later, Dobbs gave the ball back to Army again as he was stripped by McNary and Stephen Anderson recovered the loose ball at the Army 48. The Black Knights methodically moved the ball down the field, taking it 49 yards in 11 plays. On first and goal from the Navy three, Steelman tried to power his way into the end zone, but senior linebacker Tyler Simmons and senior outside linebacker Jerry Hauburger met Steelman at the two yard line and Simmons' knocked the ball from Steelman's hands. The ball popped up in the air and flew right to Middleton who raced 98 yards for the back-breaking touchdown.

Army took the opening kickoff of the third quarter and drove 47 yards on 12 plays with Alex Carlton capping the drive with a 42 yard field goal to make the score 24-10. Navy put the game away with a 13 play, 87 yard, 9:03 scoring drive to start the fourth quarter with slot back Gee Gee Greene waltzing in from the 25 to make it 31-10. Dobbs led the Navy offense with 54 yards rushing on 20 carries. He completed six of his 11 passes for 186 yards with two touchdowns and one interception. Slot back Aaron Santiago had two catches for 54 yards, while wide receiver Greg Jones caught two passes for 23 yards. Simmons paced the Navy defense with 13 tackles and two forced fumbles, while sophomore Matt Warrick, making his first-career start, had 13 tackles and a pass break up. Aaron McCauley had 11 stops, a sack and 2.5 tackles for a loss, while Middleton chipped in nine tackles, two fumble recoveries and a pass break up to go with his 98 yard touchdown return.

2010 ARMED FORCES BOWL

Josh McNary scooped up a fumble and returned it 55 yards for a touchdown and Army held on to beat SMU 16-14 in the Armed Forces Bowl on Thursday, giving the Black Knights their first winning season since 1996. The Black Knights led 16-0 at halftime on SMU's home field, then ran out the game's final 4 minutes after Matt Szymanski was wide left on a 47 yard field goal attempt that would have put the Mustangs ahead.

2011 Army Black Knights

The Black Knights were led by third-year head coach Rich Ellerson. They finished the season 3–9 and were outscored by their opponents by a combined total of 339 to 298. In the annual Army–Navy Game, the Black Knights lost to Navy, 27-21.

Trent Steelman led the team in passing with 424 yards. Raymond Maples led the team in rushing with 1,066 yards. Steelman led with 12 rushing touchdowns. David Brooks led the team in receptions with 10 for 179 yards. Steelman led the team in scoring with 74 points.

Home games were played at Michie Stadium

9/3/2011	ARMY	@	Northern Illinois (11-3)	26	49	L
9/10/2011	ARMY	vs	SAN DIEGO STATE (8-5)	20	23	L
9/17/2011	ARMY	vs	NORTHWESTERN (6-7)	21	14	W
9/24/2011	ARMY	@	Ball State (6-6)	21	48	L
10/1/2011	ARMY	vs	TULANE (2-11)	45	6	W
10/8/2011	ARMY	@	Miami-Ohio (4-8)	28	35	L
10/22/2011	ARMY	@	Vanderbilt (6-7)	21	44	L
10/29/2011	ARMY	vs	FORDHAM	55	0	W
11/5/2011	ARMY	@	Air Force (7-6)	14	24	L
11/12/2011	ARMY	vs	RUTGERS (9-4)	12	27	L
11/19/2011	ARMY	@	Temple (9-4)	14	42	L
12/10/2011	ARMY	vs	NAVY (5-7)	21	27	L
Coach: Rich Ellerson			**Season Record >>**	298	339	3-9

Schedule Source: Steve's Football Bible LLC

Selected game(s) highlights

NORTHWESTERN

Army quarterback Trent Steelman rushed for three touchdowns to lead the Black Knights to their first victory of the season. Steelman led Army in rushing for a second straight week with 108 yards on the ground. Army dominated the time of possession battle, doubling up Northwestern at 40:19–19:41. Army's defense held strong all game, as the Wildcats only converted 3 of 12 third downs after averaging 50 percent their first two games.

TULANE

Tulane only needed three plays to score its first points of the game, however those would be the only six points they scored all day as Army scored the next 45 points to defeat the Green Wave 45–6. Army quarterback Trent Steelman threw for 70 yards and a touchdown and then ran for another 54 yards and two rushing touchdowns. Army's defense held Tulane to just 199 yards of total offense, their lowest output of the season. Raymond Maples rushed for a career-high 141 yards and a touchdown for the Black Knights.

Air Force

Army's Scott Williams was twisting his way toward the goal line when Air Force defensive back Josh Hall punched the ball out of his arms and out of the back of the end zone for a touchback in the waning seconds of the first half. It was the kindling for the Falcons' rally from a two-touchdown halftime deficit and a 24-14 win over the Black Knights. With the win, Air Force retained the coveted Commander-in-Chief's Trophy. After being outgained on the ground by 230 yards in the first half, the Falcons (5-4) outscored the Black Knights 21-0 in a third-quarter blitz that included two field goals, two touchdowns, a two-point conversion and two takeaways. Parker Herrington kicked a career-high three field goals for the

Falcons, who recovered fumbles that allowed them to start drives at the Army 29, 19 and 14 in the second half.

NAVY {@ FedEx Field, Landover, MD}

Senior Jon Teague kicked fourth quarter field goals of 23 and 44 yards as Navy defeated Army, 27-21, for a record 10th-consecutive year, in front of a crowd of 80,789 at FedEx Field that included President Barack Obama and Vice President Joe Biden. Navy jumped out to a 14-0 lead thanks to a pair of Army fumbles. Army's Raymond Maples fumbled a pitch and senior defensive end Jabaree Tuani recovered the ball at the Army 26 on the Black Knights' second possession of the game. Six plays later, senior quarterback Kriss Proctor scored from the four to give Navy the early advantage. After the two teams traded punts, Army's Jared Hassin was stripped of the ball by Tuani and junior outside linebacker Brye French recovered the ball at the Navy 45. On the first play after the Army fumble, Proctor scrambled for 32 yards down to the Army 23. Six plays after that, Proctor executed a perfect double option on third-and-eight from the 10 pitching to senior fullback Alexander Teich for the touchdown. Army, however, would come right back and cut Navy's lead in half, as quarterback Trent Steelman directed an eight play, 67 yard drive that was capped off by a 34 yard touchdown run to make the score 14-7. After the Navy offense went three and out, Army was back in business moving 63 yards in seven plays with Malcolm Brown diving over from the three to tie the game at 14 with just 49 seconds left in the first half.

Navy took the opening kickoff of the second half and moved 48 yards in five plays to retake the lead at 21-14. After Teich's 48 yard kickoff return put the Navy offense in business at the Army 48, backup fullback Delvin Diggs had back-to-back carries that picked up 18 yards down to the Army 30. Junior slot back Gee Gee Greene ran for 20 more yards on first down and, after a Teich eight yard run down to the two, Proctor scored his second TD of the day. Once again Army would come right back, marching right through the Navy defense in six plays with Steelman hitting Brown with a 25 yard touchdown pass on third-and-seven to tie the game at 21. After a Proctor fumble turned the ball back over to Army at the Navy 45, the Black Knights short circuited their opportunity to take the lead with an illegal block and a delay of game penalty forcing them to punt. The Midshipmen would take advantage of the opportunity by driving 75 yards in 18 plays with Teague capping the drive with a 23 yard field goal to give Navy a three-point lead. The Midshipmen were forced to kick a field goal after lineman Graham Vickers jumped on third-and-goal from the Army 1. The Midshipmen got the ball right back on the ensuing kickoff when freshman Noah Copeland forced Army returner Scott Williams to cough up the ball and Navy freshman Jordan Drake recovered it at the Army 27. Teague would turn the Army miscue into points with a 44 yard field goal to give Navy a 27-21 lead. Army got the ball back and quickly moved down the field and had the ball first-and-10 at the Navy 28 when the Navy defense came up big.

After Brown rushed for four yards on first down, Army tried to catch Navy napping by throwing the ball, but Steelman was dropped by junior linebacker Matt Warrick for a loss of five yards. Steelman would pick up four yards on third down as Tra'ves Bush came flying up from the safety position to make the stop and then on fourth down Steelman was sacked for a loss of one by Warrick to give the ball back to the Midshipmen with 4:31 left. The Navy offense was able to clinch the game by burning 4:29 off the clock as the Midshipmen picked up two first downs, including one where they drew Army offside on a fourth-and-one from the Army 48.

2012 Army Black Knights

The Black Knights were led by fourth-year head coach Rich Ellerson. They finished the season 2–10 and were outscored by their opponents by a combined total of 424 to 291. In the annual Army–Navy Game, the Black Knights lost to Navy, 17-13.

Trent Steelman led the team in passing with 667 yards. Steelman led the team in rushing with 1,248 yards **and tied the single season record with 17 rushing touchdowns.** Chevaughn Lawrence led the team in receptions with 21 for 357 yards. Steelman led the team in scoring with 104 points.

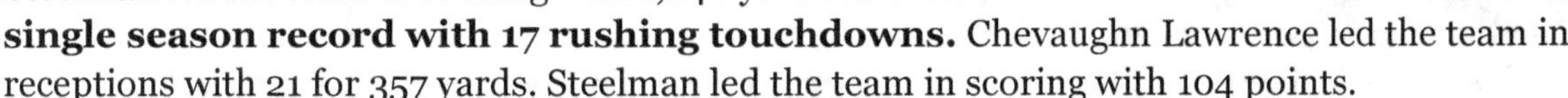

Home games were played at Michie Stadium

9/8/2012	ARMY	@	San Diego State	7	42	L
9/15/2012	ARMY	vs	NORTHERN ILLINOIS	40	41	L
9/22/2012	ARMY	@	Wake Forest	37	49	L
9/29/2012	ARMY	vs	STONY BROOK	3	23	L
10/6/2012	ARMY	vs	BOSTON COLLEGE	34	31	W
10/13/2012	ARMY	vs	KENT STATE	17	31	L
10/20/2012	ARMY	@	Eastern Michigan	38	48	L
10/27/2012	ARMY	vs	BALL STATE	22	30	L
11/3/2012	ARMY	vs	AIR FORCE	41	21	W
11/10/2012	ARMY	@	Rutgers	7	28	L
11/17/2012	ARMY	vs	TEMPLE	32	63	L
12/8/2012	ARMY	vs	NAVY	13	17	L
Coach: Rich Ellerson			**Season Record >>**	291	424	**2-10**

Schedule Source: Steve's Football Bible LLC

Selected game(s) highlights

BOSTON COLLEGE

Trent Steelman rushed for 141 yards and scored three times, including a decisive 29 yard touchdown run with 45 seconds left, and Army beat the Eagles 34-3. Fullback Larry Dixon had 128 yards rushing on just 13 carries and added another touchdown, and Dan Grochowski kicked two field goals for Army, which finished with 516 yards rushing and held the ball for more than 37 minutes. Raymond Maples led Army with 184 yards rushing 34 carries. It was the fourth game this season Army's potent triple option has had two or more players go over 100 yards, the first time the Black Knights have accomplished that since 1948. After Grochowski's 20 yard field goal gave Army a 27-24 lead with 9:04 left, Boston College awoke after a listless third quarter. Chase Rettig hit Johnathan Coleman for 30 yards and a 5 yard run by Andre Williams put the Eagles at the Army 24. On the next play, Alex Amidon, who had five catches for 85 yards, darted around from the left side, took a handoff, and with Rettig leading the way raced untouched along the right side to give the Eagles a 31-27 lead with 6:11 left. Army drove back to the BC 1 with just over 2 minutes left, but Maples was gang-tackled just shy of the goal line on a fourth-down pitch left. The much-maligned Army defense then forced a punt after three downs, giving Steelman one last chance with 69 seconds left, and he delivered with a stunning burst left after a poor BC kick had given Army a first down at the 38. It took Army just 18 seconds to score.

AIR FORCE

Trent Steelman rushed for 101 yards and scored twice, the Army defense held Air Force's high-powered offense in check for three quarters, and the Black Knights beat the Falcons 41-21 to snap a six game losing streak in the series. Army also stopped a 13 game skid in service academy games and stayed in the hunt for its first Commander-in-Chief's Trophy since 1996. The Army defense intercepted three passes, stopped a fourth-down run from its own 1, forced Air Force to punt four times, and recovered a fumble in the end zone for a touchdown. Air Force, which had only punted 15 times in its first eight games, finished with 103 yards rushing on 43 carries

NAVY {@ Lincoln Financial Field, Philadelphia, PA}

Freshman quarterback Keenan Reynolds extended Navy's dominance against Army, scoring the winning touchdown late in the fourth quarter in a 17-13 victory in the 113th playing of America's Game. Navy captured its 11th consecutive victory over Army and in doing so won the Commander-in-Chief's Trophy which is awarded to the team with the best record in games among the three service academies. Army and Navy each beat Air Force, putting the prestigious trophy up for grabs in the regular-season finale for the first time since 2005. In front of 69,607 fans and Vice President Joe Biden at Lincoln Financial Field, Navy caught a break when Army missed a late field goal attempt. Reynolds quickly found Brandon Turner down the sideline for a 49 yard gain. Reynolds then escaped a rush and followed with the eight yard touchdown run with 4:41 left in the game.

Unlike previous games over the last decade, the Black Knights were in this one until the final drive. Army had driven to the Navy 14 when fullback Larry Dixon fumbled on a sloppy exchange with quarterback Trent Steelman. Junior nose guard Barry Dabney recovered the fumble and the Midshipmen' sideline went wild as the CIC trophy was coming back to the Naval Academy for a record 13th time after a two-year stint at Air Force. Before Navy started its 11 game winning streak, the longest winning streak in a series that started in 1890 was only five games by either team. Late in the third quarter, Army's James Kelly stripped the ball from Reynolds and linebacker Alex Meier recovered to give the Black Knights the ball at Navy's 37. Eric Osteen kicked a 21 yard field goal 10 plays later for a 13-10 lead. Osteen, however, was wide left on a 37 yard attempt with 6:57 left in the game. Navy made them pay on Reynolds' score. The Midshipmen now lead the series 57-49-7.

After a scoreless first quarter, Army and Navy swapped rushing TDs in the second. Navy fullback Noah Copeland plowed straight up the middle for a 12 yard score. Trent Steelman matched him with an 11 yarder for his program-tying 17th TD run of the season, then saluted the cadets after the score. Freshman kicker Nick Sloan put Navy up 10-7 with a 31 yard field goal late in the second, but Army answered when Osteen's 41 yarder as the first half expired hit the upright and bounced in to tie the game at 10. Reynolds was named the Philadelphia Sportswriters Most Valuable Player, rushing for 43 yards and a touchdown and completing 10 of his 17 passes for 130 yards. Sophomore fullback Noah Copeland rushed for 99 yards and a touchdown on 22 carries, while senior slot back Gee Gee Greene caught three passes for 23 yards. Junior linebacker Cody Peterson led the Navy defense with a career-high 14 tackles, while senior outside linebacker Keegan Wetzel recorded 11 tackles, 1.5 tackles for a loss and one sack. Senior Matt Warrick was also in on 11 stops, while sophomore outside linebacker Josh Tate, senior linebacker John Michael Nurthen and Dabney all recovered fumbles.

2013 Army Black Knights

The Black Knights were led by fifth-year head coach Rich Ellerson. Following the loss to Navy on December 14 and finishing the season 3–9, Ellerson was fired. The Black Knights were outscored by their opponents by a combined total of 359 to 293. In the annual Army–Navy Game, the Black Knights lost to Navy, 34-7.

Angel Santiago led the team in passing with 597 yards. Terry Baggett led the team in rushing with 1,113 yards. Santiago led with 10 rushing touchdowns. Xavier Moss led the team in receptions with 35 for 468 yards. Santiago and Dan Grochowski led the team in scoring with 60 points.

Home games were played at Michie Stadium

8/30/2013	ARMY	vs	MORGAN STATE	28	12	W	
9/7/2013	ARMY	@	Ball State	14	40	L	
9/14/2013	ARMY	vs	STANFORD	20	34	L	
9/21/2013	ARMY	vs	WAKE FOREST	11	25	L	
9/28/2013	ARMY	vs	Louisiana Tech	35	16	W	
10/5/2013	ARMY	@	Boston College	27	48	L	
10/12/2013	ARMY	vs	EASTERN MICHIGAN	50	25	W	*-Baggett 304 rush yds
10/19/2013	ARMY	@	Temple	14	33	L	
11/2/2013	ARMY	@	Air Force	28	42	L	
11/9/2013	ARMY	vs	WESTERN KENTUCKY	17	21	L	
11/30/2013	ARMY	@	Hawaii	42	29	L	
12/14/2013	ARMY	vs	NAVY	7	34	L	
Coach: Rich Ellerson			**Season Record >>**	293	359	3-9	

Schedule Source: Steve's Football Bible LLC
*-Single game record

Selected game(s) highlights

MORGAN STATE

Angel Santiago rushed for 120 yards and three touchdowns and passed for another score, and Army opened its season with a 28-12 victory over Morgan State. Army scored the first three times it had the ball to gain a 21-0 lead as Morgan State repeatedly self-destructed, getting called for eight penalties for 60 yards in the first half alone. Santiago scored on a 33 yard run to cap Army's first possession of the game. He burst off left tackle and then cut back toward the middle to score untouched with 6:17 left in the first quarter. Santiago also scored runs of 3 yards and 1 yard and hit Chevaughn Lawrence for an 18 yard score. Army's Larry Dixon rushed for 107 yards on 12 carries.

Louisiana Tech

Terry Baggett rushed for 143 yards and two touchdowns, and the Black Knights rolled up 414 yards on the ground in a 35-16 victory that was twice delayed by storms. Baggett finished Army's 85 yard opening drive with a 9 yard score after the start of the game was pushed back an hour when a storm hit the Cotton Bowl about 30 minutes before kickoff. He scored again five plays after a 45-minute delay late in the first quarter. Angel Santiago had 77 yards rushing and a touchdown, and Trenton Turrentine added 81 yards on the ground.

EASTERN MICHIGAN

Terry Baggett ran for four touchdowns -- including a 96 yard score -- **and a school record 304 yards,** as Army came back to beat Eastern Michigan 50-25. Larry Dixon added 69 yards and a score for the Black Knights, who went up 22-15 on Trenton Turrentine's one yard touchdown with 9:46 left in the second and never looked back. Turrentine finished with 92 yards.

Air Force

Anthony LaCoste rushed for a career-high 263 yards and scored three touchdowns, helping Air Force snap a seven game skid by holding off Army 42-28. LaCoste finished with the second-most yards rushing for a program that's known for its ground game, just shy of Chad Hall's school-record 275 yards against Army in 2007. The elusive LaCoste had TD runs of 73 and 78 yards, along with a 1 yard burst. Angel Santiago scored three touchdowns on a sore ankle and Terry Baggett had 121 yards rushing and a score for Army.

NAVY {@ Lincoln Financial Field, Philadelphia, PA}

Navy quarterback Keenan Reynolds ran for 136 yards and scored three touchdowns (47, 11 and 1 yard) to lead the Midshipmen to a 34-7 victory, their 12th straight in the series. Reynolds scored on runs of 47 yards, 11 yards and 1 yard. The sophomore has 29 rushing touchdowns, breaking the single-season mark for a quarterback previously held by Ricky Dobbs (Navy, 2009) and Collin Klein (Kansas State, 2011), both of whom had 27. Navy won the Commander-In-Chief's Trophy for the second consecutive season and ninth time in 11 years. The trophy is awarded to the service academy with the most victories in games between Navy, Army and Air Force. The Midshipmen haven't lost to Army since 2001 and lead the series 58-49-7. Navy's 12 game run is the longest in the history of the rivalry that began in 1890. Head coach Ken Niumatalolo became the second coach in Navy history to start his coaching career 6-0 against Army, matching Paul Johnson (2002-07).

Army fumbled five times and was intercepted once in its fifth straight defeat. The snow that was forecast in the morning hours began during the pregame pageantry that makes this game a one-of-a-kind spectacle. Army quarterback A.J. Schurr fumbled on the first two drives, the second recovered by Navy at its own 38. Following the turnover, Quinton Singleton burst through a hole in the middle and ran 58 yards to the Army 4, setting up a field goal for a 3-0 lead late in the first quarter. Midway through the second period, Noah Copeland ran 39 yards for a touchdown to make it 10-0. With 2:38 left in the half, Reynolds gingerly picked his way through the Army defense on his record-tying touchdown run. Navy went into halftime leading 17-0.

In the third quarter, the snow turned to rain and Army quarterback Angel Santiago did his best to make a game of it. After throwing a 29 yard pass to Xavier Moss, the junior quarterback scored on a 4 yard run to get the Black Knights to 17-7. Reynolds answered with an 11 play drive that produced a field goal. Army then failed to convert a fourth-and-3 from its own 42, a futile gamble that all but assured the Black Knights another frustrating loss against their far more successful service academy rivals. Reynolds scored his record-breaking touchdown with 6:22 left, and the conversion pass from wide receiver Brendan Dudeck made it 28-7.

2014 Army Black Knights

The Black Knights were led by first-year head coach Jeff Monken. They finished the season 4–8. The Black Knights were outscored by their opponents by a combined total of 395 to 299. In the annual Army–Navy Game, the Black Knights lost to Navy, 17-10.

Angel Santiago led the team in passing with 488 yards. Larry Dixon led the team in rushing with 1,102 yards. Santiago led with 10 rushing touchdowns. Edgar Poe led the team in receptions with 10 for 199 yards. Josh Jenkins led the team with 4 interceptions. Santiago led the team in scoring with 60 points.

Home games were played at Michie Stadium

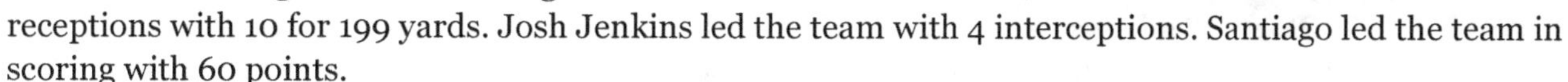

9/6/2014	ARMY	vs	BUFFALO	47	39	W
9/13/2014	ARMY	@	Stanford	0	35	L
9/20/2014	ARMY	@	Wake Forest	21	24	L
9/27/2014	ARMY	@	Yale	43	49	L
10/4/2014	ARMY	vs	BALL STATE	33	24	W
10/11/2014	ARMY	vs	RICE	21	41	L
10/18/2014	ARMY	@	Kent State	17	39	L
11/1/2014	ARMY	vs	AIR FORCE	6	23	L
11/8/2014	ARMY	vs	Connecticut	35	21	W
11/15/2014	ARMY	@	Western Kentucky	24	52	L
11/22/2014	ARMY	vs	FORDHAM	42	31	W
12/13/2014	ARMY	vs	NAVY	10	17	L
Coach: Jeff Monken			**Season Record >>**	299	395	**4-8**

Schedule Source: Steve's Football Bible LLC

Selected game(s) highlights

BUFFALO

Larry Dixon ran for a career-high 174 yards and two touchdowns, one of six Army players to score as the Black Knights gained 341 yards rushing in a fitting end to a hard-fought 47-39 victory over Buffalo. It seemed so easy for the better part of the game as Army built a 47-17 lead on 4 yard scoring runs by Angel Santiago and Matt Giachinta early in the fourth quarter. Joe Licata led the Bulls on a furious 22-point rally that made it a one-possession game. Buffalo recovered an onside kick and a fumbled pitch, and Licata took advantage, throwing three TD passes, two to Devin Campbell and one to Marcus McGill. Campbell's 8 yard catch with 2:42 left was the final score. The Bulls had one more chance, but Licata threw two incompletions, and they fell a yard short of a first down.

FORDHAM

Josh Jenkins and Lamar Johnson-Harris forced a wild punt block for a touchdown in the closing seconds of the first half, giving Army the lead for good in a 42-31 victory over the Rams. Larry Dixon tied a career high with three touchdowns on 158 yards to become the fourth player in school history with 3,000 yards rushing for the Black Knights. Terry Baggett added 52 yards rushing and a score, and quarterback A.J. Schurr ran for 70 yards off the bench as Army topped Fordham for the fourth time in four meetings. The Black Knights relied on a fake punt of their own, a John Voit pick, and the blocked punt to build a 14-10 edge at halftime.

AIR FORCE

Kale Pearson hit tight end Garrett Griffin for a 54 yard touchdown early in the third quarter to break open a tense game, Will Conant kicked three field goals, and Air Force beat Army 23-6 to win the

Commander-in-Chief's Trophy for a record 19th time. Leading by just a field goal at halftime, Pearson hit Griffin over the middle on Air Force's first possession of the second half, and he raced untouched into the end zone for a 13-3 lead. Stymied the entire first half, the Falcons had struck in just three plays that took 48 seconds after forcing Army into a three-and-out. Pearson secured the victory with a 2 yard touchdown pass to Griffin midway through the fourth quarter. Pearson, who finished 8 of 12 for 141 yards and gained 41 yards rushing, also hit Colton Huntsman for 17 yards and Jalen Robinette for 29 on consecutive plays to set up Conant's 26 yard field goal with 5:13 left on the clock before halftime. Conant boosted the Air Force lead to 16-3 when he nailed a 50 yard field goal midway through the third. Army managed just two field goals by Daniel Grochowski, 42 yards in the first quarter for a 3-0 lead and 46 yards in the third.

NAVY {@ M&T Bank Stadium, Baltimore, MD}

The game was over, and it was time for Navy to celebrate its 13th straight victory over Army. After the Midshipmen stood respectfully for Army's alma mater, defensive ends Paul Quessenberry and Will Anthony along with nose guard Bernard Sarra hoisted Ken Niumatalolo on their shoulders to give the winningest football coach in Navy history a free ride in the wake of a 17-10 triumph. Niumatalolo broke a tie with George Welsh for most wins at Navy. He also became the first to win his first seven games against Army. The streak remained intact because of Navy's unrelenting defense and quarterback Keenan Reynolds' versatility.

The Cadets went up 7-0 in stunning fashion, holding Navy to four yards on its first series before Josh Jenkins blocked a punt and Xavier Moss scooped up the ball and sprinted seven yards into the end zone. Navy senior Pablo Beltran never had a punt blocked before that play - it was his 151st kick - and it marked the first time since 2009 that Army scored first against the Midshipmen. It was a horrid first quarter for Navy, which gained 15 yards on three straight three-and-outs. Army maintained the upper hand in the second quarter, but the momentum turned when Cadets quarterback Angel Santiago was stuffed on a fourth-and-1 from the Navy 30 with just over two minutes left. The Midshipmen then turned to a seldom-used weapon - the forward pass - to pull into a tie at the break. Reynolds completed a 39 yard pass to Jamir Tillman to the Army 31 and connected with Ryan Williams-Jenkins for 12 yards before throwing a 9 yard TD pass to Tillman with 18 seconds to go before halftime.

Navy opened the third quarter with a 41 yard kickoff return by Williams-Jenkins. That led to a 45 yard field goal by Austin Grebe for a 10-7 lead. Army then wasted a 50 yard drive, moving to the Navy 30 before Daniel Grochowski hooked a field goal try to the left. Reynolds subsequently directed a 12 play march that lasted nearly eight minutes and ended with the 5-foot-11 junior bulling over the goal line for a 10-point cushion. The two teams traded fumbles and a 52 yard field goal by Grochowski made it 17-10 with 1:51 left, but Navy recovered the ensuing onside kick. The 13 game run by Navy is the longest in the history of a series that began in 1890. Before the Midshipmen went on their unprecedented streak, neither team in this storied rivalry had won more than five in a row.

Navy leads the series 59-49-7. In the previous 12 games, the Midshipmen outscored Army 400-132 - including 34-7 last year. Although the score in this one was closer, the result was the same. The Cadets haven't defeated the Midshipmen since 2001. First-year coach Jeff Monken became the sixth coach to lose to Navy over that span.

2015 Army Black Knights

The Black Knights were led by second-year head coach Jeff Monken. They finished the season 2–10. The Black Knights were outscored by their opponents by a combined total of 334 to 265. In the annual Army–Navy Game, the Black Knights lost to Navy, 21-17.

Ahmad Bradshaw led the team in passing with 429 yards and threw 5 touchdown passes. Aaron Kemper led the team in rushing with 551 yards. A.J. Schurr led with 7 rushing touchdowns. Edgar Poe led the team in receptions with16 for 441 yards and 6 TD receptions. Dan Grochowski led the team in scoring with 49 points.

Home games were played at Michie Stadium

9/4/2015	ARMY	vs	FORDHAM	35	37	L
9/12/2015	ARMY	@	Connectcut	17	22	L
9/19/2015	ARMY	vs	WAKE FOREST	14	17	L
9/26/2015	ARMY	@	Eastern Michigan	58	36	W
10/3/2015	ARMY	@	Penn State	14	20	L
10/10/2015	ARMY	vs	DUKE	3	44	L
10/17/2015	ARMY	vs	BUCKNELL	21	14	W
10/24/2015	ARMY	@	Rice	31	38	L
11/7/2015	ARMY	@	Air Force	3	20	L
11/14/2015	ARMY	vs	TULANE	31	34	L
11/21/2015	ARMY	vs	RUTGERS	21	31	L
12/12/2015	ARMY	vs	NAVY	17	21	L
Coach: Jeff Monken			**Season Record >>**	**265**	**334**	**2-10**

Selected game(s) highlights

Eastern Michigan

Joe Walker and Aaron Kemper had touchdown runs and Army never trailed in ending a season opening losing streak with a 58-36 victory over Eastern Michigan. The win was Army's first as a true road team since November 2010 and ended a 21-game string of losses away from home. Walker's 63 yard run early in the game gave the Black Knights the lead for good and Kemper added a 56 yard scoring run in the second quarter to help Army lead 29-17 at the half. The Eagles trailed 36-30 late in the third quarter but Army answered with two Drue Harris' touchdown runs. A.J. Schurr, who stepped in for injured starting quarterback Ahmad Bradshaw, added a pair of keepers for scores. Kemper had 147 yards on 13 carries to lead Army, which got a touchdown run from John Trainor. Ahmad Bradshaw had a 10 yard touchdown pass to Edgar Poe.

BUCKNELL

A.J. Schurr came off the bench to run for two touchdowns and threw for the winning score to help scuffling Army to a 21-14 win over Bucknell. Schurr connected with Edgar Poe, who won an underthrown jump ball over Nick O'Brien and ran all the way to the end zone for a 68 yard score, to put Army up with 4:44 left. Chris Carnegie intercepted R.J. Nitti on Bucknell's ensuing drive to clinch it.

Air Force

Karson Roberts threw two TD passes to tight end Garrett Griffin, Air Force's defense turned in a dominating performance and the Falcons won their school-record 11th straight home game by beating Army 20-3. Air Force's smothering defense limited Army to 169 total yards and just nine first downs. Army's Ahmad Bradshaw was held to 42 yard rushing. He also completed 2 of 8 for 45 yards, including one to Edgar Poe that went for 33. While Army's offense struggled, the defense actually kept the team in the game against an Air Force squad that's scored 100 points the last two weeks. The Falcons finished with 196 yards rushing, well below their average of 353.4,

NAVY {@ Lincoln Financial Field, Philadelphia, PA}

With a shot at history at stake, Keenan Reynolds ended his Navy career with a clean sweep against Army. Reynolds rushed for two touchdowns and threw for another score to lead the #21 Midshipmen to their 14th straight win over the Black Knights, 21-17, at Lincoln Financial Field. Reynolds' second rushing TD was his 85th career score, the most for any FBS or FCS Division I player (he ended his career with 88). He is the first quarterback over the 116 game series to go 4-0. Head coach Ken Niumatalolo improved to 8-0 against the Black Knights.

Army's Daniel Grochowski missed a 29 yard field goal early in the quarter. Chris Carter lost a fumble at the Navy 34 yard that was recovered by linebacker Ted Colburn. Navy had two interceptions - one off a trick play - on two straight drives to preserve the lead. Army's Hail Mary on the final play of the game fell short. Niumatalolo tied former Army coach Earl "Red" Blaik (8-8-2) for most wins in the series. Reynolds showed why he was a late contender for Heisman Trophy consideration. Reynolds, the only player in team history with two 1,000 yard rushing and passing seasons, put the Midshipmen up 21-17 with a 50 yard TD pass to Jamir Tillman late in the third. A three-touchdown favorite, Navy had it tougher than usual in one of the most storied rivalries in college sports. The Midshipmen won the CIC trophy, awarded to the team with the best record in games among the three service academies. Navy beat Air Force 33-11 this season. The Black Knights got a field goal on the game's opening drive and Tyler Campbell scored on a 29 yard run make it 10-7 in the first. Carter hit Edgar Poe for a 39 yard TD pass with 2:08 left in the half to make it 17-14 and give Army its first halftime lead since 2009. Army had a lead. It just didn't have Reynolds. Reynolds scored on runs of 58 yards and 1 yard to keep Navy in the game, and then used his arm to find Tillman in the third for the lead.

2016 Army Black Knights

The Black Knights were led by third-year head coach Jeff Monken. They finished the season 8–5 and defeated Navy for the first time since 2001 in the Army–Navy Game. They were invited to the Heart of Dallas Bowl where they defeated North Texas in overtime.

Ahmad Bradshaw led the team in passing with 703 yards and threw 4 touchdown passes. Andy Davidson led the team in rushing with 961 yards and 12 rushing touchdowns. Edgar Poe led the team in receptions with 16 for 336 yards. Davidson led the team in scoring with 74 points.

Home games were played at Michie Stadium

9/3/2016	ARMY	@	Temple	28	13	W	
9/10/2016	ARMY	vs	RICE	31	14	W	
9/17/2016	ARMY	@	Texas-El Paso	66	14	W	
9/24/2016	ARMY	@	Buffalo	20	23	L	
10/8/2016	ARMY	@	Duke	6	13	L	
10/15/2016	ARMY	vs	LAFAYETTE	62	7	W	
10/22/2016	ARMY	vs	NORTH TEXAS	18	35	L	
10/29/2016	ARMY	@	Wake Forest	21	13	W	
11/5/2016	ARMY	vs	AIR FORCE	12	31	L	
11/12/2016	ARMY	vs	Notre Dame	6	44	L	
11/19/2016	ARMY	vs	MORGAN STATE	60	3	W	
12/10/2016	ARMY	vs	Navy	21	17	W	
12/27/2016	**ARMY**	**vs**	**North Texas**	**38**	**31**	**W**	**Heart of Dallas Bowl**
Coach: Jeff Monken			**Season Record >>**	**389**	**258**	**8-5**	

Schedule Source: Steve's Football Bible LLC

Selected game(s) highlights

Temple

Andy Davidson ran for 121 yards and two touchdowns in his first game at fullback and Army piled up 329 yards on the ground to beat Temple 28-13. Three other Army players gained at least 50 rushing yards for the Black Knights. Trailing 10-7 at halftime, Army drove right down the field to start the third quarter with Davidson's 3 yard TD plunge capping a 12-play, 77 yard series that chewed nearly seven minutes off the clock. After a Temple field goal pulled the Owls within one, the Black Knights again went on a long drive with Tyler Campbell scoring on a 12 yard run on the 14th play of the series to put Army ahead 21-13 with 9:38 left in the contest. Kenneth Brinson sealed the win with an interception with 3:11 remaining

Wake Forest

Ahmad Bradshaw scored on an 11 yard keeper with 11:45 left to help Army beat Wake Forest 21-13 as part of a dominant fourth-quarter effort. Darnell Woolfolk added a TD run of his own with 2:54 left for what amounted to a clinching score.

AIR FORCE

Arion Worthman passed for 195 yards and one touchdown and rushed for 63 yards and another score, and Air Force beat Army 31-12 to win the Commander-in-Chief's Trophy. Air Force limited Army to 144 yards on 40 rushes. Kell Walker had a 32 yard touchdown run for the Cadets.

NAVY {@ M&T Bank Stadium, Baltimore, MD}

The Army football team and its fans around the world can finally rejoice. No longer will they have to listen to barbs from Navy or lament another missed opportunity in the biggest game of the year. At long last, The Streak is over. Army ended a 14-year run of frustration against the Midshipmen, using an overpowering running game and opportunistic defense to carve out a long overdue 21-17 victory Saturday. With future commander in chief Donald Trump looking on, the Black Knights blew a 14-point lead before quarterback Ahmad Bradshaw scored on a 9 yard run with 6:42 left to give Army the win it had been waiting for since 2001. The Black Knights' 14 game losing streak was the longest by either academy in a series that began in 1890. Army (7-5) now trails 60-50-7 in one of the nation's historic rivalries. Navy was coming off a physical 34-10 loss to Temple in the American Athletic Conference title game and had only one week to prepare for Army with a new quarterback, sophomore Zach Abey, who was making his first college start. Abey took over Will Worth, who broke his foot against Temple. Abey ran for two touchdowns but passed for only 89 yards and was intercepted twice. Navy had four turnovers, three in the first half. This senior class at Navy has accounted for 37 wins, most ever at the Academy over a four-year period. But they'll never forget this defeat. That was a mantra chanted by the Black Knights for the past 14 years. Not anymore. By halftime, Army led 14-0 and owned a 14-1 advantage in first downs. After watching from the Navy side of the field before halftime, Trump visited the TV booth on the Army side in the third quarter. The interview with the president-elect coincided with a big shift in momentum. Andy Davidson lost a fumble on the Black Knights' first possession of the second half and the Midshipmen recovered at the Army 32. A screen pass for 16 yards set up a 1 yard touchdown run by Abey to get Navy to 14-7. Minutes later, the Midshipmen got a field goal after a replay overturned a lost fumble by Abey at the Army 11. A 41 yard touchdown run by Abey gave Navy the lead with 12:42 remaining. But Army wasn't done. The Black Knights put together a 12 play, 80 yard drive that lasted nearly seven minutes and ended with Bradshaw's TD. Bradshaw went 2 for 4 for 35 yards and an interception in Army's first win in Baltimore since 1944. Davidson ran for 87 yards and two first half scores, and Kell Walker carried 16 times for 94 yards. Some teams might fold after letting a two-touchdown lead vanish. Not Army.

2016 HEART OF DALLAS BOWL

Jordan Asberry took a toss and scored Army's sixth rushing touchdown in a 38-31 win over North Texas on Tuesday in a rematch at the Heart of Dallas Bowl. The Black Knights finished with 480 yards rushing, including 119 yards and two TDs by Darnell Woolfolk. Asberry's score was the 46th rushing touchdown this season, breaking the school record held by the 1945 national championship team. North Texas had its chance in overtime. But after Alec Morris scrambled for 4 yards and Jeffery Wilson lost 3, consecutive incomplete passes followed.

2017 Army Black Knights {Commander-Chief-Trophy}

The Black Knights were led by fourth-year head coach Jeff
Monken, finished the season 10–3, winning the Commander-in-Chief's Trophy for
the first time since 1996 after sweeping service academy rivals Air Force and Navy.
They were invited to the Armed Forces Bowl where they defeated San Diego State.
Following the season, they were chosen as the 2017 ECAC Division I Football Subdivision Team of the
Year.

Ahmad Bradshaw led the team in passing with 285 yards. **Bradshaw led the team in rushing
with 1,746 yards, setting a new single season Army record.** Bradshaw and Darnell Woolfolk tied
with 14 rushing touchdowns. Kell Walker led the team in receptions with 5 for 111 yards. Bradshaw led the
team in scoring with 86 points.

Home games were played at Michie Stadium

9/1/2017	ARMY	vs	FORDHAM	64	6	W	
9/9/2017	ARMY	vs	BUFFALO	21	17	W	
9/16/2017	ARMY	@	Ohio State	7	38	L	
9/23/2017	ARMY	@	Tulane	17	21	L	
9/30/2017	ARMY	vs	TEXAS-EL PASO	35	21	W	
10/7/2017	ARMY	@	Rice	49	12	W	
10/14/2017	ARMY	vs	EASTERN MICHIGAN	28	27	W	
10/21/2017	ARMY	vs	TEMPLE	31	28	W	
11/4/2017	ARMY	@	Air Force	21	0	W	
11/11/2017	ARMY	vs	DUKE	21	16	W	
11/18/2017	ARMY	@	North Texas	49	52	L	
12/9/2017	ARMY	vs	Navy	14	13	W	
12/22/2017	**ARMY**	**vs**	**San Diego State**	**42**	**35**	**W**	**Armed Forces Bowl**
Coach: Jeff Monken			**Season Record >>**	**399**	**286**	**10-3**	

Schedule Source: Steve's Football Bible LLC

Selected game(s) highlights

BUFFALO

Darnell Woolfolk scored on a pair of 1 yard runs and Army rallied past the Bulls 21-17 as the Black
Knights avenged their most painful loss from last season. Woolfolk's game-winner came on fourth down
with 4:53 left after Kell Walker was ruled out-of-bounds before reaching past the right pylon on the
previous play. Safety Jaylon McClinton forced a fumble by Buffalo quarterback Tyree
Jackson and Andrew McLean recovered for Army midway through the third quarter with the Bulls
driving, and that helped turn the tide as the Black Knights converted to get back in the game. Woolfolk's
plunge from inside the 1 narrowed the Buffalo lead to 17-14 on the first play of the fourth.

DUKE

Ahmad Bradshaw scored on an 18 yard run, Javhari Bourdeau returned a blocked punt for
another touchdown, and Army beat mistake prone Duke 21-16 to finish the season unbeaten in six games
at Michie Stadium. It's the first Army team to be perfect at home in a season since 1996. After falling
behind 3-0, Army drove 80 yards in 11 plays to gain a lead it never relinquished, with Andy
Davidson rushing for 37 yards on four carries to help set up Darnell Woolfolk's 3 yard touchdown. Army
then forced the Blue Devils to punt, and Davidson used his expertise on special teams to block the kick.
Bourdeau, a freshman defensive back, quickly scooped it up and returned it 25 yards for a touchdown and
a 14-3 lead early in the second quarter. Bradshaw stunned Duke with his only throw of the game, hitting a
wide open Kell Walker down the left side for 42 yards on a third-and-9 play. Two plays later, Bradshaw
scored untouched over right tackle for what proved to be the decisive score.

Air Force

Quarterback Ahmad Bradshaw rushed for a career-high 265 yards and Army's defense ended Air Force's 306 game scoring streak with a 21-0 win. Army kept Air Force (4-5) off the board midway through the fourth quarter when the defense stopped the Falcons on downs deep in Army territory. After the offense went on a time-consuming scoring drive, the defense finished off the shutout by forcing an Air Force punt with around 33 seconds remaining. The Falcons missed a 47 yard field goal in the first quarter. Kell Walker scored twice for the Black Knights, who earned their first win at Falcon Stadium since 2005. The Falcons finished with 95 yards rushing.

NAVY {@ Lincoln Financial Field, Philadelphia, PA}

Bennett Moehring narrowly missed a 48 yard field goal in the swirling snow on the final play and Army held off Navy 14-13 to win its first Commander-in-Chief's Trophy since 1996. Army earned its second straight win over Navy following 14 straight losses in the series. Ahmad Bradshaw pushed over the goal line on a quarterback sneak with 5:10 remaining and Blake Wilson kicked the extra point to put Army ahead. Quarterback Malcolm Perry, who ran for 250 yards and a 68 yard score in the second quarter, then led Navy to the Army 31 with 3 seconds left. Navy elected to try a field goal, and after about 10 players used their feet to clear the steady snow during a timeout, Moehring's kick was long enough but drifted barely left. Army cut its deficit in the series to 60-51-7 in a matchup of bowl-bound teams. The Black Knights claimed the Commander-in-Chief's Trophy thanks to an earlier victory over Air Force. In a game that included only three passes - Army completed its lone toss - the Black Knights produced a 13 play, 65 yard to take a late lead. John Trainor tiptoed the sideline for 8 yards one play before Bradshaw's 12th touchdown of the season.

Navy took advantage of the ensuing kickoff going out of bounds and moved down the field. Perry dropped a shotgun snap on fourth down at the Army 37 but picked up the ball and ran for a first down. But Navy committed two false start penalties, making the final field goal attempt more difficult. Snow started falling in the late morning on the 29-degree day, leaving a coating on the field. Workers used blowers to uncover the lines and hashmarks during timeouts as a light snow fell throughout. The weather made one of sports' biggest rivalries an even more physical contest. Army's all-white uniforms - a nod to the 10th Mountain Division of World War II - served as almost camouflage in the snow. Perry's shifty 46 yard run to the Navy 11 early in the third quarter put him over 1,000 yards for the season and led to Moehring's second field goal, from 24 yards, to make it 13-7.

2017 ARMED FORCES BOWL

Darnell Woolfolk scored on a 1 yard run with 18 seconds left, Kell Walker converted a go-ahead 2 point run and Army added a last play defensive touchdown for a 42-35 victory over San Diego State on Saturday in the Armed Forces Bowl. After Rashaad Penny's fourth touchdown run of the game gave San Diego State a 35-28 lead with 5:47 to play, Army drove 72 yards for the tying score and winning conversion. On the Aztecs' final play, they made multiple laterals from their 40. The final lateral was grabbed by Army's Elijah Riley, who returned it 29 yards for a touchdown. The Black Knights tied a school record for wins set by the 1996 team. Penny ran for 221 yards, his fifth straight game of at least 200 yards. His scores came on runs of 81, on his first carry, 31, 49 and 4 yards. Juwan Washington added the Aztecs' other touchdown on a 78 yard kickoff return in the first half's closing seconds. Army dominated the time of possession. The Black Knights ran 91 plays to the Aztecs' 30 and held the ball for 46:00 to San Diego State's 13:53.

2018 Army Black Knights {Lambert Trophy} + {Commander-Chief-Trophy}

The Black Knights were led by fifth-year head coach Jeff Monken and played their home games at Michie Stadium. Following their 28–14 victory over Colgate in Week 12, Army entered the AP Poll at No. 23 and the Coaches' Poll at No. 24, the first time Army had entered the national rankings since finishing the 1996 season at No. 25 in the AP and No. 24 in the Coaches'. On December 2, Army accepted an invite to participate in the Armed Forces Bowl against the Houston Cougars of the American Athletic Conference. On December 8, Army defeated its archrival Navy by a score of 17–10, increasing their Army-Navy Game win streak to three in a row and winning the Commander-in-Chief's Trophy for the second straight year. With the win the Black Knights also secured their second straight 10-win season, the first time that had been accomplished in the Academy's long and storied history. In the Armed Forces Bowl, they defeated Houston by a score of 70–14 to tie NCAA bowl game records for points scored and margin of victory. Their 11 wins are the most in one season in program history. As a result of his team's 2018 accomplishments, Coach Monken was awarded the George Munger Collegiate Coach of the Year Award by the Maxwell Football Club, the Vince Lombardi College Football Coach of the Year Award by the Lombardi Foundation, and the President's Award by the Touchdown Club of Columbus. Army finished the season with a ranking of No. 19 in the AP Poll and No. 20 in the Coaches' Poll, their highest finish in both polls since Pete Dawkins's Heisman Trophy-winning season in 1958 where the Cadets finished No. 3 in both polls. Following the completion of the season, the Black Knights were awarded the 2018 Lambert Trophy by the Eastern College Athletic Conference (ECAC) and Metropolitan New York Football Writers, signifying them as the best team in the East in Division I FBS. This was the eighth overall time the Lambert Trophy had been awarded to Army, and the first since 1958. Kelvin Hopkins led the team in passing with 1,026 yards and threw 6 touchdown passes. Hopkins led the team in rushing with 1,017 yards **and 17 rushing touchdowns, tying the single season record**. Kell Walker and Jordan Asberry led the team in receptions with 11. Asberry led with 219 yards receiving. Hopkins led the team in scoring with 102 points. **Hopkins tied the single game rushing touchdowns with 5 in the Armed Forces Bowl vs Houston. Hopkins set the single season team record for total offense with 2,143 yards.**

FINAL RANK: #19 AP/#20 UPI							
Home games were played at Michie Stadium							
8/31/2018	ARMY	@	Duke	14	34	L	
9/8/2018	ARMY	vs	LIBERTY	38	14	W	
9/15/2018	ARMY	vs	HAWAII	28	21	W	
9/22/2018	ARMY	@	Oklahoma	21	28	L	
9/29/2018	ARMY	@	Buffalo	42	13	W	
10/13/2018	ARMY	@	San Jose State	52	3	W	
10/20/2018	ARMY	vs	MIAMI-OHIO	31	30	W	
10/27/2018	ARMY	@	Eastern Michigan	37	22	W	
11/3/2018	ARMY	vs	AIR FORCE	17	14	W	
11/10/2018	ARMY	vs	LAFAYETTE	31	13	W	
11/17/2018	ARMY	vs	COLGATE	28	14	W	
12/8/2018	ARMY	vs	Navy	17	10	W	
12/22/2018	ARMY	vs	Houston	70	14	W	Armed Forces Bowl
Coach: Jeff Monken			Season Record >>	426	230	11-2	

Schedule Source: Steve's Football Bible LLC

Selected game(s) highlights

HAWAII

Hopkins rushed for a team high 110 yards and two touchdowns and completed 6-for-10 passes for 162 yards as Army knocked off unbeaten Hawaii and extended its home winning streak to nine games. The junior scored a pair of 1 yard touchdown runs to give Army a 14-7 lead with 12:54 left in the first half. The quarterback's second touchdown was the first time that Hawaii had trailed in a game this season. Linebacker Cole Christiansen broke up McDonald's pass in the end zone with 54 seconds left to seal the win for Army. Junior fullback Connor Slomka added a career-long 48 yard touchdown in the second quarter. Darnell Woolfolk's 3 yard touchdown extended Army's advantage to 28-14 with 9:07 left.

AIR FORCE

Army used a ball-control offense early and then held off Air Force late for a 17-14 win over the Falcons at a sold-out Michie Stadium. After Air Force won the toss and deferred, Army held the ball for nearly the entire first quarter. The Black Knights opened the game with a 21 play, 75 yard drive that ended with a one yard run by Darnell Woolfolk. Late in the second quarter, Woolfolk broke a career-long 52 yard run on fourth-and-one to set up a Kelvin Hopkins' six yard touchdown run. The Black Knights took a 14-0 lead into halftime. After the Falcon defense held the Black Knights in Army territory, Jeremy Fejedelem blocked a punt, giving the Falcons the ball at the 34 yard line. The offense responded with a nine play, 34 yard drive as Donald Hammond III, who replaced Isaiah Sanders after halftime, scored on a one yard run. Air Force missed the extra point for a 14-6 lead after three quarters. Army (7-2 overall) answered with a 13 play, 62 yard drive that consumed 7:19 off the clock and culminated in a John Abercrombie 30 yard field goal as the home team built a 17-6 lead with 8:35 remaining. The Falcons responded with a scoring drive of their own. With the ball at midfield, Hammond threw a short pass, against-the-grain, to Cole Fagan and the fullback took it 30 yards to the Army 14. Three plays later, Joseph Saucier took a pitch around the right side for his second rushing touchdown of the season. Saucier then converted the two-point conversion to cut the Army lead to 17-14 with 5:19 remaining.

NAVY {@ Lincoln Financial Field, Philadelphia, PA}

The #22 Black Knights recovered two fumbles in the fourth quarter, Kelvin Hopkins Jr. had two rushing touchdowns and Army beat Navy 17-10 on Saturday to win its third straight game in the series. President Donald Trump attended the 119th game between the rivals and flipped the coin before spending a half on each side in a show of impartiality. With Navy down 10-7, quarterback Zach Abey lost a fumble on fourth-and-12 deep in its own territory. Hopkins would score on a 1 yard run to make it 17-7 and give Army the cushion it needed to win in front of 66,729 fans at Lincoln Financial Field.

2018 ARMED FORCES BOWL

Army quarterback Kelvin Hopkins Jr initially ran right before cutting back the other way and eluding a tackler. He sent two other defenders sliding to the ground when he switched directions again and took off toward the end zone. That nifty 77 yard run was one of his Armed Forces Bowl-record five rushing touchdowns as the #22 Black Knights overwhelmed Houston 70-14 on Saturday to reach 11 wins for the first time in program history. The Black Knights' (11-2) 56-point win tied the FBS record for largest margin of victory in a bowl game. Army scored 70 points in a game for the first time since 1955, when it scored 81 against Furman. Hopkins ran 11 times for 170 yards before coming out of the game midway through the third quarter when it was 49-7. He also completed the first 1,000 yard passing season for Army since 2007. He was 3-of-3 passing for 70 yards, including a 54 yarder that set up one of his three 1 yard TD plunges. He also had a 2 yard TD run. Army got 507 of its 592 total yards on the ground.

2019 Army Black Knights

The Black Knights were led by sixth-year head coach Jeff Monken. Due to playing an away game at Hawaii and the NCAA's "Hawaii Exemption", the Black Knights played a 13-game regular season in 2019. They finished the season with a record of 5–8, finishing in third place for the Commander-in-Chief's Trophy following losses to Air Force and Navy, and missing out on a bowl game for the first time since the 2015 season.

Kelvin Hopkins led the team in passing with 577 yards and threw 4 touchdown passes. Hopkins led the team in rushing with 710 yards. Sandon McCoy led with 10 rushing touchdowns. Camden Harrison led the team in receptions with 25 for 433 yards. McCoy led the team in scoring with 60 points.

Home games were played at Michie Stadium

8/30/2019	ARMY	vs	RICE	14	7	**W**
9/7/2019	ARMY	@	Michigan	21	24	**L**
9/14/2019	ARMY	@	Texas-San Antonio	31	13	**W**
9/21/2019	ARMY	vs	MORGAN STATE	52	21	**W**
10/5/2019	ARMY	vs	TULANE	33	42	**L**
10/12/2019	ARMY	@	Western Kentucky	8	17	**L**
10/19/2019	ARMY	@	Georgia State	21	28	**L**
10/26/2019	ARMY	vs	SAN JOSE STATE	29	34	**L**
11/2/2019	ARMY	@	Air Force	13	17	**L**
11/9/2019	ARMY	vs	MASSACHUSETTS	63	7	**W**
11/16/2019	ARMY	vs	VIRGINIA MILITARY	47	6	**W**
11/30/2019	ARMY	@	Hawaii	31	52	**L**
12/14/2019	ARMY	vs	Navy	7	**31**	**L**
Coach: Jeff Monken			**Season Record >>**	370	299	**5-8**

Schedule Source: Steve's Football Bible LLC

Selected game(s) highlights

RICE

Army converted five third downs on an 18 play, game winning drive that took over 9 minutes of the fourth quarter and left the Owls in a hole they couldn't climb out of in the season opener for both teams. Hopkins hit Kell Walker with a 17 yard touchdown pass with 3:48 left and Army escaped with a 14-7 victory at Michie Stadium. The Owls threatened one last time, driving into Army territory. Quarterback Wiley Green lost the ball while scrambling and Army's Jacob Covington nearly covered it before Aston Walter fell on it for Rice with just over a minute left. A last-gasp sideline pass on fourth down by Green was broken up by Jaylon McClinton at the Army 15 with seconds to play. Hopkins gave the Black Knights a 7-0 lead on a 2 yard run midway through the second quarter, and big plays set up the score in a drive that took 16 plays and lasted nearly 10 minutes. After Army converted twice on third down and once on fourth, wide receiver Christian Hayes ran a reverse right for 35 yards on a third-and-9 play. One play later Hopkins hit Hayes again, this time along the left side for 17 yards to set up the score.

Michigan

Jake Moody made a 43 yard field goal, and the seventh ranked Wolverines forced and recovered a fumble to hold on for a 24-21 double overtime win over the Black Knights. In overtime at the quiet Big House, Black Knights quarterback Kelvin Hopkins ran for a go-ahead, 6 yard touchdown and Michigan extended the game with Zach Charbonnet's third TD. Hopkins was sacked and lost a fumble to end the game in the second overtime. Aidan Hutchinson hit Hopkins to jar the ball loose and Kwity Paye recovered the fumble to seal the win.

Air Force

The Air Force Academy football team completed a goal line stand in the final minute of the game to defeat Army West Point, 17-13, at Falcon Stadium. The Falcons finished with a one yard advantage in total offense, 344-343. The Falcons controlled the ground game, rushing for 328 to Army's 129. AF was also a perfect 3-for-3 in the red zone, while the Black Knights were 1-for-3. Needing a TD to take the lead after the missed extra point earlier, Army went to work on their drive. They worked their way all the way down to the five, but Air Force's defense was up to the task again, forcing an incomplete pass on fourth down, sealing the four point win.

VIRGINIA MILITARY INSTITUTE

Kelvin Hopkins responded by rushing for a career-high 208 yards and a touchdown on just 16 carries as Army's triple option overwhelmed VMI 47-6. Senior Connor Slomka scored three times on short runs and classmate Kell Walker added a touchdown on a 59 yard scamper off a pretty pitch to the outside from Hopkins midway through the third quarter as Army won its second straight. After Grant Clemons kicked a 37 yard field goal midway through the second quarter to move the Keydets within 7-6, Hopkins gave the Black Knights a needed jolt just before halftime, taking a keeper right for 42 yards to set up Slomka's 3 yard scoring run for a 14-6 lead with 3:08 left in the second.

NAVY {@ Lincoln Financial Field, Philadelphia, PA}

Malcom Perry dominated Saturday afternoon's affair as he led the #23 Midshipmen to a 31-7 win over Army, ending the three game losing streak to their rival. Perry rushed for 304 rushing yards and two touchdowns, and those 304 rushing yards are the most by any player in the 120 game history of The Army-Navy Game. Things started out well for Army as it put together an incredible 18 play, 78 yard touchdown drive that melted 10:41 off the clock in the first quarter ... but that was it. Army managed only 74 yards of offense in the final three quarters. Compare that to Navy, which ran only four plays for eight yards in the first quarter and finished the day with 396 total yards.

2020 Army Black Knights {Lambert Trophy} + {Commander-Chief-Trophy}

The Black Knights were led by seventh-year head coach Jeff Monken. In a season impacted by the COVID-19 pandemic, the Black Knights compiled a 9–2 regular season record. They defeated the Midshipmen of Navy and the Air Force Falcons to secure Army's ninth Commander-in-Chief's Trophy, their third in four seasons.

On October 24, the Black Knights became the first team of the 2020 season to accept a bowl invitation, to the Independence Bowl. However, that bowl was canceled on December 20, due to a lack of available teams, leaving Army without a bowl game. Athletic director Mike Buddie said that "the team will continue to look for an opponent." On December 21, the Black Knights were named to the Liberty Bowl, after Tennessee had to withdraw due to positive COVID-19 testing within their program. Army went on to lose to West Virginia in the bowl, finishing the season with a 9–3 record.

Following the completion of the season, the Black Knights were awarded the 2020 Lambert Trophy by the Eastern College Athletic Conference (ECAC) and Metropolitan New York Football Writers, signifying them as the best team in the East in Division I FBS. This was the ninth overall time the Lambert Trophy had been awarded to Army, and the second in three years (2018).

Christian Anderson led the team in passing with 215 yards. Tyhier Tyler led the team in rushing with 578 yards. Sandon McCoy led with 10 rushing touchdowns. Michael Roberts led the team in receptions with 7. Tyrell Robinson led with 117 receiving yards. McCoy led the team in scoring with 60 points.

Home games were played at Michie Stadium

9/5/2020	ARMY	vs	MIDDLE TENNESSEE	42	0	W	
9/12/2020	ARMY	vs	LOUISIANA-MONROE	37	7	W	
9/26/2020	ARMY	@	Cincinnati	10	24	L	
10/3/2020	ARMY	vs	ABILENE CHRISTIAN	55	23	W	
10/10/2020	ARMY	vs	THE CITADEL	14	9	W	
10/17/2020	ARMY	@	Texas-San Antonio	28	16	W	
10/24/2020	ARMY	vs	MERCER	49	3	W	
11/14/2020	ARMY	@	Tulane	12	38	L	
11/21/2020	ARMY	vs	GEORGIA SOUTHERN	28	27	W	
12/12/2020	ARMY	vs	NAVY	15	0	W	
12/19/2020	ARMY	vs	AIR FORCE	10	7	W	
12/26/2020	ARMY	vs	West Virginia	21	24	L	Liberty Bowl
Coach: Jeff Monken			Season Record >>	321	178	9-3	

Schedule Source: Steve's Football Bible LLC

Selected game(s) highlights

GEORGIA SOUTHERN

Army West Point completed an incredible come-from-behind victory to defeat visiting Georgia Southern, 28-27 to remain unbeaten at Michie Stadium. The Black Knights went down 14-0 early in the first quarter as Georgia Southern took advantage of some early Army miscues. However, the Black Knights battled back, capping off a 15-play, 75 yard, eight minute drive, with a one yard touchdown rush by Sandon McCoy. The extra point by Quinn Maretzki made it a 14-7 contest. The back-and-forth battle ensued, as Georgia Southern pulled out to a 21-7 lead on a 24 yard touchdown pass from Shai Werts to Cam Brown with 9:24 left in the half. Three fumbles lost in the first half played a big part in the 21-7 deficit at the half for the Black Knights as they outgained the Eagles 147 total yards to 137 yards in the half. Braheam Murphy had a 12 yard rushing touchdown to cap off an 11-play, 52 yard drive to pull within seven, 21-14. Then, Fabrice Voyne blocked a Georgia Southern punt, which was recovered and returned by Kemonte Yow 15 yards to the Georgia Southern two yard line. All it took was McCoy one play to rush two yards for his second score of the day, and the extra point by Maretzki made it a 21-21 game. The back-and-forth ballgame continued, as Georgia Southern a 39 yard touchdown pass from Werts to Logan Wright put them up, 27-21. The extra point attempt by Alex Raynor was blocked by Army's Andre Carter, the second blocked kick of the day. The Black Knights went on an 18 play, 71 yard drive that ate up 10 minutes and 50 seconds and scored on a two yard rush by Jakobi Buchanan, tying the game up 27-27. Kicker Maretzki connected on the key extra point to give Army a 28-27 lead with 8:16 left in the game. The defense then came up big with huge stops down the stretch.

NAVY

Tyhier Tyler scored on a 4 yard run early in the fourth quarter, the Army defense stoned Navy with a goal-line stand in the third, and the Black Knights beat their archrival 15-0 at fog-shrouded Michie Stadium. It was the first meeting between the teams at West Point since a 13-0 Navy shutout in 1943. The game was moved to Michie Stadium from Philadelphia because COVID-19 regulations in Pennsylvania would not have allowed the Corps of Cadets and Brigade of Midshipmen to attend. The game turned in the third quarter with Army clinging to a 3-0 lead and on its heels after Arline ripped off a 52 yard run. He was poised to cross the goal line when Cedric Cunningham ran him down and pushed him out of bounds at the 2. When two runs netted nothing, Navy coach Ken Niumatalolo called timeout. The Army defense then rose to the occasion again, with senior linebacker Jon Rhattigan stopping Arline inches of the goal and West stopping Nelson Smith on fourth down. Army went up 3-0 on Quinn Maretzki's 37 yard field goal early in the second quarter, set up by Tyler's 28 yard completion to Tyrell Robinson, just the second completion of his career. Tyler scored after a Navy turnover, the only one of the game, and Daryan McDonald tacked on a safety late in the fourth when he tackled Navy wide receiver Mark Walker in the end zone on a reverse. Maretzki added a 40 yard field goal.

AIR FORCE

In another epic chapter to the rivalry, Air Force football was on the wrong end of the score, falling 10-7 to Army at Michie Stadium. Army rallied late with the game-winning touchdown with 1:13 left to play. Fullback Jakobi Buchanan punched it in from one yard out on fourth down to give the Black Knights the win and CIC Trophy. Army led 3-0 after a field goal in the second quarter. The Falcons got on the scoreboard with 15 seconds left in the third quarter, when sophomore quarterback Haaziq Daniels found sophomore tight end Kyle Patterson in the end zone from 10 yards out for the go-ahead score. The Falcons were unable to maintain the lead, as Army rallied back with the TD drive, which took 16 plays and 80 yards in seven minutes. Air Force got the ball back with just over a minute left, but Daniels threw a game-ending interception on the first play of the drive.

2020 LIBERTY BOWL

The Army Black Knights fell 24-21 to West Virginia in the 62nd AutoZone Liberty Bowl on Thursday evening in Memphis, Tenn. The Black Knights went down 3-0 in the first quarter but rebounded and led 14-10 at the half and 21-16 in the third quarter but were shutout in the fourth quarter as the Mountaineers scored eight to push them over the top. The defense set the tone early, forcing two turnovers in the first half, including an interception of West Virginia quarterback Seth Doege by senior cornerback Javhari Bourdeau on West Virginia's second drive of the game. The Mountaineers got on the board first, however, as Tyler Sumpter drilled a 31 yard field goal with 1:47 left in the first quarter after he missed a 37 yard field goal attempt on the first drive of the game. Quarterback Tyhier Tyler answered back with a drive of 74 yards on 14 plays that ate up 7:12 as he capped things off with a one yard rush for the first touchdown of the day. An extra point by Quinn Maretzki followed and the Black Knights took a 10-7 lead with 9:31 left in the first half. West Virginia answered back however, with a sustained drive of their own, going 77 yards on 12 plays as quarterback Jarret Doege connected with T.J. Simmons on a five yard touchdown pass to take the lead back, 10-7. Army's defense came up with a huge play, the second turnover of the first half as Malkelm Morrison sacked Mountaineer quarterback Doege and caused a fumble, which was recovered by Ryan Duran at West Virginia's seven yard line. The Black Knights cashed in on that Mountaineer turnover, taking two plays and Tyler rushed for six yards for his second touchdown of the day. The extra point by Maretzki put the Black Knights up, 14-10 and that score carried into the half.

The Black Knights extended their lead to 21-10 after an eight minute drive to open the third quarter, as Tyhier Tyler tied the Liberty Bowl record with his third touchdown of the day, this one a two yard rush. The Mountaineers were not going to go down easy however, and eventually scored 14 unanswered points down the stretch that proved to be the difference in the game. A three yard touchdown pass from backup quarterback Austin Kendall to Mike O'Laughlin with 3:23 left in the third pulled the Mountaineers within five after the missed two-point conversion. A second touchdown came with 5:10 left in the fourth quarter, as Kendall hit receiver T.J. Simmons on a 20 yard route for their third touchdown of the day. Reese Smith rushed for two on the conversion to make it a 24-21 game. The Black Knights had a chance to tie the ballgame up, as they drove the field and with 1:50 left in the game had kicker Maretzki lined up for a 39 yard field goal attempt. However, he missed the kick wide left. The Army defense got the ball back one more time, and with 1:28 left the Black Knights started with the ball on their own 31 yard line, however, on a last-chance fourth-and-seven, quarterback Christian Anderson on intercepted on a desperation heave, ending the Black Knight's chances.

2021 Army Black Knights

The Black Knights were led by eighth-year head coach Jeff Monken. The Black Knights finished the season with a record of 9–4, sharing the Commander-in-Chief's Trophy with Navy and Air Force after all three service academies finished with 1–1 records against each other. They were invited to the Armed Forces Bowl where they defeated Missouri, 24–22.

Christian Anderson led the team in passing with 773 yards and 5 passing touchdowns. Anderson led the team in rushing with 652 yards. Jakobi Buchanan led the team with 13 rushing touchdowns. Isaiah Alston led the team in receptions with 25 and 479 yards receiving. Alston and Tryrell Robinson led with 3 touchdown receptions. Buchanan led the team in scoring with 78 points. Andre Carter II led the team with 16.5 sacks.

Home games were played at Michie Stadium

9/4/2021	ARMY	@		Georgia State	ESPNU	43	10	**W**
9/11/2021	ARMY	vs		WESTERN KENTUCKY	CBSSN	38	35	**W**
9/18/2021	ARMY	vs		CONNECTICUT	CBSSN	52	21	**W**
9/25/2021	ARMY	vs		MIAMI-OHIO	CBSSN	23	10	**W**
10/2/2021	ARMY	@		Ball State		16	28	**L**
10/16/2021	ARMY	@		Wisconsin	BTN	14	20	**L**
10/23/2021	ARMY	vs	#18	WAKE FOREST	CBSSN	56	70	**L**
11/6/2021	ARMY	vs		Air Force	CBS	21	14	**W**
11/13/2021	ARMY	vs		BUCKNELL	CBSSN	63	10	**W**
11/20/2021	ARMY	vs		MASSACHUSETTS	CBSSN	33	17	**W**
11/27/2021	ARMY	@		Liberty		31	16	**W**
12/11/2021	ARMY	vs		Navy	CBS	13	17	**L**
12/22/2021	**ARMY**	**vs**		**Missouri**	**ESPN**	**24**	**22**	**W**
Coach: Jeff Monken				**Season Record >>**		**390**	**251**	**9-4**

Schedule Source: Steve's Football Bible LLC

Selected game(s) highlights

WESTERN KENTUCKY

Christian Anderson rushed for a career-high 119 yards and passed for a touchdown and Army survived a Western Kentucky rally to take a 38-35 victory. Trailing 35-14 midway through the second quarter, WKU closed the gap to seven points on Bailey Zappe's 14-yard pass to Jerreth Sterns with just under five minutes remaining in the game. But Army recovered a WKU onside kick and Cole Talley kicked a 31-yard field goal, giving the Black Knights the cushion they needed after the Hilltoppers scored a touchdown with 21 seconds left. Jakobi Buchanan ran for a pair of Army touchdowns. Army rushed for 339 yards and almost doubled the Hilltoppers in time of possession.

MIAMI-OHIO

Christian Anderson ran for a pair long first-half touchdowns and Army remained undefeated with a 23-10 victory over Miami-Ohio. Anderson sprinted 72 yards on Army's third play then eclipsed that personal best with a 75-yard score in the second quarter. He had a career-high 236 yards rushing on 15 carries. It was a 42-yard run by Anderson in which he broke free of tacklers near the Army goal line that might have been the game's big play. Anderson's scamper came after a goal-line stand and was part of a 18-play drive that took nearly 11 minutes and ended with Anthony Adkins' 4-yard score early in the fourth quarter for a 23-3 lead. A 21-yard field goal by Cole Talley after Reikan Donaldson blocked a RedHawks punt made it 17-3 at halftime. Army gained all its 384 yards on the ground with five pass attempts incomplete.

Wisconsin

Army trailed 13-7 and had the ball when Leo Chenal delivered a punishing hit that knocked the ball loose from quarterback Jabari Laws. Wisconsin's Keeanu Benton recovered the fumble at Army's 1-yard line with 2:55 remaining. On the next play, Graham Mertz scored on a quarterback keeper for his second touchdown run of the night. Army cut the lead to 20-14 on A.J. Howard's 6-yard touchdown run with 38 seconds left, but Jack Sanborn recovered the ensuing onside kick to seal the victory.

WAKE FOREST

Sam Hartman threw for a career-high 458 yards and five touchdowns in a big-play display and ran for another score, and No. 16 Wake Forest defeated Army 70-56 to remain unbeaten in front of a sellout crowd at Michie Stadium. Hartman was unstoppable and rarely pressured, completing 23 of 29 passes and hitting touchdown passes of 41, 54 and two of 75 yards as he matched the Michie Stadium record for scoring passes. Jaquarii Roberson had eight catches for 157 yards and three touchdowns and A.T. Perry had six catches for 146 yards and one score. Army never led, and a costly interception return for a touchdown in the third quarter gave the Demon Deacons the breathing room they needed. Two touchdown passes by Army's Jabari Laws, a 21-yarder to Isaiah Alston late in the third, and a 25-yarder to Tyrell Robinson midway through the fourth, made it a one-possession game again until Hartman scored on an 8-yard run with 6:57 left. Army rushed for 416 yards and finished with 595 yards offensively as the teams combined for 1,233 yards in a game that featured just one punt. Anthony Adkins raced 71 yards for an Army score and Hartman responded with a 75-yard strike to Ke'Shawn Williams. Army matched the Demon Deacons on the scoreboard in the first half until Christian Beal-Smith scored on a 13-yard run up the gut of the Army defense with 35 seconds left in the second quarter to give Wake Forest a 28-21 halftime lead.

Air Force {@ AT&T Stadium – Arlington, TX}

Jordyn Law recovered teammate Christian Anderson's fumble at the goal line for an overtime touchdown and Army defeated Air Force 21-14. After Law's game-saving recovery, the Black Knights denied the Falcons the end zone when Jabari Moore broke up Haaziq Daniels' fourth-down pass. Air Force tied the game on Matthew Depore's second field goal of the game, a 30-yarder with 23 seconds left in regulation. They had reached the Army 11 before a 15-yard chop-block penalty stalled the drive. After a scoreless first half, Army took the second-half kickoff and with the help of a 39-yard pass from Tyhier Tyler to Tyrell Robinson, scored on Tyler's 9-yard run. Air Force responded with Dapore's 39-yard field goal and Army came right back with a 79-yard pass play from Christian Anderson to Robinson and a 13-3 lead after three quarters. Air Force closed the gap to 14-9 early in the fourth on Daniels' 4-yard toss to Dane Kinamon with the key play on the drive a 31-yard completion to David Cormier.

Liberty

Jakobi Buchanan ran for three touchdowns and Christian Anderson threw for a score and Army beat Liberty 31-16. After Liberty turned it over on downs in five plays to start the game, Cole Talley kicked a 26-yard field goal to give Army 3-0 lead. The Black Knights followed up defensively when Bo Nicolas-Paul intercepted Max Morgan. On Army's ensuing drive, Anderson threw a 34-yard scoring pass to Braheam Murphy for a 10-0 advantage just before the end of the first quarter. The Flames continued turning it over on downs doing so on their next two possessions which resulted in Buchanan scoring runs of 19 and 1 yards for a 24-0 lead. His 7-yard scoring run came with 6:45 left in the third for a 31-3 lead. Malik Willis threw a 14-yard touchdown pass to Noah Frith for Liberty's first touchdown of the day with 4:35 left in the third, and then Willis ran it in from seven yards seconds before the third ended to cut the deficit to 31-16.

NAVY {@ Met Life Stadium, East Rutherford, NJ}

Quarterback Tai Lavatai ran for two touchdowns and Navy's defense limited Army to 57 second-half yards and a season-low 232 overall in a 17-13 victory Saturday in a game played at the Meadowlands to commemorate the 20th anniversary of the 9/11 terrorist attacks. Navy dominated against bowl-bound Army after giving up an early touchdown. It outgained them 278 yards to 232, including 196-124 on the ground against the nation's No. 2 rushing offense. The Middies held the ball for 34:25 and converted three big plays, including a fourth-down, fake punt in the fourth quarter that wasn't supposed to be a fake punt. Cole Talley added field goals of 31 and 32 yards in helping Army take a 13-7 halftime lead. The Black Knights generated little after that. Navy took over in the second half, taking the kickoff and going 74 yards in 10 plays with Lavatai scoring from 2 yards out. The drive featured a 26-yard run by Chance Warren on fourth-and-4 that got the ball to the 2. It was supposed to be a pass to Lavatai, but Warren saw it wasn't open, so he ran.

2021 ARMED FORCES BOWL

Cole Talley kicked a 41-yard field goal as time expired and Army rallied to beat Missouri 24-22 in the Armed Forces Bowl. After the Tigers took a 22-21 lead on a touchdown with 1:11 to play, third-string quarterback Jabari Laws led Army downfield to the Missouri 24-yard line, setting up Talley's game-winner. Army backup quarterback Tyhier Tyler came on after starter Christian Anderson injured an ankle late in the third quarter and threw a 14-yard touchdown pass to Brandon Walters to give the Black Knights their first lead, 21-16. Anderson and JaKobi Buchanan scored on TD runs of 22 and 10 yards, respectively, for Army. Redshirt freshman quarterback Brady Cook threw a 6-yard touchdown pass to Keke Chism with 71 seconds left to put the Tigers ahead, but his two-point conversion pass sailed over the head of an open Dawson Downing in the end zone. Cook also ran for a 30-yard score in his first collegiate start.

2022 Army Black Knights

The Black Knights were led by ninth-year head coach Jeff Monken. Army finished the season with a 6-6 record. The highlight was a double overtime win over Navy, 20-17. Army was not invited to a Bowl Game, after two straight Bowl game appearances.

Cade Ballard led the team in passing with 363 yards and two touchdown passes. Tyhier Tyler led the team in rushing with 621 yards. Isaiah Alston led the team in receiving with 16 receptions for 269 yards. Tyler led the team in scoring with 72 points. Marquel Broughton led the team with 3 interceptions. Andre Carter II led the team with 3.5 sacks.

Home games were played at Michie Stadium

9/3/2022	ARMY		@		Coastal Carolina		28	38	L
9/10/2022	ARMY	vs			TEXAS-SAN ANTONIO	CBSSN	38	41	L
9/17/2022	ARMY	vs			VILLANOVA	CBSSN	49	10	W
10/1/2022	ARMY	vs			GEORGIA STATE	CBSSN	14	31	L
10/8/2022	ARMY	@	#14		Wake Forest	ACC	10	45	L
10/15/2022	ARMY	vs			COLGATE	CBSSN	42	17	W
10/22/2022	ARMY	vs			LOUISIANA-MONROE	CBSSN	48	24	W
11/5/2022	ARMY	vs			Air Force {@ Arlington, TX}	CBS	7	13	L
11/12/2022	ARMY	@			Troy	NFL	9	10	L
11/19/2022	ARMY	vs			CONNECTICUT	CBSSN	34	17	W
11/26/2022	ARMY	@			Massachusetts		44	7	W
12/10/2022	ARMY	vs			Navy {@ Philadelphia} {2 OT}	CBS	20	17	W
Coach: Jeff Monken					**Season Record >>**		343	270	6-6

Schedule Source: Steve's Football Bible LLC

Selected game(s) highlights

TEXAS-SAN ANTONIO

Frank Harris threw for 359 yards and three touchdowns, including the game-winner to JT Clark in overtime, rallying UTSA to a 41-38 victory over Army. The Roadrunners missed a 41-year field-goal attempt on the final play of regulation and Army took the lead on the first possession of overtime on Quinn Maretzki's first field goal of the season before Harris brought back UTSA again. Trailing 28-14 midway through the third quarter, Harris directed the Roadrunners to three straight touchdowns, taking the lead 34-28 with Brenden Brady's 1-yard run. Army's Cade Ballard, who left the game midway through the third quarter with leg cramps, returned to throw a 42-yard score to Tyrell Robinson with just over a minute left in regulation. Army led 21-14 at halftime. Tyhier Tyler, who had a 77-yard TD pass to Ay'Jaun Marshall for the game's first points, reentered the game for Ballard, and scored on a 16-yard run for a 14-point lead midway through the third quarter. But Harris threw 9 yards to Zakhari Franklin for a score and Brady added a pair of 1-yard scores.

COLGATE

Jemel Jones ran for two touchdowns in his first start this season and Army defeated Colgate 42-17 on Saturday. Jones made his first start of the season and finished with 113 yards rushing on 12 carries including a 75-yard run that gave Army its first points. Jones' 1-yard TD capped an eight-minute drive to open the second half and Leo Lowin's interception set up Markel Johnson's 24-touchdown run for a 42-17 lead heading in the fourth quarter. Johnson came in with 19 yards on four carries this season.

LOUISIANA-MONROE

Jemel Jones scored a career-high three touchdowns and Army rallied in the second half to beat Louisiana-Monroe 48-24 on Saturday. Jones started his second straight game and rushed for 96 of Army's 441 yards on the ground. After Quinn Maretzki tied the game at 17-all with a field goal early in the third quarter, the Black Knights scored twice more in the period to pull away. Leo Lowin's interception led to Jones' third touchdown, a 6-yarder, to take the lead. Ay'Jaun Marshall's 36-yard catch - one of two completions for Army - set up the Black Knights at the ULM 9 and Tyson Riley scored from the 3 in the final minute of the third. Bryson Daily capped Army's 34-point second half with a 64-yard run late in the game. Chandler Rogers threw for two touchdowns and was intercepted once for the Warhawks. He threw a 12-yard scoring pass to Boogie Knight and Andrew Henry ran for a 10-yard score in the second quarter.

Air Force {@ Arlington, TX}

Brad Roberts carried it 33 times for 135 yards, Camby Goff intercepted a pass with 19 second left and Air Force edged Army 13-7 on Saturday at Globe Life Field for it first Commander-in-Chief's trophy since 2016. Air Force was stopped for a loss on a third-and-3 run near midfield with 1:46 left, giving Army a chance at a game-winning touchdown drive. The Black Knights converted one fourth down on the drive but threw an interception on fourth-and-2 as Goff cut in front of Ay'Jaun Marshall along the Army sideline for his third pick of the season. The Falcons clinched a record 21st trophy - awarded to the academy with the best record in the round-robin competition. Haaziq Daniels was 6-of-13 passing for 98 yards with an interception and he carried it 14 times for 89 yards and a touchdown for Air Force. Daniels' 17-yard touchdown early in the third quarter gave Air Force a 10-7 lead and Matthew Dapore made his second short field goal to cap the scoring with 12:06 left in the fourth. Jemel Jones passed for 67 yards and rushed for 37 and a touchdown for Army.

CONNECTICUT

Braheam Murphy ran for 124 yards and a touchdown to lead Army to a 34-17 victory over Connecticut. Murphy ran along the left hashmark and bolted 75 yards untouched into the end zone to give Army a 20-17 lead midway through the third quarter. Quarterback Tyhier Tyler's 4-yard touchdown run stretched the Black Knights' lead to 27-17 late in the third. UConn's last possessions ended with two punts and two interceptions. Tyler attempted just one pass and finished with 70 yards rushing for Army (4-6). He scored on a 2-yard run in the fourth. Army's Miles Stewart returned a blocked punt 19 yards into the end zone just two minutes into the game.

Navy {@ Philadelphia, PA}

The Army Black Knights downed the Navy Midshipmen in a 20-17 double overtime victory on Saturday, the first overtime game in the rivalry's history. With possession in the second overtime, Navy committed a costly turnover when running back Anton Hall Jr. fumbled on the one-yard line. Getting possession back, Army kicker Quinn Maretzki was able to boot a 39-yard field goal to finish it off for the Black Knights. This game was the exact defensive struggle that you would imagine with both familiar foes fighting to impose its will on the other. Navy held onto a 3-0 lead late into the second quarter before a Navy punt block was returned by Jabril Williams for a touchdown to give the Black Knights a 7-3 advantage heading into the half. Hall would turn the game on its head in the third quarter, breaking off a 77-yard touchdown run to put Navy back on top. That surprisingly marked the longest touchdown score in the rivalry's history. With its back against the wall deep into the fourth quarter, Army managed to get into Navy territory to set up a 37-yard field goal by Maretzki to tie the game with 1:53 to go. We were treated to a fireworks show to begin the overtime period. Markel Johnson broke off a 25-yard touchdown run on the first play for Army and Navy immediately followed that up when Xavier Arline hit Marquel Haywood on a wheel route for a touchdown on its first play. Following that was Hall's costly fumble, setting up the game-winning kick for Army.

2023 Army Black Knights {Commander-In-Chief Trophy}

The Black Knights were led by 10th-year head coach Jeff Monken and played their home games at Michie Stadium in West Point, New York. They competed as an independent and finished with a 6–6 record—the team was not invited to a bowl game as they had not met bowl eligibility requirements when bowl matchups were announced in early December, and even if they had accumulated six wins at that time, two of their wins were against FCS opponents. This was the Black Knights' last season competing as an independent, as Army joined the American Athletic Conference as a football-only member beginning in 2024.

Bryson Daily led the team in passing with 913 yards and 7 touchdown passes. Daily led the team in rushing with 901 yards and 7 rushing touchdowns. Noah Short led the team with 18 receptions. Isaiah Alston led the team with 266 receiving yards. Tyson Riley led with 3 touchdown receptions. Quinn Maretzki led the team in scoring with 61 points. Quindreling Hammonds and Bp Niclaus-Paul led the team in interceptions with 3. Leo Lowin, Jimmy Ciarlo and Jackson Powell led the team in sacks with 3.0.

Home games were played at Michie Stadium

9/2/2023	ARMY	@		Louisiana-Monroe	NFL	13	17	L
9/9/2023	ARMY	vs		DELAWARE STATE		57	0	W
9/15/2023	ARMY	@		Texas-San Antonio	ESPN	37	29	W
9/23/2023	ARMY	@		Syracuse	ACC	16	29	L
10/7/2023	ARMY	vs		BOSTON COLLEGE	CBSSN	24	27	L
10/14/2023	ARMY	vs		TROY	CBSSN	0	19	L
10/21/2023	ARMY	@	#19	Lsu	SEC	0	62	L
10/28/2023	ARMY	vs		MASSACHUSETTS	CBSSN	14	21	L
11/4/2023	ARMY	vs	#17	Air Force {@ Denver}	CBSSN	23	3	W
11/11/2023	ARMY	vs		HOLY CROSS	CBSSN	17	14	W
11/18/2023	ARMY	vs		COASTAL CAROLINA	CBSSN	28	21	W
12/9/2023	ARMY	vs		Navy {@ Foxborough}		17	11	W
Coach: Jeff Monken				**Season Record >>**		246	253	6-6

Schedule Source: Steve's Football Bible LLC

Selected game(s) highlights

Texas-San Antonio

Hayden Reed and Jakobi Buchanan had first-quarter touchdown runs, and Army never trailed in a 37-29 victory over UTSA. Reed scored from a yard out midway through the quarter and Buchanan punched it in from the 10 with 1:15 left to give the Black Knights a 14-0 lead. Robert Henry had a 19-yard touchdown run early in the second quarter to get the Roadrunners on the scoreboard. Quinn Maretzki followed with 23- and 45-yard field goals to push Army's lead to 20-7. Eddie Lee Marburger connected with Tykee Ogle-Kellogg for a 46-yard touchdown on the final play of the quarter to pull UTSA within 20-14 at halftime. Maretzki added a third field goal, but Marburger hooked up with Joshua Cephus for a 44-yard score and the Roadrunners trailed 23-21 with 7:04 left in the third quarter. It took the Black Knights just two plays — a 55-yard completion from running back Markel Johnson to Isaiah Alston and a 25-yard scoring strike from Bryson Daily to Noah Short — to retake a two-score lead. Daily scored on a 3-yard run with 6:45 left to play, but Marburger connected with Devin McCuin for a 72-yard score and the pair teamed up again for the two-point conversion to get the Roadrunners within 37-29 just 33 seconds later. The UTSA defense forced a three-and-out and Army's defense did likewise. Daily twice ran for first downs in the final three minutes to wrap up the victory. Daily completed 7 of 17 passes for 133 yards. Reed rushed 20 times for 107 yards, while Daily added 100 on 24 carries.

Air Force {@ Denver}

Army wrecked No. 17 Air Force's perfect season — and then some. Quarterback Bryson Daily ran for 170 yards and two touchdowns, Army's swarming defense forced six turnovers, and the Black Knights knocked Air Force from the list of undefeated teams with a 23-3 win. A stunned and staggered Falcons team never got on track in front of 52,401 fans at Empower Field at Mile High in Denver. The mistake-prone Falcons had four fumbles, threw two interceptions, missed a 32-yard field goal and turned the ball over twice on downs as their best start since 1985 came to a halt. Daily set the tone early with a 62-yard TD run less than two minutes into the game. Leo Lowin led a menacing defensive performance with 12 tackles, a sack, two forced fumbles and a fumble recovery.

HOLY CROSS

Tyrell Robinson scored on a 14-yard run, Elo Modozie returned a blocked punt for another touchdown and Army defeated Holy Cross 17-14 on Saturday. Matthew Sluka's 8-yard touchdown pass to Jalen Coker with two minutes left got the Crusaders within three points, but Army recovered an onside kick and was able to run out the clock with the help of a fourth-and-1 conversion. Quinn Maretzki's 26-yard field goal with five minutes left in the game made it 17-7. Less than three minutes into the game Modozie scooped and scored for a 12-yard run after Jamil Williams blocked a punt. Robinson's touchdown made it 14-0 early in the second quarter. Sluka threw a 24-yard pass to Justin Shorter early in the fourth quarter for the Crusaders' other score. Bryson Daily thew for 79 yards and rushed for 83 for Army.

Navy {@ Foxborough}

Army held its ground on a goal-line stand in the final seconds to send Navy mascot Bill the Goat — and Navy superfan Bill, the G.O.A.T. — home disappointed. Army linebacker Kalib Fortner scored on a fourth-quarter strip sack and then helped stuff quarterback Tai Lavatai inches from the end zone with 3 seconds left to lead the Black Knights to a 17-11 victory over Navy on Saturday and win the 124th meeting of the nation's oldest service academies. Bryson Daily ran for 84 yards and threw Army's first touchdown pass against Navy since 2015 to help the Black Knights claim the much-coveted bragging rights for the sixth time in eight tries. Kanye Udoh ran for 88 yards for Army, which also claimed the Commander-in-Chief's Trophy. Lavatai came off the bench in the second quarter and rushed for 74 yards, completing 16 of 26 passes for 176 yards — the most passing yards for a Navy quarterback against Army since 2010. Jayden Umbarger caught six passes for 75 yards and a touchdown that made it 17-9 with 2:47 left. The Black Knights opened a 17-3 lead with less than five minutes to play before Lavatai drove Navy for one score and then took the Midshipmen to the Army 6 in the final minute. He threw two incompletions before hitting Alex Tecza, who was tackled in bounds at the 2. With no timeouts and no opportunity to spike the ball — it was fourth down — Navy scrambled to line up and get the play off. Lavatai surged forward as his whole team pushed, ahead of him and behind, but Army held on; replay confirmed that the ball never crossed the goal line. To kill the remaining 3 seconds, Daily took a shotgun snap, hesitated, and stepped out of the end zone for an intentional safety.

2024 Army Black Knights

The Black Knights were led by 11th-year head coach Jeff Monken. This was the first season that Army played in the American Athletic Conference {AAC}. They won the AAC Championship game beating Tulane, 35-14 at Michie Stadium. Army was invited to the Independence Bowl where they played Louisiana Tech of Conference USA. With the defeat of Louisiana Tech, the Black Knights won 12 games for the first time in school history.

Bryson Daily {QB}, Bill Katsigiannis {G}, Brady Small {TE} and Max DiDomenico {S} were selected to the AAC All-Conference First Team. Daily was named the AAC Offensive Player of the Year. Jeff Monken was named the AAC Coach of the Year and won the Buddy Teevens Coach of the Year Award. The Offensive Line won the Joe Moore Award. Bryson Daily led the team in passing yards with 1,007 yards and 9 touchdown passes. Daily led the team in rushing with 1,659 yards and 32 rushing touchdowns. Casey Reynolds led the team in receptions with 20 and 457 yards receiving. Reynolds and Noah Short had 3 touchdown receptions. Daily led the team in scoring with 192 points. Casey Larkin and Jaydan Mayes led the team with 4 interceptions. Elo Modozie led the team with 6.5 sacks.

FINAL RANK: #21 AP/#21 UPI

Home games were played at Michie Stadium

Date	Rank			Opponent	TV				
8/30/2024		vs		*LEHIGH*	CBSSN	42	7	W	
9/7/2024		@		Florida Atlantic	CBSSN	24	7	W	
9/21/2024		vs		RICE	CBSSN	37	14	W	
9/28/2024		@		Temple	ESPN	42	14	W	
10/5/2024		@		Tulsa	ESPNU	49	7	W	
10/12/2024		vs		ALABAMA-BIRMINGHAM	CBSSN	44	10	W	
10/19/2024	#23	vs		EAST CAROLINA	espn2	45	28	W	
11/2/2024	#21	vs		*AIR FORCE*	CBS	20	3	W	
11/9/2024	#18	@		North Texas	espn2	14	3	W	
11/23/2024	#18	vs	#6	*Notre Dame {@ Yankee Stadium}*	NBC	14	49	L	
11/30/2024	#25	vs		TEXAS-SAN ANTONIO	CBSSN	29	24	W	
12/6/2024	#24	vs		**Tulane**	ABC	35	14	W	*-AAC Championship
12/14/2024	#22	vs		Navy {@ Landover, MD}	CBS	13	31	L	
12/28/2024	#22	vs		**Louisiana Tech**	ESPN	27	6	W	**Independence Bowl**
Coach: Jeff Monken				**Season Record >>**		435	217	12-2	*-Daily 5 rush TD's

Schedule Source: Steve's Football Bible LLC

Selected game(s) highlights

EAST CAROLINA

Bryson Daily rushed for a career-high five touchdowns and set Army's single-season record for rushing TDs, helping the No. 23 Black Knights beat East Carolina 45-28. Daily had 171 yards on 31 carries in his sixth straight 100-yard rushing game. Army opened the scoring on Daily's 13-yard touchdown pass to running back Miles Stewart. The Black Knights extended their lead to 24-0 at halftime on Daily touchdowns runs of 17 and 31 yards and Trey Gronotte's 23-yard field goal. East Carolina managed only 95 yards in the first half. But Katin Houser threw for three second-half touchdowns and finished with 282 yards passing.

AIR FORCE

Kanye Udoh rushed for 158 yards and two touchdowns Saturday to help No. 21 Army to a 20-3 victory over Air Force. Army's defense limited Air Force to only three red zone plays on the day and picked off three Falcons' passes in the fourth quarter. Udoh ran seven times for 48 yards on Army's opening drive of the second half. The sophomore finished the possession off with a 12-yard touchdown run. Max DiDomenico's interception sealed the victory for Army with 1:51 left. DiDomenico returned the interception 69 yards to Air Force's 25. Udoh scored his second touchdown on the next play. Trey Gronotte kicked two field goals in the first half for a 6-3 Army lead at halftime.

#6 Notre Dame

Jeremiyah Love scored three touchdowns, tying a school record with his 11th straight game with a rushing TD, and the No. 6 Fighting Irish ended No. 18 Army's 13-game winning streak with a 49-14 victory on at Yankee Stadium. Love had TD runs of 68 and 14 yards, finishing with 130 yards on seven carries, and leaped over a defender at the goal line to finish a 6-yard scoring pass from Riley Leonard. Leonard threw for two TDs and Jadarian Price ran for two scores for the Irish. Army quarterback Bryson Daily ran for 139 yards and both touchdowns. Notre Dame beat Army for the 16th straight time in the first matchup where both teams were ranked since 1958, the Black Knights' last victory. Notre Dame took a 14-0 lead on TD passes by Leonard on its first two possessions. Army cut it to 14-7 on Daily's 4-yard run early in the second quarter, but the Irish went up by two TDs again on Love's 14-yard run.

TEXAS-SAN ANTONIO

Bryson Daily tied the American Athletic Conference record for single-season touchdowns and threw for a season-high 190 yards and a score to lift No. 25 Army to a 29-24 win over UTSA. Daily rushed for 147 yards and two touchdowns. Casey Larkin sealed Army's 10th victory of the season, picking off Owen McCown at the Black Knights' 10 with 1:14 left. Kalib Fortner and Chance Keith combined to stop Brandon High short on 4th-and-1 from UTSA's 16 on the first play of the fourth quarter. Five plays later, Bryson Daily scored his 24th touchdown of the season from one yard out to give Army a 22-17 lead. Collin Matteson picked off McCown for his first career interception with 11:17 left in the game. Daily scored his conference-tying 25th rushing touchdown, a 42-yard run on the second play following Matteson's pick with 10:26 remaining in the game. Trey Gronotte made a career-high three field goals. Gronotte's 35-yard kick tied the game at 10-10 as time expired in the first half.

2024 AAC CHAMPIONSHIP

Bryson Daily rushed for four touchdowns to tie the American Athletic Conference championship game record, and No. 24 Army completed a perfect first season in the league by beating Tulane 35-14. Kanye Udoh rushed for 158 yards, including a 72-yarder to set up a Daily TD, and a score. Daily added 126 yards on the ground for the Black Knights. Daily had touchdown runs of 5, 3, 4 and 7 yards. Darian Mensah threw two touchdown passes for Tulane. Army gained 335 on the ground and went 4 for 5 on fourth down. Daily's 4-yard run made it 21-0 before Tulane finally got on the board on Mensah's 42-yard pass to Mario Williams with 44 seconds left in the half.

Navy {@ Landover, MD}

Blake Horvath outplayed Bryson Daily at quarterback, accounting for 311 yards and four touchdowns to help Navy beat No. 19 Army 31-13 on Saturday. Horvath threw for 107 yards and two touchdowns and ran for 204 yards and two TDs. Daily threw a touchdown pass of his own, but he was intercepted three times. Army fell behind 14-0 in the second quarter and never completely recovered. In front of a crowd that included President-elect Donald Trump at the Washington Commanders' home stadium in Landover, Navy took the opening kickoff and drove 65 yards, reaching the end zone on a 1-yard run by Horvath. Daily, who had been intercepted only once all season, had a pass picked off in the second quarter by Dashaun Peele. The Midshipmen took advantage of a short field, going ahead 14-0 on an 18-yard pass from Horvath to Brandon Chatman. Daily answered with a TD pass of his own — 23 yards to Hayden Reed. After a field goal made the score 14-10, Horvath connected with Eli Heidenreich, who broke free up the left sideline for a 52-yard touchdown. Daily missed an open Casey Reynolds in the end zone early in the fourth, and Army settled for a field goal. Navy then faced fourth down near midfield, but Landon Robinson — normally a nose guard — ran 29 yards on a fake punt. Although Robinson fumbled at the end of the play, the Midshipmen were able to recover. Horvath's 1-yard scoring run made it 28-13, and Daily was intercepted twice more before the end of the game.

2024 INDEPENDENCE BOWL

Bryson Daily broke the FBS record for touchdowns by a quarterback in a season with 32, running for three scores in No. 19 Army's 27-6 victory over Louisiana Tech in the Independence Bowl. Daily ran for 127 yards on 27 carries and was 2-of-9 passing for 65 yards to help Army set a program victory record at 12-2. Hayden Reed added 114 yards rushing and a TD on 20 carries. Army set an Independence Bowl record with a 21-play drive, going 75 yards in the second quarter to take a 21-3 lead. Daily scored on an 8-yard run to end the drive that had two third-down conversions and three fourth-down conversions. Drew Henderson made field goals of 27 and 44 yards for Louisiana Tech.

2025 Army Black Knights

The 2025 Army Black Knights football team was led by Jeff Monken in his 12th year as head coach. Army finished the season with a 7-6 record and beat Connecticut in the Fenway Bowl, 41-16.

Brady Small {C} was selected to the First Team AAC All-Conference team. Cale Hellums led the team in passing with 694 yards and 4 TD passes. Hellums led the team in rushing with 1,223 yards and 18 rushing TD's. Noah Short led the team with 32 receptions for 438 yards. Short and Brady Anderson each had 2 TD receptions. Casey Larkin and Gavin Shields each had 2 interceptions to lead the team. Eric Ford and Jack Bousum tied for the team lead with 4.5 sacks. Hellums led the team with 108 points scored.

Home games were played at Michie Stadium

Date			Opponent	TV				
8/29/2025	vs		*TARLETON STATE*	CBSSN	27	30	L	
9/6/2025	@		*Kansas State*	ESPN	24	21	W	
9/20/2025	vs		NORTH TEXAS	CBSSN	38	45	L	
9/25/2025	@		East Carolina	ESPN	6	28	L	
10/4/2025	@		Alabama-Birmingham	ESPNU	31	13	W	
10/11/2025	vs		CHARLOTTE	CBSSN	24	7	W	
10/18/2025	@		Tulane	ESPNU	17	24	L	
11/1/2025	@		*Air Force*	CBS	20	17	W	
11/8/2025	vs		TEMPLE	CBSSN	14	13	W	
11/22/2025	vs		TULSA	CBSSN	25	26	L	
11/29/2025	@		Texas-San Antonio		27	24	W	
12/13/2025	vs	#23	Navy {@ Baltimore}	CBS	16	17	L	
12/27/2025	**vs**		**Connecticut**	**ESPN**	**41**	**16**	**W**	**Fenway Bowl**
Coach: Jeff Monken			**Season Record >>**		**310**	**281**	**7-6**	

Schedule Source: Steve's Football Bible LLC

Selected game(s) highlights

TARLETON STATE

In one of the most historic upsets in the program's history, Tarleton State defeated Army 30−27 in double overtime on August 29, 2025. This marked the Texans' first-ever road victory against an FBS program and handed the defending American Athletic Conference champions a shocking home-opening loss at Michie Stadium. The game was a story of two halves, with Army dominating early but failing to put the game away. The Black Knights built a 24−10 lead midway through the third quarter. Quarterback Dewayne Coleman and backup Cale Hellums led a rushing attack that seemed to have the Texans on their heels. Trailing by 14, Tarleton State stayed patient. Caleb Lewis cut the lead to seven with a 6-yard touchdown run. In the fourth quarter, quarterback Victor Gabalis found Dawson Hearne for a 15-yard touchdown strike to tie the game at 24 and silence the West Point crowd. Army had a chance to win in the final seconds of regulation, but freshman kicker Dawson Jones missed a 43-yard field goal attempt wide right as time expired. Both kickers were perfect under pressure. Tarleton's Brad Larson drilled a 28-yarder, and Army's Dawson Jones redeemed himself with a 40-yarder to force a second extra period tied at 27. The Army offense stalled, and Jones missed a go-ahead 35-yard field goal. This left the door open for Tarleton. After a short series of runs, Brad Larson stepped up and nailed a 37-yard walk-off field goal to seal the 30−27 victory.

Kansas State

In one of the most stunning upsets of the early 2025 season, Army defeated Kansas State 24−21 at Bill Snyder Family Stadium. Coming off a loss to Tarleton State just a week prior, the Black Knights used a masterclass in time management and ball control to shock the Wildcats in Manhattan. Army utilized its triple-option attack to perfection, essentially removing the Kansas State offense from the game in the second half. In the second half, Army held the ball for 26:59, while Kansas State had it for only 3:01. This was the lowest second-half time of possession for an FBS team in over 15 seasons. Army finished with a total time of possession of 40:44 compared to K-State's 19:16. Junior quarterback Cale Hellums made his first career start and put on a legendary performance. Hellums carried the ball 41 times for 124 yards, the most rushing attempts by any player in Army history. Trailing 21–17 in the fourth quarter, Army recovered a squib kick that deflected off a K-State player. Hellums then led a 14-play, 56-yard drive, capping it with a 14-yard go-ahead touchdown run with 2:52 remaining. Hellums accounted for all three Army touchdowns (two rushing, one passing).

Air Force

In a classic service academy defensive battle, Army defeated Air Force 20–17 at Falcon Stadium. The game was decided on the final play when Army kicker Dawson Jones drilled a 27-yard field goal to break a late tie and secure the Black Knights' third consecutive victory over the Falcons. The game remained a one-score affair until a frantic sequence in the closing minutes. With 2:10 remaining, Air Force's defense made a massive stop, stuffing Army quarterback Cale Hellums on a 4th-and-1 sneak at the Army 26-yard line. Taking over with elite field position, Air Force quarterback Liam Szarka orchestrated a quick drive, capped by his own 2-yard touchdown sneak with 1:26 left. Following a successful PAT, the game was tied at 17–17. On the ensuing drive, with just 24 seconds on the clock, Hellums threw a deep 42-yard pass to Brady Anderson, who beat the Air Force secondary over the middle. This play set the Black Knights up at the Air Force 10-yard line, leading to Jones' walk-off field goal as time expired. Hellums accounted for nearly 200 yards of offense, rushing 26 times for 98 yards and a touchdown while throwing for 102 yards and another score.

TEMPLE

The Black Knights defeated Temple 14–13 at Michie Stadium. The defining moment of the game occurred in the fourth quarter. After Temple punted with 9:53 remaining, Army took possession at their own 42-yard line and never gave the ball back. Army ran 18 plays (all on the ground), converted two critical 4th-and-1 situations, and drained all 9:53 off the clock. Quarterback Cale Hellums reached the Temple 4-yard line and chose to slide and take a knee rather than score, ensuring the Owls' offense stayed on the sideline until the clock hit zero. The contest was a defensive slugfest from the start, with the two teams combining for only seven total possessions in the first half. Army struck first in the second quarter with a 73-yard drive capped by a 7-yard TD run from Jake Rendina. Temple responded with a touchdown pass from Evan Simon to Colin Chase. A field goal on the final play of the half gave Temple a 10–7 lead at the break. Army took the opening kickoff of the third quarter and marched 75 yards over eight minutes, with Hellums scoring on a 3-yard run. Temple answered with a 31-yard field goal to cut the lead to 14–13, but they would not see the end zone again.

Texas-San Antonio

In a thrilling regular-season finale at the Alamodome, Army defeated UTSA 27–24. The victory snapped UTSA's 25-game home winning streak against conference opponents. The game featured several major momentum swings, with Army erasing an early deficit before surviving a late UTSA rally. The Roadrunners jumped out to a 10–0 lead early in the second quarter. The highlight was a trick play where wide receiver David Amador II threw a 4-yard touchdown pass to tight end Patrick Overmyer. The Black Knights responded with 17 unanswered points before halftime. Noah Short ignited the comeback with a spectacular 81-yard touchdown run. Shortly after, Jaydan Mayes intercepted a tipped pass and returned it 73 yards for a "pick-six," giving Army a 17–10 lead at the break. After a field goal extended Army's lead to 20–10, UTSA quarterback Owen McCown orchestrated a comeback. He threw two touchdown passes in the fourth quarter—one to Overmyer and a 7-yard strike to Jamel Hardy Jr.—to give UTSA a 24–20 lead with 9:00 remaining. Facing a must-score situation, Army QB Cale Hellums led a 13-play, 75-yard drive that lasted over six minutes. On 4th down, Hellums connected with Parker Poloskey for a 4-yard touchdown with 2:49 left. It was the first touchdown catch by an Army tight end in 17 years

#23 Navy {@ Baltimore, MD}

In a defensive masterpiece at M&T Bank Stadium in Baltimore, No. 22 Navy defeated Army 17–16 on December 13, 2025. The victory allowed the Midshipmen to sweep the service academy series and claim their second consecutive Commander-in-Chief's Trophy. Trailing 16–10 in the fourth quarter, Navy quarterback Blake Horvath orchestrated a legacy-defining drive. Navy faced a daunting 4th-and-goal from the 8-yard line with 6:32 remaining. Horvath stood calm in the pocket and fired a strike to his favorite target, Eli Heidenreich, on a slant in the end zone. The touchdown and subsequent PAT gave Navy a 17–16 lead. After the Navy defense forced a quick punt, Horvath and the offense converted a crucial 4th-and-inches near midfield with 2:00 left. With Army out of timeouts, Navy was able to kneel out the clock.

2025 FENWAY BOWL

Army dominated UConn 41–16 at a frigid Fenway Park. The Black Knights relied on a punishing ground game and a breakout performance from a freshman running back to secure Jeff Monken's sixth bowl victory in 12 years. Army rushed for a staggering 368 yards, setting a new Fenway Bowl record for the most points scored in a single game. Entering the game with only 25 yards on the season, freshman Godspower Nwawuihe became the star of the afternoon. He scored on a 43-yard burst in the second quarter and followed it with a 70-yard tackle-breaking touchdown early in the third quarter, the longest run in the bowl's history. The Huskies struck first, with Cam Edwards scoring on a 12-yard run to take a 7–0 lead. However, UConn struggled to keep pace while playing without star QB Joe Fagnano (NFL Draft opt-out) and under interim coach Gordon Sammis. Army QB Cale Hellums was nearly perfect, completing 7-of-8 passes for 108 yards (all to Noah Short) and a touchdown, while adding two rushing scores of his own in the second half.